Women, Gender and Labour Migration

Migration is one of the foremost social issues of our times. European countries are now as multicultural as the United States, Australia or other migrant-settler societies. Refugee movements, involving just as many women and children as men, have become one of the most outstanding contemporary human rights issues.

The statistics are striking. In the second half of the twentieth century the proportion of the world's population who lived in cities doubled, and in all but the poorest of developing countries the urban population now exceeds the rural. This has meant an enormous social transformation, but just how new are the features we associate with modern migration?

Until the mid-1980s virtually no attention had been paid to female migrants at all: they were assumed to be dependent family members who followed their husbands. *Women, Gender and Labour Migration* provides the historical context for the recognition that many female migrants were actually autonomous agents.

The contributors indicate that women's involvement in long distance and international migration for work purposes is not a new phenomenon. They track women's paths in all five continents, from wet nurses in eighteenth-century Spain to women workers crossing the international borders of Southern Africa, and trace the historical antecedents for the transnational lives of many families. In so doing, a picture emerges of the historically separate but intrinsically connected movements of men and women in labour migrations.

Pamela Sharpe is Queen Elizabeth II Research Fellow in the History Department at the University of Western Australia. She has published *Adapting to Capitalism: Working Women in the English Economy 1700–1850* (1996), co-edited *Chronicling Poverty: The Voices and Strategies of the English Poor 1640–1840* (1997) and edited *Women's Work: The English Experience 1650–1918* (1998).

Routledge Research in Gender and History

1 **The Women's Movement and Women's Employment in Nineteenth-Century Britain**
Ellen Jordan

2 **Gender, Sexuality and Colonial Modernities**
Edited by Antoinette Burton

3 **Women's Suffrage in the British Empire**
Citizenship, nation and race
Edited by Ian Christopher Fletcher, Laura E. Nym Mayhall and Philippa Levine

4 **Women, Educational Policy-Making and Administration in England**
Authoritative women since 1800
Edited by Joyce Goodman and Sylvia Harrop

5 **Women, Gender and Labour Migration**
Historical and global perspectives
Edited by Pamela Sharpe

Women, Gender and Labour Migration

Historical and global perspectives

Edited by Pamela Sharpe

London and New York

First published 2001
by Routledge
11 New Fetter Lane, London EC4P 4EE

Simultaneously published in the USA and Canada
by Routledge
29 West 35th Street, New York, NY 10001

Routledge is an imprint of the Taylor & Francis Group

Typeset in Baskerville
by Florence Production Ltd, Stoodleigh, Devon
Printed and bound in Great Britain
at the University Press, Cambridge

British Library Cataloguing in Publication Data
A catalogue record for this book is available from the British Library

Library of Congress Cataloguing in Publication Data
Women, gender, and labour migration: historical and global perspectives/Pamela Sharpe.
p. cm.
Papers presented at the International Economic History Congress, 1998, Madrid. Includes bibliographical references and index.
1. Women—Employment—Congresses. 2. Women alien labor—Congresses. 3. Minority women—Employment—Congresses. I. Sharpe, Pamela. II. International Economic History Congress (1998: Madrid)
HD6052 .W5634 2001
331.4–dc21 00–067068

ISBN 0–415–22800–X

Contents

List of figures vii
List of maps viii
List of plates ix
List of tables x
Notes on contributors xii
Note on the Japanese text xv
Foreword by Sheila Rowbotham xvi
Acknowledgements xviii

1 Introduction: gender and the experience of migration 1
PAMELA SHARPE

2 Women migrants as global and local agents: new research strategies on gender and migration 15
CHRISTIANE HARZIG

3 Leaving home to help the family? Male and female temporary migrants in eighteenth- and nineteenth-century Spain 29
CARMEN SARASÚA

4 Labour migration, family and community in early modern Japan 60
MARY LOUISE NAGATA

5 Women and long-distance trade migration in the nineteenth-century Netherlands 85
MARLOU SCHROVER

6 Nowhere at home? Female migrants in the nineteenth-century Habsburg Empire 108
SYLVIA HAHN

7 Gender, family, work and migration in early nineteenth-century Scotland 127
DAVID TIDSWELL

8 Wives or workers? Single British female migration to colonial Australia 145
JAN GOTHARD

9 A historical perspective on female migrants: motivations and strategies of nineteenth-century Hessians 163
SIMONE A. WEGGE

10 When the migrants are men: Italy's women and transnationalism as a working-class way of life 190
DONNA GABACCIA

11 Gender and twentieth-century Irish migration, 1921–1971 209
ENDA DELANEY

12 Maids on the move: images of femininity and European women's labour migration during the interwar years 224
BARBARA HENKES

13 Female migration and the farm family economy in interwar Japan 244
JANET HUNTER

14 Migrancy, marriage and family in the Ciskei reserve of South Africa, 1945–1959 259
ANNE MAGER

15 Women and migrants: continuity and change in patterns of female migration in Latin America 275
PAULINA DE LOS REYES

Bibliography 290
Index 315

Figures

4.1 Probability of service out-migration, 1720–1860, a) Shimomoriya, b) Niita, c) Nishijō 66
4.2 Changes in the type of service out-migration over time, 1721–1862, a) Shimomoriya, b) Niita 68
4.3 Age at service out-migration, a) Shimomoriya, b) Niita, c) Nishijō 70
4.4 Changes in labour migration destinations of Nishijō villagers over time, 1772–1869 79
6.1 Age and household position of immigrant women, Wiener Neustadt, 1869 114
6.2 Age and household position of native-born women, Wiener Neustadt, 1869 115
6.3 Gender and place of origin of foreigners in the Habsburg Empire, 1890 118

Maps

3.1 Map of Spain showing significant places mentioned in this chapter 31
4.1 Map showing locations of Nishijō in Mino Province, Niita and Shimomoriya in Nihonmatsu Domain in early modern Japan 61
5.1 The Westerwald showing origins of migrants 88
5.2 The Utrecht districts in the nineteenth century 96
5.3 Regions from which German migrants came to the Netherlands 99
9.1 The German Confederation exclusive of Austria, 1815 167
14.1 South Africa: sites of African reserves, 1954 260

Plates

3.1	Late nineteenth-century postcard of Pasiego wet nurses	35
3.2	View of the new cart built for transport inside the city, Cádiz, 1804	41
5.1	Westerwalder girls	92
8.1	Poster advertising government emigration to Sydney, *c.*1880s	149
8.2	Poster recruiting young women to Canada	157
12.1	German station worker (*Bahnshofsmissionarin*) in action, *c.*1930	229

Tables

3.1 The job ladder of Cádiz dockworkers 43
4.1 Marital status of male villagers on leaving for service out-migration, Shimomoriya, Niita and Nishijō, 1721–1790 and 1791–1860 71
4.2 Marital status of female villagers on leaving for service out-migration, Shimomoriya, Niita and Nishijō, 1721–1790 and 1791–1860 71
4.3 Male relations to head before service out-migration, Shimomoriya, Niita and Nishijō, 1721–1790 and 1791–1860 73
4.4 Female relations to head before service out-migration, Shimomoriya, Niita and Nishijō, 1721–1790 and 1791–1860 73
4.5 Male relations to head on return from service out-migration, Shimomoriya, Niita and Nishijō, 1721–1790 and 1791–1860 75
4.6 Female relations to head on return from service out-migration, Shimomoriya, Niita and Nishijō, 1721–1790 and 1791–1860 75
4.7 Top ten destinations from which Nishijō villagers did not return, by sex 77
6.1 Female employees in selected occupational positions according to place of origin, Wiener Neustadt, 1869 and 1880 117
6.2 Occupation of female employees in personal and domestic service, Wiener Neustadt, 1869 and 1880 119
6.3 Women working in personal and domestic service, place of origin and status, Wiener Neustadt, 1869 120
6.4 Women working in personal and domestic service, place of origin and position in household, Wiener Neustadt, 1869 121
7.1 Occupations of suspects and witnesses where known in early nineteenth-century Scotland 130
7.2 Inter-sectoral movements of suspects and witnesses in early nineteenth-century Scotland 131

7.3 Inter-sectoral movements of Scots and Irish in early nineteenth-century Scotland 131
7.4 Inter-sectoral movements of occupational groups in early nineteenth-century Scotland 132
7.5 Links of suspects and witnesses in early nineteenth-century Scotland 133
7.6 Links of Scots and Irish in early nineteenth-century Scotland 133
7.7 Links of occupational groups in early nineteenth-century Scotland 133
7.8 Links in rural and urban places (of those with known occupation) in early nineteenth-century Scotland 134
9.1 Examples of records in the emigrant permit lists, Hesse-Cassel, 1832–1857 169
9.2 The recording of women in the Hesse-Cassel emigrant permit lists, 1832–1857 170
9.3 Characteristics of male and female emigrants, Hesse-Cassel, 1832–1857 173
9.4 Age distribution of Hese-Cassel emigrants, 1832–1857 175
9.5 Cash statistics of Hesse-Cassel emigrants (in Thaler) 176
9.6 Cash statistics of Hesse-Cassel emigrants (in Thaler, no zeros) 176
9.7 Common occupation of female emigrants in Hesse-Cassel 177
9.8 Year of departure for Hesse-Cassel emigrants, by per cent of total (cumulative) 179
10.1 Annual rates of Italian emigration, by region, 1876–1914 193
10.2 Percentage of all Italian emigrants going to the US, by regional origin, 1876–1914 193
10.3 Percentage female of all Italian emigrants, by province, 1876–1925 194
11.1 Irish emigration, 1852–1921 210
11.2 Average annual Irish net migration, by gender, 1926–1971 211
11.3 Estimated percentage of each age cohort 'lost' from the Republic of Ireland as a result of net migration up to 1971 212
13.1 Number of workers employed in Japanese textile manufacturing, by process, 1920–1940 246
13.2 Value of textiles as a percentage of total Japanese exports, 1920–1940 246
13.3 Gender distribution of workers in silk reeling, cotton spinning and weaving, 1920–1940 246
13.4 Percentage of female workforce under 20 years of age, 1920–1940 247
13.5 Family origins of spinning workers in Osaka, 1927 248

Contributors

Paulina de los Reyes holds a Ph.D. in Economic History. She is a Senior Researcher and Lecturer in the Department of Economic History at Uppsala University, Sweden. She is currently conducting a research programme on diversity in work organisations. She has written widely on the position of women in the labour market in Latin America and on the historical construction of gender and ethnicity in Sweden. Among her publications are *The Rural Poor: Agrarian Changes and Survival Strategies in Chile 1873–1989* (1992) and *The Problematic Sisterhood* (1998).

Enda Delaney is Lecturer in Social and Demographic History at The Queen's University of Belfast. He has published a number of articles on twentieth-century Irish migration, and his book *Demography, State and Society: Irish Migration to Britain, 1921–71*, was published in 2000. He is currently working on a study of Irish migrants in twentieth-century Britain.

Donna Gabaccia is Charles H. Stone Professor of American History at the University of North Carolina at Charlotte. She is the author and editor of many books on migration and gender history including *From Sicily to Elizabeth Street* (1984), *Seeking Common Ground* (1992), *From the Other Side* (1994), *We Are What We Eat* (1998) and *Italy's Many Diasporas* (2000).

Jan Gothard is Senior Lecturer in History at Murdoch University in Perth, Western Australia. She has published a number of major articles and chapters on female migration and her book *Blue China: Single Female Migration to Colonial Australia*, will be published in 2001. Her present research interests include restrictive immigration practices in twentieth-century Australia, focusing on disability and health.

Sylvia Hahn teaches at the University of Salzburg. Her publications include *Aufbruch in der Provinz* (1989) and *Frauenarbeit vom ausgehenden 18. bis zum 20. Jahrhundert* (1994). Her current projects concern gender-specific labour migration in the Habsburg Empire and widows in modern Europe.

Christiane Harzig is Assistant Professor at Bremen University, Germany where she teaches North American History. She has published on nineteenth-century migration (as editor of *Peasant Maids, City Women* (1997)), on German-American women and on labour migration. She is presently finishing a book on post-Second-World-War immigration policies in Europe and North America.

Barbara Henkes teaches at the University of Groningen and works as a postdoctoral researcher at the Meertens Institute in Amsterdam, where she is studying the construction and development of folklore studies in the Netherlands between 1920 and 1950. She has published in the fields of oral history, women's history, migration and national socialism. Her main focus is the making and unmaking of cultural and political identities during the twentieth century. She is an editor of the *Dutch Yearbook of Women's History*.

Janet Hunter teaches economic history at the London School of Economics. She is the editor of *Japanese Women Working* (1993), and has written extensively on various aspects of Japan's economic development. She is currently completing a monograph on the female labour market in pre-war Japan.

Anne Mager teaches history, gender and development studies at the University of Cape Town. She has worked extensively in non-governmental organisations. Her first book, *Gender and the Making of a South African Bantustan: A Social History of the Ciskei, 1945–1959* was published in 1999.

Mary Louise Nagata was born in California and went to Japan to study violin pedagogy in 1975. In 1977 she entered the International Christian University in Mitaka, Japan. She received a BGS from the University of Maryland in 1983, an MA from the University of Hawaii in 1992 and a Ph.D. from the University of Hawaii in 1996. She worked at the International Research Center for Japanese Studies in Kyoto, Japan as a JSPS research fellow from 1996 to 1998. She now lives in Switzerland, and since June 1999 she has been a *membre associé* at the Centre de Recherches Historique in the Ecole des Hautes Etudes en Sciences Sociales.

Carmen Sarasúa studied history at the Complutense University, Madrid, and Labour Economics at the New School for Social Research, New York, as a Fulbright scholar. She has a Ph.D. in History, from the European University Institute, Florence and is currently Professor in the Department of Economic History, Universidad Autónoma de Barcelona, Spain. She is the author of *Criados, nodrizas y amos. El servicio doméstico en la formación del mercado de trabajo madrileño, 1758–1868* (1994).

Marlou Schrover has published on the food industry, Jewish entrepreneurship, female entrepreneurship, cartel formation, the interaction between demographic variables and changing employment opportunities, and on food and ethnicity. She completed her Ph.D. on labour relations in the food industry in 1991. She co-edited *Women Workers and Technological Change* (1995). She currently works at Utrecht University.

Pamela Sharpe is Queen Elizabeth II Research Fellow at the University of Western Australia. She gained a Ph.D. in Demographic and Economic History at the Cambridge Group for the History of Population and Social Studies. She has published *Adapting to Capitalism: Working Women in the English Economy 1700–1850* (2000), co-edited *Chronicling Poverty: The Voices and Strategies of the English Poor 1640–1840* (1997) and edited *Women's Work: The English Experience 1650–1918* (1998). She has just completed a historical micro-study of Colyton in Devon.

David Tidswell was born in Portland, Oregon and is a graduate of Lewis and Clark College and the University of Edinburgh. He recently worked at Lancaster University on an ESRC project concerning the history of crime and migration in northwest England and the Basque Country. He is currently an Associate Lecturer with the Open University in Scotland, researching Scottish and Basque history.

Simone A. Wegge is an Assistant Professor at the City University of New York. During 1999/2000 she was a German Marshall Fund grant recipient and a visiting scholar at various academic institutions, including the Hoover Institution at Stanford University. A nominee for the 1997 Gerschenkron dissertation prize, she has published articles on international migration in the *Journal of Economic History* and *Explorations in Economic History*.

Note on the Japanese text

For Chapters 4 and 13, this book follows the standard practice for Japanese studies. Citations written in Japanese follow Japanese name order for authors whereas works written in English follow Western name order.

Foreword

Sheila Rowbotham

This collection demonstrates how wrong it is to imagine that nobody moved about the world before 'globalisation' was invented during the 1980s. Not only the rich have travelled; the migrant worker has a long history. Even before the eighteenth century, when this book begins, adverse economic circumstances had forced poor people to set off in search of mythical cities paved with gold.

Men have usually been seen as the prime movers; women have often been assumed simply to have followed their menfolk as dependants. In the United States especially a feminist-inspired social history has been restoring the woman immigrant and reframing the history of immigration. Many young women were among those dreaming of prosperity and freedom who sailed past the Statue of Liberty to arrive on Ellis Island, where the camera caught their faces filled with bewilderment, fear and anticipation. Like the men, they came to earn higher wages than they could at home, in the teeming clothing workshops and factories of New York.

But, as *Women, Gender and Labour Migration* shows, this was not the only story of female emigration. The women in this book can be seen travelling through the nineteenth century and into the twentieth, not just to the US but in Europe, Japan, Australia, South Africa. German women stone traders venture to Holland; a Scottish woman hawker arrives in Liverpool; Japanese women are drawn to the new textile factories.

One reason for the lack of visibility has been the nature of female migrants' occupations. In many cases they went into domestic service or served as wet nurses – activities which have never been regarded within the prevailing definitions of 'work' or the 'economy' and have thus defied statistical reckoning. This is a gendered obscurity in a double sense. The women leave no traces because they are female *and* because the framework of who is to be seen has been biased towards the male.

Another reason for the obscurity of the poor migrant woman, however, crosses gender. They belong to that great host of the ignoble who are not 'known' to history. In recent decades these exclusions have been challenged by social historians who have examined a much wider range of sources in order to document lives that have been passed over. Ingeniously reading the sources against the grain, the contributors to *Women, Gender and Labour Migration* uncover the forgotten hopes and fears of women whose existence would have otherwise gone unrecorded.

These historical perspectives on women migrants in many lands are not only fascinating in themselves; they have an urgent contemporary relevance. In our era capital moves at lightning speed, emptying sites of labour and devastating sources of livelihood. Yet the human beings whose lives have been disrupted and who seek better economic conditions are forced to travel dangerously and encounter many obstacles, from state officials to other workers who feel threatened by their arrival. This is likely to be one of the most explosive issues of the future; the grim secret of globalisation. Women, who constitute a majority of the world's poor, are a crucial element in this harsh drama.

So we do well to remember that the boundaries between nations have always been semi-permeable and that women have always been part of the shifting populations driven by need to explore elsewhere. *Women, Gender and Labour Migration* opens up a global perspective which prompts readers to look back at their own heritage, not simply the long process of mixing which makes a nation, but even the more personal family history. After all, so many of us are descended from people who came from somewhere else.

Acknowledgements

This book originated with a 'call for papers' for the International Economic History Congress to be held in Seville in 1998. In the event, the conference was cancelled, and then reconvened in Madrid. We lost some contributors along the way, but happily most of the planned papers appear in this volume and I am very grateful to those academics who kept their faith in this as a worthwhile, collaborative project. My own route during the two years after the conference took me from Australia to Spain, via Sweden, back to the UK and then back to Perth, Australia as an international migrant. I thank the Swedish Council for Research in Humanities and Social Sciences for funding my stay in the Economic History Department of Uppsala University, for it was there that I was able to formulate the organisation of the book. In Bristol, Heather Hernandez gave me considerable help. At University of Western Australia, my fellowship is funded by the Australian Research Council and I am grateful to Judy Bolton and Martin Greenacre for some last-minute assistance. Last but not least, this book was edited using internet files and messages – the invisible threads that now connect our global lives. These connectivities crucially rely on technology and mine failed me at the last minute. As a result I am, as ever, immensely grateful to Derek Pennington for his techno-mastery and his support with what I came to see as the Olympics of book editing.

Sections of Chapter 14 'Migrancy, marriage and family in the Ciskei reserve of South Africa, 1945–1959' were originally published in Chapters 6 and 7 of *Gender and the Making of a South African Bantustan: A Social History of the Ciskei* by Anne Kelk Mager (Heinemann, Portsmouth, NH, 1999) and are reprinted here with permission.

1 Introduction

Gender and the experience of migration

Pamela Sharpe

Migration trends and twentieth-century history

A surge of human migration might be seen as one of the outstanding social phenomena of modern history. While history teaches us to be wary of modernising narratives, every type of statistical evidence and contemporary comment provides a firm basis for the sense that migration has become more pervasive as an element of society. Seemingly no region is now untouched by the widening and deepening reach of the migration process. Yet there is still a popular perception that migration is somehow a disruption or a historical aberration. It remains the task of historians to show just how enduring migration has been through time.[1]

The twentieth century has marked a turning point towards far greater female migration over long distances. In fact, the enormous increase in the female labour force has partly resulted from the greater number of women migrants.[2] Today women account for approximately half of all global migrants. In terms of labour migration their numbers have expanded in all areas other than construction or heavy industry.[3] Men comprise the majority of migrants to developing countries and those reliant on migrant labour, but to developed countries and those that are suitable for permanent settlement, the greatest number have been women. The largest number of legal migrants in the world still go to the United States, and there women have predominated in migration flows since the 1930s. Nevertheless, it is important to make gender distinctions within the developing countries, rather than categorising them together. Historically, migration in Africa, south and southeast Asia and the Caribbean has been male-dominated, whereas in Latin America there have been more women in migratory flows. However, as some of the studies mentioned here will show, women's migration has been increasing within Asia and the Caribbean.[4] In Asia an increasing proportion of this migration consists of autonomous females. The estimated 10,000 Filipino maids who congregate in Statue Square in Hong Kong every Sunday, could be no better illustration of this.[5]

Before progressing very far, however, it is necessary to review what labour migration actually comprises in the contemporary world. In considering the experience of migrants since the Second World War, it is difficult to characterise much of the movement as purely labour migration. This does not simply reflect the fact that straightforward Marxist interpretations are no longer adequate and we must now apply a more sophisticated label to the migrant labourer. The war created an enormous number of refugees and expelled persons who eventually settled in occupations in other countries, but had a more complex history than that reflected in the label 'labour migrant'. Again, in the last quarter of the twentieth century,

> Unfortunately in the grim 1970s and 1980s labour migration became increasingly hard to separate from the torrents of men, women and children who fled from, or were uprooted by, famine, political or ethnic persecution, war and civil war, thus forcing the countries of the First World equally committed (in theory) to helping refugees and (in practice) to preventing immigration from poor countries, with severe problems of political and legal casuistry.[6]

Whereas poor countries have many people keen to take up jobs in rich countries, wealthier nations have a demographic structure now weighted towards the elderly and low birth rates. The dilemma these countries face is whether they should allow immigration, thus risking political problems, or simply close down the shutters. Until recently the United States, Canada and Australia have been most willing to take up the challenge of immigration whereas European countries have been more restrictive but, nevertheless, with the opening of boundaries within the European Community, these 'old world' nations are now as multicultural as migrant-settler societies of the New World. One effect in all these countries, however, has been an upturn in illegal, temporary and restricted migration resulting in many human rights quandaries and a perception that immigrants or refugees are second-class citizens. As a result asylum-seeker issues – affecting just as many women as men – have become one of the outstanding political and social justice problems of our day. The difficulties of categorising modern-day migrants as labour migrants is apparent, but, as we will see, historical analysis of women's migration suggests that a broadening of the definition should apply more generally through time.

Looking to the future, with a shift away from heavy industry but towards global capitalism within advanced countries, the movement of workers for manual jobs is less likely to be needed and access to cheap labour overseas may be at a greater premium.[7] Meanwhile, a revolution in transport and communications, and the increasing disparity between earnings in rich and poor countries, makes a 'transnational' existence far more common than has been the case before. As the studies in this book show, however, it is not the case that, as some anthropologists seem to assume, transnationalism can be viewed as an entirely new invention of modern societies. As Gabaccia's chapter in this book shows, in the huge nineteenth-century migrations to the United States, Italy's men and women provide us with an early example of transnational lives involving the construction of family economies that crossed national borders. Transnationalism can have a special impact on the way we view women's labour migration. As Momsen describes migration in the Caribbean,

> for women, migration is not a matter of people leaving the island to live and work but a matter of extending the domestic unit, so that it includes people working in migration destinations, in some cases thousands of miles away. The idea of the household, not necessarily being a residential unit, but rather a tight network of exchanges of support seem to be commonly accepted on most island communities.[8]

Some of the countries that historically produced many migrants are now receiving them. Italy, historic provider of the great migration flows to the New World in the nineteenth century, is now the destination for many Africans.[9] In mid-2000, thousands of Sub-Saharan Africans were found to be following the old routes of Moroccans across the Mediterranean to Spain.[10] In one reported case, Maria and her three-month-old daughter were arrested, eight months after she left her Nigerian village to trek across the Sahara. She remarked that the birth of her daughter had not been easy and commented on the dangers that women faced on such long journeys, such as being raped by bandits or border guards. Was it the pregnancy that had driven Maria from her home? Or was it the perception of better economic conditions elsewhere? Or were her motives entirely different? Maria's astonishing migration apart, this book will reveal many stories, not all are so dramatic but they are similar in that they reveal reasons for women's migration that are mixed and cannot readily be defined as labour migration: they are perhaps partly political, partly social and partly economic. Nevertheless, one aim of the chapters presented here is not to lose sight of the individual when describing the lives of migrants within an overarching global system.

Female labour migration in historical perspective

The sheer numbers of people involved justifies historical analysis of migration. Before the First World War, some ten million labourers migrated across international boundaries within Europe and another forty-one million went to the Americas.[11] Migration has made a major impact on urbanisation and since 1950 the proportion of the world's population who live in cities has more than doubled. In all but the poorest of developing countries, the urban population exceeds the rural. Yet the urbanising impulse, and the role of migrant labour in that, has a much longer heritage.

With some significant exceptions, most of the chapters in this book consider women's historical experience of migration using both qualitative and quantitative approaches. The contribution of economic historians is to make an assessment, with some specificity, of the population of female migrants, the money they took with them and other measurable aspects of the migration experience. As Wegge shows, this has some surprising results, such as the number of wealthy widows who migrated to the United States. The book considers long-distance migration, but none of the chapters focuses on citizenship. Indeed, national boundaries sometimes seem non-existent between the micro-level of women's lives in their neighbourhoods and the global sphere of their movements.

It appears that until the mid-1980s the circumstances of female migration were little discussed by anthropologists, sociologists or policy makers. Since then substantial accounts have been written about the invisibility of the female migrant and the ingrained assumption that the typical migrant was young, single and male with economic motivations for moving.[12] The migration of women was assumed to be for family reasons, to accompany male migrants. And there has been a perception (if not always an actuality) that women and children predominate in refugee flows. Some of the mid-1980s recognition that many women were, and probably always had been, autonomous migrants came from analysis of the contemporary situation. In the United States, over 28 per cent of those women who migrated under occupational preference categories in the 1970s entered with highly skilled occupations such as nurses, managers, teachers or administrators. Of course, some of this skilled migration is impossible to ascertain from national statistics. In Australia, for example, the Bosnian woman who has entered as a refugee might be working for a cleaning agency until she finds a job in her previous profession as an economist. Some professional Filipinos, working outside the country, also earn more as migrant domestic workers than in their own occupations. As Kelson and Delaet comment 'Clearly many women migrated to fulfil labour needs in low-wage job sectors. Nevertheless, these figures also indicate that a significant number of women migrated to perform skilled jobs with higher wages'.[13]

As Delaney points out in his chapter, the historical study of gender-specific migration was adopted from the social science disciplines and has only recently been seen as a valid subject of historical analysis. It is also the case that the approach to female migration has been a series of case studies, with few attempts at synthesis, and this book is no departure from this trend. As Doreen Indra remarks in her recent collection about forced migration, there is a central issue of 'a tension in dealing with the universal versus the specific concerning gender and forced migration through time and space'.[14] This comment is equally applicable to voluntary migration. As Gabaccia observed in 1996, 'historical studies of international female migration scarcely exist'.[15] Those studies that have been carried out have an overwhelming emphasis on the great migrations to North America, and this book will widen the geographical focus of this academic enquiry.

The emphasis here will be on long-distance migration rather than the movement between village and town that was commonplace in early modern and, especially, industrialising Europe.[16]

As these chapters show, and as is particularly stressed by Harzig in Chapter 2, the emphasis is no longer on the mere existence of female labour migrants but rather their historical agency and the wider context of their migration. Henrietta Moore has written of anthropological studies of female migration:

> it is important to note that migration is often not a single discrete event, but part of a strategy for coping with economic change, an opportunity which depends on multiplex links being established between rural and urban areas[17]

Many women who are resident in towns in fact form part of a wider family group based in rural areas. Izzard's study of Botswana showed that over a third of the women she interviewed received money, goods or food from their daughters who were working in towns, mainly because they were looking after their daughters' children.[18] Moore concludes that,

> the significance of recent research on female migrants, in Africa, is the emphasis on the importance of mother–daughter links across the rural–urban divide, as part of strategies of household survival.[19]

Moore's remarks have wider relevance than the African case. Within migration studies, historians can still learn to shape their investigations by listening to other disciplines and considering evidence from a range of countries and cultures.

In fact, several of the chapters in this book, but particularly those by Sarasúa for Spain and Hunter and Nagata for Japan, show that both male and female migration reflects not just individual motivation but also family strategies. Hunter is able to provide a very clear indication of the value of migrant income to the household. Of course, in similar studies, the limitations of historical sources mean it can be difficult to analyse what is happening within the family: Did they have shared interests or were they following the man's plan? In how many cases was migration a strategy for survival or was it a means towards upward social mobility? Sarasúa shows that peasants increasingly relied on migration to sustain the farm at home, bearing out Anne Phizacklea's comments in *One Way Ticket*: 'Nearly all labour migration is characterized by compulsion'.[20] Sarasúa's chapter is very valuable in showing that distant motherhood is hardly a new phenomenon as we might imagine from some contemporary sociological and anthropological studies.[21] The movement of wet nurses that she describes compares with that from Slovenia to Egypt in the second half of the nineteenth century, where the women concerned earned the special name of 'alexandrinke' because most of them undertook migrations to Alexandria that, unlike those to Madrid, would last a lifetime.[22]

The movements of ordinary people are also analysed by Tidswell, who uses the pre-trial statements of suspects and witnesses to allow him to examine the migrations of the Scottish labouring poor, providing a means to compare the migration experiences of men and women. As a comparable study, of the peregrinations of an English labouring family, has shown 'migration was a fundamental life event which can only be understood in the context of complete life histories'.[23] Tidswell shows that a migration for economic reasons might often disguise a significant social impetus for moving, such as the family breakdowns also identified by Mager for Southern Africa. Another factor common to several studies is that it is the case that women were far less likely than men to be categorised according to what work they did in official records. Indeed, the problems of historical sources are highlighted by many of these chapters because motivation for moves is often difficult to discern, so that the evidence cannot therefore convincingly reveal migrant strategies.

Hahn's chapter describes the type of long-distance migration which reflects the distant hopes and desires of men and women for a better job and way of life. She is able to analyse the connection between distance of migration and occupational position in the hierarchy. Her chapter raises the important issue of social control of migrants in local communities and the loss of their legal standing when they migrated. Nagata shows the close connections between migration and the demographic and environmental situation in particular regions, but also highlights the role of political and social policy (in a way which might compare with the Settlement Laws, enforced in Britain from the late seventeenth to the nineteenth century).

Gothard, in arguing for the need to reconsider patterns of colonial immigration and immigrant experience in terms of gender, demonstrates that single women are certainly visible in the government records of nineteenth-century Australia, but their economic role has been ignored anyway. Like Hahn, Gothard's chapter underlines how domestic service is central to understanding women's historical migration. This fact is now being recognised in anthropological and sociological studies of migration, but it is only recently that domestic service has been the subject of significant study in the historical context.[24]

In Ireland, the male–female balance of migrants turned early. From the 1870s more women than men migrated to the United States, whereas the male predominance elsewhere lasted to at least the First World War.[25] Although many accounts suggest that young women left Ireland to secure a marital partner, Delaney's study gives little support for this. On this point his results echo those of Gothard. Delaney shows that in rural Ireland women were expected to find an occupation that would give them an independent income. This reinforces a stream of recent research in anthropology and geography suggesting that the migration of women might be to gain independence or emancipation. It is evident in contemporary research on illegal migration, for example from Central America to California, that, as Kelson and Delaet point out, 'The evidence that large numbers of women have migrated illegally in a variety of countries poses serious challenges to the pervasive image of the undocumented migrant as a male worker'.[26] Again, drawing on contemporary social science research we can see that migration allowed women to take up employment opportunities, acquire skills or achieve financial autonomy. Prostitutes in Nairobi have been shown to send back cash to the villages that they come from, but some also create capital investments and make a financial outlay to set up a permanent residence in the city.[27]

The picture sketched by Delaney might be compared to that of the Eastern European women migrants, especially the Jewish women who made an enormous contribution to the development of garment industries in New York, Chicago and Philadelphia.[28] The combination of traditional and modern motivations for these women's migration is well described by Kathie Friedman-Kasaba, who writes that the time-honoured path for the young Russian-Jewish woman to empower herself was through marriage but she needed a dowry to marry. In the case where her father was unable to afford this,

> migration emerged as a non-traditional means of satisfying a traditional rite of 'passage' into female adulthood. For them, saving for a ticket to America was synonymous with accumulating a dowry, but in this case, migration offered the possibility of making a more satisfactory free-choice marriage, as the distance between fathers and daughters widened.[29]

Similar reasons for migrating emerged in the Italian case, where partible inheritance meant that landholdings were no longer viable. In this situation, temporary overseas migration was a means to an end: financing the purchase of more land.[30] As a result,

> Becoming a 'person' in New York City for single women, both Italian and Russian-Jewish, meant first of all, becoming an important wage earner in her household. This was a source of self-esteem, pride, and accomplishment for many women, although never a free choice.[31]

As Moore has reminded us, gender relations and particularly conflict are a key part of understanding why women migrate.[32] Feminist research has shown the ways in which women experience social and economic pressures differently from men, and they often migrate as a result of divorce, which can result in them losing the right to land, or the death of a parent, meaning they need to send money to the widowed parent. Premarital pregnancy or infertility might be other reasons for women's migration.[33] Anne Mager analyses a common theme in women's migration – the breakdown of families – and finds that 'female migration stemmed from the increased viability of independent livelihoods for women and women's ability to develop strategic responses to social change'. As Mager shows, women did not receive patriarchal sanction for leaving home but paradoxically, this gave them more independence. Statistical analysis has shown the greater number of separated, divorced and widowed women in labour migrations compared with men of the same status.[34]

Nevertheless, de los Reyes' chapter takes on a much wider geographical area than any other in the book and interrogates the idea of modernity often applied to migrants. Her article brings the historical analysis right up to date and shows how the image of the young, single female migrant needs, in itself, to be redefined because increasingly, within Latin America, migrants are mothers. Overall, work clearly emerges as a major reason for women's movement through these studies, although sometimes we need to dig below the surface of official preconceptions to penetrate women's career moves and economic agendas. At the same time, other important reasons for women's migration must form part of the story of scattered livelihoods.

Migration and identity: future directions for research

This book will take further some of the research on gender and migration, but there are many areas that still need to be examined. In particular, historical analysis of migration and identity will be a fruitful area of future research. In a perceptive article, Mary Chamberlain shows that men and women's language about the migration experience can be very different.[35] Whereas men present the decision to migrate as autonomous, she finds that women see migration as a more collective endeavour and represent the experience within a set of family relationships. Women's movements might involve as much calculation as male migrations, but women viewed their plans as one element in a larger picture, often involving family support. She shows that Barbados has a culture of migration; moves are not undertaken in isolation.

One future area of enquiry, inadequately covered in this book (except when considering the attitudes of fathers to their daughters' migrations, as Mager does), is masculinity and migration. Dorothy Louise Zinn, in a useful collection on migration and identity, looks at how Sengalese men, who often work as peddlers in Bari in Italy, reconcile their participation in the informal street economy through their gendered responsibility to be providers in the home context with male-sanctioned codes of travel and wanderlust: 'In the Sengalese discourses, manhood –

construction of adult gender identity – figures as part of a triad with travel and knowledge as the other two legs'.[36] Analysis of masculinity would deepen many of the studies of male international labour migration.[37]

What is the identity of independent female migrants, often perceived as 'modern' in the societies in which they live? How does it connect with the meanings of femininity in these societies? Can migrant women really liberate themselves or are traditional gender roles perpetuated? Teresa Barnes refers to Southern African women migrants as 'agents of the new, perhaps the unconventional, sometimes the outrageous'.[38] Gabaccia shows that Italian migrant women became active resisters in labour organisations. The meanings we may attach to the identity of migrants are very specific nevertheless. Some Asian countries, such as Singapore, impose pregnancy regulation on domestic workers who are migrants. In the Hausa area of northern Nigeria, the migration of young women is thought automatically to imply that they have become prostitutes.[39]

Women migrants are sometimes used as a way of defining a collective identity, to secure the boundaries of a community.[40] In this book, Henkes explores images of femininity in the process of migration from Germany to the Netherlands and asks whether migrating women were in fact the vulnerable victims of male lust that they were portrayed to be in public debate, or whether they were ever regarded as self-confident, enterprising young women? This northwest European migration had a long history as Olwen Hufton has shown.[41] Schrover's chapter also shows how female migrants had earlier crossed the border to the Netherlands and settled in particular urban enclaves, near to those who came from similar areas.

Future studies will continue to probe both the regionalism of migration and the interface between race and gender within the migration process. Historically, in the West, many migrants have entered segmented labour markets, but since the Second World War immigration has largely been a state-sponsored response to labour shortage and, as a result, immigrants entered the same labour market as natives thus leading to tensions between both new migrants and the established population, and between different groups of immigrants.[42] How did caste, gender and dominant power structures determine migration in colonial societies? From the late eighteenth century low-caste female migrant labour was extensively used on the plantations of South India, often drawing women from villages affected by famine, with those who had converted to Christianity being found work by missionaries. On the face of it, this is a classic case of capitalist power and subservient workers. How do gender identities and preconceptions influence this situation?

The short- and long-term emotional and physical impact of migration has also been little explored. Henkes says that Mrs Vanvliet crossed the Germany–Netherlands border in 1920 'with a feeling of sensational expectation'. Shortly after arrival, emotions could be much more mixed.

In discussion with me, a Chinese doctor who arrived in Australia in the 1970s, with no English or Cantonese, reported spending the first year constantly in and out of hospital, sometimes suffering from pneumonia, oftentimes experiencing much despair. What are the longer-term psychological impacts of migration and those across generations? This question has not been much studied by anthropologists or historians.[43] Paula Aymer has looked at regional migration within the Caribbean of domestics to the oil enclave of Aruba. As Aymer comments:

> Aruba is not the apex of some women's migration aspirations but many women never find a way of fulfilling their most cherished migration goals. Migrant domestics get stuck on Aruba, mired down in the pseudosecurity of regularly received wages, exchanged for grinding, menial, domestic labor. Some women can neither move on, nor manage to go back home. The years of separation from relatives in the sending countries erode connections, take their toll on relationships, and eventually make returning to the sending country an unattractive retirement option for many women.[44]

It was not even necessary to cross the sea to lose touch. A woman I interviewed in Essex in England as part of an oral project in 1991, was born to a poor family in the East End of London in 1911, and moved around the country as a domestic servant obtaining most of her jobs through charity agencies. She had six sisters and three brothers and commented on how difficult it was to keep in contact with her kin. Given a lack of resources, within a few years of leaving home she had lost contact with most of her siblings, who were also in migratory situations.

Recently more attention has been given to those who are left behind in the migration process – previously a neglected topic in history and anthropology, with the exception of such studies as Caroline Brettell's detailed survey of Lanheses in Portugal since 1700.[45] Rodenburg, in a detailed study of North Tapanuli, Indonesia, found that the effect of a migrant's absence could be positive or negative. It might enhance the decision-making power and influence of wives who do not move, but ultimately 'It devalues women since they are left in the "traditional" sector and excluded from the "modern" world of men, which entails migration'.[46] Nevertheless, it is difficult to obtain a balanced, gendered view simply because it is very hard to find men who are 'left behind'. Momsen concludes that where women are highly mobile (in Peru, the Caribbean, Ghana and Thailand), men are even more mobile.[47]

Investigation of those left behind reflects an increasing need to study migration in terms of the wider community implications: What societies did migrants leave and what were the communities formed and gained? To date, this is the real contribution of historical studies considering women. In 1992 Weinberg argued that in most immigrant studies:

> we do not learn about the texture of women's lives: how did they see themselves, socialize their children, participate in community life, maintain kin relationships, establish sex-linked ties, and create their own sense of values within home and neighbourhood?[48]

Gabaccia provides an exemplar of how to examine such issues in this volume. On a larger scale, Harzig *et al.* who followed the lives of migrant women through from their origins in different rural areas of Europe to Chicago provide a model study. Whereas the migration process is usually studied alone, Harzig *et al.* study both the effect of migration on the region from which migrants are drawn and consider the assimilation of women into the city. They find that, for example, 'Migration changes the rural gender system in that it introduces additional elements of choice, legitimate alternatives for women'.[49] Yet regional difference was important. Migration produced no sharp disjuncture in Dalshund in Sweden, where there was already a long history of seasonal migration.[50] Once in Chicago, the Swedes seemed readily to adapt to continuing mobility as the residents of the suburb of Lake View commonly took in other Swedish women as lodgers.

Kathie Friedman-Kasaba's perceptive study, which centres on whether international migration was coercive or empowering, also considers the wider context. Commenting on the recent historiography, she notes that she aims for her work to be a corrective to a situation where:

> In the otherwise praiseworthy attempt to correct previous omissions, migrating women have been reduced to genderless, cultureless units of labor power, as researchers liberated them from kinship, household, community, and all other non-market relationships.[51]

And later she comments,

> However essential a global perspective is to understanding the relation between migration and women's status, reductionist interpretations that analyse migration only as an economic phenomenon, or depict immigrant women's experiences only with regard to their role in social reproduction, or discount systemic hierarchical relations based on nationality/race/ethnicity and gender merely repeat the unproductive polarizations of previously discussed approaches.[52]

There may have been great diversity but women 'were active participants in the migration process and engaged subjects of their own lives'.[53]

There is still a popular conception of the international migrant as the young, lowly, white male who made good in a new land, becoming the revered entrepreneur hallowed in history. In a rural context, the successful migrant was the pioneer who tamed the alien landscape and established a thriving farm or sent remittances to allow others to do so. On the shoulders of such mighty individuals rests the popular history of the development of frontier-settler societies like Australia. This book is part of an alternative history of migration that recognises the contribution of women to the process in many diverse ways. It also suggests that the study of gender alongside migration might bring out a more realistic story, one that considers failure alongside success within the mix of human motivations and emotional impacts that provide a broad context for migration. In a wider sense, as the global economy develops and the communication revolution advances, we may approach a time when the labour migration of both males and females is a topic only for historical study. The implications of this for both developed and less developed regions have yet to become apparent.

Notes

1 This is a point made strongly by J. Lucassen and L. Lucassen (eds), *Migration, Migration History, History: Old Paradigms and New Perspectives* (Peter Lang AG, Bern, 1997): p. 9.
2 R. J. Simon and C. B. Brettell (eds), *International Migration: the Female Experience* (Rowman and Allanheld, Totowa, NJ, 1986): p. 4.
3 G. A. Kelson and D. Delaet (eds), *Gender and Immigration* (Macmillan, 1999): p. 2.
4 S-J. A. Cheng, 'Labor Migration and International Sexual Division of Labor: a Feminist Perspective' in G. A. Kelson and D. Delaet (eds) *Gender and Immigration*: pp. 38–59. The fact that there are increasing numbers of autonomous women in Asian migration flows is discussed in S-E. Khoo, P. C. Smith and J. T. Fawcett, 'Migration of Women to Cities: the Asian Situation in Comparative Perspective' *International Migration Review*, Vol. XVIII (1984): 1247–1263 and with more detail in their book J. T. Fawcett, S-E. Khoo and P. C. Smith, *Women in the Cities of Asia: Migration and Urban Adaption* (Westview Press, Boulder, CO, 1984). See also T. Lauby and O. Stark, 'Individual Migration as a Family Strategy: Young Women in the Philippines' *Population Studies*, 42 (1988): 473–486.
5 V. C. W. Tam, 'Foreign Domestic Helpers in Hong Kong and their Role in Childcare Provision' in J. H. Momsen (ed.) *Gender, Migration and Domestic Service* (Routledge, London, 1999): p. 263.
6 E. Hobsbawm, *Age of Extremes: the Short Twentieth Century 1914–1991* (Abacus, London, 1994): p. 364.
7 A. Sivanandan, 'Casualties of Globalism' *Guardian Weekly*, 17–23 August 2000: p. 11.
8 J. H. Momsen, 'Gender Selectivity in Caribbean Migration' in S. Chant (ed.) *Gender and Migration in Developing Countries* (Belhaven Press, London, 1992): p. 83.
9 D. L. Zinn, 'The Sengalese Immigrants in Bari: What Happens When the Africans Peer Back' in R. Benmayor and A. Skotnes (eds) *Migration and Identity* (Oxford University Press, Oxford, 1994): pp. 53–69.
10 R. Carroll, 'Tide of Refugees Floods Spanish Beaches' *Guardian Weekly*, 31 August – 6 September 2000: p. 5.
11 D. Gabaccia, 'The "Yellow Peril" and the "Chinese of Europe": Global Perspectives on Race and Labor, 1815–1930' in J. Lucassen and L. Lucassen (eds) *Migration, Migration History, History*: p. 178.

12 For one example, M. Morokvasic, 'Birds of Passage are also Women . . .' *International Migration Review*, Vol. XVIII (1984): 886–907.
13 Kelson and Delaet, *Gender and Immigration*: p. 6.
14 D. Indra, *Engendering Forced Migration: Theory and Practice* (Berghahn, New York and Oxford, 1999): p. xiii.
15 D. Gabaccia, 'Women of the Mass Migrations: from Minority to Majority 1820–1930' in D. Hoerder and L. P. Moch (eds) *European Migrants: Global and Local Perspectives* (Northeastern University Press, Boston, 1996): p. 91.
16 For an overview, see B. Hill, 'Rural–urban Migration of Women and their Employment in Towns' *Rural History*, 5, 2 (1994): 185–194.
17 H. L. Moore, *Feminism and Anthropology* (Polity Press, Oxford, 1988): p. 96.
18 W. Izzard, 'Migrants and Mothers: Case-studies from Botswana' *Journal of Southern African Studies*, 11, 2 (1985): 258–280 cited in Moore, *Feminism and Anthropology*: p. 97.
19 Moore, *Feminism and Anthropology*: p. 97.
20 A. Phizacklea (ed.), *One Way Ticket: Migration and Female Labour* (Routledge & Kegan Paul, London, 1983): p. 7.
21 B. S. A. Yeoh and S. Huang, 'Singapore Women and Foreign Domestic Workers: Negotiating Domestic Work and Motherhood' in J. H. Momsen (ed.) *Gender, Migration and Domestic Service*: pp. 277–300.
22 A. Barbič and I. Miklavčič-Brezigar, 'Domestic Work Abroad: a Necessity and an Opportunity for Rural Women from the Goriška Borderline Region of Slovenia' in J. H. Momsen (ed.) *Gender, Migration and Domestic Service*: pp. 164–178.
23 C. Pooley and S. D'Cruze, 'Migration and Urbanization in North-West England circa 1760–1830' *Social History*, 19, 3 (1994): 339–358.
24 For European early modern studies see L. C. van de Pol, 'The Lure of the Big City: Female Migration to Amsterdam' in E. Kloek, N. Teeuwen and M. Huisman (eds) *Women of the Golden Age: an International Debate on Women in Seventeenth-century Holland, England and Italy* (Hilversum, Verloren, 1994): pp. 73–82. Some of these migrants came from afar. J. Lucassen, 'The Netherlands, the Dutch, and Long Distance Migration in the Late Sixteenth to Early Nineteenth Centuries' in the same volume (p. 161) cites the study by S. Sogner of the migration of female servants from Norway to Amsterdam ('Young in Europe around 1700: Norwegian Sailors and Servant Girls Seeking Employment in Amsterdam' in J.-P. Bardet *et al.* (eds) *offerts à Mesurer et comprendre. Mélanges Jacques Dupaquier* (Presses Universitaires de France, Paris, 1993), pp. 515–532) and suggests a link between female servant migration and male labour migration from the region of Stavanger to Amsterdam. See also T. Meldrum, *Domestic Service and Gender 1660–1750: Life and Work in the London Household* (Pearson, London, 2000): pp. 18–21. For more contemporary surveys see J. H. Momsen (ed.) *Gender, Migration and Domestic Service* and J.K. Lintelman, 'Making Service Serve Themselves: Immigrant Women and Domestic Service in North America, 1850–1920' and S. Wehner, 'German Domestic Servants in America 1850–1914: a New Look at German Immigrant Women's Experiences', the latter two both in D. Hoerder and J. Nagler (eds) *People in Transit: German Migrations in Comparative Perspective 1820–1930* (Cambridge University Press, Cambridge, 1995). For a recent contemporary study see B. Anderson, *Doing the Dirty Work: the Global Politics of Domestic Labour* (Zed Books, London, 2000).
25 W. Nugent, 'Demographic Aspects of European Migration Worldwide' in D. Hoerder and L. P. Moch (eds) *European Migrants*: p. 76. Harzig remarks in this volume that overall women formed 30–40 per cent of migrants to the United States during the period 1850 to the 1920s.
26 Kelson and Delaet, *Gender and Immigration*: p. 8.
27 Luise White's research cited in Teresa Barnes 'Virgin Territory? Travel and Migration by African Women in 20th-century Southern Africa' in S. Geiger,

J. Allman and N. Musisi (eds) *Women and African Colonial History* (Bloomington, Indiana University Press, forthcoming). Paper presented at a conference on Africa's Urban Past held at the School of Oriental and African Studies, University of London, June 1996).

28 Nugent, 'Demographic Aspects': p. 77.

29 Kathie Friedman-Kasaba, *Memories of Migration: Gender, Ethnicity, and Work in the Lives of Jewish and Italian Women in New York, 1870–1924* (State University of New York Press, New York, 1996): p. 61.

30 ibid.: p. 85.

31 ibid.: p. 173.

32 Moore, *Feminism and Anthropology*: p. 95.

33 This has been a common theme of studies of Africa but see also for India, S. Sen, 'Gendered Exclusion: Domesticity and Dependence in Bengal' in A. Janssens (ed.) *The Rise and Decline of the Male Breadwinner Family?* (*International Review of Social History Supplement*, Cambridge University Press, Cambridge, 1998): pp. 65–86.

34 M. Morokvasic, 'Women in Migration: Beyond the Reductionist Outlook' in A. Phizacklea (ed.) *One Way Ticket*: pp. 13–32.

35 M. Chamberlain, 'Gender and the Narratives of Migration' *History Workshop Journal*, 43 (1997): 87–108.

36 Zinn, 'The Sengalese Immigrants in Bari': p. 59.

37 For example, S. Marks and P. Richardson, *International Labour Migration: Historical Perspectives* (Maurice, Temple and Smith, London, 1984).

38 Barnes, 'Foreign Women and Virgin Territory': p. 23.

39 S. Chant and S.A. Radcliffe, 'Migration and Development: the Importance of Gender' in S. Chant (ed.) *Gender and Migration:* pp. 1–29.

40 D. Abdulrahim, 'Defining Gender in a Second Exile: Palestinian Women in West Berlin' in G. Buijs (ed.) *Migrant Women: Crossing Boundaries and Changing Identities* (Berg, Oxford, 1993): pp. 55–82.

41 O. Hufton, *The Prospect Before Her: A History of Women in Western Europe, Vol 1: 1500–1800* (HarperCollins, London, 1995): p. 494 on North German migrants to Amsterdam as domestic servants.

42 Hobsbawm, *Age of Extremes*: p. 309. For some background to this see Gabaccia, 'The "Yellow Peril"'.

43 See Introduction to L. Baldassar, *Visits Home: Ethnicity, Identity and Place in the Migration Process*' (Melbourne University Press, Melbourne, 2001).

44 P. L. Aymer, *Uprooted Women: Migrant Domestics in the Caribbean* (Praeger, Westport, CT and London, 1997): p. 77.

45 C. B. Brettell, *Men who Migrate: Women who Wait: Population and History in a Portugese Village* (Princeton, NJ, Princeton University Press, 1986).

46 J. Rodenburg, *In the Shadow of Migration: Rural Women and their Households in North Tapanuli, Indonesia* (KITLV Press, Leiden, 1997): p. 202.

47 Momsen, 'Gender selectivity': p. 83.

48 S. S. Weinberg, 'The Treatment of Women in Immigration History: a Call for Change?' in D. Gabaccia (ed.) *Seeking Common Ground: Multidisciplinary Studies of Immigrant Women in the United States* (Praeger, Westport, CT, 1992): p. 11.

49 C. Harzig, M. A. Knothe, M. Matovic, D. Mageean and M. Blaschke (eds), *Peasant Maids, City Women: from the European Countryside to Urban America* (Cornell University Press, Ithaca, NY and London, 1997): p. 4.

50 ibid.: pp. 135–6.

51 Friedman-Kasaba, *Memories of Migration*: p. 16.

52 ibid.: p. 28.

53 ibid.: p. 178.

2 Women migrants as global and local agents

New research strategies on gender and migration

Christiane Harzig

Though it has been more than fifteen years since the *International Migration Review* published its special issue on 'Women and Migration' and M. Morokvasic (1984) in her overview drew attention to women participating in international migration processes, every reflection on women and migration still begins by stating that women have generally been ignored by migration research.[1] And since the classical *homo migrans* is still defined in male terms (young, single, independent and unattached, endlessly mobile, in the prime of his physical strength) there is truth in this almost mantra-like complaint. However, migrating women or women in migration processes, whether as stayers or movers, are no longer invisible. The vast amount of case study research and the growing body of theoretical and conceptual reflections on *femina migrans* point to that fact. But it is often argued that migrant women and their (mostly female) chroniclers have not yet made it into mainstream migration research and analysis.

> The 'state of the art' is then that a majority of male authors write about migration in mainstream literature as if gender did not matter, while many women authors deliver fatal criticism of main (male!) stream research from a gender perspective but are little read outside their own circle and their criticism makes little impact on the main body of knowledge.[2]

Despite 'malestream' neglect migration is none the less a gendered process, that is a process which reflects the different positions of women and men in society.[3] This chapter attempts to bring together the conceptual findings of migration research with results from women-specific case studies. I am guided by the assumptions that, on the one hand, many of the 'women-centred' case studies have produced results which entice us to rethink and reconceptualise migration processes in general and their agent, the *homo migrans*, in particular, and on the other hand that new concepts in migration studies are very well suited to analyse the meaning of gender on the move. Migration here is conceived as the process encompassing conditions in the homeland, travel, as well as settlement at a point of arrival. Throughout my writing I will be guided by a *femina migrans* who has a timeless and spaceless disposition but who is imbued with a goodly portion of agency.[4] It is her task to keep me on track and focused on a gendered perspective. She will present herself as (i) part of various migration systems and subsystems; in which (ii) she will take on numerous roles and functions; (iii) she will participate in the building and maintenance of social and personal structures pertaining to migration, and (iv) she will reflect on her decision-making strategies. Throughout the process she will present her position in migration historiography.

From linear moves to migration systems

For a long time migration researchers, historians, sociologists, political scientists, have perceived migration along the push–pull paradigm, by which people moved from one place (culture/region of origin) to another place (receiving culture), mainly for social and economic, sometimes for religious and political reasons. The process was seen as linear, one-directional, with a beginning in one culture and an end in another. The migrant tried to insert him/herself into one new culture, creating a hyphenated identity, bicultural at the most. Central to this perception was the male pioneer, daring to venture into the unknown, scouting out the terrain, setting up structures for the woman to follow. With this push–pull paradigm North America and Europe figured as the main, if not the only, sending and receiving sides of the equation. If we follow with Pedraza the general historiography, immigration to (North) America proceeded along four waves:

> that of northwestern Europeans who immigrated up to the mid-nineteenth century; that of southern and eastern Europeans at the end of the nineteenth and beginning of the twentieth centuries; that of black Americans, Mexicans, and Puerto Ricans from the South to the North, precipitated by two world wars; and that of immigrants mostly from Latin America and Asia from 1965 on.[5]

Each of these movements with their various subgroups had specific gender compositions the implications of which we are only beginning to analyse.[6]

Rather than perceiving migration in a linear perspective with the occasional return migration, we are beginning to see people as multiple movers in more than one direction, being part of larger and more complex structural relationships than the push–pull paradigm implies. Migration-systems theory perceives migration as movement with complex trajectories. Referring to Moch and Jackson, Hoerder describes systems as ‘connecting two or more societies, each composed of various hierarchical groups of different interests, economic positions and political systems’.[7] It involves clustered moves in groups over time spans and is informed and nourished by personal and semi-public information. Within these often well-established systems people move along mental maps which may signify well-trodden paths, and may be quite different from geographic maps. 'Potential migrants, rightly or wrongly, perceive comparatively fewer constraints and increased opportunities at the destination'.[8]

The concept of migration systems enables us, for example, to move beyond the Euro-centred perception of the peopling of North America, pointing toward world-encompassing processes. Next to the 'dual Euro-Atlantic System' in which Southern Europeans move primarily to Central and South America and Northern Europeans to North America, and in which transoceanic migrations are related to intra-European migrations to industrial centres, there is an 'Afro-Atlantic system' constituted mainly by the slave trade, a 'transpacific system' which, surpassing racial and exclusionary policies, gained great momentum in the 1980s, and an 'intra-American system' in which migrants move mainly in the bicultural Hispanic-Anglo regions of the American Southwest (Texas and California).[9] It may not be of particular importance to *femina migrans* to know that she is part of one of these larger systems as long as she can negotiate the mental map which makes up the system. However, it has been the relational analysis of migration processes, informed by Gender Studies, which has brought forward the concept of systems and has made us aware of the more than linear aspect of migration decisions.

In each of these larger systems there are subsystems (waves, streams, movements) which are differentiated by time, origin, goal and purpose. People may leave rural areas in Europe (Sweden, Germany, the Ukraine) to settle in rural areas in North America (Minnesota, Wisconsin, the Canadian Prairies). These so-called settler migrations are usually dependent on a balanced sex ratio, the family being the basic unit of movement, and success of long-term settlement very much depended on the (reproductive and productive) input of women. The most intensive period of Prairie settlement in the United States (1840s to 1860s) saw more than 40 per cent female migrants[10] and in the late 1890s, when the Canadian Minister of Agriculture and Immigration was looking for people to settle the Canadian Prairies, he was looking for sturdy peasants with wives, being well aware of the necessary labour performed by women to secure long-term settlement.

With industrialisation gaining momentum in the second half of the nineteenth century people from rural as well as urban areas began to migrate to industrialising urban centres whether in Europe (Berlin, Vienna, London, Paris) or North America, in search of wage labour. This (labour) migration came to signify all subsequent migration with the male, independent young migrant in search of economic advancement being its most significant agent. It was generally assumed that it was the more adventurous man, less confined by traditions and conventions and reproductive responsibilities who wanted and was able to venture abroad, seeking and making use of better employment opportunities in industrial centres. Here the stereotype of the male pioneer and the female follower took shape.

However, the picture has turned out to be much more complex. As research has shown, because of the gendered labour market women too were in demand as labourers (pull factors), albeit in smaller numbers, and they often had the same incentives to move as men (push factors). Women who had moved from the Swedish countryside to Stockholm to work as maids or in the textile trades and then decided to move on to Chicago were as much aware of their labour market value and the higher wages they could realise abroad as their male counterparts.[11] The same is true for the young German women seeking employment in households in the neighbouring Netherlands during the 1920s to 1950s.[12] Not only did the service sector (a never-failing employment opportunity), the textile industry or the growing white-collar occupations provide employment opportunities for women, these sectors were also less sensitive to seasonal and business cycles, leading to a more steady movement of female labour migrants.

A combination of factors: the growing demand for female employment and a decline of the industrial sector combined with a change in immigration legislation, led to a steady rise in female immigration to the US, the 1930s being the turning point. The decade saw 55.3 per cent female migrants arriving in the US, rising to 61.2 in the 1940s. In both decades the absolute numbers were small. However, the trend remained steady, with women making up a stable 53 per cent of over four million by the 1980s.[13] Tyree and Donato pick up where Gabaccia left off, giving a demographic overview of worldwide labour migration systems of the 1960s and 1970s. Data show that though men dominate by numbers in all of these systems, from the Mediterranean periphery to the North European centres, to Latin America, within Africa, including the Arabic countries, women account for large portions of international migrants and they are in the majority to countries like Israel, Argentina and the United States. Once they moved, however, women tended to stay. The return migration rate for women from the US is significantly lower and the original sexual imbalance for migration into Germany, for example, becomes less pronounced when short-term immigration is discounted. And they show a much larger labour market participation rate than the women in the receiving cultures, as again is shown in the Turkish–German case for the 1970s.[14] Though many women may not have started out as independent labour migrants (though one-third of the labour migrants into Germany in the early 1960s were female) they certainly soon became part of the immigrant work-force.

As to refugee migration, nobody seems to question the preponderance of women, though it is rarely considered conceptually significant. It is estimated that of the *c.* 20 million refugees today 80 per cent are women.[15] Again it is the concept of the (well-educated) isolated, mature, politically persecuted male which informed the Geneva Convention definition of refugees and which still structures and guides the refugee determination system of most 'Western' countries.[16] What is considered 'political persecution' is also very much informed by a male understanding, which makes it often very difficult for women to be recognised as political refugees. Gender also determines the migratory choices of women. Often due to fewer resources being made available to them by family and support networks, women have fewer options for seeking refuge, usually escaping to neighbouring countries. As a rule of thumb we may say that the further the distance between the country of refuge and the country of asylum, the smaller the number of women in the refugee movement. The discrepancy between reality and concept, which arises from the dominant presence of women in refugee movements resulting from wars, civil wars, ethnic cleansing raids, ecological catastrophes and internal feuds on the one hand and the restrictive (male) definition of the Geneva Convention and asylum-granting bureaucracies on the other is especially disheartening.[17]

Roles and functions in migration processes

In each of these systems and movements, whether settler, labour or refugee movements, women perform vital functions and take up specific roles. They were pioneers, as in the case of Caribbean domestics to Canada in the late 1950s,[18] who, due to the very gender-specific labour demand for house-maids, were able to spearhead subsequent migration movements. Or they were, indeed, followers as in spouses migration,[19] their migration being sponsored by family unification policies – as in the subsequent migration of Turkish women into Germany; or by the war bride act of 1945, allowing war brides from Korea or Germany to follow their soldier husbands.[20] They may be considered as members of a family group – mothers, daughters – doing consumer-work, managing the family income, often establishing the private realm of family and household as their sphere of interest (in contrast to the women of the receiving society).[21] As single women they may seek factory work, and perhaps get involved in strike activities resulting, for example in the most active and radical 'International Ladies Garment Workers Union' of the many Italian and Jewish immigrant women in New York in 1909;[22] or they may opt for the secure and familiar employment of domestic service, as many German women chose to do for a period of time which often ended in marriage.[23]

Today, as well-educated women, being part of the 'brain drain' migration, they may hope to find qualified employment related to their previous education and training. However, not all 'South–North' movement of well-educated people (women) should be considered brain drain. At the moment India produces an 'abundance' of female software programmers who experience few problems emigrating to Canada. Or they may be refugee women either organising survival for their kin groups in refugee camps or negotiating status, credibility and acceptance in the bureaucratic regime of asylum-granting (or not) countries. The social activist Mary Jo Leddy (1997) has brought together in her book *At the Border Called Hope* a very telling collection of stories by refugee women she has helped to fight for justice. These life-stories provide moving insights into the everyday negotiations for survival in a 'safe' country, even when life is not immediately threatened. It is through these roles and functions that migrant women interact with the receiving societies and it is in these interactive processes that new identities are formed or changed.

Most of the research on women in the migration process during the past two decades has focused upon roles and functions in the immigrant communities, and here the most interesting and far-reaching results were brought forward. US labour historians almost inevitably had to discuss issues of race, ethnicity and immigration when trying to analyse working-class culture. In doing so they discovered complex forms of co-operation and conflict, resistance and incorporation among immigrant men and women.[24] US women's history, in contrast, took much longer, and still has not completely succeeded in conceptualising 'the immigrant woman' into its analysis of the women's movement. However, in the many sub-fields of American (social) history – labour, urban, African-American, family history – migrants are no longer considered as 'the other', the deviant, whose incorporation into Anglo-dominated society has to be explained. Rather, their experience has come increasingly to signify the base material which structures and shapes American history and culture.[25]

At the same time that Americans began to rewrite their history from a multicultural perspective, people in Europe (the Netherlands, Germany, Sweden, France, Britain) began to notice the 'foreign woman' among them. In Germany she entered the scene as a pathological case, as a research object for educators, social workers and the medical profession, where gynaecologists were especially concerned with assimilating immigrant women to child-bearing processes in high-tech hospitals.[26] Migrants of the guestworkers movement were constructed as the 'other' and often the question was how the co-existence of migrant and 'native' population could be negotiated in such a way as to enable their return to the homeland. It was generally assumed that women had followed their men into structures men had created for them. While the Netherlands and Sweden began to perceive themselves as immigrant countries and France and Britain attempted to come to terms with their colonial past, Germany remained in a state of denial, while at the same time allowing for a broad range of community formation and multi-ethnic cultural development.

Building transnational communities

This will bring us forward to the issue of community formation. After we have seen *femina migrans* as a member of larger migration systems, as participant of more specific subsystems, as taking up a number of roles and functions within these subsystems, using these functions in interaction with the receiving society, we have come to realise that she plays the decisive role in the community-building process. Without a crucial number of women in the migration wave, it is safe to say there will be no community-building process, or as Tyree and Donato put it: 'The presence of a large number of women in immigration populations appears to signal settlement rather than transiency.'[27]

The concept of community has provided a useful framework in which to discuss a number of aspects of the migrants' life. Not only have women proven to be essential to the community-building process, migration itself has been seen as the terrain where gender relations are renegotiated. Under the heading of 'community' (and neighbourhood)[28] we may consider the changing reality of material culture in the migration process, i.e., adjustment to living conditions, eating habits, dress.[29] It is also easy to see how women's agency as household workers, consumers and care givers is essential in adjusting past experience to present reality.[30] Another aspect concerns the emergence of an organisational structure which negotiates a 'before' and 'after' experience, that is, mediates between 'old world' values, customs, habits and traditions and the demands of the modern-industrial-urban 'new world'. Mutual aid and benefit societies, charity organisations, recreational groups (such as choirs or gymnastics societies known as 'turners'), 'Landsmanschaften' or groups based on region of origin (not only organised by Jewish groups) and – most important – the church, provide a (semi-)public space for immigrant women, a space situated between the traditional confines of the home and the demands for public representation of the receiving society. The next step would be into the ethnicity-based activities in formations provided by the corporate society – unions, political parties. The third aspect which may be discussed against the background of community is identity formation, i.e., changing concepts of national identities, creation of hyphenated identities, usage of different identities in different settings for different purposes, and again, changing gender relations.

So far analysis of immigrant communities has focused on one or more ethnic groups in one space (Chicago's North Side, New York's Lower East Side, Vienna's 10th District). Now we begin to see migrants living in diasporas or transnational communities, recognising the fact that migration is a process involving multiple moves and relationships. Transnational communities are occupied by diaspora populations which may have to satisfy three minimal criteria:

> First, the population is dispersed from a homeland to two or more other territories. Second, the presence abroad is enduring, although exile is not necessarily permanent, but may include movement between homeland and new host. And third, there is some kind of exchange

> – social economic, political or cultural – between or among the spatially separate populations comprising the diaspora.[31]

The agents of these diasporas or transnational communities also have to be perceived in multi-relational terms. They have to come to be understood as transmigrants who 'develop and maintain multiple relations – familial, economic, social, organisational, religious and political – that span borders'. Accordingly the transmigrants' experience is described as transnational, emphasising 'the emergence of a social process in which migrants establish social fields that cross geographic, cultural and political borders'.[32]

Whereas the idea of diaspora goes back to the Greek word signifying 'dispersion' and the Jewish experience of some 2500 years ago,[33] the concept of transnationalism/transmigrants has been developed by anthropologists interested in presentday migration experiences. The concept has been derived from looking at today's Caribbean, Filipino and Hispanic populations in New York, assuming that global capitalism and modernday processes of transportation and communications are, if not prerequisites for, then facilitators of transnational identities. However, it is easy to see how these ideas can also be applied to historical immigration experiences. As much as Filipinas send home duty-free *balikbayan* boxes,[34] Irish-American maids transferred money to support families at home or sent pre-paid tickets to enable 'chain-migration'.[35] As much as Haitians remain involved in island politics while working and living in New York, Polish-American women saw it to be their patriotic-feminist duty to support liberation of Poland from Prussian rule and to instil and maintain love for the homeland while bringing up their offspring, thus educating transnational identities.[36] But though form and content of transnational and transmigratory encounters may be carried across historical time and space, it is the different experience of contemporary time, the vastness of transspatial processes, which may lend a different quality to today's transnational experiences.

The gender-informed analytical perceptions in relational terms: keeping contact, maintaining relationships, upholding communications, storing knowledge about personal histories, preserving tradition and adjusting cultural practices, help us perceive the larger complexities of migration processes not as bi- or multicultural but as transcultural processes.

Decision-making processes on the meso level

After we have situated *femina migrans* as a global player in multidirectional and multilayered migration processes, we should want to know how the decisions as to why, when and where to go are formed. I argue that her actions are most likely guided by careful reflection, selecting and weighing her options. Historical research on immigrant women has shown that the decisions to emigrate were usually made within the context of the family, guided by the needs of the family economy, informed through letters and reports from earlier migrants. Labour market prospects, the relationship between qualification and opportunities, marriage markets and possible family formation, responsibilities for family care, all these elements had an impact on the decision. In addition, we may suppose a widespread culture of migration in late nineteenth- and early twentieth-century (as much as in the last decades of the twentieth century) Europe with well-established information and transportation networks. There was also a widespread popular culture of novels, stories, tales, songs and poems celebrating the trials and glories of emigration and (successful) return.[37] Within this migration culture Irish mothers encouraged their daughters to leave; Swedish families did not stand in the way of their daughters' wanderlust; and Polish girls were sent abroad to earn cash and to find a husband.

What was common then is even more widespread today. Women's migration very much relies on extended networks. As Hillmann in her analysis of women migrants from Somalia, Peru and the Philippines in Italy has pointed out, all of these women primarily migrated for economic reasons and the internal organisation of the process very much relied on the embeddedness of the migrants in family and household strategies. It is these household and family strategies and considerations which at first confused the individually based rational-choice models of the sociologists who were trying to explain emigration. What appears rational to a Western-acculturated, economically informed (single) researcher may not appear rational to the Somali woman who decides to migrate to Italy in order to earn money so her brother can migrate to Sweden in pursuit of better educational facilities.[38] Migration of Filipino women is very much guided by a system of reciprocal social relations, deeply rooted in Filipino culture, which determines the instigation and continuity of migration.[39]

In order to provide an analytical home for the concepts of strategies and networks which have proven to be so important for understanding female migration patterns, historians and sociologists have introduced the meso-level as an analytical realm. It relates the individual experience and motivation to the larger social, economic and political structures. Thus, to better understand the relationship between movers and stayers as players in migration processes we may work on three levels of analysis: the micro-level of rational choice, the macro-level of migration systems theory and the meso-level of social relations between the individuals in kin-groups, households, neighbourhoods, friendship circles and formal organisations. Crucial categories of meso-level analysis are 'social ties' and 'social capital' in social networks. Social capital is created in exchange relationships, reciprocity, trust, and solidarity.[40]

The more historically grounded approach by Hoerder also uses the meso-level to analyse the negotiation between the worldwide systems and the life course of the individual.

> The worldwide systems approach requires adaptation to local circumstances or specific groups. Networks of families, larger kin groups, and neighbourhoods integrate individuals into local units that form societal segments. Migration offers spatial options in other parts of the world for specific family economies and village or neighbourhood groups, for members of specific crafts, and for families active in commerce.[41]

On the meso-level we may analyse the migrants' decision-making strategies as well as their incorporation into segmented systems of the receiving society. The relationship between the individual migrant and the state, i.e., entry permissions, residence permits (Germany), landed immigrant status (Canada), Green Cards (United States), denizen or citizenship status may also be negotiated and analysed on the meso-level. In recent years the relationship between the state and the migrant has received growing attention. Citizenship and immigration policy have been shown to produce different sets of relations to the state for men and women migrants.

Derivative citizenship, a political concept stemming from the eighteenth-century idea of coverture, here implying that a woman should follow her husband's citizenship in bi-national marriages, remained dominant in most countries until the 1950s. In her detailed and thoughtful analysis of US legislation (1907–1934) Bredbenner has shown yet another very striking example of the gendered construction of nationhood: an American woman marrying a foreigner was considered a patriotic threat, yet a foreign (immigrant) woman marrying a US citizen would, it was assumed, always be grateful for having gained entry to this superior nation and thus would gladly fulfil her patriotic duty when raising her children. Thus, in the first case the woman was expatriated; in the second case the woman received US citizenship when signing the marriage licence. While these ideas become evident looking at congressional debates (among men), the study of law suits shows the often unexpected detrimental consequence for thus expatriated women, not being able to vote or being threatened with deportation if they become dependent on charity. After gaining the right to vote in 1920 with the passage of the 'Anthony Amendment', politically active women's groups made it their prime object to fight for 'a nationality of their own' and a revision of the law.

While the study of immigration policy (entry control, permission to stay, naturalisation) has a historical dimension – outlining the various restrictionist legislations directed against unwanted 'races' (Chinese, Japanese, East Indians) and ethnic groups (Eastern and Southern Europeans) leading up to the Quota laws[42] in the mid-1920s, for example – it remains the most prominent concern of contemporary migration studies. Today immigration policies in Europe and North America not only influence migration processes – direction, demographic and occupational composition, legality – they also impose themselves on the migrants' identities, maybe more so than even race, class, or gender.[43] Whether a migrant is seeking asylum and/or has had it granted, whether s/he has the right to work or an indefinite right to stay, whether s/he is negotiating legality, is hiding from or fighting against deportation, whether access to citizenship is made difficult or granted as a prerequisite for the subsequent integration process, all of these aspects influence his or her position in the transnational community, influence subsequent migration networks and strategies, and affect gender relations in the diaspora. A woman may very well decide, for example, that it is worth her while to give over her children to the family network and seek work as a domestic in Canada for two years. During her time as a maid she may decide not to send all of her savings back home but rather to invest into building up a household in Canada, thus delaying thoughts of return. Afterwards she may apply for landed immigrant status and thus be able to sponsor the subsequent immigration of her children. All of these decisions may be analysed on the meso-level, relating individual goals to national policies.

Conclusion

Detailed knowledge of the various immigration policies is the most valuable capital of 'travel' agencies aiding (legally or illegally) the migration process. Every decision by industrial countries to make immigration more restrictive increases the profit margin for these agencies. But while 'travel agencies' are more flexible in responding to the market of migrating women[44] and men, immigration policy makers have so far failed to realise the complexity of migrants' decision-making strategies. Any legal arrangement providing for the individual migrant with (labour) marketable skills which fails to account for the mental maps of transnational migrants, the multiple layers of decision-making strategies and the complexities of transnational communities, will be unable to control migration 'waves'. An immigration policy which considers family sponsorship and family unification the exceptional form of entry rather than the rule does not reflect the realities of transmigrants' lives. It inevitably has to fail.

As migrants of past and present show, migration works within transworld migration systems which are formed not only by global capitalism but by well-informed global players – the migrants themselves – performing multiple gendered functions, deciding about their moves in transnational communities, considering their assets on the global labour market and relying on networks formed by family, kin, friendship and neighbourhood/village. Within these transnational processes women are often decisive agents pursuing their own agenda at the local and global levels, negotiating gendered strategies and options.

Notes

1 See for example the otherwise very good article by S. Prodolliet, 'Ohne Migrantinnen geht wirtschaftlich nichts', *Widerspruch* 19, 37 (1999): 95–106. For a recent analysis providing a conceptual introduction see P. Hondagneu-Sotelo, 'Gender and Contemporary U.S. Immigration', special issue, *American Behavioral Scientist* 42 (1999): 4.
2 G. Bjerén, 'Gender and Reproduction' in T. Hammar *et al.* (eds) *International Migration, Immobility and Development: Multidisciplinary Perspectives*, Oxford: Berg, 1997, pp. 224–225.
3 ibid., p. 221.
4 Despite my attempt to be as encompassing as possible, I have to acknowledge the fact that I know most about Euro–North American migrations in the nineteenth and twentieth centuries.
5 S. Pedraza-Bailey, 'Immigration Research: a Conceptual Map', *Social Science History* 14, 1 (1990): 49–50.
6 R. Cohn, 'A Comparative Analysis of European Immigration Streams to the United States during the Early Mass Migration', *Social Science History* 19, 1 (1995): 61–89; D. Gabaccia, 'Women of the Mass Migrations: From Minority to Majority, 1820–1930' in D. Hoerder and L. P. Moch (eds) *European Migrants: Global and Local Perspectives,* Boston: Northwestern University Press, 1996, pp. 90–111.
7 D. Hoerder, 'From Immigration to Migration Systems: New Concepts in Migration History', *Magazine of History* 14, 1 (1999): 5–12.
8 ibid., p. 6.
9 ibid., p. 8.
10 Gabaccia, 'Women of the Mass Migrations', p. 91.
11 M. Matovic, 'Maids in Motion: Swedish Women in Dalsland' in C. Harzig (ed.) *Peasant Maids–City Women: from the European Country Side to Urban America,* Ithaca, NY: Cornell University Press, 1997, pp. 99–142.
12 B. Henkes, *Heimat in Holland. Deutsche Dienstmädchen 1920–1950*, Straelen/ Niederrhein: Straelener Manuskripte, 1998.
13 Gabaccia, 'Women of the Mass Migrations'.
14 A. Tyree and K. Donato, 'A Demographic Overview of the International Migration of Women' in C. Brettell and R. J. Simon (eds) *International Migration: the Female Experience*, Totowa, NJ: Rowman & Allanheld, 1986, pp. 21–44. This may very likely have changed in the 1990s due to the restructuring of the labour market which showed a strong decline in the low-skill job bracket, i.e., the textile industry in Europe and North America.
15 S.F. Martin, *Refugee Women*, London: Zed Books, 1995.
16 The question as to whether women constitute a 'social group' and whether gender-specific persecutions may be considered is another important issue for discussion.
17 On the life of refugee women in the receiving cultures, for Europe, see M. Schöttes and M. Schuckar (eds) *Frauen auf der Flucht*, 2 vols, Berlin: Edition Parabolis, 1994. For Canada see W.Giles, H. Mussa and P. van Esterik (eds) *Development and Diaspora: Gender and the Refugee Experience*, Dundas, Ontario: Artemis Enterprises, 1996.
18 C. Harzig, '"The Movement of 100 Girls." 1950s Canadian Immigration Policy and the Market for Domestic Labour', *Zeitschrift für Kanada Studien* 19, 2 (1999): 131–146.
19 As to the complexity of marriage migration see S. Sinke, 'Migration for Labor, Migration for Love: Marriage and Family Formation', *Magazine of History* 14, 1 (1999): 17–21.

20 R. Eßer, '"Sprache kein Hindernis"– Kriegsbräute in der deutschen Presse 1945–1949', paper presented at the Summer Institute on Migration, Humboldt University, Berlin, 1997.
21 S. Prodolliet, 'Ohne Migrantinnen geht wirtschaftlich nichts', *Widerspruch* 19, 37 (1999): 95–106.
22 M. S. Seller, 'The Uprising of the Twenty Thousand: Sex, Class, and Ethnicity in the Shortwaist Makers' Strike of 1909' in D. Hoerder (ed.) *'Struggle a Hard Battle': Essays on Working-class Immigrants*. DeKalb, IL: Northern Illinois University Press, 1986.
23 S. Wehner-Franco, *Deutsche Dienstmädchen in Amerika, 1850–1914,* Münster: Waxmann, 1994.
24 See for example the proverbial radicalism of Jewish female textile workers in New York, one of the earliest 'discoveries' of ethnicity conscious labour history. See also the chapter 'Working Together' in D. Gabaccia, *From the Other Side: Women, Gender and Immigrant Life in the U.S., 1820–1990*, Bloomington: Indiana University Press, 1994.
25 Gabaccia, *From the Other Side.*
26 See the early entries in M. Schulz (ed.), *Fremde Frauen. Von der Gastarbeiterin zur Bürgerin*, Frankfurt a.M.: Verlag für Interkulturelle Kommunikation, 1992.
27 Tyree and Donato, 'A Demographic Overview', p. 40.
28 In a more extended version one could discuss the relationship between the 'material' neighbourhood and the 'ideal' community.
29 Gabaccia, *From the Other Side.*
30 Harzig, *Peasant Maids–City Women.*
31 N. Van Hear, *New Diasporas: the Mass Exodus, Dispersal and Regrouping of Migrant Communities,* Seattle: University of Washington Press, 1998, p. 6.
32 N.G. Schiller, L. Basch and C. Blanc-Szanton, 'Towards a Definition of Transnationalism', in *Annals of the New York Academy of Science* vol. 645, 6 July 1992, *Towards a Transnational Perspective on Migration*, 645, p. ix.
33 R. Cohen, 'Rethinking "Babylon": iconoclastic conceptions of the diasporic experience', *New Community* 21, 1 (1995): 5–18 provides a useful analysis of the emergence of the diaspora concept.
34 Schiller, Basch and Blanc-Szanton, 'Towards a Definition of Transnationalism', p. 4.
35 H. Diner, *Erin's Daughters in America,* Baltimore, MD: Johns Hopkins University Press, 1983. J. Nolan, *Ourselves Alone: Women's Emigration from Ireland 1885–1920*, Lexington: University of Kentucky Press, 1989.
36 W. J. Galush, 'Purity and Power: Chicago Polonian Feminists, 1880–1914', *Polish American Studies* 67 (1990): 5–24.
37 My private collection of (German) emigration novels containing titles such as 'A German Emigrates' or 'A Rascal in America' show large editions of 30,000 to 40,000 copies in the 1920s and 1930s. The Irish 'wake' mourning the departure of emigrants has become a standard item of Irish folk culture.
38 F. Hillmann, *Jenseits der Kontinente: Migrationsstrategien von Frauen nach Europa*, Paffenweiler: Centaurus Verlag, 1996, p. 185.
39 Hillmann, *Jenseits der Kontinente,* p. 141, dedicates a large section to discussing the women's own perceptions of the migration process and the related strategies.
40 T. Faist, 'The Crucial Meso-Level' in T. Hammar *et al.* (eds) *International Migration, Immobility and Development*, pp. 187–218.
41 D. Hoerder, 'Segmented Macrosystems and Networking Individuals: the Balancing Functions of Migration Processes' in J. Lucassen and L. Lucassen (eds) *Migration, Migration History, History: Old Paradigms and New Perspectives*, Bern: Peter Lang AG, 1997, p. 78.

42 For newer research and analysis see E. Lee, 'Immigrants and Immigration Law: a State of the Field Assessment', *Journal of American Ethnic History* 18, 4 (1999): 85–114.

43 C. Harzig, 'A Migrant is a Migrant is a Migrant: Immigration Policies in Post-World-War-II Europe', *Magazine of History* 14, 1 (1999): 22–25.

44 Hillmann, *Jenseits der Kontinente.*

3 Leaving home to help the family?

Male and female temporary migrants in eighteenth- and nineteenth-century Spain

Carmen Sarasúa

In peasant societies based on family farms, temporary and seasonal migrations were a resource on which most households periodically relied, one of the few sources of cash apart from the sale of dairy goods and other forms of domestic production.

In eighteenth-century Europe, factors relating both to the demand for (increasing labour opportunities in industry and, due to city growth, services) and to the supply of (growing need for peasant families to make payments in cash for taxes, etc.) labour led to an increasing dependence of peasant families on these migrations. As a result, 'migration time' became an essential part of the peasants' life-cycle, playing a fundamental role in the process by which peasants adapted themselves to urban and new working environments and fundamentally shaping their skills, income and possibilities of social mobility.[1]

Differences between female and male workers involved in flows of temporary migration have been described with reference to the decision to migrate itself, the distance of the migration and the age at which the migration started.

First, the decision to migrate: in some places migration appears as almost totally a male experience. This seems to have been the case in regions where migration was usually across the sea,[2] and it has been explained by three reasons: first, the single man's greater need to obtain resources in order to establish his own family. In areas where the inheritance system or the property system prevented men from having access to sufficient resources, out-migration would have functioned as an alternative means of achieving these resources. Second, men have greater access to family and external financial (credit) resources, for instance, to buy boat passages. The third explanation given is men's greater chance of finding a job as a migrant worker, and their higher salaries which, in theory, make 'man's migration' the best family strategy.

It is not only long-distance migration that has been defined as mostly male, however. In mountain areas of Europe, seasonal and temporary short- and medium-distance migration was apparently mostly male too, since most of the growing demand for labour from urban centres was for male workers (stonemasons, masons, etc.).[3]

A second difference is distance travelled to find work. Where both female and male migration existed, female migration tended to be over short distances with male migration over longer distances. Ravenstein (1885) made of this one of his laws of migrations.

The third difference is that women appear to have migrated at a younger age than men.[4] This seems to be related to the greater importance of employment in domestic service for women (both girls and boys were taken into domestic service at a very young age), and the earlier age of marriage for women.[5]

However, although they have been noted, sex-differentiated migration patterns have not been examined with a view to determining male/female role and status differences. In this chapter I argue that an analysis of this type requires an understanding of the experience of men and women migrants, including not only the nature of the task involved but also the social relations under which work was carried out. As a contribution to such an analysis, the chapter focuses on temporary migrations as mechanisms for gaining access to resources, here conceptualised as economic resources and also the skills and experience that were to prove fundamental for workers' later conversion to permanent waged work.

Emphasis on the conditions and relations under which temporary migrations took place is important, since peasant women and men who undertook temporary migrations (temporary work for wages) did so as members of families, as heads of households or as wives, that is, as components of an established relationship in which duties and rights were defined in terms of both consumption and production. They did not go as individuals choosing to undertake certain activities at different moments of their lives.

The position of the migrant within the family relationship conditioned his or her access to wage labour in two ways: first, it determined entrance into the labour market. In some places, women were precluded from participating in seasonal and temporary migratory flows which were primary sources of earnings in their local economies, in what could be seen as an antecedent of the nineteenth-century construction of wage labour as a male realm.

Second, the intent is to determine the migrants' access to the earnings derived from their migration. This chapter analyses two internal migratory flows existing in Spain during the eighteenth and nineteenth centuries, originating in the same area, the northern province of Santander. The first one was a female flow, to work as wet nurses in Madrid, at a distance of about 400 km. The second was a male flow, to work as dockworkers at the southern seaport of Cádiz, at about 1,000 km.

Both were well-established flows, well known to contemporaries. In both cases, the workers involved in them were adult members of peasant families,

Map 3.1 Map of Spain showing significant places mentioned in this chapter

married (married migrants tended to be temporary and seasonal migrants, while for single migrants temporary movements often meant the first step towards permanent migration, which included getting married), travelling to an urban centre to work for some years for wages that were intended to be invested in the family farm. Yet the cases analysed show that working as temporary migrants, spending an important period of their adult lives working away from home, had rather different effects for women and men workers, especially in regard to their respective capacities to use the earnings generated by their own migration and those generated by the migration of family members.

The construction of migration as male

'The deeply seated image of women in these times as sedentary, as tied to home and family, is simply not true for the lower classes; that is, the majority of the population.'[6]

This image is due partially to the sources traditionally used to study migration.[7] But it also reflects a reality: women had no access to most long-distance migratory flows. Highland areas all over Europe, like the region studied here, were important sources of temporary emigration.

The gender pattern of these migratory flows was always very similar: during the winter months men would leave for the plains to work as artisans, stonecutters, woodcutters, clockmakers.[8] Excluded from apprenticeship by guild regulation and social custom, women had no access to these migratory flows; instead they went into domestic service or remained at home working in domestic textile industries or agriculture. The special difficulties of identifying domestic workers further reinforce the invisibility of women as migrants for the historian.

Women's participation in agricultural migratory flows, on the other hand, was directly regulated. A good example of such external regulation is provided by the sustained attempt to exclude women from the gangs of Gallego harvesters. Migration to Andalusia and Castile to harvest attracted each year some 25,000 to 30,000 young women and men, and was the main source of income for inland areas without access to the fisheries. Female participation apparently accounted for about a third of this flow of migration. This became, during the eighteenth century, a matter of deep concern for authorities. In an attempt to put an end to it, a series of prohibitive measures were enacted.[9]

Prohibitions came from the State, the city councils and the Church. In 1736, emigration of single women to Castile 'who go in the company of their fathers, uncles or brothers, as well as for married women, not in the company of their husbands' was forbidden. The town councils also tried to prohibit the migration of those women who 'with the pretext of going to work' abandoned Galicia (1748). Meijide Pardo (1960) mentions 'endless announcements in all the parishes'. Also in 1748 jail sentences or the confiscation of property for those contravening the prohibition were announced.

In 1754 an order from the administrative authority of Galicia revealed that women were emigrating in men's clothes:

> That no gang boss nor other person who goes to the works of Castile takes any woman, under penalty of twenty *ducados* for each one taken, and of ten years of jail in one of the presidiums of Africa; that no husband, father, brother, or relative or master, permits his wife, daughters, sisters, relatives or servants who are under his custody, to go to such works, under the same penalty; that justices and officials be vigilant in the observance of this and let it immediately be known when any woman from their parish is missing, and take and place an embargo on the properties of the person under whose custody she is. If the justices do not enforce this law they must pay fifty ducados and thirty to the officials; in cases of women being found going to the work dressed in men's clothes, besides the said penalties, she and the man taking her must be punished by public shaming.[10]

In 1766 a new order by the minister Aranda recalls the endless regulations to impede women from migrating to Castile 'in men's gangs'.

The notion of restricting women's mobility was widespread. Describing the province of Santander, an enlightened author complained in 1798 that

> in the valleys of Camargo, Piélagos, and villages of the Abadía, there are perverse women whose excessive behaviour runs to coming to Santander [town] with small bundles of fagots on their heads and that for the eight or ten *quartos* they make for each of them, they tear their clothes to gather the fagots and they never know in practice the spindle or the distaff. For a wage of a real it is possible to find women ready to go thus loaded two or three miles, but no one who wants to spin even if the price be doubled. It follows from this a distraction from their proper work, the fact that they get accustomed to idle loafing, to eating and drinking in the taverns, to the crowds that the roads provide to seduce their ignorance rather than to a modest behaviour; and finally that they escape from spinning, weaving, and sewing, and every labour that restricts them to the home.[11]

The ideal of domestic seclusion was in sharp contrast to the activities that women had traditionally undertaken. But it inspired Catholic opinion, propagated every week in the churches, and, above all, policies and regulations concerning the labour market. At the beginning of the nineteenth century, women migrants found employment only in domestic service.

However, it was not only a matter of occupational segregation. Regulation or direct prohibition of women's participation in flows of temporary or seasonal migration denied them access to the most dynamic part of the emergent market economy, thus preventing them from improving their working skills, earning wages, and achieving social mobility through wage labour.

Migration of women from La Montaña to Madrid to work as wet nurses

The region between the Basque country and Asturias was part of the province of Burgos until the mid-nineteenth century and was known as 'the Mountain'. The economy of the interior part of this Cantabric region consisted of a mix of arable and dairy farming. The marginal character of most of the land meant low productivity, and the egalitarian system of inheritance (after continuous partition) resulted in very small plots. For these reasons, Galicia, Asturias, Cantabria and the Basque country, which were mountainous regions, became, during the nineteenth century, main sources of temporary, seasonal and permanent migrant workers.

The valley of Pas, located in the interior part of the province of Santander, is a good example of such an economy. The isolation resulting from bad communications and distance from urban centres was overcome by the initiative of its inhabitants, who tirelessly walked roads which no animals could traverse to transport their dairy produce to the local markets. This short-distance movement (to sell dairy produce or for smuggling), played an important role in accustoming Pasiego people to mobility and giving them contact with towns and urban markets.[12]

Pasiego women became famous nationwide as wet nurses, an activity that they performed in most northern capitals and, above all, in Madrid, where they were wet nurses to the offspring of the royal family. Wet nurses of the royal family had traditionally come from Castile. King Fernando VII (1814–1833) was the first to choose a Cantabric wet nurse to nurse one of his children, reflecting a change in the demand in the Madrid market for wet nurses.

In the second half of the eighteenth century, a series of changes in the wet nursing market increased the opportunities for women from the northern regions. Influenced by the criticisms of doctors and politicians of the high rates of infant mortality (due, according to them, to the practice of taking the babies to the wet nurse's village), urban middle- and upper-class families began hiring and bringing wet nurses into their homes and this occasioned a shift in the geography of the market: wet nurses no longer needed to be from areas near the cities, so women from distant regions gained access to the wet nursing market.[13] A particular preference for northern women, who were considered healthier and also of the purest blood (not contaminated by Protestant or by Muslim blood, as was often the case in the southern regions), eventually became a main feature of the Madrid market. The fact that the royal family chose its wet nurses from these regions further reinforced the demand.

As a result of this confluence of supply and demand factors, by the end of the eighteenth century most wet nurses employed by the well-to-do families of Madrid were from the northern regions. Although women from Asturias were by far the majority of them, the most sought after were from the Cántabro valleys, especially from the Pasiego valley. Pasiego wet nurses became so famous that the term Pasiega is still synonymous with wet nurse.[14] Writer Emilia Pardo Bazán explained this identification at the end of the nineteenth century:

> The litoral of our Cantabric Sea provides Madrid mostly with this human commodity, which most advantaged type is produced in the famous Pas Valley, from which the name 'pasiega' cames, with which we designate all wet nurses, although the natives of Bierzo in the Mountains of León are equally good.[15]

I have studied the temporary migration of wet nurses to Madrid through the *Diario oficial de Avisos de Madrid*, a journal that began publication in 1758.[16] The flow of Pasiego women to Madrid started in the last decades of the eighteenth century. The first advertisement of a wet nurse identifying herself as Pasiega appeared on 4 November 1786, though it is likely

Plate 3.1 Late nineteenth-century postcard of Pasiego wet nurses

that others were already working as wet nurses in Madrid. In any case, this was the beginning of a migration that rapidly organised itself and that would last over 150 years.[17]

> The purpose of getting employment as wet nurses is what brings these peasant women to Madrid, a few weeks, or even days, after giving birth. 'They walk the road with bread and wine', goes the old Spanish saying, and a Pasiega fulfils that saying in her trip to Madrid, considering herself very lucky if she can add to those foodstuffs some other nutritious substance that neither her wealth, nor the assortment of the wayside inns provide. Half dressed, halfshod, walking during the day, and sleeping during the night on the hard soil, these unhappy women make their journey. But their health, their robustness, and strong nature resist everything, and they arrive at Madrid as ruddy and fresh as if they had not undergone any deprivation.[18]

Group movements, characteristic of seasonal and temporary migrations, appear also in the flow of Pasiego wet nurses to Madrid. Unlike other migrations, though, the rhythm of this depends on a personal circumstance, the timing of a baby's delivery. Women from the same village who had decided to look for a job as wet nurse in town would wait for each other to recover from a birth to travel together.[19] In order to keep their milk, they carried a puppy with them:

> They undertake with virile resolution the path to the Court, either alone segregated in a covered wagon, or together walk in group. The first thing they do, until, as they say, they find an arrangement, is to provide themselves with a newly born puppy, which during the expedition works as a baby and applying it to the breast, keeps and maintains the nutritious juice, object of speculation.[20]

The hiring process

Once in Madrid, if they did not already have lodgings, they would go to the square of Santa Cruz, near Plaza Mayor, the town's centre. Surrounded by arcades with fabric stores, this place was an outdoors labour market:

> At the plaza de Santa Cruz, in Madrid, there is a daily market in human flesh, one whose effect on social custom has yet to be considered. Those who pass, look, see a group of Pasiegas sit on the floor, or on the stones that form the edge of an entrance hall, some with a baby, others without, and without paying more attention, or thinking about it, continue on their way [. . .] What are these poor and robust Pasiegas doing here, some eating crumbs of bread, others with an envious face?[21]

From at least the second half of the eighteenth century this place was also frequented by Pasiego itinerant sellers, men and women, who sold in Madrid the fabrics, especially muslins, that they smuggled in from the fiscally exempted Basque provinces. Pasiego wet nurses probably arrived in Madrid with these itinerant sellers and were helped by them at the beginning of their stay in the capital. An advertisement for fashion fabrics that appeared in the *Diario* on 30 September 1802, refers to the stall as 'the stall that Pasiego women have': 'In the stall that Pasiego women have in the plaza de Santa Cruz there is a great assortment of fine spotted muslin of high quality and fashion designs'. These Pasiego women sellers of fabrics acted probably as the link with the Pasiego women who arrived to work as wet nurses, some decades later.[22]

Different means of hiring were used:

> They come to the Court, they stand in the plaza de Santa Cruz and trusting their ruddy complexion and robust appearance, among other qualities proper to wet nurses, they insert in the Diario de Avisos an advertisement, the content of which is with small variations as follows: 'X., 23 years old, with milk four months old, wants to find a nursling at the parents' home; she is robust and has some one to recommend her. A reference will be given at Barquillo street.' Through this means, or by effect of private recommendations and after the necessary arrangements, the Pasiega enters the home of an opulent family, of a

> noble Grande de España perhaps, or the Royal Palace itself, with the object of breastfeeding one or more children successively.[23]

Once a family had contacted the wet nurse, she had to go through a medical examination, which was determinant of the choice, and is described in all the gynaecology books. Indeed, there is evidence that women were instructed by colleagues and friends on how to respond to the doctors' questions. The importance of the nurse's physical condition, and of the quality of her milk, explains how doctors and midwives became heavily involved in the hiring process, often as mediaries.[24]

Working conditions of wet nurses in Madrid

The resident wet nurse became a characteristic figure of the nineteenth-century urban theatre. The rise in demand for such women increased their wages, and to have such a nurse became a status symbol. Part of the wet nurse's working day was spent at public places like parks, where she, sometimes with the help of a young assistant, took the baby. A key element of this new social figure was the uniform, a mystified version of the northern peasant costume that proclaimed the origin, and, hence, the cost, of the wet nurse.

> It is six o'clock. Let us walk towards the Puerta del Sol, but not without first stopping for a while in the gardens in the first part of Alcalá street. They are full of children playing, of servant girls, of wet nurses with dresses with blue and red fringes, carrying on their backs, in a bamboo basket covered with a bright scarf, a baby lying in its covers.[25]

The pattern of employment at the parents' home had two main variations: families that could afford it kept on the wet nurse for around two years, the period for which she was physically able to breastfeed and that was viewed as an appropriate weaning time. She then went back to her village and bore another child, returning to Madrid after each new delivery:

> The Pasiega Santos Diega, just arrived, solicits a nursling at the parents' home: milk two months old; having breastfed at the homes of the *Secretario de Cruzada* and the *Contador de Espolios y Vacantes*, twenty months in the first one and two years in the second. They will inform on her good behaviour and quality.[26]

When the wet nurse was kept only for some months she had to find a new home:

> Antonia de Villegas, Montañesa, looks for a nursling at the parents home: she is *primeriza* [had her first baby], and with milk six months

> old; just finished feeding a girl at D. Vicente Goldoni's, silver maker, who lives in Olivo Baxo Street, 13, where she currently is, and there the best references will be given.
>
> (3 January 1805)

Cases where the same wet nurse appears in different advertisements at intervals longer than a year indicate either a very long period of breastfeeding or two different migration periods. The following advertisement appeared on 13 November 1860: 'María Mazón, a native of the province of Santander, wants a child to feed'. She had already so advertised on 3 July 1859, sixteen months before.

In any case, there existed a clear tendency among the wet nurses who had travelled from distant regions to prolong breastfeeding as long as possible to maximise the profit derived from their emigration. Time away from home was time for the accumulation of money.

Wet nurses were among the best-paid of all servants, probably the best-paid of all female servants after cooks. Pasiego wet nurses were the highest-paid of all wet nurses in Madrid. Few advertisements included information about wages offered or requested. In the period 1758–1799 only two mentioned the wage offered: 60 and 150 reales per month. Taking the latter as the better indicator of wages paid to Pasiego wet nurses, this monthly wage meant an annual income of 1,800 reales around the end of the eighteenth century. In the same years, a master mason or carpenter was paid 14 reales at day (equivalent to a monthly income of 280, considering twenty working days per month, and an annual income of 2,800, considering ten months of work per year), while a mason apprentice was paid 7–8 reales (140–160 reales per month, 1,400–1,600 per year) and a carpenter apprentice 10 reales (200 a month, 2,000 reales a year). These figures are consistent with the idea that in this period women's highest wages were similar to those of male apprentices.

But comparison between wages of servants and other workers is meaningful only if the monetary equivalent of the payment in kind (food, lodging, clothes) that servants received is included. If we do so, despite the longer working day, domestic service appears as a good choice for women, even in the last decades of the nineteenth century, and as a less good choice for men, who had many other opportunities, with higher wages and fewer working hours.[27] Benefits and premiums were also frequent. In the case of wet nurses, for example, parents were generous if their babies blossomed.

Royal wet nurses were in addition generously rewarded when they finished the nursing, and recompensed with the title of hidalguía for themselves, their husbands and descendants. While working, they occupied a privileged place in public ceremonies according to protocol, and they exerted their influence also in a public way by eliciting favours.[28]

Evidence exists about strong links of affection developing between the wet nurse and the family she worked for. It was not uncommon, for instance, for the wet nurse to stay at the former parents' house while looking for a new family in subsequent migrations. Former employers usually provided references and even placed the new advertisements, in some of which they offered to show the wet nurse's portrait. If the wet nurse was literate, her correspondence was often kept and the children raised by her considered her a second mother, sometimes visiting her at her village. This personal relation seems to have had important material consequences: the baby's parents became protectors of the wet nurse's family and helped her and the members of her family to solve bureaucratic problems or to start a small business in Madrid.

Living conditions of wet nurses in Madrid

As was the case for all domestic servants, the standard of living enjoyed by Pasiego wet nurses in Madrid depended not only on their wages but on the family for which they worked and on the personal relationship they managed to develop with that family.

Wet nursing meant the permanent care and feeding of a baby, and a heavy daily workload. Babies had to be fed every three or four hours, bathed, put to sleep and taken care of; their clothes had to be changed and washed, etc. The nurses shared the room with the baby so as to feed and comfort it at night. Wet nurses spent time out for the baby's daily walks and, in general, on any occasion decided by the family, such as visits to relatives, summer trips, etc.[29] Unlike male immigrants of rural origin, for whom the urban working experience included a pattern of socialising centred around the drinking tavern, wet nurses were precluded from access to such public places and thus from such patterns of workers' sociability.

On the other hand, this physical proximity to the family's baby was advantageous for the wet nurse in terms of clothes and, more so, food. Satirical articles in the press suggested that wet nurses' access to food had no limits, since the parents believed a rich diet was good for the baby.[30] They were also very well dressed, since the external appearance of wet nurses was part of the family's visible status. In fact, wet nurses wore uniforms the family chose for them. In many respects, and setting aside the emotional tug of home and of babies left behind, these years may have been the most comfortable of their lives.

Wet nurses and their families

Their stay in Madrid finished, wet nurses returned to their land and to their families. Although single mothers were not uncommon among wet nurses, this seems to have been rarely the case among Pasiegos. In every case during almost two centuries, they were married women who migrated as a part of a family strategy to increase the family income. They intended to invest the capital saved on the family property.

The saving capacity of wet nurses working at the parents' home was very high, amounting to almost all their wages, since they had no free time to spend, and clothes, food and lodgings were provided by the family.

> Wet nurses [. . .] when they finish raising the little angel, go back to their lands bringing the husband some onzas, with which he buys a couple of cows and devotes himself to the expansion and enlargement of his property, while the hapless wife gives birth to another offspring, whose breastfeeding will be taken care of by a woman neighbour for a meagre amount, and she returns to the Court, where she will find, by recommendation of the parents of her first nursling, another similar home, which after a year she will leave again to bring the lucky husband a similar or greater amount, with which the number of cows will be increased, and some lucrative speculation made.[31]

This capital input was the most important financial resource of the Pasiego family. In fact, migration of Pasiego women to Madrid (and other cities) to work as wet nurses became during the nineteenth century perhaps the most important source of capital for Pasiego families. Most Pasiego families invested the wife's savings after working as wet nurses in the purchase of cattle, since this was, indeed, the basis of the local economy. As a result of this investment in cattle, a complete transformation of the cattle-rearing economy took place during the second half of the nineteenth century. A woman's time away from her family translated into a general economic advancement of her family.

Migration of men from La Montaña to Cádiz to work as dockworkers

A tradition of male migration existed from the same area to a more distant point, the southern seaport of Cádiz, where men from La Montaña, usually involved in commercial activities, were known as *jándalos*.[32]

Seaports were main centres of economic activity in pre-industrial Europe. Merchants were ready to pay high wages to guarantee that expensive commodities were unloaded as quickly as possible to prevent deterioration, but also to unlock capital. They became a source of male employment and often attracted men from distant regions.[33]

From the time of Colón's second expedition, the seaport of Cádiz was the point of departure and arrival for the expeditions between Spain and the New World. The monopoly of transoceanic trade between Spain and its colonies was granted by the Crown to Seville and its two nearby seaports of Sanlúcar de Barrameda and Cádiz, and a long fight for the privilege began. During the seventeenth century, Cádiz merchants complained that most ships already being over 200 metric tonnes were at risk at the sand bar of Sanlúcar and could not go up the river without great effort and loss of time to arrive at the docks of Seville. In 1717 the long dispute was finally resolved in favour of Cádiz, and a period of expansion and sustained demographic growth started with 41,000 inhabitants in 1700, 50,500 in 1750 and 71,500 around 1786.[34]

Cádiz dockworkers were organised in the Compañía del Palanquinado (1566–1836), in two different 'companies', the Compañía de Carros y Trabajadores de la Real Aduana and the Compañía de Aljameles.[35] There is evidence of the first having ninety members, at least from 1797 to 1821, while the second had fifty-two members during those same years, 142 workers in total.[36] There were also *jornaleros*, workers who were not yet members of the companies.

The work consisted of the unloading and transportation of commodities '*a pie como a caballo*', by foot and by horse. In 1805 horses were replaced by small hand-drawn carts or two-wheel horse-drawn carts.

> For the delivery of the effects through the city, and for the unloading of the ships that import and export them, there are some groups of gallegos who carry sometimes on their backs, sometimes in two-wheels carts, to the point of destination,

wrote Madoz in his famous mid-nineteenth century dictionary.[37]

Besides working in the carrying and transportation of the merchandise from the ships to the warehouses, or to stores in different parts of the town, members of the company also performed other tasks. *Jornaleros* worked at the repair of carts, like Diego Pérez, 38, who declared in 1799

Plate 3.2 View of the new cart built for transport inside the city, Cádiz, 1804

that he was working 'in making the new wheel barrows that he has been ordered to'. All members were responsible for the horses and mules allotted to them. The most privileged among them were appointed by the superiors to travel to other towns to buy horses or grass for them.

The company organisation: the hiring process

The hiring process started with the announcement of vacancies:

> to proceed in the vacancies that have occurred in the positions of Workers of the Palanquinado [. . .] to choose an individual suitable in every way for the work [. . .] if he is or is not able to serve and perform with his strength and Robustness all the works and tasks, by foot as much as by horse, in which he will have to alternatively occupy himself.

Candidates for vacancies had to write their names on a piece of paper and put it in a *cántaro*, a jug acting as a ballot box, from which the name of the appointed was drawn.

In the election of 1754 there were twenty-nine certificates or *cédulas*,

> and on each of them written the Name of each of the participants [. . .] and well folded they were put into a hat, which once covered, the said certificates were shuffled and one by one three certificates were taken out by the second overseer of Aduana, Juan Domingo de Quirós, and of them, without opening them or reading them, Sr. Prior chose one that happened to contain the name of Bentura González upon whom the remaining vacancy was conferred.[38]

The new member was 'from the Cabuérniga valley [. . .] in the Mountains of Burgos, and thirty years old'.

In August 1811 a conflict arose during the hiring process of a candidate who, not being a native from the mountains of Santander, was backed by Patricio Gutierrez de Terán, overseer of one of the societies, who 'insists on the placement of this individual against the will of the two companies'. Other officials complained that candidates had always been 'Young men, agile and from the Mountains, from which country and not from any other it has been the custom and tradition of these companies' to recruit their members.[39]

The basic structure of the two companies was similar, with a small group of 'proprietors' of the jobs and *jornaleros* or day labourers who worked for long years waiting their turn to became proprietors. The company had developed a complex system of benefits to be granted to members who retired or had become disabled by accidents. In order to pay for these benefits the company created an intermediate position between the *jornaleros*

Table 3.1 The job ladder of Cádiz dockworkers

Name	*Age*	*Years of work*		
		as jornaleros	*as* terceristas	*Total*
At applying for access as terceristas:				
Son of Josef Gutiérrez		3		
Francisco González	22	3		
Manuel Rodríguez		8		
Antonio Clemente	28	3		
Domingo de Montes				
Recommended by:				
Diego Pérez	38	15		15
Manuel Huyán		10		10
Pedro Sánchez		3	4	7
Josef Gutiérrez		6	13	19
At retirement:				
Antonio Díaz de Casa Ferniza		7	16	23
Francisco Sánchez Rubin		7	19	26
Francisco García de la Vega	63			34
Juan González Adán	65			
Manuel Viana de Tezanos				27
Francisco Balbás Rebollo	60			34
Josef Díaz Ruiloba	49	6	22	28
Antonio Salceda	60			25
Diego Pérez	60			30
Diego Gutiérrez del Dosal				43

and the proprietors, called *terceristas*, workers who were to became proprietors of one of the positions and who, in the meantime, were paying for these future benefits.

In June 1799, there were twenty-seven *terceristas* with sixteen or more years of work as such ('working for merits'). The documents presented by the candidates usually described long years of work for the company, as Table 3.1 shows.

Dockworkers started as day labourers or *jornaleros*. There were *quatro quadrillas*, four groups of four men each, working as *jornaleros* in the Real Aduana, but there were also men working *sin estar en cuadrilla*, out of the group, like Pedro Luzán, 22, who also applied to be included in the selection. The career of those already at the top of the ladder is described by Josef Gutiérrez in a document presented in 1792 on behalf of his son. He had worked 'as a Jornalero six years and as Aljamel five and a half, and thirteen that I work in the said Real Aduana', that is, a total of twenty-four and a half years working for the company.

The job ladder can be identified with the working life-cycle. Dockworkers consistently tried to have their sons hired by the company, and sent for them to come from their home towns. As a result, the work was seen as hereditary.

In theory, age and seniority defined the way up the job ladder, but family relations and contacts within the company structure seem to have played a major role. Access to a position which was a 'property' was difficult and only achieved after many years of work, first as day labourer and then as *tercerista*, or through the intervention of powerful friends. In fact, in the process of hiring a new worker, support from friends and relatives was fundamental. Having a relative, especially father, as a member of the company was an important comparative advantage in relation to other candidates. Workers' sons seem to have had a preferential right to be hired. The father himself could apply on behalf of the son, like Josef Gutiérrez de San Juan, worker for over twenty-five years, who in 1792 applied for a position for his son, already a *jornalero* for three years.[40]

Domingo de Montes, for his part, complained in 1799 of working as a *jornalero* for eleven years, 'having not been able to succeed in that time in being included in the poll by the company for not having a sponsor'.

Wages, benefits, pensions

The company functioned rather like the guilds: it was highly protective of the members, and had a well-structured internal organisation.

Very little is known about wages. They were paid by the company, since in cases of debts to families or private people the debtors would directly address their complaints to the company, which in turn would deduct from the worker's pay the amount of the debt. In 1792, Bernardo de la Peña was obliged to send a third of his annual benefits to his family in Santander. This third part was established as 1,200 reales, from which we can deduce an annual income of 3,600 reales.[41]

But more important than wages were the other forms of benefits and pensions, which were exceptional for the time. The system guaranteed important benefits to its members, who for their part were expected to pay for them during their working lives. Entrance to the company was costly, and most dockworkers were indebted for years. The main expense was the horse or mule that the company gave the new member.

> He who is received as a new member has to pay for the horse or the mule that he is given and when he leaves, he gets reimbursed [. . .] the current value is between 4,500, 4,000 and 3,500 [. . .] he who temporarily leaves [. . .] can be assisted on occasion of his leaving with a loan of 750 reales, which he will pay back with that which he will earn on his return.[42]

In case of sickness and accidents, which were very frequent occurrences, an entire year with 'the entire part', that is, full wage, was granted. In

1819, Diego Ruiz de Celis asked for this one-year licence 'receiving the entire part that is due to me so that I can sustain and recover my poor health' (it was denied for reasons of drunkenness).

Age of retirement was regulated in 1820 at 60 or after twenty-five years of service, if solicited. There are instances, however, of workers retiring after much longer periods, like Diego Gutiérrez del Dosal, who retired in 1799 after forty-three years. Retirement pension was fixed at 'the third part of what corresponds to a worker' until the time of his death, that is, 1,200 reales per year. This was the same percentage that seven years before the company had decided Bernardo de la Peña should send his family back in La Montaña.[43]

Living conditions

The town at which these Montañeses arrived was one of the most dynamic and wealthy in Spain. Around 1842 it was described as 'one of the cities of Spain in which the manners of people are sweeter, and the habits of life more agreeable', in the dictionary published by Madoz.

The dock occupied the centre of the town's economic and cultural life. In the mid-nineteenth century Madoz wrote:

> the position of the seaport of Cádiz is one of the most convenient for grand scale trade. Placed at the entrance of the Atlantic Ocean [. . .] Foreigners of all nations had their factories on it, their houses and warehouses; ships from all over the world continuously arrive, and there were always from 500 to 600 ships on its bay [. . .] from cereals to legumes; meats, wines, woods, coals, irons, paper, threads, cottons, silks, fabrics, every thing is the action of its commerce [. . .] Tobacco, sugars, spices, arrive at Cádiz as a deposit point, to be distributed later through Spain.

A cigar factory employing over 1,220 women provided inspiration to Romantic travellers. There were also hundreds of small workshops: 'there are as many establishments with door open to the street as the number of buildings in the town, among them nine coffee shops, fifteen inns, 200 shoe makers, 104 barbers', Madoz wrote.[44]

In this environment, dockworkers seem to have enjoyed a good deal of freedom of movement. Working outdoors allowed them to ignore the permanent control to which indoor workers were subjected and allowed them to spend time at the taverns, the main spaces for male socialising. Instances of heavy drinking are documented frequently. Some workers were denied the right of retirement by their companions in cases of accidents, on the basis of the many days of work lost because of their drunkenness.

Socialising was highly gendered, with most public places and opportunities for consumption reserved for men. Besides taverns and tobacco, prostitution and gambling were the main sources of expenses. A pattern of high expenditure on consumption seems to explain the inability of men to save in nineteenth-century urban centres, and this is to be contrasted with female migrants, mostly in domestic service, who seem to have managed to save most of their earnings.

Demands and complaints to the company often mention unpaid debts of workers. In 1810, the owner of a food store denounced four dock-workers who had debts from food purchases; in 1791, the president of one of the confraternities, the Hermandad de Gracia, demanded a dock-worker pay a debt of 300 pesos, borrowed to put in the company's fund when he first joined.[45]

The status of head of the household enjoyed by married men granted them the opportunity of travelling at least every three years back to Santander, which meant crossing the whole of Spain. However, some of them never came back to their families, finding other jobs, probably through acquaintances made in the course of these long journeys.[46] For the male absentees then, that work gave them new personal freedom and money. It is unclear how much of this money was seen by their families back home.

Dockworkers and their families: the State's intervention to guarantee maintenance

For the State, dockworkers were in the first place heads of households and their rights as workers depended on the fulfilment of their duties as such. To guarantee this, the Compañía del Palanquinado obliged them to return to their homelands every three years and after retirement.[47]

Although most dockworkers adhered in part to the rules, members of the companies seem to have refused to return to their homes, or to return at the periods fixed by the law, and to fail consistently to bring with them the certificates extended by the local priests and the written agreement from the wives, a situation tolerated by the authorities.[48] According to the edict on retirement of 8 May 1807, 'some individuals from these Companies that obtained their retirement have abused of this grace, keeping themselves out of the towns of their domicile and separated from their families'. They will have to prove their permanence in their countries 'as the head of their families' or 'they will be deprived forever of the said benefit'.[49]

Instances of intervention of the company's authorities to oblige the workers to periodically return to their families are frequent. On 30 May 1807,

> The major overseer of the Company of the Real Aduana and the official of the Company of Aljameles will let the compañeros of the said their respective companies, Juan González de los Ríos, Juan Pérez

> González, Antonio de la Mata Linares, Antonio González Camberas, Franc[cis]o de la Llera y Manuel Rubín know that in the precise term of eight days they must come to this Tribunal del Consulado to obtain their respective licenses to travel to their homes to live and remain there with their families for an entire year; for they are married in their home lands and have been absent from them for the three years permitted by the Real cédula of 6 April 1783 issued by the Supremo Consejo de las Yndias. If they do not do so within the said term, they will be suspended; and if by the day 15th of June next they have not left this town in use of their licenses, they will remain deprived of their positions, which will be immediately announced. The same deprivation of their position and subsequent announcement will take place if within mid-July they would fail to send, by hand of the said overseer and official, certification for their respective parish priests, legalized by *escrivanos*, that attest that they are with their families, with mention of the day that they have checked it; and at their return they have to present another similar document, also legalized, in which it is said that they have lived and remain united to their families for an entire year, without including the days of their round trip; and also that they return to serve their positions on renewed agreement of their wives; if they fail to do so, they will be deprived of their position.[50]

Despite the legal obligation, and despite claims by dockworkers themselves to be heads of households and to have family responsibilities in order to get hired,[51] it is unlikely that most of them actually maintained their families in Santander. In some cases this was due to an inability to save, like Domingo de Montes, who after working for eleven years as a day labourer declared himself 'in most need, unable to maintain his family, which obliges him to have his wife serving in a House, not only in the present times, but in time of peace'.[52] In other cases it was due to an interruption of contact with the family.

It is interesting, however, that wives actively exerted their rights over their husbands' salaries. Among the dossiers kept by the Consulado 'on demands, claims, and other matters related to the Companies of the Palanquinado', from 1790 to 1820, it is possible to find the cases of workers denounced for failing to send any money to their families. For example, on 29 September 1790, Bernardo de la Peña asked the authorities that his wife Bárbara Gutiérrez de Celis be obliged to leave Cádiz and to return to the mountains to take care of their daughters. The wife had travelled to Cádiz to claim abandonment. She appears to have stayed for, on October of the same year, an agreement was signed: the overseer would ensure that Bernardo would receive just one-third of his salary, while the second third would be for his wife and the remaining third to be kept by D. José de Oviedo 'so that by his hand the debts contracted up to last July begin to be repaid'.[53]

'Persuaded by the Prior' (the highest authority of the Consulado), husband and wife agreed to put aside a third part of Bárbara's share 'for the help of their daughters who are in the Mountains, until the said Bárbara returns there, which she said she would do around May, whence she will take her third part entirely'.

On 11 August 1792, Bernardo de la Peña sent a memoir denouncing his wife and seeking the order granting her the third part to be annulled, because

> for my wife and my two single daughters that remained in the Mountain, to maintain themselves 100 silver ducados [around 1,000 reales] are enough, of which still something must be left, for she does not need to pay for a house, having land to cultivate according to the custom of the country, and cattle at her disposal, in which circumstances there is no reason why I must be robbed of the proceeds of my work any longer.[54]

A decree of 17 August 1792 certifies that 'the said Bernardo de la Peña remains from now obliged to help by his hand his wife with 1,200 reales a year, sending them to her by the transport drivers, half in the season of San Juan (24 June) and half in the season of San Miguel (29 September).'[55]

Despite the agreement, Bárbara issued from Santander an authorisation to a legal representative in Cádiz to claim 'before the person or persons in charge of the satisfaction and payment of that third part of utility that belongs to me, so that he perceives and collects it, at the times and occasions accustomed'. In September 1792, Bárbara's legal representative is denied the dossier of the case since 'the authorisation that he presents has been conferred by a married woman without competent licence'.[56] In fact, married women had no legal capacity to represent their interests in court. This is precisely the cause of many of the problems faced by the wives of absent migrant men.

In a second case in 1797, Antonio Morante, of Cádiz, brought an action to oblige the retired Juan de Prío, his son-in-law, to pay for the maintenance of Juan's daughter:

> for ten years he has under his responsibility a granddaughter named Ysabel de Prío, whom he has been maintaining and sustaining in clothing and shoes to a decent level [. . .] and the said Ysabel de Prío has as her father the named Juan de Prío who was here in the Company of Workers of the Real Aduana, and five years ago he retired to the Mountains with the third part, where he is to this day, and when he left this town he was a widower and up to the present he has made in the said Mountain two marriages: and the said Antonio Morante his father-in-law having asked with the good reasons he gives for the

> maintenance of the said Ysabel, never succeeded [. . .] he has written to him during all this time different letters which have even been handed in personally: and he has pretended to be deaf and mute before all of them, not having wanted to respond to any of them, being that the principal that still remains in the said Aduana belongs to the said Ysabel de Prío, for it was her mother's, may she rest in peace, her father Juan de Prío, having taken his half of the principal when he left for the Mountain.[57]

In another case, Josef Santiso, of Saja, is granted his pension on 16 March 1805

> with the precise condition that immediately he has to return to his country, in which he has to enjoy with his wife Rosa Sánchez the product of the third part that remains to him of the utilities of the entire position he has served; if he does not do so, or gives motive for new complaints from his wife, he will be deprived absolutely of the said third part, and he will be considered separated and excluded from the said Company.[58]

A complaint by his wife, Rosa Sánchez, is attached, in which she states that

> five years ago he left me in the said town destitute, with no property, and he has neither fulfilled the order to come and cohabit with his wife. Nor has he even contributed money for my food, clothes, payment of the room (that I use out of charity), royal and town charges, for I only survive (though very miserably) with the small produce of my hands, and the charity of my neighbours, who (if I fall in some sickness) will have to assist me through piety or Justice. All of which, if you doubt, you can be informed by Juan González Adán, Antonio de Salzeda and Antonio González Camberas, my neighbours and from other compañeros.[59]

Rosa Sánchez begs a third part of the husband's income or, in case he is still paying the principal, a third of the two parts he receives, to be given to one of these neighbours. A note at the side of the wife's complaint explains that, in fact, Santiso is still paying former debts, and

> no doubting the truth of what his Wife Rosa Sánchez says in view of the evidence of the two Parish priests and because Santiso himself has acknowledged it as well as the said Casa Ferniza [. . .], from next week [. . .] 15 reales will be weekly discounted from the said Santiso and the said discount will be given to Juan González Adán, so that through him it arrives to the hands of the said Rosa Sánchez.[60]

In 1815, Manuel Sánchez, living in Cádiz and native of Serdio in 'the mountains', complains that his sister (another) Rosa Sánchez, married to José del Valle, who 'although is retired, has secured the part that corresponds to him, lives in Seville, where also he works and gains'. He is acting on behalf of his sister, who on 22 December 1814, wrote him a letter (also included in the dossier): 'my husband sends to me nothing nor does he return to his house to maintain his family.' The resolution appears at the margin: 'that all that exists at present produced by the said third part, and all this third part will produce from now onwards, the mentioned official ensures that it will be forwarded to Rosa Sánchez, wife of the said Valle'.[61]

In fact, Josef González del Valle had asked for his retirement fifteen years before, in December 1800. It was granted on the condition that

> as soon as the roads to his homeland become traversible he has to do so, and subsist there and not in this one nor in other towns around; if he does not, he must remain excluded from the position, and this requirement he will bear in his Licence so that he cannot allege ignorance.

On 24 January 1801 he is in Seville, from where he sends an authorisation to his cousin to sign the agreement, since 'for my poor health' and 'the absence of means' he is unable to travel to Cádiz.[62]

More frequent seem to have been instances of dockworkers refusing to travel to their families every three years. They themselves often asked to have their licence for temporary return cancelled, for different reasons: in 1804 eight of them succeeded in having their temporary licences cancelled after alleging the epidemic in the northern regions.[63] In 1807, Juan González de los Ríos, de Los Tojos, 65, asked for the suspension of his temporary licence for 'having some interests of consideration among some people who owe him, which he needs to receive without retiring from this'.[64]

Leaving home to help the family?

In this chapter, I have presented two flows of temporary migration to work for wages. By comparing them it is possible to see that male and female temporary migrants differed in their skills (all dockworkers could read and write while their wives could not), their legal status, their access to public spaces, their access to family resources, level of consumption and obligations towards the family unit.[65] These differences reflected their relative status as members of a family. They were daughters or wives, sons or husbands, and they migrated as such.

In the period studied here, the disruptive effects that individual wages could potentially have on the family organisation of labour failed to materialise for two reasons: first, because access to migratory flows and wage labour was not open to all members of the family, and second, because heads of the families had a legal right on the earnings of family members, which was not reciprocal.

Families redistributed the earnings of their members according to principles which were founded not upon need or work done, but maintenance of a hierarchy, which in turn reflected a power relation. This explains why, as the cases described here show, families could coexist with completely different standards of living under the same laws, types of production, inheritance rules and demographic patterns. With a husband working as a dockworker, two similar families could live an easy life or be dependent on charity; two wet nurses working for the same period for the same wages could see their family patrimony increase or disappear, given that back home it was in the hands of their husbands.

Some of the changes experienced by wives of male migrants have been pointed out by the literature: increased workload, a general worsening of living conditions, increased dependence on local lenders, etc. Yet male out-migration had also positive aspects for wives, who gained a new control over the family resources (farm, cattle, land), scarce as these could be. Paola Corti speaks of a 'progressive change of the relationships between the sexes' in the alpine areas which remained in the hands of women for long months during the year or long years. Rose Duroux of 'the powers of women left alone'.[66] One significant indirect indicator of the positive consequences of male migration for women was social criticism, the 'sarcastic references to the customs of these women without men' (Corti), to their idleness, the disorder and dirtiness of their homes. And, of course, to the shameful consequences of the lack of sexual control: adultery, illegitimate births (interestingly, social criticism affected both migrants' wives and female migrants: it was probably the temporary rupture of the family, which always involved an important degree of 'world turned upside down', that was at stake).

The documents discussed in this chapter throw new light on the living situation of the wives of male migrants who remained behind. It is probably true that long-distance and long-term migration of their husbands turned into a new situation for them, into more freedom. But things were not that easy. Their legal status as married women remained unchanged: they could not defend themselves, their children or their property legally; they faced the pressure of both local public opinion and the in-laws, who carefully watched over these 'women without men'.

In the cases seen here, the economic and social instability of migrants' wives originated with the desertion of their husbands. But in other cases the conflicts arose because the husband resented the new situation of the wife. In July 1799, in the Alfoz de Lloredo valley, in La Montaña, doña Antonia Isabel Sánchez was killed in her house.[67] In the long trial that followed the crime, her husband for nineteen years, don Domingo García, was accused of having instigated and paid for the murder. Domingo García was a *jándalo*, as male migrants from Cantabria to Andalucía were called. Together with a friend from the same village, Udías, he owned two food stores in Seville, where he was at the time of the crime, and witnesses described him as bearing the external signs of economic success in their visits to the village (a horse, good clothes, spending money . . .). The declarations of the witnesses speak of constant physical and psychological abuse of his wife, public death menaces and also his public preference for their female servant. But at the bottom of this and similar cases involving violent male migrants was the resentment felt by husbands due to the inversion of roles in their marriage caused by their absence. In the hard times of the last two decades of the eighteenth century in Spain, difficulties were increased for the wives of male migrants, who had to cope 'with the interruption of money sent by husbands, decreasing rents generated by the family properties, and decreasing capacity to generate income through her own work'.[68] The different strategies developed by these women to face the situation, be they new, more independent, positions in the labour market or increasing reliance on more powerful male relatives or neighbours, were all seen by husbands as endangering their traditional power, and their wives' traditional dependence on them.

It is usually assumed that families functioned with their members pooling their earnings and having equal access to the fund. The documents analysed here show that while female migrants, particularly married ones, were legally forced to pool their earnings, married men could easily refuse to do so. There is an obvious contradiction between the model (the ideal situation, the norm, represented by the laws and by the company rules, and supported by the idea that men had had a preference for having access to higher wages just because their families depended upon them) and the practice, in which men acted as they wanted.

Wives clearly viewed themselves as entitled to a part of their husbands' earnings. This supposition was backed by the law and the State's institutions, to whom deserted wives or daughters complained and went for help. In the case of Cádiz dockworkers, the company itself established the part that families were legally entitled to ask for as one-third. Although this seems to have been difficult or impossible to enforce, some wives, with the help of the parish priests, seem to have succeeded in having the authorities intervene in their favour.[69]

Women's economic and social benefits from migration were invested in the household: married women's migration was an important source of income for their husbands and families, as evidenced by the massive investment in milk cows made possible by Pasiego women's employment as wet nurses in Madrid. Savings were also used, for example, to build a new house, pay for a son's education or to buy him out of military service. And since most of the skills acquired through migration were related to domestic work or to children, women's work as carers and housewives was reinforced. This investment of savings and skills was not a choice: married women were legally obliged to return to their husband's place of residence and did not have the right to spend the money themselves.

Married men's return to their family home, on the contrary, depended on their will, and was unlikely to take place if they had established a new family. In such cases, the original families were almost unavoidably pushed into poverty: while the absence of the husband left the wife with sole responsibility for the daily running of the family farm, her legal incapacity prevented her from doing it successfully, being either forbidden or impeded in the selling and buying of cattle and land, attendance at cattle markets, taking decisions on the organisation of family labour, etc. Instances of male relatives intervening in favour of children whose fathers never returned are common, since the legal defence of the property against neighbours could not be undertaken by the mother. These gendered differences were backed by a legal system which had a fundamental role in structuring them.

In the northern region where the two migratory flows studied here came from, the fundamental institution of local power was the *Concejo*, the town council to which all married men belonged. The *Concejo* often overruled higher institutions, and governed local life with the help of a body of rules called *Ordenanzas municipales*. The domestic process of decision-making cannot be explained without reference to this instance, where 'anomalous' situations, like households in which women had greater decision-making power than men, were corrected. One example will allow us to understand women's position in the same village and during the same years that the migratory flows studied here were taking place.

On 17 November 1876, Doña Serafina Abascal Crespo, of Vega de Pas, the region where the most celebrated wet nurses came from, appeared as plaintiff before the local judge. She was a married woman, 'devoted to the occupations proper of her sex', and she was accompanied by don Manuel Abascal Crespo, her brother, 'not appearing the husband of the plaintiff for being incapacitated and without sense'. Don Juan Oria Ortiz, her neighbour, a married proprietor, appeared as defendant. 'It was requested by the plaintiff that the defendant be punished for having made highly injurious statements publicly against the plaintiff's honour, repeating and telling to Juan Oria and to Bernardo Abascal, husband of the plaintiff, that her daughter is not her husband's daughter.' The defendant answered that 'if the plaintiff does not have a permission from her husband, she completely lacks the faculty to appear at a trial, and the trial cannot occur, and the Judge should not have admitted the complaint, therefore he protests this trial'.[70]

In fact, the new Civil Code enacted in 1889 repeated these norms: 'the husband must protect the wife and the wife must obey the husband' (art. 57, title IV, 'Of marriage'). 'The husband is the representative of the wife. She cannot, without his licence, appear at a trial by herself or by means of an attorney' (art. 60). One century before, in the first case seen above, relating to Bernardo de la Peña and Bárbara Gutiérrez de Celis, Bárbara's legal representative was denied the dossier of the case since 'the authorization that he presents has been conferred by a married woman without competent licence'.

Differences in saving practices, commitment to family needs and legal ability to earn and to spend, account, among other factors, for a very distinctive male/female pattern of contribution to, and use of, family earnings. Male and female migration, and earnings made through migration, are key to an understanding of the economic workings of marriage.

Notes

1 A first version of this chapter was presented to the Conference on *The Historical Construction of Working Time*, organised by Olwen Hufton at the European University Institute, Florence, in 1994. I am indebted to Olwen Hufton and sociologist Mary Daly for their helpful comments.

2 C. B. Brettel, *Men who migrate, women who wait: Population and History in a Portuguese Parish*, Princeton, NJ, Princeton University Press (1986). For Spain, C. Yáñez, *Saltar con red: La temprana emigración catalana a América, 1830–1870,* Madrid, Alianza (1996) and C. Soldevilla Oria, *La emigración de Cantabria a América. Hombres, mercaderías y capitales*, Santander, Estudio (1996). For Italy, P. Corti, 'Donne che vanno, donne che restano. Emigrazione e comportamenti femminili'. *Annali dell'Istituto 'Alcide Cervi'*, 12 (1990): 213–235.

3 See for Spain, B. Alonso Ruiz, *El arte de la cantería. Los maestros trasmeranos de la Junta de Voto*, Santander, Universidad de Cantabria (1991), and for Italy, P. Audenino, 'Le custodi della montagna: donne e migrazioni stagionali in una communità alpina' in P. Corti (ed.), 'Società rurale e ruoli femminili in Italia tra Ottocento e Novecento', *Annali dell' Istituto 'Alcide Cervi'*, 12 (1990): 265–287.

4 In the nineteenth century, 'British female rural-to-urban migrants were younger than their male counterparts during the 1840s. Among emigrants from Ireland at the turn of the twentieth century, males also tended to be older than females.' T. Guinnane, 'Age at Leaving Home in Rural Ireland', *The Journal of Economic History*, 52, 3 (1992): 651. The age difference was probably reversed among transoceanic migrants, women not being able to migrate without spending a previous period in domestic service to save for the passage money.

5 A. Chatelain, 'Migrations et domesticité féminine urbaine en France, XVIIIe siècle–XX siècle', *Revue d'Histoire Economique et Sociale*, 47, 4 (1969): 506–528.

6 L. C. van de Pol, 'The Lure of the Big City: Female Migration to Amsterdam' in E. Kloek, N. Teeuwen and M. Huisman (eds) *Women of the Golden Age: an International Debate on Women in Seventeenth-century Holland, England and Italy*, Hilversun, Verloren (1994), pp. 73–86. An image originally 'meant for the middle classes of society, the nucleus of calvinist, affluent burghers of the cities of Holland', is still alive for it 'fits in with the preconceptions of women's lives of modern historians', p. 74.

7 For a critique of the use of marriage registers to study immigration to urban centres, L. C. van de Pol, 'The Lure of the Big City'.

8 From eighteenth-century Bellino, in the Italian Alps, departed every year for six months in summertime men who worked in the fields, as masons, itinerant sellers and artisans, and others in the wintertime to work as hospital workers at Toulon, shoe cleaners, etc. Women found work in agriculture, spinning or in the domestic service. A. Dionigi, M. Dossetti and S. Ottonelli, 'Società ed

emigrazione nell'alta valle Varaita in età moderna', *Bolletino Storico Bibliografico Subalpino*, 86 (1988): 117–169. On temporary migrations of French and Swiss clockmakers, D. Landes, 'The Round of Horological Migrations', in *Le migrazioni in Europa, secc. XIII–XVIII*, Istituto internazionale di Storia economica F. Datini, 25 (1993): 561–566.

9 A. Meijide Pardo, 'La emigración gallega intrapeninsular en el siglo XVIII', *Estudios de Historia Social de España*, CSIC, IV, 2 (1960): 463–606. See esp. pp. 532–533, and for 'female exodus', pp. 532ff.

10 Meijide Pardo, 'La emigración gallega', p. 534. Dressing in men's clothes to enlist in the army or to sign on to the fleet was almost a tradition for poor women in Northern European countries. In seventeenth-century Holland, 'a man could always become a sailor or a soldier and was thereby assured of at least housing and food. Women, who were already at a disadvantage because of far fewer possibilities to work and far lower wages, had no such last resort.' R. Dekker and L. van de Pol, *The Tradition of Female Transvestism in Early Modern Europe*, London, Macmillan (1989), p. 32.

11 J. Manso [1798], *Estado de las fábricas, comercio, industria y agricultura en las Montañas de Santander*, ed. T. Martínez Vara, Santander, Librería Estudio (1979), p. 244. The tradition of the identification of activities to be performed at home as the activities more suitable for women can be traced back to the theoreticians of the Middle Ages. In the sixteenth century, fray Luis de León (1527–1591) wrote in *La perfecta casada* that 'the house [. . .] is the space around which the woman has to stir her feet, and the places for which she has to walk and [. . .] the field of her course, that is her own house, and not the streets nor the plazas, nor the orchards, nor the extraneous houses'. Fray Luis de León, *La perfecta casada*, Madrid, Espasa-Calpe (1980), p. 128. For an analysis of this work, M.A. Durán, 'Lectura económica de Fray Luis de León', in *Nuevas perspectivas sobre la mujer*, Seminario de Estudios de la Mujer de la Universidad Autónoma de Madrid (1982).

12 A more comprehensive description of the Pasiego community in the eighteenth and nineteenth centuries can be found in C. Sarasúa, 'Understanding Intra-family Inequalities. The Montes de Pas, Spain, 1700–1900', *The History of the Family*, 3, 2 (1998): 173–197.

13 Throughout Europe, the demand for wet nurses generated important flows of female migration during the eighteenth and nineteenth centuries. They were mostly internal flows, from rural to urban areas, but there is also evidence of migration of wet nurses from country to country, such as from different Italian regions to France and Egypt. P. Corti, 'Donne che vanno', p. 227. For internal migration of wet nurses in Italy, D. Perco (ed.), *Balie di latte. Una forma peculiare di emigrazione temporanea*, Milan, Feltre (1984).

14 The process by which women from some regions developed a specialisation as wet nurses and eventually became identified with this activity seems to have occurred in most European countries. In Paris, women from Normandy were most sought after, while in the German cities Saxon wet nurses were much in demand. V. Fildes, *Wet-nursing: a History from Antiquity to the Present*, Oxford, Basil Blackwell (1988).

15 M. Bretón de los Herreros, 'La nodriza', in *Los españoles pintados por sí mismos*, Madrid (1851), p. 36. 'Asturias, Galicia, and the Mountains of Santander send annually to Madrid an endless amount of mothers ready to be such of the first that appears [. . .] This does not mean that only those countries produce wet nurses; the rest of the provinces of Spain also produce them, but from here comes the main number', explained *El cascabel. Periódico para hacer reír*, in 1864.

16 C. Sarasúa, *Criados, nodrizas y amos. El servicio doméstico en la formación del mercado de trabajo, Madrid, 1758–1868*, Madrid, Siglo XXI (1994).

17 'Reference will be given in San Benito street, house of the Cars master. And she is Pasiega.' The same year advertisements of women defining themselves as 'native of the Mountain' or 'Montañesa' began to appear. Anthropologist S. Tax Freeman interviewed in the 1970s some Pasiego women who had worked as wet nurses in different cities. She suggests that their migration started in the first decades of the nineteenth century: 'This form of temporary migration of women grew, flourished, and diminished in approximately one century, beginning in the 1830s if not slightly earlier.' S. T. Freeman, *The Pasiegos: Spaniards in No Man's Land*, Chicago, Chicago University Press (1979), pp. 146–147.
18 *Teatro social del siglo XIX*, vol. II, Madrid 1846, quoted in A. García Lomas, *Los pasiegos. Estudio crítico, etnográfico y pintoresco (años 1011 a 1960)*, Santander, Estudio (1977), p. 167.
19 Escolástica Suárez, 19, and Antolina Martín, 20, from Iglesuela, in the Castilian province of Toledo, arrived together in Madrid, advertised themselves in the *Diario* the same day (1 March 1868) and gave the same address. One of them had milk three months old, the other four months old.
20 A. García Lomas, *Los pasiegos*, p. 167.
21 ibid., pp. 166–167.
22 'A wet nurse of total satisfaction and healthiness solicits a nursling for her place: reason can be found in Toledo street, store of linen from Entrambasaguas.' *Diario*, 2 December 1801. Entrambasaguas is a village near the Pas valley.
23 A. Esperón, 'El Pasiego' in *Semanario pintoresco español* (1851), pp. 390–392. Wet nurses working for the royal family were chosen by the doctors in their own towns.
24 In France doctors were very actively involved in the business, and they owned the most important private agency for wet nurses in Paris. F. Fay-Sallois, *Les nourrices à Paris au XIXe siècle*, Paris, Payot (1980).
25 L. Teste, 'Paseo por Madrid' in *Viaje por España* (1872). On 19 August 1795 the *Diario* announced: 'On sale. A Pasiega dress, of fine cloth, bordered with stripes of fine gold.'
26 *Diario de Avisos*, 22 June 1804. The mentions refer to court positions of prestige.
27 In Paris, the value of the payments in kind to servants amounted to around 850 annual francs, when female servants received 480 in wages, and male servants 720. T. McBride, 'The Modernization of Woman's Work', *Journal of Modern History*, 49 (1977): p. 240ff. The different significance that domestic service had for men and women helps to explain the feminisation of the sector in all European countries since the seventeenth century.
28 In 1715, the town of Tembleque, in Toledo, solicited the king through Bárbara de Flores, 'Wet nurse who has been of S.A. Príncipe de Asturias and of the Serenísimo infante D. Felipe', that a Company of Flanders Guards that was installed in the town would abandon it. The king accepted. In Archivo Histórico Nacional, section Estado, legajo 2675, documentation on royal wet nurses corresponding to the period 1708–1840 can be found. The reports of the doctors of the Palace after their trips in search for wet nurses, in the archive of the royal palace, sección histórica. Cf. also L. Cortés Echánove, *Nacimiento y crianza de personas reales en la Cortede España*, Madrid, Consejo Superior de Investigaciones Científicas (1954).
29 In early twentieth-century Barcelona, bourgeois families sent their wet nurses with the babies and other servants to the opera performances scheduled for children in the mornings. 'The juridical condition of the [Liceo] boxes as private property had repercussions on the audience. Children invaded them on Saturday with governesses and retainers, and even wetnurses'. W. McDonogh, *Good Families of Barcelona: a Social History of Power in the Industrial Era*, Princeton, NJ, Princeton University Press (1986), p. 196.

30 Chocolate was included in some advertisements asking for servants as part of their wages.
31 *El cascabel*, Madrid, 1864.
32 The source for the study of this migration flow is Archivo General de Indias (AGI), in Seville, section Consulado, legajos 1775 to 1786, and books 1167 to 1169. In fact, this is the source for all the quotes taken from male migrants to Cádiz in this chapter. See A. Herrera Heredia, *Inventario de los fondos de Consulados del Archivo General de Indias*, Ministerio de Cultura (1979), p. 11.
33 Men from Galicia, for example, migrated to work at the Portuguese seaports of Lisbon and Porto, where they spent most of their working lives with short intervals at home. 'Tous les travaux qui demandent de la force se font par des galiciens qu'on peut appeller les portefaix et les forts de la halle de Lisbonne', wrote the English traveller Murphy around 1789 (quoted in A. Meijide Pardo, 'La emigración gallega', p. 551).They continued to participate in these temporary migrations until they were about 50, when, if they had not formed a new family, they would return to Galicia. Typically, Gallego men migrants to Portugal were water carriers, stonemasons, etc.
34 M. Bustos, *Burguesía de negocios y capitalismo en Cádiz: los Colarte (1650–1750),* Cádiz, Diputacíon Provincial de Cadiz (1991), p. 22. For the history of the merchant institution, A. Herrera Heredia, 'Apuntes para la historia del Consulado de la Universidad de cargadores a Indias en Sevilla y Cádiz', *Anuario de Estudios Americanos*, XXVII (1967): 219–279.
35 'Palanquín', hand chair, from the Portuguese 'palanquim', hindu 'palaki', bed. M. Moliner, *Diccionario de uso del español.* 'Aljamel' is Andalusian for 'Alhamel', 'mozo de cuerda o arriero que se alquila para llevar carros', J. Corominas, *Diccionario crítico etimológico de la lengua castellana.*
36 AGI, Consulados, leg. 1778.
37 'Gallego', or native of Galicia, in northwestern Spain, was a generic name for northern immigrants in the nineteenth century, but the use of the expression here is due to the existence of a third company called *Compañía de gallegos*, as all its workers were from this region. It functioned from 1791 to 1832 and was also called *Compañía de la puerta de Sevilla y San Carlos* for it was in charge of the unloading of merchandise through these two doors of the town. AGI, Consulados, leg. 1781 and books 1167 and 1168.
38 AGI, Consulados, leg. 1778.
39 Leg. 1778, 'Expedientes de nombramientos y elecciones (1789–1830)', cuadernillo nº 5, 1811.
40 'having been the said his father in the said Real Aduana as a Jornalero six years and five and a half as Aljamel and thirteen that he is at the present working in the said Real Aduana and this be sufficient so the said my son enters in the jug' (AGI, Consulados, leg. 1778).
41 As was seen above, top annual salaries of Pasiego wet nurses in Madrid amounted to 1,800 reales.
42 Decree of 1815 establishing the way of adjusting the account to the individuals entering or leaving the Compañía de Aljameles.
43 'Individuals of the Company who want to retire having twenty-five years of service in it, or sixty of age, will be considered as retired workers, and will receive the third part of what corresponds to workers at the moment of their death', Cádiz, 24 October 1820.
44 Madoz' *Diccionario*, under 'Cádiz' (1842).
45 AGI, Consulados, leg. 1782.
46 AGI, Consulados, leg. 1779, 'Titles and forms and licences of individuals to temporarily leave Cádiz'.

47 By a Real Cédula of 6 April 1783, the Supremo Consejo de las Yndias ordered the members of the Companies who were married in their countries to return to their families at least every three years. On 8 May 1807, a decree was published that 'the Retired workers of the Companies of Palanquinado go to enjoy the benefits of their Retirement to their Domiciles, or in union to their Families'.

48 In 1807 the Company announced that 'This Consulate, understanding that the individuals of the Companies of workers of Aduana and Aljameles Francisco González Cavanzón, Bruno de la Torre, Miguel Yglesias Coballes, Feliciano González, Francisco González Cordero, Antonio Callejo Palenque, Francisco Guivar and Lorenzo Elguera have returned from their countries working at the said Companies, not having presented the certificates of the parish Priests [. . .] nor the one that justifies that their wives agree on their return to the said Company [. . .] the Consulate permits that these continue working at their positions (and) must present within two months the said documents [. . .] so that in the future they do not proceed with the indifference shown until now in the obeying of the [thing] ordered by this Tribunal about the presentation of the said certificates', Cádiz, 20 December 1807.

49 AGI, Consulados, leg. 1778.

50 ibid.

51 Manuel Huyán, who had been working as a day labourer for ten years, affirms in his application for a position in 1792 to have invested 'all his little gains in Feeding his poor parents, that have no other shelter, Wife and Family'. Pedro Luzán, 22, from Ucieda, 'in the Mountain, with obligation to sustain his elderly Parents', declared himself to have been serving as a day labourer in Cádiz for some years; or Antonio Clemente de la Madrid, 28, working three years as a day labourer, 'and with the anxiety of remedying the urgent needs of his poor and old parents'.

52 10 June 1799.

53 AGI, Consulados, leg. 1779.

54 ibid.

55 ibid.

56 ibid.

57 AGI, Consulados, leg. 1780.

58 ibid.

59 ibid.

60 ibid.

61 ibid., folder year 1815.

62 AGI, Consulados, leg. 1780, dossiers regarding retirements.

63 For they had no money to pay for the trip and 'a Province that in the day only offers calamities, hunger and misery, and where its inhabitants only present sickness, nudity and all the qualities of a famine and contagious illness, those representing do not believe its mention be desirable to any rational, mostly when for the penury of goods, their habitation in such a Theatre would only serve to increase the number of victims sacrificed to such penury.'

64 AGI, Consulados, leg. 1780.

65 One of the wife's legal obligations regarded precisely her mobility: 'The wife is obliged to follow her husband wherever he establishes his residence', an obligation of which the tribunals could exempt her if he moved abroad or to a foreign country (Civil Code 1889, title IV, chapter I, art. 58).

66 P. Corti, 'Donne che vanno', p. 223. R. Duroux, 'The Temporary Migration of Males and The Power of Females in a Stem-family Society: the Case of 19th-century Auvergne', *The Journal of Family History*, forthcoming.

67 T. Mantecón, *La muerte de Antonia Isabel Sánchez. Tiranía y escándalo en una sociedad rural del Norte español en el Antiguo Régimen*, Alcalá de Henares, Centro de Estudios Cervantinos (1997).

68 ibid., p. 89. See note 62.

69 The right of deserted wives to use the summary courts against their husbands for maintenance was not possible in England until 1878. The English Common Law recognised the husband's obligation to maintain as a counterpart, since at matrimony, the law 'conferred on the husband total economic dominion over his wife, by depriving her both of rights against him and resources of her own'. M. Finer and O. R. McGregor, 'The History of the Obligation to Maintain', appendix 5 to Department of Health and Social Security, *Report of the Committee on One-Parent Families*, vol. 2, London (1974), p. 96. Yet 'while recognising the husband's obligation, the common law refused recognition of any corresponding right on the part of the wife to enforce the obligation against him', since 'it would have amounted to an invasion of the spiritual jurisdiction', p. 98. Cf. also L. Holcombe, *Wives and Property. Reform of the Married Women's Property Law in Nineteenth-century England*, Toronto and Buffalo, University of Toronto Press (1983).

70 Archivo Municipal de Vega de Pas (Santander), box 1, oral trials.

4 Labour migration, family and community in early modern Japan

Mary Louise Nagata

In this study of the labour out-migration patterns in early modern Japan, I argue that labour migration patterns were the result of a combination of environmental factors, all of which were necessary in creating the conditions for out-migration. I show the relation between labour migration patterns and environmental factors as I contrast the migration patterns of three villages in two regions as they changed over time. The environmental factors important to producing the labour migration patterns are: demographic system, economic development, family systems, village structure and the policies of the regional political authorities.

Labour migration has been studied from a number of angles resulting in different interpretions of the phenomenon. Scholars have discussed push and pull factors and family strategies. Migration has been described as a necessary method for getting rid of extra unused labour and as a way of balancing internal population pressure and maintaining population stability.[1] Some of these scholars have looked to migration patterns to explain the overall demographic system.[2] At the same time, others have seen the needs of the labour market as the main factor behind labour migration. In this latter view, urban and economic development produce a kind of population vacuum pulling labour out of the countryside or redistributing labour according to the needs of the economy.[3]

Much of the above research has focused on economic and demographic structural explanations for the aggregate behaviour of individuals. This focus assumes labour migration to be an individual action. Research on labour migration in modern countries, however, has suggested that it can be viewed as a family economic strategy. Instead of individuals choosing to migrate for individual reasons informed and constrained by demographic and economic factors, families choose to send individual members out to work and rely upon the wages they send back as part of the family income.[4]

Labour migration in early modern Japan was a family strategy for survival and economic prosperity. The environmental factors listed above influenced which family members were sent where and for how long, but labour contracts show that the decision was ultimately made, or at least endorsed, by the family. The household head of the employee's family

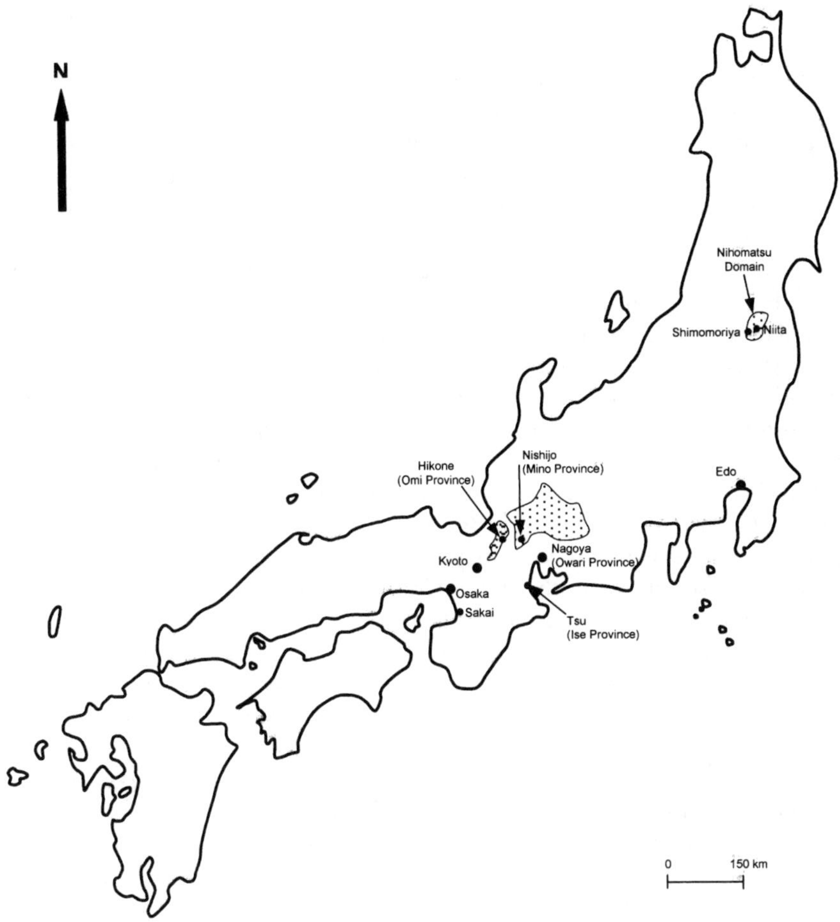

Map 4.1 Map showing locations of Nishijō in Mino Province, Niita and Shimomoriya in Nihonmatsu Domain in early modern Japan

nearly always endorsed labour contracts in early modern Japan, and the head was held responsible for any trouble caused by the employee.[5] Social networks were also an important part of the system as they influenced the direction of migration by providing introductions to employers and possible guarantors for labour contracts. I found that social mobility also depended upon the overall equation, as I will show below. The role of gender, especially for women, was another factor in the general equation making up the framework of migration and gender roles in the family and the society. My analyses are designed to contrast male and female migration patterns and I will make some general inferences about gender from these analyses.

Labour migration in early modern Japan has shown complex regional patterns and numerous differences between regions. Using the migration data from the population registers of several villages in central Japan, Hayami Akira has shown that labour migration was quite common in this region.[6] The ages for labour migration in the villages he studied suggest a pattern of life-cycle service, but although some of this migration was circular, much was not. Moreover, his work with data from an urban neighbourhood in the same region shows a constant and rapid population turnover from migration and mortality.[7] Hayami therefore argues that the stable urban population was maintained only by constant in-migration from the rural hinterland, and the higher fertility of the rural population was consequently balanced by out-migration.[8]

If we assume that labour migration to urban communities was the result of industrialisation, or proto-industrialisation, then Osamu Saitō's findings for southwestern Japan are somewhat contradictory. Saitō suggests that proto-industrial development in rural villages led to a reduction in labour migration as the former excess local labour force was utilised at home.[9] While the nature of proto-industry and labour structures found in central and southwestern Japan could explain part of this disparity, the economic and labour structures in the two regions were not so very different. Rural cottage industry was common in both regions. Moreover, the manufacturers in central as well as southwestern Japan tended to use daily wage and seasonal labour. This kind of labour usually would not appear in population registers as migration because the workers were only away for a few days or months at a time and would be present on registration day.[10]

Economic development, the needs of the local labour market, demographic system and family strategies have therefore been the main environmental factors considered by scholars as shaping labour migration. However, the contrast between the findings of Hayami for central Japan and Saitō for southwestern Japan suggests that other factors were equally important. After all, both regions had a surplus labour population and growing proto-industrial development. Why should this combination lead to more migration in one area and less migration in the other? I suggest that there are other factors necessary to the equation.

To address this issue I compare three villages in two regions of early modern Japan that have a similar type and quality of data on labour migration. The three villages are Shimomoriya and Niita in Nihonmatsu in northeastern Japan, and Nishijō in central Japan. I chose to compare these three villages for several reasons. First is that the data sources for these villages are of excellent quality and overlap in time span. Second, the northeastern villages share a common village structure, political environment, climate and demographic system in contrast to Nishijō, the village in central Japan. On the other hand, Nishijō and Niita share certain economic traits, such as location near major highways and easy access to urban areas of commercial development. Moreover, the Nihonmatsu administration encouraged proto-industrial development from the late eighteenth century. Although the region was never to become as affluent as central Japan, proto-industrial development certainly benefited the economy during the nineteenth century. These economic differences, similarities and changes lead me to expect certain differences, similarities and changes in the labour migration patterns of the three villages.

Data and methodology

For data I use the population registers of each village. The Nishijō registers, called *Shūmon Aratame Chō* (SAC), are literally religious population registers. Each village resident, whether domicile or temporary servant, is listed as a member of a household in relation to the household head. Each household is also listed according to its temple and religious sect of registry. Each household listing records members according to whether they are actually present in the household on the day of registration each year or are domicile members living outside the household. These outside listings record where the outside member is currently residing and why he or she is outside (marriage, adoption or service, etc.) and these listings continue to trace the outside member until he or she dies or moves domicile registration elsewhere. One probable reason for maintaining these listings is that the household head was ultimately responsible for guaranteeing contracts of marriage, adoption and service.

The population registers of villages in Nihonmatsu, including Shimomoriya and Niita, are quite similar in form to those of Nishijō except that they do not record religious or temple affiliation. They are popularly known as Ninbetsu Aratame Chō (NAC), but their actual title is Hito on Aratame Chō, both titles meaning population register. For labour migration data, the NAC can be considered identical to the SAC.[11] I chose the registers of these three villages, first, because of the quality of their information, as explained above, second, because they are comparable data sources, and third, because of the extremely long series of yearly registers available for each village in overlapping time periods. The Shimomoriya data includes yearly registers 1716–1869 with only nine missing years (1720, 1729, 1846, 1850, 1858 and 1864–1867). The Niita data registers run yearly 1720–1870 with only five missing years (1742, 1758, 1796 and 1857–1858). The Nishijō run is shorter, 1773–1872, with five missing years (1829, 1838, 1845 and 1870–1871). Altogether, I have around 150 years of data for the two northeastern villages and ninety-nine years of data for Nishijō.

Population declined in northeastern Japan during much of the eighteenth century, stabilising only after 1790 and recovering after 1840. The administration of Nihonmatsu domain was very much aware of this decline and enacted a number of policies to encourage population growth. One such policy was a prohibition of migration outside the domain.

Such policies were not always successful. Tatsuno domain in western Japan had such a policy, but was unable to enforce it in the face of the strong draw from the brewing and textile industries in neighbouring provinces.[12] In Nihonmatsu villagers frequently 'absconded', meaning they left without informing the authorities where they went. The NAC of Shimomoriya and Niita have long lists of such people who probably left for out-domain labour migration. Without further information as to where they went, however, I cannot include them in this analysis, except to mention here that many of these runaways later returned. These people will undoubtedly be a topic for future analysis.

For this analysis I am interested only in villagers who leave for service migration. My reasons for thus limiting the discussion are as follows: first, there is no information on where the runaways went or what they did, although labour migration is one likely answer. Second, other types of employment, such as daily wage labour in breweries or other manufactories, would not appear on the registries. All forms of contract labour lasting any duration of time longer than six months was known as 'service', hence my use of the term instead of 'labour'. Moreover, I am not interested in outsiders who have come to the village as servants and later leave when their service term is completed, so I limit the enquiry to people who appear in a kin relation to a family at least once in the data.

The administration of Nihonmatsu reversed its economic policies from discouragement to encouragement of proto-industry in the late eighteenth century.[13] In an earlier paper of mine on naming and the stem-family in Shimomoriya, I found evidence of major changes in village practice after about 1790.[14] In a later paper, I divided the Shimomoriya data at 1790 and found differences between the earlier and later periods in naming and inheritance practices that may have been related to a combination of demographic and economic differences.[15]

Because of the way the data overlaps, and the many economic, demographic and social changes occurring in Shimomoriya village and Nihonmatsu domain after 1790, I have divided the data period as follows. The Shimomoriya and Niita data are split between t1 (1721–1790) and t2 (1791–1860). I use only the Nishijō data corresponding to t2 (1791–1860). I chose to begin t1 in 1721 to allow for differences in data overlap between Shimomoriya and Niita. I chose to end t2 in 1860 to make the two data periods equal in length. Moreover, this cut-off means that we can observe villagers that emigrated during t2 for at least ten years beyond the data period. Ten years is a reasonable period for observation because many labour contracts lasted for ten years or less. Longer contracts were more likely to belong to people who would not return.[16]

I have arranged my data analysis around four questions. First, I ask who is most likely to leave for service migration. This will include questions of age, sex, marital status, relation to head of household and the general probability of service migration. The second question is who returns in the same categories of sex, marital status and relation to head. The third question is who does not return, controlling for those who died before they could return. The fourth and final question is about geographical patterns of out-migration, networks and possible social mobility. I will present and discuss my conclusions in the final section.

Why leave the village for service out-migration?

The political, social and economic backgrounds of the three villages lead me to expect certain differences in the level of labour out-migration between villages and between periods. Nihonmatsu domain authorities discouraged the development of proto-industry during much of the eighteenth century, but then changed their policy to encouraging it after about 1790. There is no sign that proto-industry developed in either Shimomoriya or Niita, so villagers would have had to migrate out to take advantage of this new income source. Of course, the labour market for the developing industries would have been important. Silk textile and lacquer industries developed in the villages near Shimomoriya, so I would expect that labour migration would increase during t2 (1791–1860). Moreover, Niita had easy access to two communities that urbanised during t2 and incorporated as towns in 1824 suggesting that labour migration would increase for Niita as well during t2.[17]

Nishijō, on the other hand, was in a region of early industrial development with several cities and other growing urban communities. Minō province, which included the Nōbi plain where Nishijō was located, was well known for its manufacture of paper and cotton textiles. The local highway was the main road connecting Kyōto with Edo, thus giving Nishijō villagers easy access to Ōsaka, Kyōto, Nagoya and Edo as well as more local towns. Moreover, the three rivers flowing through the Nōbi plain were major transportation routes that connected the coastal plain with mountainous regions inland.[18]

In short, I expect that service out-migration was more common in Nishijō than in Shimomoriya or Niita. I expect that Shimomoriya and Niita villagers would show a higher probability for out-migration in t2 than in t1. I also expect the Niita t2 levels to be close to the Nishijō levels.

Investigation of the general probability for service out-migration, however, shows unexpected results (see Figures 4.1a–c). Villagers in Shimomoriya and Niita were far more likely to migrate for service in the early part of the data period and the tendency to migrate declines over time. When the Nishijō data period begins, Niita and Shimomoriya have higher levels of out-migration, but these levels soon fall to a level even with Nishijō and then below that of Nishijō. The probability of out-migration in Shimomoriya, however, declines far more rapidly than in Niita. In Nishijō, there is no clear trend. Instead, out-migration fluctuates around a steady level possibly related to the needs of the labour market.

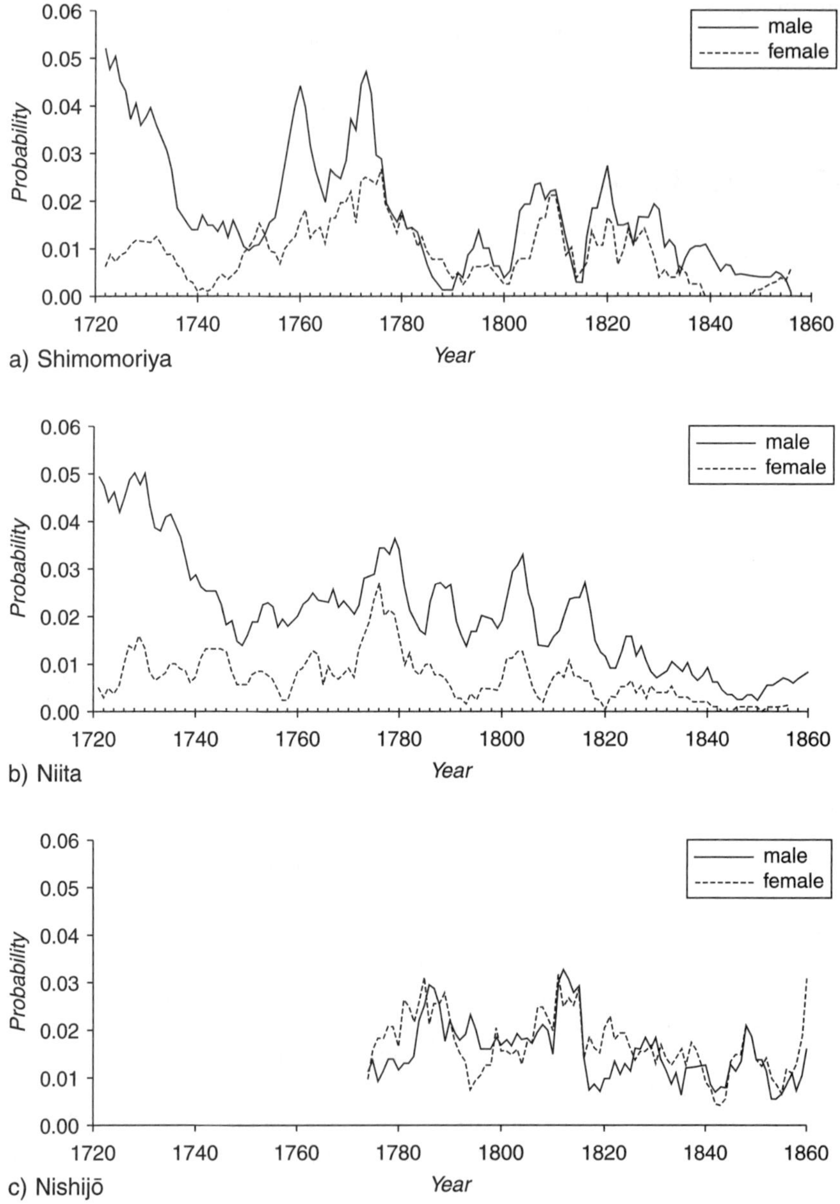

Figure 4.1 Probability of service out-migration, 1720–1860

Closer examination of out-migration from Shimomoriya and Niita also reveals a secondary peak around 1775 for both villages and an earlier peak around 1760 for Shimomoriya. Although I have little secondary information regading the 1760 peak, the 1775 peak came at a time of a long run of harvest failures in the region that preceded the Tenmei famine 1782–1787.[19] The three villages also show different patterns of male versus female out-migration. In Shimomoriya, male out-migration is higher until about 1775, after which male and female levels are quite similar. The major fall in out-migration appears to be largely a fall in male out-migration. In Niita, however, the male and female patterns are quite similar with male out-migration always higher than female out-migration and the two levels declining together. In Nishijō, male and female levels and patterns are nearly identical. What lies behind these differences?

One clue to these differences is the type of service involved. Figures 4.2a–b show the breakdown of types of service over time for Shimomoriya and Niita. I do not show this breakdown for Nishijō because all service in the Nishijō records was simply contract, or wage, service. In Shimomoriya and Niita, however, warrior service and pawn service were apparently the two most important types. Simple wage service, while not uncommon, was not as important to these villagers as the other two types. In Shimomoriya there are 166 cases of out-migration for wage service in the record, 340 cases for pawn service and 275 cases for warrior service. In Niita, the figures are 125 for wage service, 434 for pawn service and 445 for warrior service.[20]

The types of service neatly explain the differences between male and female service migration patterns in the two villages. The high level of male out-migration in the early part of the data period was largely warrior service by which mostly men were hired by some member of the warrior class. A common form of warrior service was for the domain lord to hire peasants to fill out the lower ranks of his retinue for official occasions.[21] In this respect, warrior service was also a kind of wage service, but the employer was the domain lord or some other member of the warrior class and provided fewer opportunities for women. The domain administration stopped hiring service from the men of Shimomoriya villages as time went on, although the men of Niita continued to serve in this capacity until the end of the period at reduced levels. Moreover, gender differences in out-migration rates in Shimomoriya largely disappear with the decline in warrior service. This change in warrior service levels probably reflects the worsening economic status of the domain government and the warrior class. The economic environment is also reflected in the levels of pawn and wage service with, again, some unexpected results.

With pawn service, the family literally put a family member in pawn as collateral for a loan. The 'pawned' member then worked for a wage, but this wage agreement was separate from the loan amount.[22] High levels of pawn service therefore reflect high levels of debt and poor economic

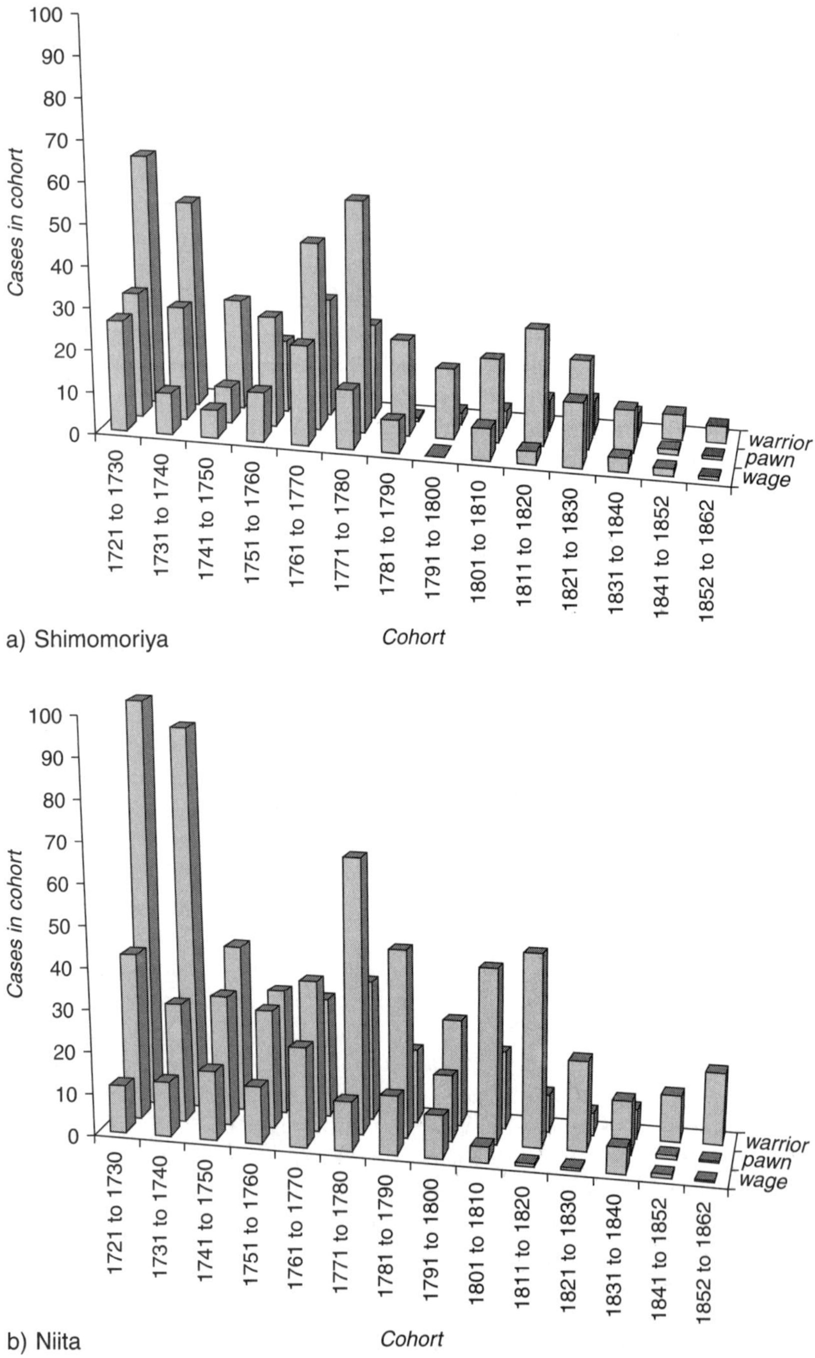

Figure 4.2 Changes in the type of service out-migration over time, 1721–1862

circumstances. The secondary peaks in the 1770s coincide with a run of poor harvests before the Tenmei famine 1783–1787.[23] Wage service, on the other hand, had no such debt relation. Therefore I would expect wage service levels to change inversely with pawn service levels. This was not the case. Although there were some periods when there was pawn service but no wage service, generally higher amounts of wage service accompanied higher amounts of pawn service. I must conclude, therefore, that both wage service and pawn service were used as family strategies for necessary income supplements in times of economic hardship in these two northeastern villages.

Who left the villages for service out-migration?

Who did families choose to send out for service migration? The age, marital status and relation to head of the out-migrants reveal important aspects of the role out-migration played in the demographic system. Equally interesting are the intentions of families revealed in who they chose to send into service.

The ages for service out-migration have an important relationship with the demographic systems of the three villages. The average age of first marriage for women in Nishijō was relatively high at 22 and the marital fertility rate was also high at 6.2 for women marrying at ages 21–25.[24] In comparison, the age of first marriage for women in Shimomoriya and Niita was 13.5 during much of the eighteenth century and rose only to 17.5 in the latter half of the century.[25] The average age of first marriage for women for the whole period was 14.8. In spite of this young age at first marriage, the marital fertility rate was also low with a total fertility rate of 2.82 for Shimomoriya and 3.17 for Niita. Marriage was also nearly universal in all three villages with only a very few women remaining unmarried and celibate in these villages.[26]

Figures 4.3a–c show the ages of out-migration in the three villages again contrasting male and female. There was no apparent difference between t1 (1721–1790) and t2 (1791–1860) in Shimomoriya or Niita, so the figures show the ages for the entire period. Instead of looking at average age, I contrasted age with cases to get the general pattern. In Nishijō the age pattern suggests life-cycle service with most service out-migration taking place in the teens to early twenties before marriage. In Shimomoriya and Niita, however, service out-migration continued throughout the productive years ages 15–50 and beyond. Indeed, the service out-migration age pattern suggests that the productive age period in these two villages continued until ages 55–60. Moreover, most of the out-migrants were probably married, since other research has shown that most people in these two villages were married by the age of 20.[27] Emiko Ochiai also noted this contrast in the marital status of out-migrants in northeastern and central Japan.[28]

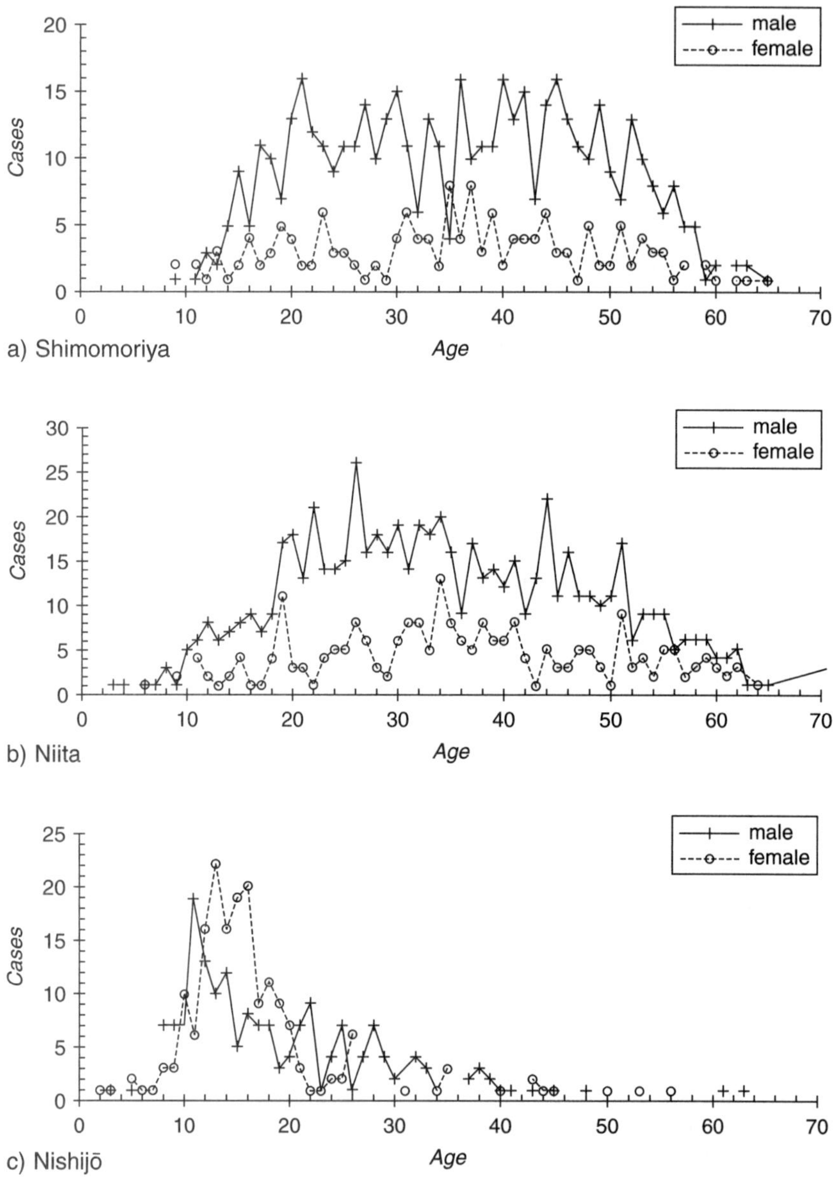

Figure 4.3 Age at service out-migration

Table 4.1 Marital status of male villagers on leaving for service out-migration, Shimomoriya, Niita and Nishijō, 1721–1790 and 1791–1860

Marital status	*Shimomoriya (%)*		*Niita (%)*		*Nishijō (%)*
	t1	*t2*	*t1*	*t2*	*t2*
Never married	14.1	16	16	18	92
Married together	54.5	57	41	46.5	5
Married separate	16.7	15	13.2	17.8	–
Formerly married	7.6	5	11.6	15.1	3
Unknown	7.2	–	18.9	1.1	1
Total (N)	*347*	*98*	*507*	*185*	*181*

Table 4.2 Marital status of female villagers on leaving for service out-migration, Shimomoriya, Niita and Nishijō, 1721–1790 and 1791–1860

Marital status	*Shimomoriya (%)*		*Niita (%)*		*Nishijō (%)*
	t1	*t2*	*t1*	*t2*	*t2*
Never married	2.8	9	9.1	2	94.9
Married together	47.6	42	40.6	45	2.3
Married separate	41.3	34	46.2	35	–
Formerly married	8.4	13	3.5	16	2.9
Unknown	–	2	0.7	2	–
Total (N)	*143*	*64*	*143*	*51*	*185*

Tables 4.1 and 4.2 show the marital status of the villagers when they left for service migration. As might be expected from the above analysis, most of the Nishijō out-migrants were never married while most of the Shimomoriya and Niita out-migrants were either married or formerly married. Moreover, I divided the married category into married living together and married living separately. In this division, about half of the men in both Shimomoriya and Niita fall into the 'married living together' category with far fewer 'married living separately'. The women, however, divide relatively evenly between the 'living together' and 'living separately' categories of 'married'. This suggests that the husband would often leave for service migration first and his wife would leave for another contract later.

The inferred difference in timing between the service out-migration of husbands and wives suggests a second reason why service out-migration generally tended to be less common for women than for men in Shimomoriya and Niita. When considered together with service types, it also suggests the reason for the decline in service out-migration from these two villages during the eighteenth century when the local economy was more stable.[29] If families sent members into service to borrow money out of necessity, then this necessity would disappear when the household economy became more stable. Moreover, if wives were the second choice for service out-migration, then of course more men would go than women did.

The service out-migration of married men and women may have been one factor behind the low marital fertility rates in Shimomoriya and Niita. Demographic research has shown that the crude birth rate for the two villages rises after 1790.[30] The men and women who left for service out-migration could have been heads of household and their wives, sons, sons-in-law and their spouses or collateral kin. Each choice possibility has different implications for the family and demographic systems of the three villages.

Of course, a wife might be 'married living separate' even when her husband was working within the village. In this case there was probably less effect on fertility as the couple could still spend time together. Nevertheless, labour migration limited the time married couples lived together. Take the case of Shime in Shimomoriya, for example. Shime appears in the data at recorded age 2 in 1766. She marries Josuke in 1783 and their first child, daughter Miyo, is born 1785 after which Josuke goes into service and does not return until 1800. Some of his service contracts during this time, however, are within the village, and a second daughter Haru is born in 1795. The couple hardly ever cohabits thereafter until 1825. Josuke, who changes his name to Sukeuemon in 1784, appears in the listing for the household in 1800, 1814 and then 1820–1828. The records show he is working outside the village in 1804–1809 and again in 1810–1814. Meanwhile, Shime also leaves the household for service within the village 1789–1795. Then she leaves her daughters with her parents as she works outside the village on consecutive contracts from 1803 to 1825 and only appears in the household list as living at home in 1807 and 1820 during this period. Although the life courses of Shime and Josuke seem rather extreme, I picked the couple at random from the data sample and there are many others like them.

Which family members went into service outside the village? Table 4.3 shows the relations to head of the male migrants the year before migration. I include fictional kin as well as blood relations in the categories. Thus, 'son' includes adopted son, son-in-law and husband of adopted daughter. I have included grandsons in this category. There is little difference between t1 and t2 in Shimomoriya, with the exception that the proportion of household heads is smaller and the proportion of fathers is larger. Since headship succession and inheritance usually occurred with the retirement of the former head and the various rights and duties were transferred over a number of years, this change could reflect earlier retirement and the retention of some duties by the former head. In Niita the change is in the opposite direction, with an approximately equal proportion of heads and sons leaving in t1 and more heads than sons

Table 4.3 Male relations to head before service out-migration, Shimomoriya, Niita and Nishijō, 1721–1790 and 1791–1860

Relations	*Shimomoriya (%)*		*Niita (%)*		*Nishijō (%)*
	t1	*t2*	*t1*	*t2*	*t2*
Head	49.6	46	38.9	49.7	9.9
Father	4.6	9	1.2	7.0	–
Son/grandson	26.5	26	38.7	22.7	71.3
Other rel.	2.3	3	2.8	3.2	11.6
Servant	17.0	16	18.5	17.3	7.2
Total (N)	*347*	*98*	*507*	*185*	*181*

Table 4.4 Female relations to head before service out-migration, Shimomoriya, Niita and Nishijō, 1721–1790 and 1791–1860

Relations	*Shimomoriya (%)*		*Niita (%)*		*Nishijō (%)*
	t1	*t2*	*t1*	*t2*	*t2*
Head	3.5	8	1.4	4	1.6
Wife	41.3	34	41.3	55	2.2
Mother	4.2	6	4.2	12	0.5
Dau./grandau.	14.7	25	24.5	16	81.0
Other rel.	2.1	–	2.1	–	12.4
Servant	34.3	27	26.6	14	2.2
Total (N)	*143*	*64*	*143*	*51*	*185*

leaving in t2. The differences between t1 and t2, however, might also be the result of differences in sample size between the two periods. In either case, the overall pattern shows that families in Shimomoriya and Niita sent heads, former heads and sons out to service migration.

Nishijō was quite different in this respect. Most of the male family members sent out to service migration were sons of the head. This finding supports the pattern of life-cycle service seen in the age at migration. Moreover, although the numbers are relatively small, Nishijō families show a higher propensity to send collateral kin out for service migration than those of Shimomoriya and Niita. I refer, in this case, to the category labelled 'other relatives'.

Table 4.4 shows the relations to head for the female out-migrants. The most important category for women in Shimomoriya and Niita was wife of the head. This was a negligible category for women in Nishijō. Instead, Nishijō women were far more likely to be daughters of the head. Again, as with the men, Nishijō families also show a relatively stronger propensity to send collateral kin into service as represented by the category 'other relatives'. From these findings, I suggest that service out-migration from Nishijō was also a method for getting rid of surplus population or labour.

Apparently, Shimomoriya and Niita were not using service out-migration as a method to get rid of surplus family members. The household head was the most important member of the household labour force and of the family. His choice to leave the family and the village for service migration suggests economic necessity rather than labour surplus. Of course, pawn service was undertaken from economic necessity. Moreover, the choice of Shimomoriya and Niita families to send married members to service migration, as well as the most important family members suggests another strategy. Families from these two villages chose the members who were most likely to return to the village. Nevertheless, the population in these two villages and the domain as a whole fell during the periods when out-migration was most common. Was service out-migration behind this fall?

Who returned from service out-migration and who didn't?

When villagers migrate from economic necessity, we might expect to find that they do not return. Moreover, there were high levels of labour migration during periods when the population fell. On the other hand, the villagers of Shimomoriya and Niita tended to leave for service out-migration after marriage, thus separating from their spouses, which was a good reason for them to return. In Nishijō, service out-migration appears to take the pattern of life-cycle service in age structure and relation to head. Does this mean that they later returned in a pattern of circular migration? Or was service migration also a way of redistributing or getting rid of surplus labour and population? What were the family strategies involved?

To answer these questions I look at the people who returned from service out-migration, asking what proportions returned and who they were. I define the base population for this analysis as having left during t1 (1721–1790) or t2 (1791–1860). The data continues until 1870 for all three villages allowing us to observe the migrants of the final years of the sample period at least ten years after departure. Since the longer-term contracts of ten to fifteen years tend to be for apprentices who would not return to the village, this extra observation period should allow us to know who intended to return.[31]

Tables 4.5 and 4.6 show the relations to head of villagers when they returned from service out-migration. The first most striking finding is that around 90 per cent of the out-migrants from Shimomoriya and Niita later returned to their villages, whereas only about half of the men and 15 per cent of the women of Nishijō returned. Also apparent is that a larger proportion of the men returning to Shimomoriya and Niita were house-

Table 4.5 Male relations to head on return from service out-migration, Shimomoriya, Niita and Nishijō, 1721–1790 and 1791–1860

Relations	*Shimomoriya (%)*		*Niita (%)*		*Nishijō (%)*
	t1	*t2*	*t1*	*t2*	*t2*
Head	52.5	48	47.6	60.5	10
Father	7.6	16	2.2	11.2	–
Son/grandson	23.3	19	33.3	18.3	63
Other rel.	4.5	3	4.3	4.7	13
Servant	12.1	14	17.6	5.3	14
Total (N)	*337*	*90*	*481*	*170*	*83*

Table 4.6 Female relations to head on return from service out-migration, Shimomoriya, Niita and Nishijō, 1721–1790 and 1791–1860

Relations	*Shimomoriya (%)*		*Niita (%)*		*Nishijō (%)*
	t1	*t2*	*t1*	*t2*	*t2*
Head	3.7	7	5.5	10	–
Wife	44.8	26	54.3	48	4
Mother	6.0	14	4.7	17	–
Dau/grandau.	13.5	23	19.7	13	65
Other rel.	2.9	–	3.2	–	19
Servant	29.1	30	12.6	12	12
Total (N)	*134*	*57*	*127*	*42*	*26*

hold heads upon return than when they left, suggesting that some, at least, returned or were called back to inherit. Because relatively few Nishijō villagers returned from out-migration, we cannot make any inferences of this sort for the Nishijō sample. At the least, most men who returned to Nishijō were not called back to inherit immediately.

Headship succession in absentia also affected the status of returning women. A number of women in Shimomoriya and Niita, particularly during t2, moved from wife of the head to mother of the head. The stronger tendency for this change in t2 suggests again that heads were choosing to retire earlier than during t1, although the difference could be merely a difference in the sample sizes. In Niita, more women returned as female head of household suggesting again that they were called back to inherit, perhaps in the absence of any other suitable heir.

In all three villages, men who returned from service were more likely to be married. The men in the never married category that returned to the village fell from 14 per cent of the leavers to 11 per cent of the return migrants in Shimomoriya during t1 and 16 per cent to 13 per cent in

Shimomoriya during t2. They also fell from 16 per cent to 10 per cent in Niita during t1 and 18 per cent to 14 per cent in Niita during t2. The same was true for Nishijō, as the never married category fell from 92 per cent of the leavers to 70 per cent of the return migrants for men and from 95 per cent to 70 per cent for women. Since most of the women of Shimomoriya and Niita who migrated out were already married before migration, differences in the never married category are negligible. All three villages had universal marriage systems, so any never married villagers who remained in their village eventually married, probably soon after return from migration if not before.[32] In any case, marriage seems to have been a powerful reason for return migration.

When considering the villagers that did not return from service out-migration, we must consider the possibility that they died before they could return. Careful though the registers are in tracing villagers through their migrations, village officials sometimes lost track of villagers living outside the village. Therefore, I focused upon those villagers whose death is recorded in the registers even though they lived outside the village. Because the number of out-migrants who did not return to Shimomoriya and Niita is so small and the patterns for the two villages are so similar, I combine the figures for the two villages t1 and t2. Of all villagers who did not return, only twelve lived outside the village more than ten years after their final departure from the village. Another twelve villagers died five to ten years after leaving and the remaining died within five years of departure. So of the over 1,500 departures for service out-migration from these two villages during the data period, only a small number left permanently out of choice and most returned to their villages if they could.

Nishijō villagers, however, made a different choice. Few of the out-migrants returned. Of the 118 whose death appears in the record, 15 died within five years after departure, 12 died five to ten years after departure and 91 died more than ten years after departure from Nishijō. The remaining villagers have no record of death in the registers and were probably still alive away from the village at the end of the data period. This finding suggests that many Nishijō villagers leaving for service migration generally had little reason for or intention of returning if they found something better outside the village. Out-migration from Nishijō was, as the analyses above suggest, an integral part of the demographic system redistributing surplus labour and population. Finally, although service out-migration from Nishijō may have been a kind of life-cycle service, it was by no means circular. Rather, most people went, but only a small group returned.

Where did they go?

Service migration from Shimomoriya and Niita was largely circular in that most migrants returned. Much of it was also either service to the domain or combined with personal debts. In the former case there is no question of the network involved. Moreover, there was little chance of real social mobility from this service, although at least one person from Shimomoriya returned from warrior service with a surname – a privilege normally reserved for members of the warrior class – and possibly higher social status.[33] In the latter case the financial network connection is apparent. Examination of the destinations of these villagers revealed that they remained largely in their local districts. Even migration to urban communities was confined to local towns in the district rather than larger and more distant urban centres. The same was true for the few permanent migrants, with only two exceptions and they only went as far as the neighbouring district.

I also examined the places the villagers went for permanent migration and found two general characteristics to the pattern true for both Shimomoriya and Niita. Migrant villagers generally stayed within their home district with only one or two exceptions. Even these exceptions only went as far as the neighbouring district. Within their home districts, however, these villagers tended to go to the rural towns or larger villages where presumably economic opportunities were greater.

The out-migration pattern for Nishijō villagers, however, was quite different. Nishijō villagers frequently migrated outside their district and to villages, towns and cities outside their province. Moreover, multiple villagers migrated to the same destinations suggesting that later migrants used the connections of earlier migrants to find employment.

Table 4.7 shows the ten most popular labour migration destinations of Nishijō villagers who did not return. These destinations easily reveal the nature of labour migration from Nishijō, so I will comment on the top four destinations.

Table 4.7 Top ten destinations from which Nishijō villagers did not return, by sex

Village/city name	*Female*	*Male*	*Total*
Nagoya	27	23	50
Ōsaka	7	15	22
Ōgaki	14	7	21
Takegahana	10	6	16
Niremata	10	6	16
Hikone	4	8	12
Kyōto	8	3	11
Tsu	7	3	10
Hongō	9	–	9
Nakamura	6	2	8

Note
Ōsaka and Kyōto are two of the three major cities of early modern Japan. Nagoya, Ōgaki and Hikone are castle towns. Tsu was a port and highway town in the neighbouring province. Takegahana was an industrial town. Hongō was a village in the neighbouring district. Niremata was the parent village of Nishijō. Nakamura was a village in the same district.

The most popular destination was Nagoya. This city was a castle town in the neighbouring province and the closest urban, commercial and industrial centre for Nishijō villagers. Ōgaki was the local castle town and Nishijō was under the management of the Ōgaki domain. Ōsaka was the second largest city in Japan and certainly the largest commercial centre. Finally, Takegahana was a local centre for the textile industry. Although we do not know what type of work Nishijō villagers found in these commercial and industrial centres, there were plenty of opportunities for employment in support and service industries as well as the more obvious commercial and manufacturing jobs. In any case, agricultural villagers who found permanent employment in urban settings were probably socially mobile in the most basic sense because they permanently changed the type of work they did.

Figure 4.4 shows the general trends and changes in the destinations of Nishijō villagers over time. The categories in this graph are as follows. Nishijō was located in Anpachi district in Minō province. 'Anpachi' thus refers to villages in Anpachi district while 'Minō' refers to communities in Minō province, but not in Anpachi district. Owari is the neighbouring province to the east and includes the city of Nagoya. Ōmi is the neighbouring province to the northwest and contains the castle town Hikone. Ise is the neighbouring province to the southwest and contains the port town Tsu. Edo, Ōsaka and Kyōto are the three major cities of early modern Japan. Sakai is a port city south of Ōsaka.

This figure shows one very important trend. Whereas villages in Anpachi were very common destinations for labour migration in the early part of the period, they nearly disappear after about 1820. Instead, most of the migration destinations are outside the Anpachi district where Nishijō was located. In a sense, this trend is similar to that of Shimomoriya and Niita villagers who only migrate within their own districts. If we limit our focus to labour migration within the same district, then labour migration falls dramatically for the population of all three villages after about 1820 (see also Figures 4.1a–b). Yet this was just the period of more proto-industrial development.

I suggest that this apparent fall in local labour migration was actually a change in the nature of employment. The population registries recorded household residence once a year. If employment practices change from long-term contracts for live-in employees to short-term contracts for commuting employees, or to using daily wage or casual labour, then local residents would not need to migrate out. The continuation of labour migration to more distant destinations then could be explained by distance because they are too far away to commute. Moreover, research on labour contracts and labour practices in other regions has suggested that this change occurred with the development of manufactories in certain industries such as dyeing, brewing and paper manufacture.[34]

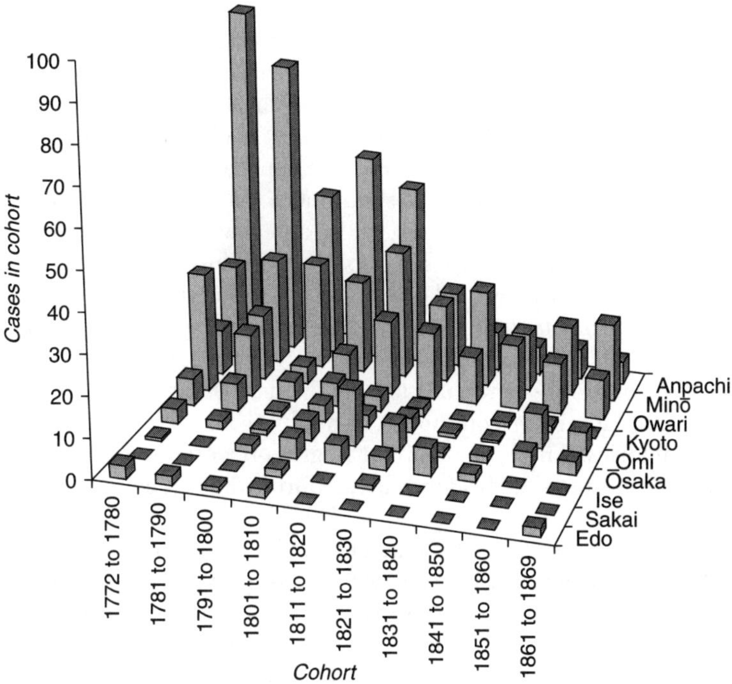

Figure 4.4 Changes in labour migration destinations of Nishijō villagers over time, 1772–1869

Conclusions

My investigation of the labour migration from and return migration to three villages in two regions of Japan produced some unexpected results. These results have led me to suggest some conclusions regarding the relation between labour migration and the demographic, economic and political environments of these villages.

Labour out-migration was common for all three villages, Shimomoriya, Niita and Nishijō. However, contrary to my expectations, labour-migration levels were much higher for Shimomoriya and Niita in the northeast than for Nishijō in central Japan. Moreover, migration from these two northeastern villages was much higher during the early eighteenth century and during periods of economic hardship than during the later period of economic and proto-industrial development. Migration from Nishijō, on the other hand, showed no such trend.

Analysis of the population registers of these three villages has provided several reasons for these different regional trends. Villagers in Shimomoriya and Niita largely migrated for warrior service in the early period, but these levels fell as the domain economy worsened. At the same time, economic hardship caused villagers to enter into pawn service contracts as their families went into debt. As the economy improved in the nineteenth century, the need for villagers to enter pawn service also fell.

The economy in the northeastern region improved with proto-industrial development. Proto-industry, however, did not replace pawn service with wage service. Nor can we assume Saitō's argument that labour was utilised at home in the proto-industries of these villages because these villages did not develop proto-industry.[35] This suggests that the improved economic circumstances of these villages related to proto-industrial development must have resulted from income from employment in proto-industry outside the villages. This seeming contradiction suggests that the employment system changed from long-term contracts for live-in workers to short-term contracts or casual labour for commuters as might occur with the development of manufactories. This type of labour migration would not appear on the yearly population registers because the labourers did not actually move away.

This supposition is supported by changes in the geographic migration pattern of Nishijō villagers after 1820. While Nishijō villagers continued to leave for labour migration, they apparently changed from preferring local destinations to preferring primarily distant destinations outside of the local district and outside of the province. This pattern is easily explained if employment practices for proto-industry changed in this region as suggested above. Migration from Nishijō could move to distant destinations outside commuting distance also partly because there were few, if any, legal restrictions on labour migration. The villagers of Shimomoriya and Niita did not have this option because of legal restrictions prohibiting distant migration. Therefore, regional differences in political policies were part of the differences in migration patterns.

The demographic systems were also a factor in these regional differences. Shimomoriya and Niita drastically lost population during the periods of economic hardship and their populations did not begin to recover until the nineteenth-century period of economic development. This population loss was behind the political policies restricting distant labour migration because political authorities feared the loss of a necessary agricultural labour force.[36] In other words, these villages could not afford to lose population or labour force. Family and village efforts to balance the need for outside income during periods of economic hardship with the need to maintain population can be seen in the choice of which family members were sent out for service. One aspect of the strategy was to send married family members into service, probably using marriage as insurance that these migrating members would return. The high rates of return migration attest to the success of this family strategy.

In contrast, Nishijō village had a demographic system that could support high rates of out-migration. The family decision to send young, unmarried members outside the village, often to distant places, for service virtually assured that the majority would not return. Instead, village families gained the benefits of extra income and an extensive network of social and economic ties. At the same time, the village shed excess labour that was redistributed throughout the region and elsewhere according to the needs of the labour market.

In all three villages labour migration patterns show a strong relation to the demographic system as well as the economic environment. The low fertility and falling population of the northeastern villages was likely a factor behind the migration of married men and women. The ensuing separation of spouses may, in turn, have been a factor behind the low fertility levels of this demographic system. This family strategy may also have been a factor behind the early age of first marriage in this system. These relations will require further investigation.

The later age of first marriage and the higher fertility rates of the demographic system in Nishijō also neatly dovetail with the migration pattern. The choice to send young unmarried villagers out to service may have been a factor behind the later age of first marriage. This method of shedding excess labour and population may also have been a factor supporting the system of universal marriage in a region that followed stem-family household formation rules and had few resources for increasing the number of households. While universal marriage meant that virtually everyone in the village eventually married, this could be rephrased for Nishijō to mean that everyone who remained in or returned to the village married. Moreover, the general lack of migration by married spouses provided an environment conducive to the higher fertility that produced the excess population necessary to the cycle.

Proto-industrial development in both regions caused changes in the migration patterns from the three villages probably related to changes in hiring practices as discussed above. These economic changes, however, influenced migration patterns in different ways as mediated by political policy and legal restrictions. The role of political policy is not often considered in historical studies of migration and also deserves more attention.

Women played an important role in these migration patterns, not very different from that of men. The only gender difference found in the analysis can largely be explained by warrior service in the northeast, which heavily relied upon male labour. Gender differences largely disappear with reductions in warrior service. There were no apparent gender differences in Nishijō, the village in central Japan. Therefore, female labour was as important to family economic strategies as male labour.

Finally, the migration patterns of these three villages are best understood as the result of family strategies for survival rather than individual actions even though the migration was of individuals rather than family groups. Families sent members into service and their strategies were determined by the need to encourage return or non-return migration. Networks determined the destinations villagers chose and this out-migration sometimes led to social mobility.

Acknowledgements

The analyses for this chapter used the Xavier and Nōbi data files of the EurAsian Project on Population and Family History created under the leadership of Hayami Akira. Ōno Yoshihiko converted the Xavier file into a DB2 database system. Morimoto Shūma further developed the Nōbi file. I particularly want to thank Hirai Shōko for helping me create the basic tables for this analysis.

Notes

1 Saitō O., *Purōto Kōgyōka no Jidai*, Tokyo, Nihon Hyōronsha, 1985, p. 250. A. Bideau and G. Brunet, 'Stay or Leave? Individual Choice and Family Logic: the Destinations of Children Born in the Valserine Valley (French Jura) in the Eighteenth and Nineteenth Centuries', *The History of the Family: an International Quarterly*, 1, 2 (1996): 159–168.

2 M. Anderson and D. J. Morse, 'High Fertility, High Emigration, Low Nuptiality: Adjustment Processes in Scotland's Demographic Experience, 1861–1914, Part II', *Population Studies*, 47 (1993): 319–343.

3 M. Oris, 'Fertility and Migration in the Heart of the Industrial Revolution', *The History of the Family: an International Quarterly*, 1, 2 (1996): 169–182. A. McCants, 'Internal Migration in Friesland, 1750–1805', *Journal of Interdisciplinary History*, XXII, 3 (1992): 387–409.

4 J. Lauby and O. Stark, 'Individual Migration as a Family Strategy: Young Women in the Philippines', *Population Studies*, 42 (1988): 473–486. A. de Haan, 'Migration as a Family Strategy: Rural–Urban Labour Migration in India during the Twentieth Century', *The History of the Family: an International Quarterly* 2, 4 (1997): 481–505.

5 M. L. Nagata, 'Commercial and Industrial Contract Labour in Central Japan, 1672–1873', University of Hawaii UMI Dissertation Services, 1996, pp. 74–84.

6 Hayami A., *Kinsei Nōbi Chihō no Jinkō, Keizai, Shakai*, Tokyo, Sōbunsha, 1992, pp. 101–120, 255–284.

7 Hayami A., 'Kyōto Machikata no Shūmon Aratame Chō: Shijō Tachiuri Naka no Machi,' in *Kenkyū Kiyō*, Tokugawa Rinsei Shi Kenkyū Sho, 1981, pp. 502–541.

8 A. Hayami, 'Rural Migration and Fertility in Tokugawa Japan: the Village of Nishijō 1773–1868', in S. Hanley and A. Wolf (eds) *Family and Population in East Asian History*, Stanford, CA, Stanford University Press, 1985.

9 Saitō, *Purōto Kōgyōka no Jidai*, p. 250.

10 Nagata, 'Commercial and Industrial Contract Labour', pp. 102–107.

11 For a comprehensive discussion of Japan's early modern population registers, see A. Hayami, 'Thank you Francisco Xavier: an Essay in the Use of Microdata for Historical Demography of Tokugawa Japan', *Keiō Economic Studies*, vol. XVI, 1–2 (1979): 65–81, and L. Cornell and A. Hayami, 'The Shūmon Aratame Chō: Japan's Population Registers', *Journal of Family History*, 11, 4 (November 1986): 311–328.

12 Nagata, 'Commercial and Industrial Contract Labour', p. 104. Yagi T., 'Kinsei Mura to Seikatsu: Nōson Yojō Rōdō wa Dekasegi ni', in Tatsuno-shi Shi Hensan Senmon Iinkai (ed.) *Tatsuno-shi Shi*, vol. 2, Tatsuno City, 1981, pp. 235–238.
13 Shōji K. *et al.*., *Nihonmatsu-shi Shi*, Nihonmatsu City, 1982, pp. 79–81.
14 M. L. Nagata, 'Name Changing Patterns and the Stem Family in Early Modern Japan: Shimomoriya', in A. Fauve-Chamoux and E. Ochiai (eds) *House and the Stem Family in EurAsian Perspective: Proceedings of the C18 Session Twelfth International Economic History Congress*, August 1998, pp. 291–319.
15 M. L. Nagata, 'Balancing Family Strategies with Individual Choice: Name Changing in Early Modern Japan', *Japan Review*, 11 (1999): 145–166.
16 Nagata, 'Commercial and Industrial Contract Labour'.
17 Okabe B. *et al.*, *Kōriyama-shi Shi*, vol. 2, Koriyama City, 1981, p. 333. Shōji, *Nihonmatsu-shi Shi*, pp. 79–81. Narimatsu S., *Kinsei Tōhoku Nōson no Hitobito: Ōshu Asaka gun Shimomoriya mura*, Kyōto, Mineruva Shobō, 1985. Narimatsu S., *Edo Jidai no Tōhoku Nōson: Nihonmatsu han Niita mura*, Tokyo, Dōbunkan, 1992.
18 Mori Y., 'Seishigyō', in Kodama Kōta (ed.) *Sangyōshi II*, Tokyo, Yamakawa Shuppansha, 1984, pp. 346–364. Hayami, 'Kyōto Machikata no Shūmon Aratame Chō'. K. Wigen, *The Making of a Japanese Periphery, 1750–1920*, Berkeley, University of California Press, 1995, pp. 25–38.
19 M. L. Nagata, S. Kurosu and A. Hayami, 'Niita and Shimomoriya of the Nihonmatsu Domain in the Northeastern Region of Tokugawa Japan', *Working Paper Series* 20, EurAsian Project on Population and Family History, 1998. Okabe *et al. Kōriyama-shi Shi*, vol. 2, p. 341.
20 In Nishijō the term used is simply *hōkō*. For Shimomoriya and Niita I combined the figures for simple *hōkō* (4 and 5 respectively) with those for *kyūtori hōkō* or wage service. Pawn service is *shichimostu hōkō*, and warrior service is *buke hōkō*. I also included the figures for *dai* and *shudai hōkō* with those for *buke hōkō* because they refer to someone substituting for another in *buke hōkō* and the figures are comparatively negligible (3–3 *dai* and 1–2 *shudai* for Niita and Shimomoriya respectively).
21 Morishita T., *Nihon Kinsei Koyō Rōdōshi no Kenkyū*, Tokyo, Tokyo Daigaku Shuppankai, 1995.
22 Okabe, *Kōriyama-shi Shi*, pp. 289–292.
23 Nagata, Kurosu and Hayami, 'Niita and Shimomoriya of the Nihonmatsu Domain'.
24 Hayami, *Kinsei Nōbi Chihō*, pp. 101–120.
25 Nagata, Kurosu and Hayami, 'Niita and Shimomoriya of the Nihonmatsu Domain'.
26 N. O. Tsuya and S. Kurosu, 'Patterns and Covariates of Fertility in 18th and 19th Century Rural Japan: Evidence from Two Northeastern Villages', *Working Paper Series* 16, EurAsian Project on Population and Family History, 1998, p. 5. Hamano K., Kurosu S. and Morimoto S., 'Tokugawa Nōson wa "Kaikon Shakai" Ka? Nōshū Nishijō mura, Shōgai Mikonritsu no Suikei', *Working Paper Series* 6, EurAsian Project on Population and Family History, 1998.
27 Tsuya and Kurosu, 'Patterns and Covariates of Fertility', p. 3.
28 E. Ochiai, 'Two Types of Stem Household System in Japan: the *ie* in Global Perspective', in A. Fauve-Chamoux and E. Ochiai (eds) *House and the Stem Family in EurAsian Perspective: Proceedings of the C18 Session Twelfth International Economic History Congress* (August), pp. 215–224.
29 Shōji, *Nihonmatsu-shi Shi*, pp. 81, 896–898.
30 Nagata, Kurosu and Hayami, 'Niita and Shimomoriya of the Nihonmatsu Domain'.
31 Employees of stem-family businesses had maximum contracts of ten to fifteen years for apprentices destined to become the skilled management members of

the business. If they stayed that long, then they usually remained in a new management capacity and would not return to their home villages. Nagata, 'Commercial and Industrial Contract Labour', pp. 29–62. Nagata, M. L., 'Who Are You? Servant Origins and Social Mobility in Early Modern Japan', *Conference Paper Series* 18, EurAsian Project on Population and Family History, 1997.

32 Tsuya and Kurosu, 'Patterns and Covariates of Fertility', p. 5. Hamano, Kurosu and Morimoto, 'Tokugawa Nōson wa "Kaikon Shakai" Ka?'

33 Nagata, 'Name Changing Patterns'.

34 Nagata, 'Commercial and Industrial Contract Labour', pp. 29–62.

35 Saitō, *Purōtō Kōgyōka no Jidai.*

36 Nagata, Kurosu and Hayami, 'Niita and Shimomoriya of the Nihonmatsu Domain'.

5 Women and long-distance trade migration in the nineteenth-century Netherlands

Marlou Schrover

Introduction

In this chapter I focus on long-distance trade migration, and especially on one group which consisted half of women and half of men – a characteristic rather uncommon for long-distance trade. The group originated from a German region called the Westerwald, and members of the group established communities in Dutch towns. One of these communities, in the Dutch town of Utrecht, is discussed here at some length. Evidence from other places shows that this community was similar to those in other Dutch towns. This article pays attention to the migration process itself, and the settlement and acculturation process that followed.

In the nineteenth century, German migration to the Netherlands was both seasonal and permanent. It consisted of migrating agricultural labourers, traders, domestics, soldiers, sailors and artisans. In the nineteenth century, as in the preceding centuries, Germans were by far the largest minority in the Netherlands. Of all foreigners in the Netherlands, 60 per cent came from German regions. In the middle of the nineteenth century, there were over 40,000 Germans in the Netherlands. This official figure only includes those born in Germany, not their offspring.[1]

In the countryside, agricultural migration was important. In the towns trade migration prevailed, as did the migration of domestic servants and artisans. The traders and artisans were mostly men, the domestics were almost all women. In the larger towns in the western part of the Netherlands, men outnumbered women two to one. The Westerwalder traders stood out amongst the other groups of traders because the number of women was equivalent to that of the men. The composition of the Westerwalder group had consequences for the settlement process.

Theory

As yet there is no comprehensive theory available which explains the long-term group acculturation process.[2] Lucassen and Penninx have described the acculturation process as the interaction between the acquisition of a position in society and its allocation.[3] Allocation refers to the mechanisms operating in society which keep a migrant in a position, impose a position or grant it. The effects on the migrant can be either negative or positive. Acquisition of a position refers to the initiatives and efforts of the migrant to acquire a good position within given circumstances. How the interaction develops depends, among other things, on the access group members have to resources that evolve from the group's cohesion, and reactions of the host society towards this cohesion. Groups of migrating families, as opposed to isolated migrants, have the advantage that members of the group can support each other. Individuals are more vulnerable, but being more dependent on the host society forces them to have more contacts with others.[4]

Success or failure of migrants in their new surroundings depends on the help and support they get from migrants who preceded them.[5] Whether new migrants really get this support is determined by the coherence of the group, which is influenced by the degree of self-organisation. Self-organisation can strengthen the position of the group, because individuals can fall back on the group's support, but it can also slow down integration when a powerful sense of group cohesion leads to segregation, to which the rest of society reacts with exclusion.[6]

The composition of the migrant group has consequences for its economic activities. It is not uncommon for migrants to cluster together in an economic niche, whereby all members of the group work in the same sector. According to Waldinger, niche formation is the logical outcome of migration.[7] Newcomers have a restricted number of contacts, mostly with people from the same regional background. The exchange of information and recruiting of personnel takes place through these restricted networks. As a result the group tends to concentrate in certain employment sectors.

Niches can evolve from the exclusive access some migrants have to certain trade goods. Migrants can act as the sole representatives of a product, or through family ties and other contacts can obtain more favourable trade conditions than outside traders.[8] A favourable access to the market can be combined with the recruitment of employees from the region of origin, who are willing to work for lower wages or longer hours.[9] Light has pointed out that the nature of niche formation is determined, amongst other things, by the possibilities it offers family members to get involved in it.[10] When both men and women can work within the niche, a much closer relationship develops between the group and the economic sector. The possibilities for family members to get involved, depend not only on the nature of the sector, but also on work options outside it. When there are many possibilities within the niche, and only a few outside it, entrepreneurs from within the group can profit from the existence of a large reservoir of cheap labour. This will strengthen the success and continuity of the niche.

Sources

The reconstruction of the Westerwalder community, and other migrant populations, as described below, is based mainly on data from the population registers. From the middle of the nineteenth century onwards, the Netherlands had population registers. The population registers were centrally organised, and administered by local governments. They were based on ten-yearly censuses. To the census data were added all changes that occurred in the ten years after the census, such as house-moving and all life events. Every ten years, there was a new census and a fresh start of the population registers.[11] The municipal population registers list name, date and place of birth, religion, marital status, occupation, date of death, previous and new addresses. The registers allow reconstruction of all life events, such as births, deaths and marriages, and all house-moving. Furthermore they allow the reconstruction of geographically based networks. The occupational information in population registers is of course far richer than that in the marriage registers, as it gives information for many more snapshots than just at marriage, and allows for reconstruction of career mobility.

For the research presented here, the whole Utrecht population register for the period from 1850 to 1859 has been worked through. All data on people born in German regions, plus data on their spouses, children and other members of their household have been recorded in a data base. The same has been done for the next population register period – that of 1860 to 1879. Separately, family reconstructions over three generations have been made for the Westerwalders and other families. Apart from the Utrecht population registers, the registers for Amsterdam, Rotterdam and Delft were also used to trace Westerwalders.

Westerwalders

The Westerwald is situated in what was, until 1866, the German Duchy of Nassau, on the right bank of the Rhine, some 200 km from Utrecht. There was migration from the Westerwald before the nineteenth century, but in the nineteenth century it increased.

The Westerwalder migrants specialised in the stoneware trade, mainly in jars and pitchers. All Westerwalders in Utrecht were engaged in this business. The production of stoneware goods in the Westerwald originated from Roman times. The clay in the Westerwald has the special quality that its particles melt together when baked at a high temperature. Clay like that from the Westerwald was found nowhere else. In theory Westerwalder stoneware could be produced outside the Westerwald, but only from Westerwalder clay. Westerwalder stoneware is water- and air-tight and therefore particularly suited for holding fluids.[12] In the nineteenth century, the stone bottles produced in the Westerwald were widely used

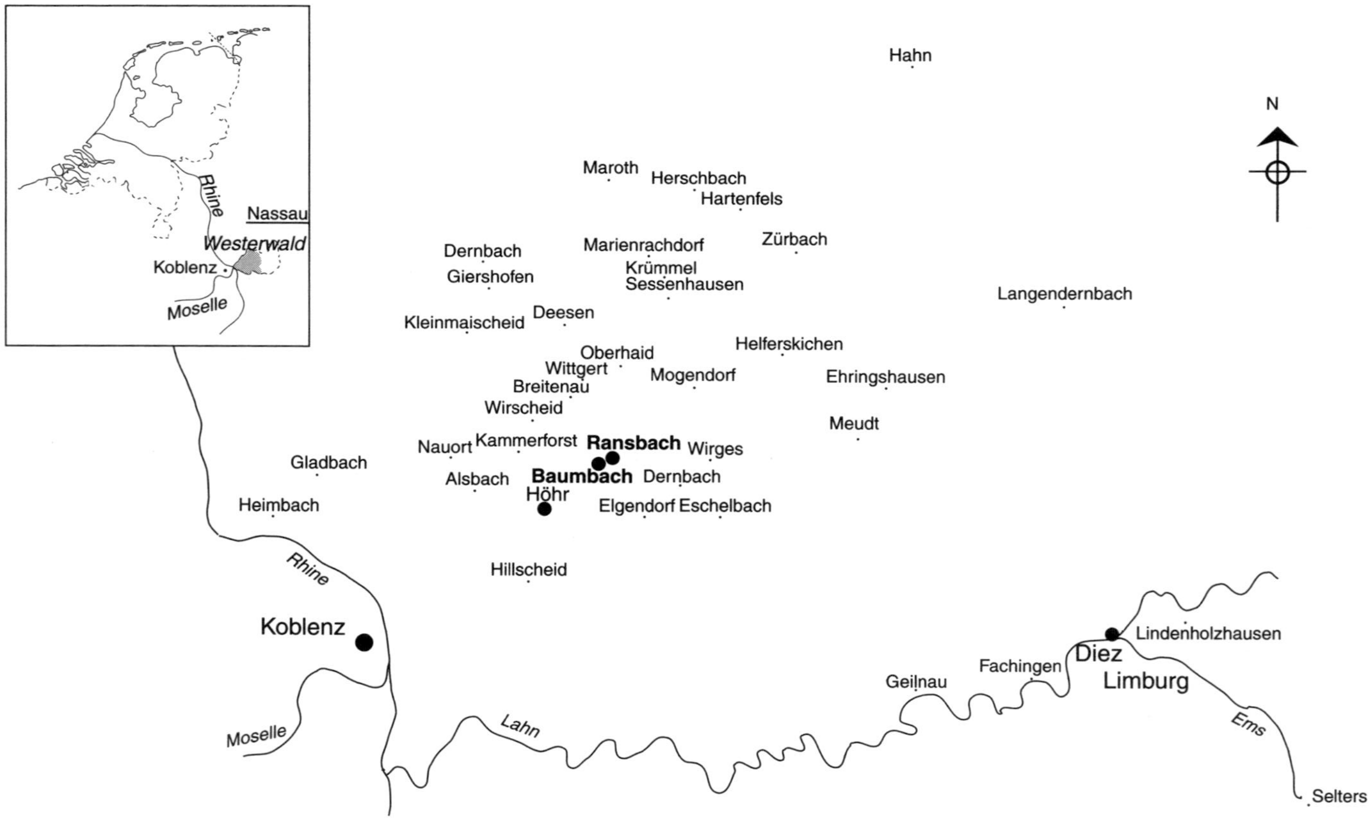

Map 5.1 The Westerwald showing origins of migrants

for natural mineral waters, as their air-tight quality guaranteed that the level of carbon dioxide was maintained. Unlike other ceramics, stoneware jars were not affected by salt or acidity and were therefore suited for pickling and preserving vegetables, meat and fish. The Westerwalder stoneware was a widely used specialised product, with its own market segment.

Already before the nineteenth century, traders from the Westerwald went beyond their region of origin to sell the jars and jugs. In the sixteenth century, stoneware was sold by the producers and their wives in the countryside surrounding the Westerwald. In the seventeenth and eighteenth centuries the trade was detached from its production and came into the hands of professional traders. The scope of the traders widened, and the wealthy Netherlands became an important market. Traders, however, also went to Belgium, France, Northern German regions, Sweden, Poland and Russia. From the seventeenth century onwards, a seasonally based, long-distance trade in stoneware developed. Trade migration evolved side by side with stoneware production. Many of the traders had family ties with the potters. The trading season for the stoneware traders was the summer. Traders were away from their home villages for nine months, leaving in spring and returning in autumn.

Stoneware is heavy and bulky. Within the Netherlands goods were transported mainly over water. From so-called pot-boats goods were sold directly on markets or hawked out on the countryside. Until the Napoleonic period, Dutch guilds had restricted the trade in stoneware. Guild rules stipulated that those from outside town could work only as wholesalers, selling their goods to the local shopkeepers.[13] In the countryside they may have been able to act as retailers. Guild regulations forbade hawking on the countryside, but outside the towns rules were less easily maintained. When a trader from outside arrived in town, guild authorities had to be notified. Local shopkeepers were then informed, and the outside trader got a restricted permit to sell to shopkeepers only.

The Westerwalder traders dealing in Utrecht not only encountered guild restrictions, but also other restraints. The Westerwalder stoneware traders were all Catholic. In 1655, Catholic migrants to Utrecht, both from within and outside the Netherlands, had lost the right to become citizens of the town. In the years after 1655 this rule was applied less strictly for migrants from within the Netherlands, but it was maintained for those from outside.[14] Guild membership was restricted to those who were burgesses of the town. Until the nineteenth century Westerwalders could be neither burgesses nor guild members.[15] After the Napoleonic period, guilds were abolished, and restrictions on citizenship disappeared. As a result the trading opportunities for the Westerwalders increased. They could now act both as wholesalers and as retailers.

The nineteenth century saw an increase in the demand for the goods in which the Westerwalders traded. A slight increase in wealth amongst the Dutch population as a whole was translated into an increased demand for kitchen and table-ware.[16] The Westerwalder traders expanded by including in their business other articles of everyday and kitchen use.[17] It was only at the end of the nineteenth century that the demand for stoneware started to decline. Glass bottles became widely used for mineral waters because they were lighter and easier to clean. At the end of the nineteenth century it furthermore became fashionable to add extra carbon dioxide to the mineral water. This increased level of carbon dioxide could be kept better in glass bottles.[18] Glass preservers replaced the stone jars which had been used to preserve fruit and vegetables.

The increased demand for the Westerwalders' goods until the middle of the nineteenth century, and its decline towards the end of the century, was reflected in the migration pattern. In the middle of the century the number of migrants was largest. Some 2,000 travelled annually from the Westerwald to the Netherlands. After 1870, this number declined sharply. This decline is not only explained by a decreased demand for stoneware, but also by more employment opportunities in the Westerwald region at the time of Germany's industrialisation.

When the trade in stoneware expanded, and the number of traders increased likewise, Westerwalder traders continued to recruit personnel in their region of origin. Originally most traders came from the neighbouring Catholic villages of Baumbach and Ransbach. When the trade expanded, servants were found in other villages in the region. Although the Westerwald was religiously mixed, the recruited servants were, like the original traders, all Catholic. Some of the servants were related to the earlier traders, others were not.

The increased demand for Westerwalder goods, in the middle of the nineteenth century, meant that more people entered the trade. Although the region from which people were recruited expanded, the trade was kept within a regionally based group, and links with the region of origin continued to exist. These ties were strengthened by the fact that many of the earlier traders had property in the Westerwald, or acquired property after trading in the Netherlands for a few years.[19] Because of their property, which consisted of houses and land, ties with the region of origin remained strong.

When the trade expanded, people with less means entered into it as well. Their attempts at the trade were stimulated by credit from the producers and wholesalers in stoneware. Originally, acquiring credit was facilitated by the fact that many of the traders had family ties with producers.[20] Traders could get their goods on credit, paying for them only when they returned from the Netherlands. Houses and pieces of land were used as security. Failure to pay the debt, because of illness or bad luck in the trade, led to the forced sale of property. This was not uncommon.[21] Once the property had been sold, the ties with the region of origin became less strong.

The barriers of entry to the stoneware trade were not high in terms of money and knowledge. Servants, both men and women, could easily set up business for themselves. Contacts were important, as well as credit from producers or suppliers. A few seasons in the trade as a servant were enough to acquire both.

Opportunities for women traders

The Westerwalders differed from other German migrants because both the seasonal and the permanent migration was group migration. Not only young men or young women migrated, but whole families took to the road.

In the middle of the nineteenth century, foreigners were free to settle in the Netherlands as long as they could show some identification, could support themselves and did not cause a public nuisance.[22] In the middle of the nineteenth century the main reason for expelling foreigners was lack of means. In the reports on these expulsions, the Westerwalders stand out because of their group migration. Most reports refer to one, two or three men being brought across the German border. Apart from the Westerwalders, the only others travelling in groups consisting of several men, women and children were groups which are described as gypsy-like bands, and traders in red chalk. The traders in red chalk are a bit of a mystery. The reports are not very clear as to where these traders came from. The traders in red chalk may have been Westerwalders. When the trade in stoneware started to decline, some Westerwalders started trading in a polishing product called wonder chalk or Viennese chalk, which may have been the same as red chalk.[23]

Migrating traders were affected by rules and regulations on migration in both the Netherlands and in Nassau. In German regions a distinction was made between permanent and seasonal migration. Until the beginning of the nineteenth century, Nassau authorities had discouraged permanent migration. When they started to encourage it in the nineteenth century, the Dutch authorities reacted with restricting measures. In the nineteenth century, there was large scale permanent migration from Nassau. The permanent migrants came from all layers of society, with an over-representation of labourers and artisans. Like the population of the Westerwald in general, they were religiously mixed. The permanent migrants mostly went overseas.

Nassau authorities allowed free permanent migration of women. Men could not migrate before they were 23 years old and had fulfilled their military duties. In order to avoid this age-bar, some men may have pretended to migrate on a seasonal basis whereas in reality they migrated permanently.[24] Furthermore, as some of the migrants going overseas had been unable to pay for their crossing, and had thus been stranded in Dutch harbour towns, the Dutch government demanded that German trading houses would guarantee the passage of these migrants. For temporary migrants, there were no such restrictions. Moreover, people tended to pose as temporary migrants, rather than as permanent migrants, because

Plate 5.1 Westerwalder girls: (left) a farewell to a girl in the Westerwald; (right) Westerwalder girl selling pots in Amsterdam

Source: Municipal Archive Amsterdam D. 38415.

those who had migrated permanently from German regions could not make claims on German poor relief if their migration proved to be a failure, and they decided to return home. The permanent migration from the Westerwald is rather well documented but the temporary migration, including that of most of the stoneware traders is not well recorded.

Whereas permanent migration was allowed, local authorities in Nassau did not regard seasonal family migration favourably. This had already been the case before the nineteenth century. At the end of the eighteenth century, fearing that the seasonal migration of whole families might lead to vagrancy, local authorities in Nassau restricted the freedom of women to travel. This restriction severely distorted the trading and migration practices that had hitherto existed.

Although the migrating groups of Westerwalders consisted of both men and women, it was the women who were actually the traders, while the men were involved in transportation of the goods.[25] The importance of women for the trade is reflected in the fact that both the German and the Dutch language had a special word for these female traders – which could be translated as 'pot-wenches' – whereas there was no male equivalent.

It is not easy to explain why women played such an important role in the stoneware trade, while in most other long-distance trades women were absent. In general, trade was gendered, like most other economic activities. Female traders sold butter, milk, vegetables, fruit, eggs, fish, flowers, earthenware, matches, sweets and songs. Male traders sold knives, scythes, copper pots, herbs, wine and vinegar, cattle, hare and rabbit skin, human hair, books, lottery tickets, textiles, rags, sieves, umbrellas and plaster figures. Both men and women sold brooms, baskets, toys, water and haberdashery. The segregation tended to be fixed both within and outside the Netherlands.[26] It is unlikely that the segregation can be explained by the weight of the goods, looking at for instance earthenware and copper pots, or milk, wine and water. The male sub-sectors were, in general, no less marginal than the female ones. Furthermore, although scythes may have been bought more by men, and milk more by women, the gender of the client does not fully explain the gender of the trader either. Some logic may be found in the fact that potters in the Westerwald region were mainly men, and this dated from before the nineteenth century. In the sixteenth century the potter's products were sold by his wife. Although this may sound plausible as a start of a tradition, the explanation becomes less likely when compared with textile production and trade. The weavers, like the potters were mainly men. Yet also the textile traders were mainly men. It can be argued that spinning may have offered added work options for women, but so did sanding, glazing and decorating the pots. A segregation in perishable goods and therefore short-distance trade on the one hand, and non-perishable goods and long-distance trade on the other, seems applicable in most cases. The earthenware and stoneware trade would then be an exception to the rule.

In the beginning of the nineteenth century, local authorities in Nassau forbade unmarried male traders and unmarried female traders to journey and work together. They forbade married women to travel at all. Married traders could take both male and female servants; unmarried traders could only take male servants. The restrictions were widely disobeyed. Married male traders, however, also formally asked permission to take their wives. They argued that they had houses in the places they went to. 'The spouses did not leave their houses, except when there was a market, when she could earn a lot.' Without their female partners income was much less, they claimed. Furthermore, the women sometimes mastered the language of the host country, while the men did not. At first, permission was granted when the couple was newly married and there were not yet any children. Later permission was also given if couples could prove that good arrangements had been made for the care of their children during the nine months they were absent from their homes. Permission was denied in cases in which the youngest children were less than two months old.[27]

Migrating traders were not allowed to take children of school age (5–14) with them. Some of the migrants took their school-aged children despite the rules, and claimed that they put them to school in the Netherlands. They even provided letters from Dutch authorities to show that children did actually attend school in the Netherlands. Local German authorities, however, did not give in. When the migrating traders took their children with them anyhow, they were fined. Traders claimed to their defence that they did not know that taking school-children was forbidden, or that the child ran after them and they only noticed when they were already half a day's walk away. 'Es war mir allerdings verboten, mein schulplichtiges Kind Georg auf den Hausierhandel mitzunehmen. Das Kind war mir aber nachgelaufen, und ich konnte es nich mehr zurückschicken!'[28] Moreover, some of the traders did not only take their own children, but also children of others, who were hired out to the traders.[29] This indicates that it was not only for emotional reasons that the traders took their children. The child traders were a real help to the trading migrants.

Providing care for children who stayed behind in the Westerwald was expensive, especially in those villages where more than half of the population went away as migrating traders. In these villages there were not enough family members to whom the care could be delegated.[30] Children were sent to distant relatives in villages further away. The sum that had to be paid for child care more or less equalled the fine that was given when traders took their children. As the fine could be partly wiped out by doing road work in the winter months, some traders rather paid a fine and took their children with them instead of paying for care.[31] Other traders went away not only for one nine month trading season, but for two or three years on end. Fines could accumulate to hundreds of Nassau guilders.[32] For the traders this will have been an incentive not to return to the Westerwald at all. Accumulated fines stimulated the transition from seasonal to permanent migration.

The Westerwalder traders were connected to each other by formal and informal ties. A married couple or a widow who lived in the Netherlands permanently or semi-permanently would recruit servants from the Westerwald. These servants could be family members or unrelated workers. The servants, both men and women, were usually between 15 and 25 years old. For the larger traders it was not uncommon to hire three men and three women. The servants could work one year for one trader, and the next for another. In the third year they could set up a business for themselves. The social distance between traders and servants seems to have been small. There were numerous marriages between servants and the adult children of their employers.

Apart from servants who were recruited by people who lived in the Netherlands there were the migrating groups of traders. These groups consisted of a married couple or widow with servants or siblings. There were also groups consisting of a married woman, without her husband, but with several female helpers or children.

An aspect of the regulation of migration that added to strengthening the group cohesion of the migrants was the German practice that temporary migrants were given papers which indicated a fixed route by which they had to travel.[33] Fixed travel routes may have added to the phenomenon that Westerwalder traders did not go to Dutch places randomly, but rather that a Westerwalder village had stable ties with a Dutch town. The Westerwalders who came to Utrecht mainly came from Baumbach and

Ransbach, Westerwalders in the Dutch town Zwolle came from Sessenhausen. In Maastricht there were traders from Höhr. The result was that Westerwalders in Dutch towns did not just have a common region of origin, but rather came from the same village. This would have strengthened group cohesion.

Apart from guild restrictions and restrictions on migration, trading opportunities for the women of the Westerwald group, like that of all other women, were affected by legal Dutch restraints on female economic activities.[34] Married women were by the Civil code, legally deemed incapable of economic action. 'Action incapability', as it was called, meant that a married woman was not to sell or buy, to pawn or to give away anything, or to hire workers without the consent of her husband. The Civil code of 1838 did in this respect not change the situation as it had existed in previous centuries. Restrictions were, however, not as rigid as they may seem at first glance. A woman became capable of independent action from the age of 23. Before that her father or guardian was legally responsible. When she married she became 'action incapable', regaining her rights when she was widowed. Although 'action incapability' restricted female economic activities, its consequences must not be exaggerated. 'Action incapability' only restricted the activities of part of the women. In the nineteenth century, half of the women in age group 25 to 29 were unmarried; in the age group 30 to 34 a third were unmarried, and in the age group 40 to 44 still a quarter.[35] Of those who did marry, more or less a third were widowed before the age of 45.[36]

For the Westerwalder women the fact that widows could be economically active in their own rights was rather important. The marital behaviour of the Westerwalders was different from that of the Dutch population at large. Amongst the Westerwalders it was not uncommon for a man in his thirties to marry a woman in her late teens. As a result there were within the Westerwalder community several women who were widowed at a young age. These widows often formed the centre of economic activity.

Law did not only make an exception for unmarried women, and widows, but more importantly, 'action incapability' did not apply to married independent female traders. An independent female trader was assumed to have been granted by her husband the right to make all agreements and contracts necessary for her work. His permission did not have to be given in writing. The permission showed, according to the law, in the cases where a female trader who had been active as such before her marriage, continued her business after her marriage. An independent female trader was not to be regarded as an assistant to her husband, and her husband was not to act in her name or to buy with her money. The permission sustained until the husband officially withdrew it, given notice of this withdrawal both in a daily newspaper, and at the Chamber of Commerce. The Cantonal court could, however, grant a married female trader her independent rights if her husband was unable or unwilling to give these to her, thus harming her in her economic activities.[37]

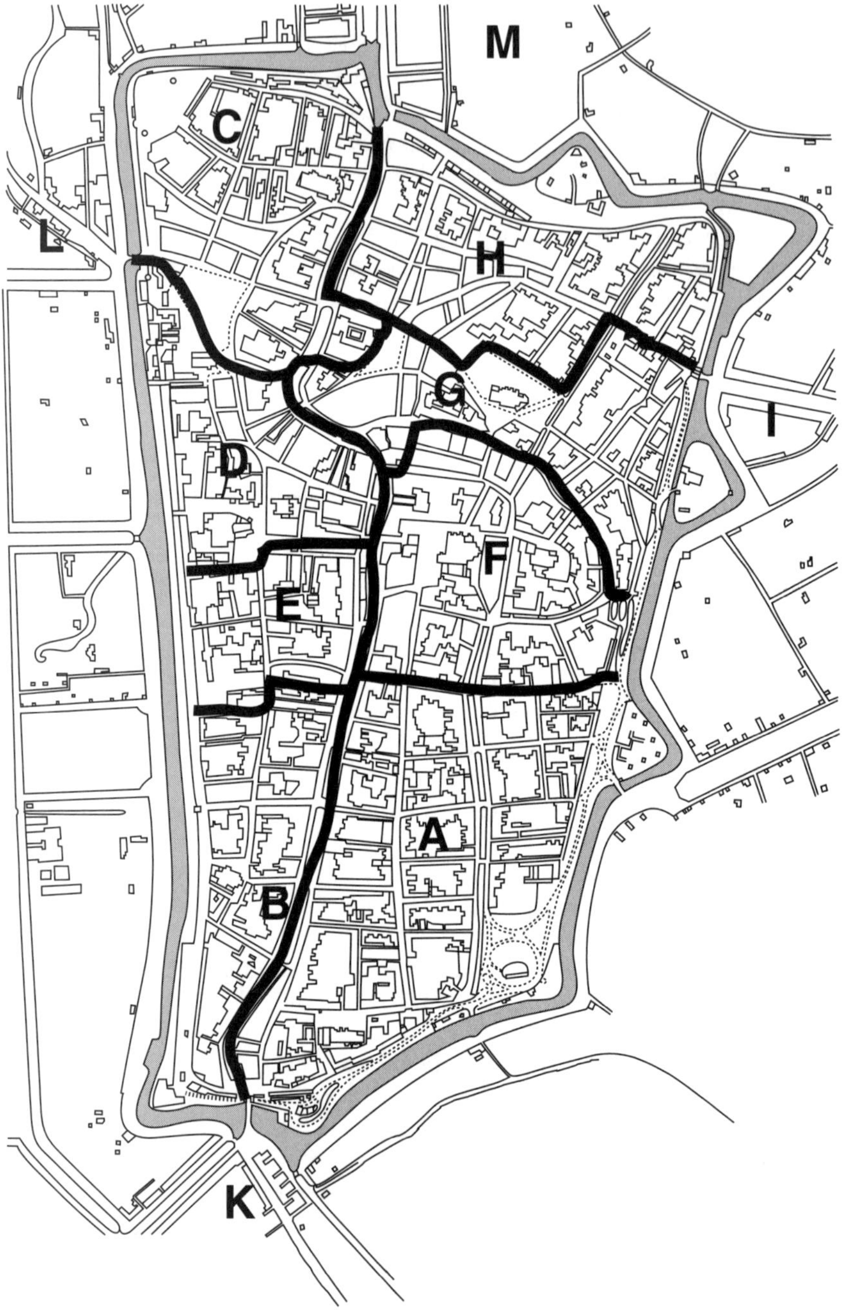

Map 5.2 The Utrecht districts in the nineteenth century

Utrecht

The Westerwalders were not the only German migrants in Utrecht. German migrants could be found in all town districts. Utrecht is located in the centre of the Netherlands. From 1856, it had a railway connection with Prussia. In 1849, Utrecht had a population of 50,000 which increased to almost three times that much in 1920. Until 1880, expansion was mainly due to natural growth; after 1880, immigration was more important.[38] In the course of the nineteenth century, the employment opportunities in industry, trade and commerce increased, whereas work in the domestic sector became less important. The number of people working in agriculture was halved between 1849 and 1930. Utrecht, because of its central position, became an important centre for trade and commerce. The occupational structure of the town influenced the nature of the migrant population.

From Napoleonic times, Utrecht was divided into twelve districts (see Map 5.2). Districts A to H lay within the city moat. Districts I, K, L and M were situated outside the moat.[39] Although the various districts were not socially homogenous H, G and especially F stand out as the richer neighbourhoods, C and K as poorer districts. By the middle of the nineteenth century houses had been built in all the space within the inner city. Expansion could only be found outside the city moat. In the inner city the number of houses remained stable at about 6,000.[40] Outside the city moat the number of houses increased from about 2,000 in 1850, to over 9,000 in 1890. In the inner city the population remained more or less stable. Outside the moat, the population grew from 11,000 in 1850 to 50,000 forty years later. At the end of the nineteenth century more people lived outside the moat than within it. Newcomers looking for a place to live were more likely to reside outside the moat than within.

Officially there were about 500 German residents in Utrecht in 1849.[41] The official figure does not describe the German community, in an analogous manner to contemporary definitions of migrant communities, because it does not include migrants' children, since children born in the Netherlands until 1892 received the Dutch nationality. Furthermore, it does not include the temporary migrants. In 1849, there were 1,700 such temporary migrants residing in the town. Temporary migrants were all those who did not have their residence registered with the civil administration. This included people who resided in town for a couple of weeks, but also ones who stayed for years on end. Students, domestic servants, traders and travelling artisans, who assumed they came only on a temporary basis, often did not change their residence officially. It is not known how many of the 1,700 temporary residents were German.

German and other migrants were not distributed evenly over the various town districts. There was no correlation between the social status of the neighbourhood and the number of German migrants. Migrants did not concentrate in the poorer districts of the town.

Religion

The numbers of Protestant and Catholic German migrants were more or less equal. About 2 per cent of the migrants were Jewish. The religious division amongst the migrants is in line with that of the Utrecht population as a whole. Utrecht was segregated in a religious sense. More Protestants lived in the inner city. In the districts outside the moat there were more Catholics. German migrants divided themselves over the town in a similar manner.

Within the German Protestant group a distinction can be made between those who belonged to the Reformed Church, which was the main Dutch Protestant church, and those who belonged to the Lutheran Church, which was a minority church in the Netherlands. Lutheran migrants could, if they wished, become members of the well-organised minority church. The Lutheran Church had its own organisations for care for the poor, orphans and the old. Almost all Lutherans in Utrecht could trace back their own or their family's history to migration from Germany. German Lutheran migration to Utrecht already existed before the nineteenth century. In preceding centuries it had even been quite considerable, so that Lutheran migrants coming to Utrecht in the nineteenth century found migrants or children from migrants that preceded them in earlier decades.

The Lutheran Church in Utrecht was an immigrant church. However, although Lutherans could be part of this well-organised community, in practice not all were. The Lutheran community was split in three. The more orthodox Lutherans found their church too liberal, and sought contacts with the small orthodox Dutch Protestant churches. The most liberal Lutherans found the Lutheran Church too conservative, and too strongly oriented on its German background, so they chose the Dutch Reformed Church. The result was that the Lutheran community was much more divided than it may seem at first glance. Although at first instance it may seem as if adherence to a minority, immigrant church might strengthen group coherence, in the case of the Lutherans this was only true for some. The ambiguous relationship of the Lutherans regarding their church is reflected in the fact that many of them married outside their church, with other Protestants, and with Catholics.

As Catholic migration had been restricted since 1655, Catholic migrants did not find a similarly established German community in Utrecht. Catholic Germans belonged to the Catholic Church in general. Unlike the Lutherans they did not have the support of an immigrant church.

Occupations

The German migrants, and other migrants, can be divided according to profession. With the professional segregation comes sex segregation. There

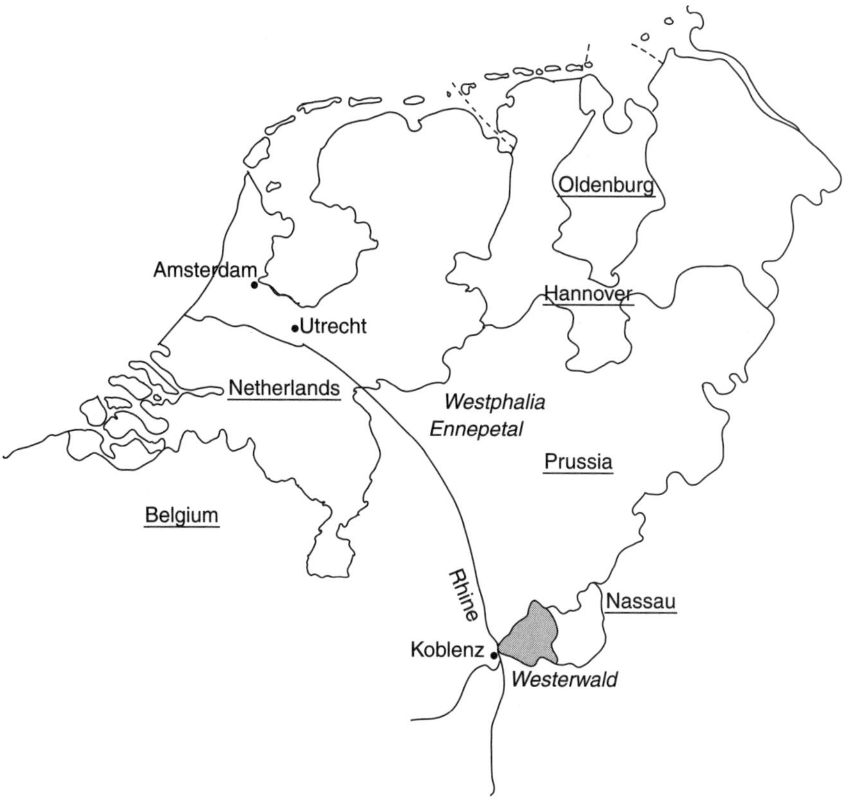

Map 5.3 Regions from which German migrants came to the Netherlands

were railway workers, stucco workers, soldiers, filemakers, brewers, hatmakers, students and scientists; these were all men. Domestic servants were all women. Traders in stoneware and to a lesser extent in textiles there were both men and women.

Railway workers lived in district M, and later also in L. The construction of the railroad had been started in 1843. The group consisted of German specialists and engine drivers, and British engineers. The British engineers were accompanied by their British born wives, children, and servants. With the German migrants, mostly skilled workers and engine drivers, migration was mostly male. The railway workers did not come from one region in Germany. Their numbers increased sharply between 1860 and 1880.

German ex-soldiers can be found in virtually all districts of the town. The Utrecht garrison included many foreign professional soldiers, of all ranks. Most of these foreign soldiers had Swiss nationality. The soldiers lived both in and outside the army barracks, which were situated in the south side of district A. Migration of soldiers took place through the transfer of army units. Although the soldiers were of course all men, migration connected to army transfers was not all male. Married soldiers came with their wives and children. Around 1850, the wives and children of soldiers in Utrecht were mostly born in the South of the Netherlands and in Belgium. This reflects army manoeuvres in these regions at the time of the Belgian uprising of 1830.[42]

In the wealthy district F we find traders in textiles, both men and women, from Oldenburg.[43] The migration pattern seems to have been permanent chain migration, rather than seasonal migration as in the case of the Westerwalders. The textile traders set up shops. Amongst the personnel they recruited for these shops were many German men and women. Although a substantial part of the workforce was German, it was by no means exclusively German.

One of the largest groups of German migrants is formed by the female domestic servants. Domestics can be found in all districts of the town, but obviously mostly in the better-off parts, like district F. Most of the domestics were Catholic. Some belonged to the Reformed Church. There were no Lutherans amongst them. The female German servants came from a few neighbouring villages in a restricted area in Westphalia. This cannot be only because this region borders on the Netherlands, because there were other border regions from which few migrating domestics came. Chain migration offers a better explanation. Chain migration is of course important for all migration. For domestics it may have been of extra concern. It was important that the employer could trust the domestic, who for instance had easy access to the family's silverware. Recommendations and family ties may have helped to create this trust.

The professional structure of Utrecht, with its wealthy traders, administrators, and academics, meant that there was a rather large demand for domestics. This had also been the case before the nineteenth century. To satisfy the demand for female domestics, it was arranged in earlier centuries that single female domestics did not have to acquire the right to inhabit the town.[44] Thus, Catholic German women could migrate as domestics even before the nineteenth century, whereas their male peers could not find similar employment. As a result migration from the Westphalian area was one-sided in the sense that it was all female.

The German domestics usually worked for Dutch employers. Although they formed a large group, German women did not monopolise the trade. There were many more Dutch women working as servants (over 2,000) than there were German women.

In district M we find the Lutheran filemakers from the Ennepetal. The Ennepetal is situated in what was later known as the Ruhr district, south of the town of Hagen on the river Ruhr. It is a region that traditionally produced iron products. As in the Westerwald region, a long-distance trade developed on the basis of this specialisation. Unlike the Westerwalders' stoneware trade, this long-distance trade involved only men. Migration was therefore migration of individuals, and groups of men, rather than that of families. Although these migrants did go to the Netherlands, the Ennepetalers who resided in Utrecht were not traders, but producers, primarily of files.

The migration of metal workers from the Ruhr district had a tradition pre-dating the nineteenth century. At the end of the sixteenth and the beginning of the seventeenth century, specialised metal workers came to Utrecht, mainly to make gun barrels and work in weapon assembly. These specialised metal workers seem to have disappeared by the end of the eighteenth century. From the registers of the Lutheran church it becomes clear that hands and journeymen metal workers from the same region continued to come to Utrecht until the end of the eighteenth century. They, however, apparently did not set up business for themselves. The cause for this may have been the high barrier to entry set up by the guilds and the unfavourable development of the trade after 1740.[45]

File making was a skilled job. Steel first had to be hardened by double conversion. Next it had to be heated to soften the area that was to be cut. Subsequently the teeth were cut with a chisel, each incision being made separately. Finally the steel was hardened again. Until the end of the nineteenth century, files were made by hand. The two types of ovens that were used in the production process created possibilities to reach economies of scale. Some capital was required to set up a business in file making. Unlike in the stoneware trade, it was therefore not easy for workers to set up their own business.

Since the Ennepetalers were producers, rather than traders dealing in products from their region of origin, it could be assumed that ties with their region of origin were less. This, however, need not have been the case. Uncut files were probably imported as half-products. It is very likely that these uncut files came from the iron producing region from which the filemakers themselves came. Like the Westerwalders, the Ennepetalers recruited their workers in their region of origin. A difference with the stoneware trade was that file making was a predominantly male profession. This meant, first, that more men migrated from this region than women. Migrants were thus forced to find marriage partners outside their own community. Second, there was no overlap between business ties and family ties. With the Westerwalders the niche was based on both family and business ties, and thus could be more easily sealed off from outsiders. As file making did not offer many employment opportunities to the women of the Ennepetaler community, they had to find employment outside it. This made the community much less isolated than that of the Westerwalders.

Filemakers lived both in boarding houses and inns, and in regular houses. They worked in the steel making district, which, because of its water polluting nature, was located at the north side of the town. There was no need for large warehouses. It was also not necessary for the filemakers to live closely together. As a result, they were spread out over the neighbouring districts M, C and H. The part of district M where most Ennepetalers were to be found was the better part of the district, and indeed one of the better parts of the town. The region in which the Ennepetalers lived also differed from that of the Westerwalders, in that many other migrants, both from inside and outside the Netherlands could be found in this neighbourhood. Since the filemakers were all Lutheran they could, if they wished, be part of a well-organised minority church. In practice they did indeed have ties with this church.

Apart from the German migrants, there were also migrants from other regions in Utrecht. In 1849, the largest group consisted of 225 Belgians. Amongst the Belgian migrants the makers of straw hats were the most conspicuous. With the Belgian straw hatmakers, men and women were roughly equally represented. The straw hatmakers originated from a few villages in Belgian Luikerland. They came for the summer months and lived near their employer, mostly in district E, with a smaller group in district G. Every year, half of these migrants left after the summer; the other half remained in Utrecht permanently.

Westerwalders in Utrecht

At the beginning of the nineteenth century, a group of Westerwalders tried to evade restrictions on group migration. A group of men, women and children profited from the confusion of the Napoleonic period and journeyed to Utrecht. This group consisted of some 200 people. Part of this group remained in Utrecht. Others went to other Dutch towns. The group formed the basis of the Westerwalder community in Utrecht. The group was larger than those in other Dutch towns at the same date.

Amongst the Westerwalders seasonal migration and permanent migration existed side by side. The Westerwalders who settled in Utrecht in the beginning of the nineteenth century, were born in the Westerwald at the end of the eighteenth century. Some of their children were born in the Westerwald. The seasonality of their stay is reflected in the births of their children which occurred alternately in the Westerwald and in the Netherlands. A third to two-thirds of the families migrated seasonally. The others were in the Netherlands more permanently. After 1870 seasonality disappeared, and the group in the Netherlands stabilised: there were no more returns to the Westerwald, and no newcomers from the Westerwald.

The Westerwalders formed the largest German minority in Utrecht.

The Westerwalders all lived in district K. Similar communities of Westerwalders existed in many other Dutch towns.[46] Possibly because of family migration, Westerwalders, contrary to other migrants, seldom stayed in boarding houses or inns. There were, of course, occasional individual travellers who stayed in an inn, but as a rule Westerwalders did not. In some towns such as Amsterdam, Westerwalders lived on their boats. Mostly, however, they had houses that they either owned or rented permanently. They stored their goods in these houses and in nearby warehouses.

Family migration as well as the need for access to water and warehouses, all combined to enforce a geographical concentration in the towns Westerwalders settled in. The Westerwalders did not live spread out over district K, but rather concentrated in one small neighbourhood consisting of some 180 houses. The choice for this neighbourhood near the waterfront was logical, as their trade goods were transported over water. Furthermore, a tax advantage could be gained by storing goods in this district. Until 1866, a tax had to be paid for goods which were brought into town.[47] District K was officially outside town. Traders who did not sell all their goods within the town, but used the town as a centre for regional distribution, could avoid taxation by storing their goods just outside the inner city. District K may have had its advantages, but it was also one of Utrecht's worst slums.[48] It is striking that the Westerwalders continued to live in this neighbourhood throughout the nineteenth century. The group lived in some 180 houses, clustered together on a small site, with many blind alleys and warehouses.

District K was a Catholic neighbourhood. The neighbourhood had held on to Catholicism despite the sixteenth century conversion of the town and its surroundings to Protestantism. Throughout the centuries, Catholics continued to meet in a clandestine church in district K. The neighbourhood formed a parish with a strong coherence, known as 'the paupers' parish'. The community consisted of Catholic Dutch horticulturists, who kept very much to themselves, and a large group of paupers. The Germans stood out amongst these paupers as the worst off. Part of the group lived in a large building, called the Arc, where families rented one or two rooms; a form of housing uncommon for the Netherlands. In the evening the Germans sat by the water, and sang German folk songs.[49]

For a whole century, the Westerwalders lived inside their neighbourhood. At the end of the nineteenth century, the community dissolved. The end of the community coincided with changes in other fields. The Westerwalders stopped working in the stoneware trade, and no new migrants came from the Westerwald. The demand for Westerwalder goods decreased. The Westerwalders in Utrecht started to marry outside their group, and moved to other parts of the town. After having existed for a whole century as a community with a great coherence, it is striking how fast the community dissolved at the end of the century.

Conclusion

The Westerwalders were successful in carving out a niche and sealing it off from outsiders. In their successful creation of a niche they were aided by the fact that they dealt in a highly specialised, regionally based product. Successful niche formation was strengthened by the fact that traders and producers had close contacts which gave the traders credit facilities, and other trade advantages. The niche of the Westerwalders was much stronger than that of other migrant communities in Utrecht. Differences between the groups indicate that the settlement process was to a large extent influenced by the composition of the group in respect to gender: migration of both men and women led to a much more coherent group, and as a result to a more isolated community, than the migration of either men or women. If, as in the case of the Westerwalders, the niche offered opportunities for both the men and the women of a group, this resulted in a group with a strong coherence, and as a result possibilities for sealing off their sector.

However, as the barrier to entry of the stoneware trade was low for those within the group, more and more people entered the trade at the time when prospects were good. The effect was self-suffocating. Successful creation of a niche seems thus not to have led to economic prosperity of the group as a whole. This notion seems to be sustained by the fact that the group lived in derelict houses in a poor neighbourhood. Housing circumstances, however, need not be the best indicator of the group's success. The Westerwalders differed from most other groups of migrants within Utrecht because of the fact that seasonal migration and permanent migration continued to exist side by side until around 1860. Ties with their region of origin remained strong because local regulations forced them to leave their children behind in the Westerwald. Furthermore, their trade was based on the regional specialised product. Unlike some of the other migrants, the Westerwalders came from a restricted and cohesive area.

The orientation of the region of origin influences the settlement process. If migrants assume to be in the host society on a temporary basis, they will be less likely to make investments that do not render an income within a short time span, or which cannot be liquidated on short notice. In general, the seeming success of migrants may be partly the result of the nature of the migration process: do successful migrants return to their country of origin, do failed migrants return leaving behind in the host country a strikingly successful group, or is there no return migration?

The Westerwalders could, in theory, invest the revenues of the stoneware trade in houses and shops in the host countries. Westerwalders, however, chose to invest in houses in their region of origin, and live under dismal or even poor conditions in the Netherlands. The stoneware trade offered opportunities for both men and women and thus strengthened group cohesion. The nature of the trade and local regulations necessitated ties with the region of origin. The result was a delayed integration.

Notes

1 Until 1892, children born in the Netherlands from a German parent automatically received Dutch nationality. E. Heijs, *Van vreemdeling tot Nederlander. De verlening van het Nederlanderschap aan vreemdelingen 1813–1992*, Amsterdam, Spinhuis, 1995, pp. 216, 229.

2 R. Penninx, *Raster en Mozaiek. Uitgangspunten voor onderzoek naar internationale migratie, etnische processen en sociale ongelijkheid*, Amsterdam, UvA, 1994, p. 5.

3 J. Lucassen and R. Penninx, *Nieuwkomers, nakomelingen, Nederlanders.* Immigranten in Nederland 1550–1993, Amsterdam, Spinhuis, 1994, pp. 99–111.

4 J. H. Jackson, 'Migration in Duisburg, 1867–1890: Occupational and Familial Contexts', *Journal of Urban History*, 8, 3 (May 1982): 235–270.

5 B.P. Mullan, 'The Impact of Social Networks on the Occupational Status of Migrants', *International Migrations*, XXVII, 1 (March 1989): 69–86.

6 S. Model, 'The Effects of Ethnicity in the Workplace on Blacks, Italians, and Jews in New York, 1910', *Journal of Urban History* 16 (1989): 29–51; E. Bonaich and J. Modell, *The Economic Basis of Ethnic Solidarity. Small Business in the Japanese American Community*, Berkeley and Los Angeles, University of California Press, 1980; J. Rath, *Minorisering: de sociale constructie van 'etnische minderheden'*, Utrecht, SUA, 1991.

7 R. Waldinger, *Still the Promised City? African-Americans and New Immigrants in Postindustrial New York*, Cambridge, MA/London, Harvard University Press, 1996, pp. 21–25, 302–304.

8 M. Schrover, 'Omlopers in Keulse potten en pottentrienen uit het Westerwald' in M. 't Hart, J. Lucassen and H. Schmal (eds) *Nieuwe Nederlanders. Vestiging van migranten door de eeuwen heen.* Amsterdam, IISG/SISWO, 1996, pp. 101–120; K. S. Chin, I. Yoon and D. Smith, 'Immigrant Small Business and International Economic Linkage: a Case of the Korean Wig Business in Los Angeles, 1968–1977', *International Migration Review* 30, 2 (1996): 485–510.

9 A. Portes, 'The Informal Economy and its Paradoxes', in N. J. Smelser and R. Swedberg (eds) *The Handbook of Economic Sociology*, Princeton, NJ, Princeton University Press, 1994, pp. 426–449, esp. p. 437.

10 I. Light and S. Karageorgis, 'The Ethnic Economy' in N. J. Smelser and R. Swedberg (eds) *The Handbook of Economic Sociology*, pp. 647–670, esp. p. 663.

11 In 1869 there was a census in Utrecht, but there was no new start of a population register. The population registers from 1860 to 1869 were continued until 1880 (with the exception of district C). Results of the 1869 census were incorporated in the 1860 to 1880 population register.

12 J. de Kleyn, *Volksaardewerk in Nederland 1600–1900*, Zeist, De Tijdstroom, 1965, pp. 36–37.

13 Municipal Archive (MA) Utrecht, 86 BA 1 Gilden, inv. nrs. 63 and 56.

14 R. Rommes, *Oost, west, Utrecht best? Driehonderd jaar migratie en migranten in de stad Utrecht (begin 16e – begin 19e eeuw)*, Utrecht, Amsterdamse Historische Reeks, 1998, p. 108.

15 MA Utrecht, 86 BA 1 Gilden, inv. nrs. 58, Register van de namen der aangenomen leden van het marslieden gild 17–24–1798.

16 A. J. Fr. van Maenen, *Petrus Regout 1801–1878. Een bijdrage tot de sociaal-economische geschiedenis van Maastricht*, Nijmegen, Centrale Drukkerij, 1959, p. 233.

17 J. Plenge, *Westerwälder Hausierer und Landgänger,* Leipzig, Dunder and Humblot, 1898, p. 204.
18 P. Zwaal, *Frisdranken in Nederland. Een twintigste eeuwse produktgeschiedenis*, Rotterdam, Stichting BBM, 1993, p. 31.
19 *Herzoglich Nassauisches allgemeines Intelligenzblatt*, 1854, pp. 10, 18, 22, 31, 115, 134, 146, 167, 197.
20 H. Fries, *Kurrimurri. Erinnerungen an die Kannenbäcker in Höhr-Grenzhausen*, Höhr-Grenzhausen, Stadt Höhr-Grenzhausen, 1993.
21 *Herzoglich Nassauisches allgemeines Intelligenzblatt*, 1854, pp. 10, 18, 22, 31, 115, 134, 146, 167, 197.
22 Heijs, *Van vreemdeling tot Nederlander*, p. 57.
23 *Algemeen politieblad*, 1850s and 1860s. See also L. Lucassen, *En men noemde hen zigeuners. . .De geschiedenis van Kaldarasch, Ursari, Lowara en Sinti in Nederland (1750–1944)*, Amsterdam, IISG, 1990, p. 361.
24 W.H. Struck, *Die Auswanderung aus dem Herzogtum Nassau (1806–1866)*, Wiesbaden, Steiner, 1966, p. 9.
25 J. van Maurik, *Toen ik nog jong was*, Amsterdam, Van Holkema and Warendorf, 1901, p. 31; Plenge, *Westerwälder Hausierer und Landgänger,* p. 39.
26 G. Barth-Scalmani, 'Salzburger Handelsfrauen, Frätschlerinnen, Fragnerinnen: Frauen in der Welt des Handels am Ende des 18. Jahrhunderts', *L'Homme Zeitschrift für Feministische Geschichtswissenschaft*, 6, 1 (1995): 23–45.
27 Hessisches Hauptstaatsarchive Wiesbaden w 241–345; F. Baaden, *Landgänger. Botschafter des Kannenbäckerlandes,* Ransbach-Baumbach, Stadt Ransbach-Baumbach, 1993, pp. 15–16.
28 Baaden, *Landgänger*, p. 30.
29 Baaden, *Landgänger*, p. 28.
30 Baaden, *Landgänger*, p. 8.
31 Hessisches Hauptstaatsarchive Wiesbaden w 241–345; Baaden, *Landgänger*, p. 26.
32 Hessisches Hauptstaatsarchive Wiesbaden w 241–345.
33 *Algemeen Politieblad,* June 1853, Neede 263.
34 M. Braun, *De prijs van de liefde. De eerste feministische golf, het huwelijksrecht en de vaderlandse geschiedenis*, Amsterdam, Spinhuis, 1992, pp. 15–32.
35 C. van Eijl, *Het werkzame verschil. Vrouwen in de slag om arbeid 1898–1940*, Hilversum, Verloren, 1994, p. 74.
36 F. van Poppel, *Trouwen in Nederland. Een historisch-demografische studie van de 19e en vroeg-20e eeuw*, AAG Brijdragen 33, Wageningen, Landbouwuniversiteit, 1992, p. 355.
37 J.J.M. Petit, *De burgerlijke rechtstoestand der gehuwde vrouw*, Zwolle, Tjeenk Willink, 1930, pp. 42–45.
38 P.D. 't Hart, *Utrecht en de cholera 1832–1910*, Utrecht, Stichtse Historische Reeks 15, 1990, pp. 297–298.
39 The letter J was not used because of the risk of confusion with the letter I.
40 C. Denig, *Utrecht van het ancien régime tot nieuwe tijd. De bewoning van de Utrechtse binnenstad in haar ruimtelijke structuur, 1793–1891*, Utrecht, Matrijs, 1995.
41 Census 1849.
42 MA Utrecht Vestigingsregister.
43 R. Miellet, *Honderd jaar grootwinkelbedrijf in Nederland*, Zwolle, Catena, 1993, p. 27.
44 Rommes, *Oost, west, Utrecht best?*, p. 141.
45 Rommes, *Oost, west, Utrecht best?*, p. 157.
46 M. Schrover, 'Groepsvorming onder Duitse aardewerkhandelaren in 19e-eeuws Holland en Utrecht', *Historisch tijdschrift Holland*, 2 (1998): 94–112; M. Schrover, 'Gescheiden werelden in een stad. Duits ondernemerschap in Utrecht in de negentiende eeuw' in J. Rath and R. Kloosterman (eds) *Rijp en Groen, Het*

zelfstandig ondernemerschap van immigranten in Nederland, Amsterdam, Spinhuis, 1998, pp. 39–60.

47 A. van Hulzen, *Utrecht en het verkeer 1850–1910*, Baarn, Bosch en Keuning, 1987, pp. 7–15.

48 H. Snellen, 'Utrechts Achterbuurten. Voordracht in de Algemeene vergadering van 25 februari 1868 Vereeniging tot Verbetering der Volksgezondheid' in MA Utrecht archief 162 Verslagen van de Vereeniging tot verbetering der Volksgezondheid, 1868; F.E. Vos, *Onderzoekingen over de cholera-epidemie van 1866 gemeente Utrecht,* Alphen aan de Rijn, 1867, pp. 84–85; 't Hart, *Utrecht en de cholera,* p. 304.

49 G.J. van Rijnsoever, *Sint Maarten in de Tolsteeg. Geschiedenis van de Sint Martinusparochie te Utrecht,* Utrecht, Spectrum, 1947, pp. 91, 127–128.

6 Nowhere at home?

Female migrants in the nineteenth-century Habsburg Empire

Sylvia Hahn

'It was an overcast winter day', as Josefine Joksch wrote in her memoirs, 'on which I set out on my first journey to assume a position as a child-maid'. Josefine Joksch, born in a small village in Bohemia, was a young woman in the 1880s when she started her journey to Vienna, the capital city of the Habsburg Empire or the so-called *k.k. Reichshaupt- and Residenzstadt.*[1] According to her memoirs, Josefine

> was glad to be leaving home. First of all, because all of those who were in the position to have to become domestic servants went away, to avoid losing the last shred of dignity and respect they had in their hometown. And Vienna had long been the object of my yearnings.

Afterwards, as Josefine tells us, 'sitting shivering in the corner of the railway car and peering out into the muted twilight of the winter morning', she 'thought about how dreary and boring such winter days had been in her hometown, and how great it was to be able to escape this eternal monotony'.[2]

These distant hopes and desires of finding a good job and perhaps a better way of life somewhere else outside of one's own small village or town are a common feature that we can find in many female and male autobiographies as well as literary essays of the nineteenth century. Most of them stress the 'myth' of the *k.k. Reichshaupt- and Residenzstadt* Vienna. There was also a song which, as Josefine noted, she 'used to sing even as a little girl, and later with increasing conviction and ever-more-ardent passion'[3] and which can be regarded as a symbolic expression of the dreams and senses of longing that many (primarily) young women and men associated with the imperial city:

There's only one imperial city,	*'s gibt nur a Kaiserstadt,*
There's only one Vienna!	*'s gibt nur a Wien!*
It must be magnificent there,	*Dort muß es prächtig sein,*
That's where I must go!	*dort muß ich hin!*

This brief glimpse into Josefine's life reveals some important aspects and main socio-economic issues of nineteenth-century society. First and foremost there is the aspect of labour migration, which can be regarded as a part of the life-experience of the life-cycle of large segments of the population. Josefine was only one of thousands of younger and older women and men who took the road from the countryside to a nearby city or to Vienna, hoping to find work and a better future. Over the course of the nineteenth century and as a result of industrial concentration, Vienna and the surrounding area became a magnet for migration. One result of the labour migration within the Habsburg Empire during these days was the rapid population growth of cities like Vienna, Prague, Triest, Graz, or of smaller towns in Upper and Lower Austria or Styria. For example, between 1840 and 1880, Vienna's population doubled from 350,000 to 700,000 and the population continued to climb to around two million by 1910, whereby 53 per cent of the growth was attributable to net migration.[4] Thus, by the second half of the nineteenth century, in many cities and towns of the Habsburg Empire the numerical percentage of the 'immigrant foreigners' who had not been born in the city had already attained the majority within the cities' population. In 1890 in Vienna, only 44 per cent, in Wiener Neustadt 37 per cent, in Graz 33 per cent, in Linz 32 per cent or in Salzburg 28 per cent of the population was born in the respective city.[5]

With regard to the geographic origin of the individuals making up this wave of migration, two distinct changes can be identified as having occurred since the eighteenth century. Up to the beginning of the nineteenth century, migration was predominantly from the area of southern and central Germany – thus, a migratory current flowing from west to east – whereas, over the course of the nineteenth century, migration was primarily from Bohemia, Moravia and Silesia (the Sudeten Germans) as well as from the eastern Habsburg lands of Galicia, Bukovina and Hungary. In other words, the migration stream which initially flowed in a west-to-east direction (Bavaria, Germany and France to Vienna) shifted in the nineteenth century to a north–south and/or an east–west flow.[6]

The second interesting point of Josefine's autobiographical notes is her employment. Working as a child-maid or generally in the field of personal or domestic services was very common for women in former centuries. The range of job possibilities was broad, from domestic live-in servants in households of farmers, craftsmen or the (petite) bourgeoisie, to such live-out domestics as laundresses or charwomen who lived in their own household but worked for other households. Generally, personal and domestic service was one of the leading employment sectors for women.[7] Although a wide variety of new, incremental jobs was created in the course of the industrialisation process in the nineteenth century, women still had available to them only a limited range of jobs. In many cases they had no alternative but to seek employment in areas considered 'women's work', such as personal and domestic service. The most important reasons for this strong orientation of female employment opportunities toward personal and domestic servant positions can be seen in connection with the role-specific assignment of women to family and household-related activities or, as a (male) contemporary observer put it in 1902: 'The home and hearth is still the true place of women's work'.[8]

Scholarly research has shown that in the nineteenth century at the latest, this employment sector underwent a process of 'feminisation' and became almost totally a woman's domain. In Vienna, for example, in the 1860s, 87 per cent of all domestic servants were female, and by the turn of the century this figure had increased to 97 per cent.[9] We can find similar results in other European cities. In Hamburg the figures for female servants increased from 73.4 per cent in 1764 to 98.4 per cent in 1900 or in Berlin from 74.5 per cent in 1830 to 98 per cent in 1895.[10] There are different opinions about when this process really started. Sarti has shown in her long-term case study of domestic servants in Bologna, Italy that the percentage of female servants increased from 55 per cent in 1581 to 62 per cent in 1617, decreased to 58 per cent in 1631 and increased rapidly again during the nineteenth century: in 1841, 69 per cent of all servants were female, 77 per cent in 1901, and 82 per cent in 1911.[11] For England, Hill has suggested that service already was feminised 'between the early eighteenth and the end of the nineteenth century'.[12] Sharpe identified this process at the end of the eighteenth century, but it was during the nineteenth century and 'the "domestic revolution" that the purely domestic, invariably female, servant emerged as an essential feature of nineteenth-century life'.[13] In his study of English servants and their employers in the eighteenth and nineteenth centuries, Schwarz suggests that the feminisation of domestic service began a great deal earlier and that it did not involve employing increased proportions of the female population.[14] For Schwarz, the 'often quoted' nineteenth-century increase 'can only be demonstrated to have taken place between 1851 and 1871, and even this depends on the definition of the term "servant" in the census.'[15] One of his main arguments is that 'female servants were, of course, far more ubiquitous but there is no strong evidence that they were proportionally more important in 1780 than in 1851' and 'that servants did not form a higher proportion of the population of England in 1851 than they had formed in 1780'.[16]

These findings are similar to my own conclusions on women working in personal and domestic service. In the Habsburg Empire, the percentage of female domestic servants as a proportion of the population decreased from 7.3 per cent in 1869 to 3.4 per cent in 1890 and 2.9 per cent in 1910, although their numbers were still very high. In Vienna, domestic servants (female and male) as a proportion of the employed population made up 15.4 per cent in 1869, 12.2 per cent in 1890 and 9.4 per cent in 1910.[17] In the smaller town of Wiener Neustadt, their share was 18.4

per cent in 1869, 8.7 per cent in 1890, and sank to 5.6 per cent in 1910. The figures for the female domestics as a proportion of all employed women were similar: in Vienna, their share was 18.3 in 1880, 12.4 in 1890, and sank to 9.0 in 1910. In Wiener Neustadt, we find this downward trend too, and to a much greater extent than in Vienna, interrupted by a slight increase in 1880. In 1869, 16.4 per cent of all employed women were domestics, in 1880 17.7 per cent, in 1890 8.3 per cent, and in 1910 5.5 per cent.

We can suggest that this downward trend, especially among live-in domestic servants, was similar to the case of males, where we can find a decreasing number of live-in apprentices and journeymen in specific crafts during the second half of the nineteenth century.[18] Although this process within the female domestic sector was rather slow compared to the male domestics or formerly live-in journeymen, we can assume a connection between the female and male trend for separated spheres of working and living, which was probably linked to migration. Beside the aspect of labour force demand[19] and the rather hard working conditions which made these jobs less and less attractive, the place of origin may well have influenced this process. Therefore, I suggest that the situation for women in the labour market was not only drastically constricted by employment handicaps ranging from role-specific assignments based on a patriarchal ideology and thus resulting in the emergence and consolidation of a dual labour market, but was also related to the place of origin of the women.

Thus, one main question that arises is whether region of origin can be regarded as an important aspect influencing social and occupational position. In other words, is there a possible connection between region of origin and occupational position on the one hand and position in the household on the other? Another central question is whether female servants and migrants during the nineteenth century really constituted a homogenous group as we generally suggest: single, young, approximately 15 to 35 years old. In regard to this aspect, I want to question if it is possible to find some differences with regard to their place of origin, position in the household and age.

The problems inherent in the sources – especially the quantitative material at the macro or state level about (female) domestic servants – have been well discussed within the field of scholarly research.[20] For this reason, a change of perspective has been called for within migration research to look more closely at internal and regional migration. A shift of perspective from the state level down to the micro level, towards a specific arena of migration of individuals, seems to me to be important, since in this way the female (young) labour migrants come into sharper focus and details of their social make-up become clearer. In this way, it might be possible to go beyond the typical spatial migration patterns which differentiate only between short-term and long-term migrants. Therefore I want to focus on the group of women who were working in personal and domestic service in an urban environment. The city I am going to concentrate on is Wiener Neustadt, a small town located just 50 km south of Vienna.[21] The sources which have served as the basis of my research are statistical material already available in printed form and my own data calculated from census lists of Wiener Neustadt which were filled out in the city in 1857, 1869 and 1880. All of these original census questionnaires[22] were compiled and evaluated by computer, and a 'record linkage' was also performed.[23]

Wiener Neustadt – a brief overview

Wiener Neustadt was one of the smaller cities of the Habsburg Empire, situated in the geographical region of the so-called Viennese Basin, an area located just to the south of Vienna. This region was – along with the industrial districts in northern Styria, Vorarlberg and Bohemia – one of the major industrial centres of the Habsburg Monarchy in the nineteenth century. Wiener Neustadt, which had been a city of craftsmen and merchants until the late eighteenth century, participated particularly in the Empire's gradual industrial expansion and became an important industrial centre in Lower Austria. As in Vienna and the surrounding area, textile production played the leading role for the industrial development of Wiener Neustadt. In 1857 about one-fifth (22 per cent) of all employees in the industrial and commercial sectors were working in textile production. Although textile production was the main industrial employer in the first half of the nineteenth century, by the end of the 1860s iron, metal and machinery production was the leading industry, with 47 per cent of the employees of the industrial and commercial sector employed in this production segment.[24]

Women made up about 30 per cent of the total workforce during this period.[25] A gender-specific breakdown among the individual sectors of the economy in 1869 and 1880 clearly shows the city's dual labour market. In the commercial-industrial sector women were strongly underrepresented, with only 9 per cent in 1869 and barely 10 per cent in 1880. The decisive factor here was the leading role of the machinery industry in the city, as well as its small-scale goods production, both of which were based almost exclusively upon male (skilled) labour and offered few employment opportunities for women in the workforce.[26]

However, a different situation was to be found in agriculture and in the service sector, in which the proportion of women was relatively high. In agriculture, 40 per cent of all employees were female in 1869 and 30 per cent in 1880. In the service sector women made up the majority of employees with 56 per cent in 1869 and 53 per cent in 1880. Among the occupational fields displaying the highest levels of employment in the service sector was 'personal and domestic service' in which 90 per cent of all employees were women. The great demand for female workers in the service sector and domestic service was generally the result of the fact that Wiener Neustadt, beside its industrial growth, remained a city of the petite bourgeoisie as well as a main military centre of the Habsburg Empire.[27] It was part of the social prestige of military officers to have at least one domestic servant in their household. Generally the service sector was an expanding branch in the nineteenth century, with demand for labour ranging from female domestic servants, transportation experts and finance specialists, medical and educational personnel down to unskilled hands.

The establishment of these new firms and the wide variety of jobs offered by the city's labour market from the beginning of the nineteenth century also brought demographic and social changes in their wake: The population rose from 7,000 in 1805 to 9,000 in 1830 and to barely 15,000 in 1857, 24,000 in 1869 and 33,000 in 1910. Above all, the city's rate of population growth in the 1860s was above the average for the province of Lower Austria. Within the Habsburg Empire in the second half of the nineteenth century, Wiener Neustadt and its surroundings trailed only certain parts of Bohemia as the region displaying the highest rate of immigration.[28]

Female migrants and position in the household

One of those migrants who came to find work in Wiener Neustadt was Maria Erhard. Born in 1843 in a village in Lower Austria, Maria Erhard arrived in Wiener Neustadt during the 1860s. She accepted a position as a domestic servant in the household of a spice dealer and in 1869 she was working and living together with another female and one male servant in the employer's household. Shortly thereafter, she must have married Leopold Fachathala, the male domestic servant. In 1880 Leopold Fachathala was working as a 'day labourer in the locomotive factory' and Maria Erhard was taking care of the household and the three children, who were born in 1873, 1876 and 1880. Two circumstances may well have eased the way for the couple to establish their own household: savings accumulated during their years 'in service' and the salaried industrial work available to the man.

Maria Erhard was in many respects a typical nineteenth-century female migrant: single, young, approximately 15 to 35 years old, having migrated alone from a small rural community to the nearest small city and then integrated into an employer's household, where she worked as a domestic servant. As we can see in Figure 6.1, immigrant women, especially in the stage of life between ages 15 and 30, lived as domestics (as so-called *Gesinde*) or as tenants in the household of a stranger. About 35 per cent[29] of this age group lived and worked as domestic servants and 11 per cent were tenants. In the next age group – those between ages 30 and 45 – there

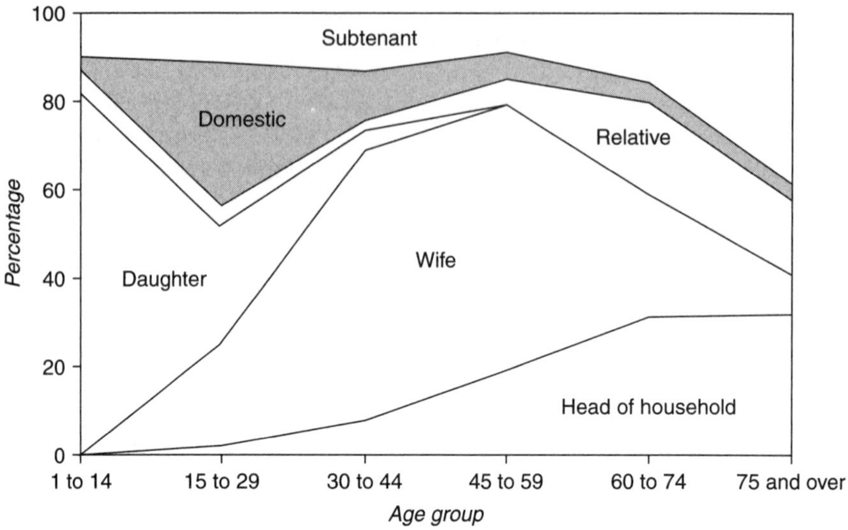

Figure 6.1 Age and household position of immigrant women, Wiener Neustadt, 1869

were still 10 per cent living as servants in the household of the employer. For those women who had not succeeded by age 40 or 45 in making the transition either to a household of their own like Maria Erhardt did, or to another form of employment, the existence as a domestic servant remained their lot until an advanced age. Only two-thirds had the chance for a life with their own family in their own household. Generally, a much larger percentage of immigrant women than native-born women had to live and work in their employer's household as domestic servants.

The situation for native-born women turned out to be quite different. As Figure 6.2 shows, only a small minority lived as a domestic servant in the employer's household. Until the age of 60, about 80 per cent of the locals lived in their own family household, either as daughter, wife or head of the household, or in old age as relatives. Within this group of native-born women, there were already young women who were daughters of immigrants and who were still living within their own family household but working as domestic servants in another household in Wiener Neustadt. Co-residents unrelated to the family likewise make up a minimal percentage in younger age groups but was significant for the older ones, as we can see in Figures 6.1 and 6.2. Slightly more native-born women lived as subtenants in the household of a stranger after the age of 45 than did immigrant women.

On the whole, Figure 6.1 shows that immigrant women were far more likely than locals to be in the position of having to live as a domestic servant or subtenant during their life-cycle in an environment populated

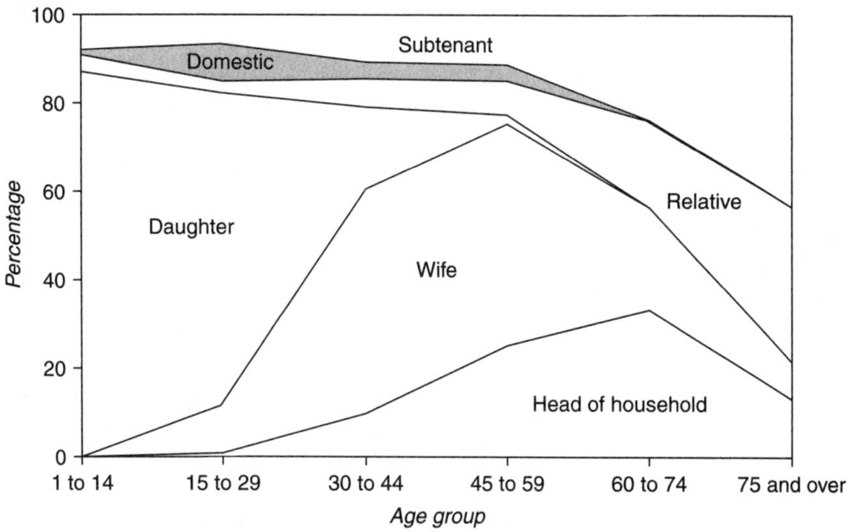

Figure 6.2 Age and household position of native-born women, Wiener Neustadt, 1869

by strangers. For the native-born female population, the prospect of living within one's own family group was relatively high at all stages of life.

Path to the city

Furthermore, Maria Erhard is also a good example of where most of these female immigrants working in the field of personal and domestic service came from. Like Maria Erhard, about 40 per cent of the female servants – and this was by far the largest group – came from villages in Lower Austria, mostly from nearby rural areas or districts in the immediate vicinity of Wiener Neustadt. The second largest group, with 25 per cent, were women who had been born in the city. The third group comprised Hungarian women; in 1869, 14 per cent and in 1880, 20 per cent came from this country. The majority of these women came from regions near the Austrian border, mostly located within 20–50 km of Wiener Neustadt.

Thus, in comparison to other towns of the Habsburg Empire, Wiener Neustadt displayed the highest proportion of Hungarian immigrants in the Austrian half of the Empire. For example, in Vienna only 5 per cent of the domestic servants were Hungarians. Wiener Neustadt, as one of the biggest cities in the immediate vicinity of these Hungarian districts, seemed to be a focal point for these labour migrants – for the female as well as the male ones – coming from this region.[30]

Nevertheless, there is also a significant percentage of female servants who can be considered as long-distance migrants coming from other districts of the Empire, like the remaining Alpine, eastern or southern provinces, as well as from other European countries. These figures were between 1 and 3 per cent. The largest subgroup within this group of longer-distance migrants were women from Bohemia-Moravia. They made up about 10 per cent, the fourth-largest group of the total. In comparison to Vienna, the female servants from Bohemia in Wiener Neustadt were a rather small group: in Vienna the group of female servants coming from Bohemia-Moravia made up about 35 to 45 per cent between 1857 and 1880.[31]

That means that Vienna was, along with Prague, one of the most important cities for female immigrants from Bohemia or Moravia. It also appears that the Danube was a symbolic watershed or frontier for these immigrants, because their proportion was very small in towns situated to the south of Vienna or generally in the southern part of the Habsburg Empire. In Graz, for example, as William Hubbard has shown in his study about this city, the proportion of female immigrants from Bohemia was only about 4 per cent. The percentage of those coming from Hungary, and – as in Wiener Neustadt – mainly from adjacent districts was a little bit higher at 7 per cent.[32]

If we analyse all female migrants[33] from Bohemia present in Wiener Neustadt in 1869, we cannot find any special region in Bohemia which predominated. The places of origin are widely spread all over the region. The districts of origin with the highest levels were districts located near the border to Lower and Upper Austria and constituted only 4 or 5 per cent. In this context, it seems to be interesting to take a closer look at the districts from which no female migrants came. These districts are situated in the area surrounding Prague and in the northeastern part of Bohemia – a traditional region of proto-industrialised textile production. Therefore, we can assume that women coming from the area around the city of Prague primarily went to Prague and, perhaps in a second step, migrated to other places and towns far away from their birthplace and family household. As a broad generalisation, we can conclude at this point that women employed in the field of personal and domestic service can be characterised mainly as short-range migrants.

Region of origin and occupational position

These findings are well in accordance with studies conducted a hundred years ago – for instance, by E. Ravenstein[34] – as well as those published in the last ten years. The main thesis is that first and foremost the path to the city of (young) migrants led to the town which was in the vicinity of their birthplace and where they lived; long-distance or medium-distance migration could follow afterwards. As Michael Mitterauer has shown in his studies of adolescent domestic servants, there was a clear relation between increasing migration distance, age and better job opportunities.[35]

However, most of these findings refer to men working in crafts[36] and trades or in the agricultural sector. Therefore I want to question now whether this is really only a gender-specific male pattern or if it is possible that a similar pattern of hierarchical occupational positions related to age and distance of migration exists in the case of women.

As Table 6.1 shows, there are two main differences connected to place of origin and occupational position. A significantly lower percentage of the higher-ranking servants were born in Wiener Neustadt, and a higher percentage of them were long-distance migrants. We can find these differences also within one household. For example, in the household of Paul Grüner, owner of a leather factory, married and father of five children, there are four female domestic servants with different regions of origin. The long-distance migrant and the oldest one was the governess Therese Larisch, 32 years old and born in Troppau, Silesia. Elisabeth Haller, age 23 and born in Oedenburg, Hungary, was the cook. The 20-year-old chambermaid Elisabeth Bohar was also born in Hungary. Johanna Manninger, the 23-year-old child-maid, came from a village in Lower Austria. Except for the governess Therese, the others can be regarded as short-distance migrants, although two of them had crossed a national

Table 6.1 Female employees in selected occupational positions according to place of origin, Wiener Neustadt, 1869 and 1880

Place of origin	*General servant*	*Higher-ranking servant*	*Day-labourer*	*General servant*	*Higher-ranking servant*	*Day-labourer*
	1869	*1869*	*1869*	*1880*	*1880*	*1880*
Wr.Neust./City	26.3	18.7	17.6	23.4	16.0	13.0
Lower Austria	39.6	40.8	37.3	37.8	39.1	35.8
Vienna	4.3	4.7	0.9	3.4	3.7	3.5
Styria	4.9	4.5	8.2	5.3	5.6	12.6
Hungary	13.5	13.9	20.6	19.0	18.3	23.6
Subtotal (Vicinity)	*88.6*	*82.6*	*84.6*	*88.9*	*82.7*	*88.5*
Upper A., Salzbg., Tyrol, Vorarlbg.	1.9	3.0	0.4	1.4	2.3	0.4
Carinthia	0.4	0.6	0.4	0.3	0.6	–
Bohemia, Moravia	8.5	10.6	13.3	7.6	9.7	9.9
Carniola, Galicia, Silesia	0.3	1.6	0.9	1.3	1.5	0.4
Foreign countries*	0.3	1.6	0.4	0.5	3.2	0.8
Total percentage	100.0	100.0	100.0	100.0	100.0	100.0
Total (N)	*912*	*510*	*233*	*1168*	*536*	*254*

Sources: Census Wiener Neustadt 1869, database Hahn.

Note
* Includes Germany, Switzerland, Italy, Netherlands, France, Great Britain.

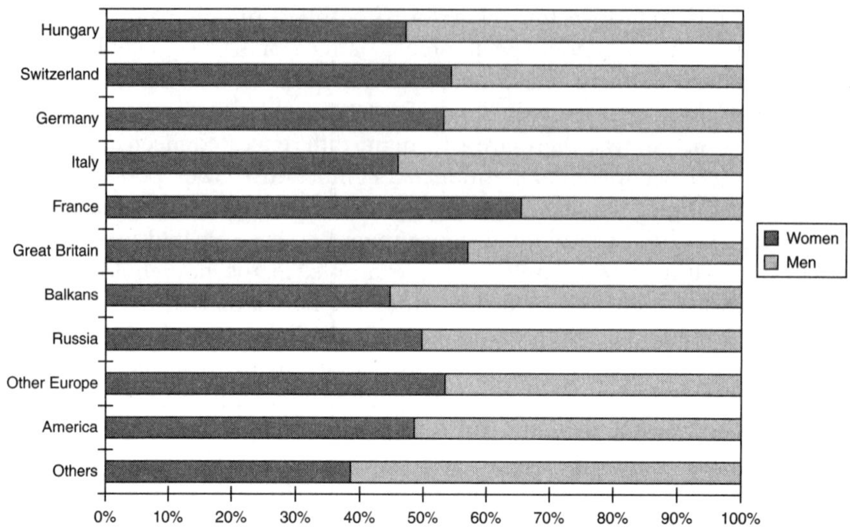

Figure 6.3 Gender and place of origin of foreigners in the Habsburg Empire, 1890

border. Although these three villages were situated in different regions and directions from the town, all of them were within a 50-km radius of Wiener Neustadt.

Thus, two general conclusions can be drawn for the migrational behaviour of the female servants present in Wiener Neustadt in the 1870s. There was a certain connection between the distance of migration and the occupational position or place in the hierarchy[37] and this was not exclusively a male phenomenon. Furthermore, I want to add that generally I believe that the myth of male-dominated migration patterns should be revised and that the long-distance migration of females until today has been overlooked or rarely acknowledged in historical studies. For example, as Figure 6.3 shows, in the year 1890 in the Habsburg Empire among all long-distance migrants coming from abroad (including all foreigners), there were more female than male migrants coming from Switzerland, Germany, France and Great Britain. Of these female foreigners 23 per cent were registered as employees, and, compared to the total female employee rate of 30 per cent, this can be regarded as a significant proportion. A small but well-known group of these well-educated long-distance migrants were the governesses,[38] most of whom came from Switzerland, France and Great Britain.

Age and occupation

If we take a closer look at the question of whether there is a possible connection between age and the hierarchy in the occupation of the female

Table 6.2 Occupation of female employees in personal and domestic service, Wiener Neustadt, 1869 and 1880

Occupation	*1869*	*1880*	*Av. age*
Kitchenmaid	39	35	24
Chambermaid	83	98	24
General servant	730	903	27
Housemaid	19	28	29
Nurse	58	47	30
Cook	253	236	30
Governess	15	17	31
Sewing/knitting	34	13	34
Laundress	75	141	45
Landlady	9	10	52
Total (N)	*1401*	*1648*	

Sources: Census Wiener Neustadt 1869, database Hahn.

servants, we also notice a hierarchy among the female servants that coincides with age. As Table 6.2 shows, the occupation of the female servants between age 20 and 30 can be categorised as common household work – kitchen-, house- or chambermaid or general servant, also called 'girl Friday' (*Mädchen für alles*). The occupational field of higher-ranking servants – such as nursemaid, cook or governess – included women of about 30 and older.

Women over the age of 30 worked as laundresses, did ironing and sewing, or rented out rooms in their homes. In comparison to the younger groups, the main difference besides age was that most of these women were no longer live-in domestic servants. Most of them were living in their own household or as subtenants and they worked on a daily wage basis either in the household of strangers or in their own homes. One of them was Maria Beck, who changed her household position but not really her duties within the time period under examination. Maria, born in 1825 in Siglos, a small village in Hungary close to the border with Lower Austria and about 25 km from Wiener Neustadt, came to Wiener Neustadt during the 1860s. On the day of the census, taken on 31 December 1869, Maria worked as a housemaid in the household of a restaurant and house owner. Besides Maria, Josef Samek, born in Bohemia, also worked as a waiter in the household and lived there. Ten years later, at the census 1880, both had left their employer's household, living now as a married couple in their own household with two unmarried male subtenants. Like Maria Erhard's husband, Josef Samek also had changed his job and worked now as a day labourer. The 1880 census lists Maria Beck's profession as 'household work', but we can imagine that besides the usual housework she also took care of the two subtenants and did the cooking and laundry for them as well. This was very common within the working class in the

Habsburg Empire and in Germany.[39] In some sense, Maria Beck's job had not changed a lot. Although she now was living in her own household, she was again working as a 'housemaid' within her own four walls for her family and the subtenants living with them.

Place of origin – position in the household

Finally, I want to consider the marital status of the female servants in relation to the four main regions of origin, and also (to broaden out the discussion) analyse the position in the household with respect to these regions. As can be seen in Table 6.3, we now get a more detailed picture which shows that the percentage of single female servants decreases with increasing distance of migration; on the other hand, the percentage of married women and widows working in the field of personal and domestic service increases with greater distance of migration. The group of female servants from Bohemia displayed the lowest proportion of single women (80 per cent) but the highest proportion of married or widowed women (20 per cent).

Along with the differences resulting from marital status, we can see in Table 6.4 some differences connected with household position. Immigrant women from Hungary comprise the group containing the highest proportion of live-in domestic servants. For nearly 75 per cent of them, workplace and living quarters were identical. Among the female servants from the vicinity of the city as well as from longer distances, about two-thirds of them were living in the household of their employer. The native-born female servants had the greatest likelihood of living in their parents' household; only one-third of them had to live as a domestic servant in the employer's household.

With the exception of females from Bohemia, living as a relative in the household was not the usual case. We can conclude that with increasing distance of migration, there was also an increase in the proportion of

Table 6.3 Women working in personal and domestic service, place of origin and status, Wiener Neustadt, 1869

Marital status	*Native*	*Vicinity**	*Hungary*	*Bohemia*	*Total immigrant*
Single	94.5	89.5	86.3	80.6	88.2
Married	1.2	2.5	3.2	6.1	2.9
Widowed	4.3	8.0	10.5	13.3	8.9
Total	100.0	100.0	100.0	100.0	100.0
Total (N)	*323*	*608*	*190*	*98*	*1047*

Sources: Census Wiener Neustadt 1869, database Hahn.

Note
* Vicinity includes the district of Wiener Neustadt, Lower Austria, Vienna.

Table 6.4 Women working in personal and domestic service, place of origin and position in household, Wiener Neustadt, 1869

Household position	*Native*	*Vicinity**	*Hungary*	*Bohemia*	*Total immigrants*
Head	3.4	5.8	6.8	7.1	6.0
Wife	–	1.3	2.1	5.1	1.7
Daughter	54.8	15.5	5.3	8.2	12.2
Relative	2.5	2.1	2.1	7.1	2.7
Domestic servant	31.3	66.1	72.6	60.2	67.0
Subtenant	8.0	9.2	11.1	12.3	10.4
Total	100.0	100.0	100.0	100.0	100.0
Total (N)	*323*	*608*	*190*	*98*	*1047*

Sources: Census Wiener Neustadt 1869, database Hahn.

Note
* Vicinity includes the district of Wiener Neustadt, Lower Austria, Vienna.

female servants who lived as head of household, as wife, relative or subtenant. The reasons for this could be the result of the migration pattern of these women: perhaps the long-distance migration of female servants was connected with family migration or chain migration. That does not preclude the possibility that some of them could have come as single migrants, perhaps in connection with chain migration. After their arrival, it seems that they were integrated into a social network which was constituted by former immigrants from the same village or region in Bohemia. Generally, and probably one result of being integrated into a social network of a family, friends etc., it was the case that women from Bohemia or Moravia, especially daughters of Bohemian immigrants, were – together with native-born women – more likely to find work in the industrial sector. We already can observe a clear trend within this group of preference for working in a factory over domestic service.[40]

Conversely, in the case of women from the vicinity of the town, the distance to their place of birth and perhaps family residence was much shorter so they could maintain their family ties. Perhaps these aspects – the short distance as well as the continuity of the family ties – did, on one hand, prevent the formation of and involvement in an immigration network; on the other hand, perhaps this factor played an important role in forcing them to live and work as domestic servants in the employer's household.

Nowhere at home?

If we take a look not only at the quantitative but also at the qualitative material which is available for us in the local archive of Wiener Neustadt about women alone in an urban society, we can recognise, for example, how important it was for women to belong to a network of relatives, friends or neighbours. Generally it seems to be the case that virtually no outsider, neither residents nor transients passing through, could escape the attention of the local population or of the municipal authorities. The numerous transcripts that have been preserved offer us a picture of strict supervision of those arriving from 'outside'. In addition, the distance maintained by the 'locals' could be generally felt quite clearly by the 'foreigners' both in their everyday life and in their dealings with each other, as well as in various different ways and levels of intensity. This had a very strong correlation to social status, occupation and gender. Above all, single women were the targets of reproach, rejection and mistrust by the locals. Here, supervision and control by the authorities did not stop short of encroachment into the private sphere. The famous author Karl Kraus described the particularly precarious situation of women as the object of state and municipal surveillance in his 1907 essay entitled 'Meldezettel' (registration form). Here he wrote: 'The state harasses women and girls not only on the street but pursues them even into their residences [. . .], desires to know whether the lady already has a child, when it was born, whether the father is circumcised, etc.'[41]

Along with literary illustrations of this sort, the numerous city police protocols available for the nineteenth century clearly show that especially younger (immigrant) women or women alone – such as female servants or widows (as well as men) – were kept under close scrutiny by the municipal control mechanism. Detailed interrogations of women 'picked up for questioning', the arrests and interrogations, such as those of female 'strangers', were often carried out in a seemingly arbitrary fashion. The grounds were invariably suspicion of prostitution, illegal peddling, failure to officially register subtenants, or vagrancy and homelessness. The subsequently imposed sentences and forms of punishment seem in many cases unjustifiably cruel in relation to the often rather trivial misdemeanours: several days, weeks or months of imprisonment, made more severe by additional measures meant to contribute to the 'moral' improvement of the prisoner. A final consequence, above all in the case of vagrancy or destitution which very often applied particularly to women, was banishment from the city.

In many cases this was the result of the legal situation and so-called Heimatrecht, which gave an individual the assurance of permanent residence in a community and the right to take advantage of the community's public social services such as welfare payments or care.[42] Women – and this was a very important aspect – lost their original Heimatrecht through marriage, which means that the Heimatrecht of the husband was automatically carried over to his wife and children as well. And most frequently, cities which had received large numbers of recent immigrants did not wish to be burdened with additional welfare responsibilities and therefore women were banished from the town. This means that the conveyance of the male's Heimatrecht to the woman (and children) and the restrictive practices of bestowing Heimatrecht led to the fact that in some ways and from a legal point of view, women were never at home anywhere.[43]

Conclusion

To summarise the results in regard to how the state treated lone, immigrant women, we can suggest that in some ways women were forced to look for a job where they were involved in a household, although it was the household of a stranger, the employer's household. Furthermore, taking into account that most of the female migrants came from rural areas, we also can imagine that they probably lacked knowledge about employment opportunities except for personal and domestic service. Generally it seems to be the case that place of origin therefore played an essential role for the women's chances in occupation as well as in household position: immigrant women were far more likely than locals to be in the position of having to live as a domestic servant or subtenant during their life-cycle in an environment populated by strangers. For the native-born female population, the chances of living within one's own family group were relatively high at all stages of life. However, there was also a certain connection between the distance of migration and the occupational position or hierarchy, and this hierarchy went along with age as well as the place of origin. Being integrated into a social network of a family, friends or migrants from the same place of origin played an important role too for the employment opportunities of female migrants in the nineteenth-century Habsburg Empire.

Notes

1 Later on Josefine became a leading figure in the labour movement and wrote a few articles about her working life and career. J. Joksch, 'Nur ein Kindermädchen (1885)' in R. Klucsarits and F. G. Kürbisch (eds) *Arbeiterinnen kämpfen um ihr Recht*, Wuppertal, Paul Hammer Verlag, (no date), p. 86.

2 Joksch, 'Nur ein Kindermädchen', pp. 86–87.

3 ibid., p. 86.

4 As a result of administrative measures which incorporated outlying communities into the city at around the turn of the century, Vienna reached the million mark in 1890. H. Fassmann, 'A Survey of Patterns of Migration in Austria, 1850–1900' in D. Hoerder (ed.) *Labour Migrations in the Atlantic Economies: the European and North American Working Class during the Period of Industrialisation*, Westport, CT and London, Greenwood Press, 1985, pp. 69–94, 78; R. Bauböck, *'Nach Rasse und Sprache verschieden'. Migrationspolitik in Österreich von der Monarchie bis heute*, Vienna, IHS, 1996, p. 3.; M. John and A. Lichtblau, *Schmelztiegel Wien – einst und jetzt. Geschichte und Gegenwart der Zuwanderung nach Wien*, Vienna, Böhlau, 1990, pp. 13–15.

5 S. Hahn, 'Different Ways – Common Experiences. Labour Migration in Nineteenth-century Austria' in D. Ebeling and S. King (eds) *Community, Locality and Life-cycle: Migration Strategies in Modern and Early Modern Europe*, Oxford, Berghahn, forthcoming.

6 Fassmann, 'A Survey of Patterns', p. 71.
7 D. Simonton, *A History of European Women's Work 1700 to the Present*, London and New York, Routledge, 1998, pp. 96–111.
8 H. Morgenstern, *Gesindewesen und Gesinderecht in Österreich. Mitteilungen des k.k. Arbeitsstatistischen Amtes im Handelsministerium*, Vienna, Verlag Alfred Hölder, 1902, p. 100.
9 H. Stekl, 'Hausrechtliche Abhängigkeit in der industriellen Gesellschaft', *Wiener Geschichtsblätter*, 30 (1975): 301–313.
10 R. Sarti, 'Notes on the Feminization of Domestic Service: Bologna as a Case Study (18th–19th Centuries)', *Acta demographica*, XIII (1997): 160–161. For Austria see M. Tichy, *Alltag und Traum. Leben und Lektüre der Dienstmädchen im Wien der Jahrhundertwende*, Vienna-Cologne-Graz, Böhlau, 1984. For Germany, R. Engelsing, 'Das häusliche Personal in der Epoche der Industrialisierung' in R. Engelsing, *Zur Sozialgeschichte deutscher Mittel- und Unterschichten*, Göttingen, Vandenhoeck & Ruprecht, 1973, pp. 225–261; U. Ottmüller, *Die Dienstbotenfrage. Zur Sozialgeschichte der doppelten Ausnutzung von Dienstmädchen im deutschen Kaiserreich*, Münster, Verlag Frauenpolitik,1978; H. Müller, *Dienstbare Geister. Leben und Alltagswelt städtischer Dienstboten*, Berlin, Dietrich Reimer Verlag, 1981; K. Walser, *Dienstmädchen. Frauenarbeit und Weiblichkeitsbilder um 1900*, Frankfurt am Main, Verlag Neue Kritik, 1986; D. Wierling, *Mädchen für alles: Arbeitsalltag und Lebensgeschichte städtischer Dienstmädchen um die Jahrhundertwende*, Bonn, Verlag J.H.W. Dietz Nachf., 1987; K. Orth, *'Nur weiblicher Besuch'. Dienstbotinnen in Berlin 1890–1914*, Frankfurt am Main and New York, Campus, 1993. For Great Britain, B. Hill, *Servants: English Domestics in the Eighteenth Century*, Oxford, Clarendon, 1996; P. Horn, *The Rise and Fall of the Victorian Servant*, Gloucestershire, Alan Sutton Publishing, 1990 (first edn 1975); L. Ross, *Weibliche Dienstboten und Dienstbotenhaltung in England*, Tübingen, Verlag J.C.B. Mohr, 1912.
11 Sarti, 'Notes on the Feminization of Domestic Service', p. 145.
12 Hill, *Servants*, pp. 36–43.
13 P. Sharpe, *Adapting to Capitalism: Working Women in the English Economy, 1700–1850*, Basingstoke, Macmillan, 1996, pp. 101–102.
14 L. Schwarz, 'English Servants and their Employers during the Eighteenth and Nineteenth Centuries', *Economic History Review*, LII, 2 (1999): 250.
15 ibid., p. 253.
16 ibid., p. 238.
17 J. Ehmer, 'Zur sozialen Schichtung der Wiener Bevölkerung 1857 bis 1910' in G. Melinz and S. Zimmermann (eds) *Wien – Prag – Budapest. Urbanisierung, Kommunalpolitik, gesellschaftliche Konflikte (1867–1918)*, Vienna, Promedia, 1996, pp. 73–83 (here: pp. 79–80).
18 See, for example, J. Ehmer, *Soziale Traditionen in Zeiten des Wandels. Arbeiter und Handwerker im 19. Jahrhundert*, Frankfurt am Main and New York, Campus, 1994.
19 T. Pierenkemper, '"Dienstbotenfrage" und Dienstmädchenmarkt am Ende des 19. Jahrhunderts', *Archiv für Sozialgeschichte*, 28 (1988): 173–201.
20 E. Higgs, 'Domestic Servants and Households in Victorian England', *Social History*, 8 (1983): 201–210; E. Higgs, 'Women, Occupations and Work in the Nineteenth-Century Censuses', *History Workshop Journal*, 23 (1987): 59–80; L. Schwarz, 'English Servants', pp. 236–256.
21 About Wiener Neustadt see in detail S. Hahn, 'Große Hallen – Enge Räume. Handwerk, Industrie und Arbeiterschaft in Wiener Neustadt im 18. und 19. Jahrhundert' in S. Hahn, W. Maderthaner and G. Sprengnagel, *Aufbruch in der Provinz. Niederösterreichische Arbeiter im 19. Jahrhundert*, Vienna, Verlag für Gesellschaftskritik, 1989, pp. 7–152; S. Hahn and K. Flanner (eds), *Die 'Wienerische Neustadt'. Handwerk, Handel und Militär in der Steinfeldstadt*, Vienna-Cologne-Weimar, Böhlau, 1994.

22 They contain the following entries for each individual present in the city: position in the household, first and last name, date and place of birth, marital status, religion, occupation, whether the individual possessed permanent right of residency, the so-called Heimatrecht, and physical impairments, if any. In the case of the absence of an individual, there followed a remark as to his current whereabouts.

23 The record-linkage carried out between the Wiener Neustadt censuses of 1869 and 1880 reveals that only about 10–15 per cent of domestic servants were present ten years later. S. Hahn and G. Sprengnagel, 'Nominative Record Linkage aus Massenquellen des 19. Jahrhunderts. Aufbau und Dokumentation der Datenbank "Wiener Neustadt im Maschinenzeitalter"' in F. Hausmann, R. Härtel and I. H. Kropac (eds) *Datennetze für die historischen Wissenschaften? Probleme und Möglichkeiten bei Standardisierung und Transfer maschinenlesbarer Daten*, Graz, Leykam, 1987, pp. 113–128.

24 In comparison, the employees in textile production dropped to 6 per cent.

25 The gender-specific breakdown of employment figures corresponded to that of other European cities. See J. Ehmer, 'Frauenarbeit und Arbeiterfamilie in Wien', *Geschichte und Gesellschaft*, 3/4 (1981): 438–473; E. Rigler, *Frauenleitbild und Frauenarbeit in Österreich vom ausgehenden 19. Jahrhundert bis zum Zweiten Weltkrieg*, Vienna, Verlag für Geschichte und Politik, 1976; W. Müller, A. Willms and J. Handl, *Strukturwandel der Frauenarbeit 1880–1980*, Frankfurt am Main and New York, Campus, 1983; U. Knapp, *Frauenarbeit in Deutschland*, Munich, 1984; H. Bradley, *Men's Work, Women's Work: A Sociological History of the Sexual Division of Labour in Employment*, Cambridge, Polity, 1989.

26 S. Hahn, 'Frauenerwerbstätigkeit in Wiener Neustadt 1869–1880' in Verband Österreichischer Geschichtsvereine (ed.) *Bericht über den siebzehnten Österreichischen Historikertag*, Vienna, Verband Österreichischer Geschichtsvereine 1989, pp. 354–357.

27 In the eighteenth century, the Maria-Theresianische Militär-Akademie, an elite educational institution for military officers, was founded. P. Melichar, 'Ästhetik und Disziplin. Das Militär in Wiener Neustadt 1740–1914' in Hahn and Flanner (eds) *Die Wienerische Neustadt*, pp. 283–336.

28 In detail S. Hahn, 'Auf dem Weg zur Industriestadt – Wiener Neustadt im 19. Jahrhundert. Ein Überblick', in Hahn and Flanner (eds) *Die Wienerische Neustadt*, pp. 203–238.

29 The exact figures are 32 per cent in 1869 and 35 per cent in 1880.

30 This was the case for the female migrants as well as for the male ones. Within the male migrants, the Hungarians made up about 10 per cent of the whole. See Hahn, 'Auf dem Weg zur Industriestadt', p. 218.

31 Stekl, 'Hausrechtliche Abhängigkeit', p. 308. About the Bohemians in Vienna see in detail M. Glettler, *Die Wiener Tschechen um 1900*, Munich and Vienna, R. Oldenbourg Verlag, 1972.

32 W. H. Hubbard, *Auf dem Weg zur Großstadt. Eine Sozialgeschichte der Stadt Graz 1850–1914*, Vienna, Verlag für Geschichte und Politik, 1984, p. 395.

33 In detail S. Hahn, 'Fremde Frauen. Migration und Erwerbstätigkeit von Frauen am Beispiel von Wiener Neustadt', *Zeitgeschichte*, 5, 6 (1993): 139–157.

34 E. G. Ravenstein, 'The Laws of Migration', *Journal of the Statistical Society*, 48 (1886): 167–235 (Part I) and 52 (1889): 241–305 (Part II).

35 M. Mitterauer, 'Gesindedienst und Jugendphase im europäischen Vergleich' in M. Mitterauer, *Familie und Arbeitsteilung. Historischvergleichende Studien*, Vienna-Cologne-Weimar, Böhlau, 1992, pp. 301–332.

36 On the migration of (male) apprentices and journeymen see, for example, J. Ehmer, 'Worlds of Mobility: Migration Patterns of Viennese Artisans in the Eighteenth Century' in G. Crossick (ed.) *The Artisan and the European Town*,

1500–1900, Aldershot and Vermont, Scolar Press, 1997, pp. 172–199; R. Reith, 'Arbeitsmigratin und Gruppenkultur deutscher Handwerksgesellen im 18. und frühen 19. Jahrhundert' in H.-G. Haupt and P. Marschalck (eds) *Städtische Bevölkerungsentwicklung in Deutschland im 19. Jahrhundert*, St. Katharinen, Scripta Mercaturae Verlag, 1994, pp. 1–26.

37 In order to allow for comparison, the group of 'female day labourers' has been included, leading to the following conclusions: within this group, the native-born females represent the smallest share and a significantly higher proportion came from nearby regions with typically agricultural character, such as Styria. Perhaps we can assume here that women originally from the agrarian countryside and perhaps having previously served as a farmhand did not take up a position as a servant in an artisan or bourgeois household.

38 I. Hardach-Pinke, *Die Gouvernante: Geschichte eines Frauenberufs*, Frankfurt am Main, Campus, 1993, pp. 206–240.

39 About the sub-tenants in Austria and Germany in the nineteenth century, see in detail J. Ehmer, 'Wohnen ohne eigene Wohnung. Zur sozialen Stellung von Untermietern und Bettgehern' in L. Niethammer (ed.) *Wohnen im Wandel*, Wuppertal, Peter Hammer Verlag, 1979, pp. 132–150; F.J. Brüggemeier, *Leben vor Ort. Ruhrbergleute und Ruhrbergbau 1889–1919*, Munich, C.H. Beck, 1984.

40 In detail, Hahn, 'Fremde Frauen', p. 152.

41 K. Kraus, 'Der Meldezettel' in K. Kraus, *Sittlichkeit und Kriminalität*, Frankfurt am Main, Suhrkamp, 1987, pp. 276–280 (here p. 278).

42 On aspects of Heimatrecht in the nineteenth-century Habsburg Empire see J. Jegierek, *Das Heimatrecht, dann das Aufenthalts- beziehungsweise Abschaffungsrecht, die Armenversorgungspflicht und der Verpflegs-, Transport- und Beerdigungskosten-Ersatz in Österreich*, Vienna, 1886; H. Rauchberg, 'Die Heimatsverhältnisse der Bevölkerung Oesterreichs nach den Ergebnissen der Volkszählung vom 31. December 1890', *Statistische Monatsschrift*, 18 (1892): 345–401. About the influences of the Heimatrecht on the immigration policy of today, R. Bauböck, 'Immigration Control without Integration Policy: An Austrian Dilemma' in G. Brochmann and T. Hammar (eds) *Mechanism of Immigration Control: A Comparative Analysis of European Regulation Policies*, Oxford and New York, Berg, 1999, pp. 97–134.

43 E. List, *Die Präsenz des Anderen. Theorie und Geschlechterpolitik*, Frankfurt am Main, Suhrkamp, 1993, p. 128.

7 Gender, family, work and migration in early nineteenth-century Scotland

David Tidswell

Introduction

Changes in home, work and family situations often coincide and create our most significant experiences in life. They usually involve a great deal of consideration and are carried out despite known drawbacks. This chapter examines evidence about the mobility and motives of people in Scotland in the early nineteenth century. It discusses the different mobility of males and females, examines the connections which migrants had with different places, and explores several individuals' histories. It argues that females and males made decisions relating to their own aspirations as well as their families' economic circumstances. It also suggests that many females' freedom to make decisions was more limited than males', but that this was less pronounced for females in industrial work.

Scotland was one of the most rapidly changing societies in Europe in the late eighteenth and early nineteenth centuries. Radical shifts in agriculture and industry saw large numbers of people move out of traditional peasant and sub-tenant roles to become landless labourers and industrial workers based in villages, towns and cities. Women, men and children moved for many reasons, usually involving work but also for new social relationships, impatient with older, traditional settings. Movement was especially directed toward urban areas in lowland regions, mainly the Central Belt between Edinburgh and Glasgow, as well as the large towns of Aberdeen and Dundee on the east coast. Most population growth occurred in the regions around these cities, and sex ratios for the whole country show the predominance of females in all regions of Scotland (in 1811 there were 0.84 males for every female); however, this changed significantly after the Peace of 1815 with the return of thousands of soldiers (0.89 in 1821).[1]

The different work and migration experiences of females and males in Europe is well known, and Scotland was no exception.[2] Yet women there were generally more mobile and more available to work than in other societies, even England. Poor law relief was not guaranteed to the able-bodied unemployed, and wages were generally low, encouraging women to work as part of family strategies. Females' seasonal and regular wages, though lower than males', allowed households to survive, particularly during periods of recession, such as after 1815. Returning soldiers and immigrant Irish then flooded the labour market, putting greater pressure on women and children to enter the lowest levels of work. This frequently involved agricultural work which, like most other sectors, was gendered with women used for harvest and domestic chores. Young Scottish women were traditionally more willing than females in other countries to leave home for agriculture and domestic service, and many continued in such work until leaving it at marriage in their mid-twenties. Agricultural servants were hired for six months at a time though many were re-hired, often staying on in one area for three to five years; payment was often in kind rather than with cash, a system which benefited servants in difficult years. However, once people had become landless servants they still had to live with the possibility of moving twice a year at least. Harvest work also brought many men and women temporarily from Ireland and the Scottish Highlands, frequently to the same districts every year. Only occasionally are women's skills known to have directed household mobility, such as in the southwest, where dairying skills were at a premium. Other options for the large number of single women included textile work, such as handloom weaving, spinning and bleaching.

While most studies draw attention to the wider economic contexts of migration, more immediate social aspects also played an important part. Work by family historians in particular, stresses the importance of migration as one of several family strategies,[3] but again individual men and, especially women, are seen as playing out an agreed upon role rather than making decisions in their own right. One thesis on the Scottish port town of Greenock touched on such aspects by discussing women's migration as a means of escape from the negative side of social life in the rural Highlands.[4] While economic opportunities grew in Lowland Scotland in this period the reasons behind movement went far beyond simple financial gain. This is the point at which short-term tactics and long-term aspirations came together.

Recent studies of gender and migration in the present also stress the central importance of the family, and the ways in which women adapted to the absences of male household members and to their own mobility.[5] Women's household and migratory roles in changing labour markets are of particular concern, especially since women carry out the bulk of daily household tasks or are more closely tied by cultural, social and economic bonds to their original families. The studies particularly emphasise family ties between movers and stayers, how migrants ended up in a particular place, and how they maintained their cultural ties with their origins. These themes can rarely be dealt with systematically in historical studies but some are highlighted in this chapter using qualitative evidence. Several case studies explore the transitions and crises experienced over the course of people's lives, especially those which involve mobility, such as leaving home, looking for work, and marriage.[6]

Source

The main source used here is known as the Precognitions of the Lord Advocate's department; it is a series of legal records used to determine the need for criminal proceedings. These are mainly pre-trial statements of witnesses and suspects but also include official correspondence about cases and occasionally some evidence, such as plans or documents.[7] The Precognitions were (and still are) produced throughout Scotland but particularly in Lowland urban areas, and only those from 1812 onwards have been retained in sufficient numbers for analysis. The series was examined for the period 1812–1821 with details taken regarding any suspects or witnesses for whom there was information regarding geographical movement, whether through their own statements or official correspondence. About two-thirds of the people found were questioned in urban locations of above 5,000 persons, while one-quarter of the people alone were questioned in Glasgow. While about one-quarter of the suspects gave information about their mobility, relatively few witnesses did so because of the nature of the interrogations. Suspects frequently provided a wealth of detail, often citing two or more moves, their activities in the places where they stayed, their reasons for moving, their family and work situations, and their personal details, such as age, nationality, place of birth and occupation(s). The series thus provides a rare opportunity to examine people's lives in this period from both quantitative and qualitative perspectives.

The period 1812–1821 was chosen partly because of the availability of the Precognitions and the fact that those of later years fail to provide full accounts of suspects' lives. More importantly, though, were the wider events of the 1810s. The unsettling nature of both the war and the post-1815 economy was likely to draw out people's support networks and resources. Such strategies were almost certain to be highlighted in criminal sources, if anywhere. Yet criminal material is not without its problems. Most of the information used here comes from the statements of suspects and witnesses, but the comments of officials also provided information. Both suspects and witnesses told lies, creating difficulties in reconstructing their paths of movement. There is little that can be done in such a situation other than to use information in later statements to correct earlier ones, or to use the information in the statements of witnesses and officials to correct those of suspects. Theoretically, this may affect all types of information but particularly any cited events, stated reasons for movement or exact locations.

Indicators of mobility

Who were the people known to have moved? Most of the suspects in the study group were Scottish (79 per cent, with 18 per cent Irish) males, between the ages of 16 and 35 (72 per cent of the 50 per cent whose age is known), questioned in urban places of more than 5,000 people, and questioned about acts of theft or violence. Witnesses were more often Scots (87 per cent, with 11 per cent Irish) and 63 per cent (of the 34 per cent known) were between the ages of 16 and 35. The known occupations of males and females differed significantly, with half of the females providing no information while the rest were predominantly in agriculture, service, textiles and hawking; males were split between textiles (primarily weaving), trades and crafts, labourers, hawkers and, for male witnesses, agriculture (see Table 7.1). About 20 per cent of the deponents specified where they were born or raised, while another 18 per cent provided information about their general origin, citing an area such as Ireland or a parish. For the purposes of analysis, such areas are assumed to be rural.

How did these people move around Scotland and the United Kingdom? Three basic indicators include the number of moves made, the length of time remaining in a place, and the distances travelled. Many deponents provided information on more than one move (39 per cent of females, 47 per cent of males), and this was higher when suspects alone are considered (60 per cent of females, 56 per cent of males). However, this merely indicates the known rather than actual number of moves. The length of time people stayed in any one place was stated infrequently (23 per cent of all stays); of those known, a high proportion were of six months or less (females 55 per cent, males 46 per cent), while a significant proportion were over two years (females 27 per cent, males 29 per cent). Finally, wider differences emerge when distance is considered; the median distances for all moves by males was 49 km, 23 km for females. When locations within Scotland and the north of England alone are considered, these

Table 7.1 Occupations of suspects and witnesses where known in early nineteenth-century Scotland

Occupational group	*Females*		*Males*		*Total*
	Suspects (%)	*Witnesses (%)*	*Suspects (%)*	*Witnesses (%)*	
Agriculture	16	29	9	21	129
Labourers	4	7	17	9	133
Servants	38	46	3	10	103
Textiles	22	4	19	10	161
Trades/crafts	0	4	18	21	157
Total	80	90	66	71	70
Total (N)	*55*	*74*	*424*	*130*	*683.7*

figures decrease to 35 km and 20 km. The figure for females also differed greatly between those suspected of theft (29 km) and those who were witnesses (18 km).

How did these people move between rural and urban places? Inter-sectoral movements between rural and urban places[8] also show important differences for males and females, but these are reduced when nationality and occupation are considered. There was not a great difference in the movements of suspects and witnesses (Table 7.2), but Table 7.3 shows that Irish female deponents stated proportionally more rural–urban and inter-urban moves (and fewer urban–rural moves) than Scottish females. Likewise, Irish males had proportionally more rural–urban moves (though fewer inter-urban moves) than Scottish males; this is probably a result of Irish males and females moving directly to Glasgow from Ireland. Females and males in agriculture had fairly similar types of movements, while female servants were more involved in inter-rural movement and less in rural–urban and urban–rural movement than male servants (Table 7.4). Finally, a major contrast is found in females working in textiles; these were far more involved in inter-urban movement and less in inter-rural movement than males in the same category.

What connections did the deponents mention having with these places? Many of the deponents provided information about their ties with the places they moved between (Tables 7.5–7.8). These links do not

Table 7.2 Inter-sectoral movements of suspects and witnesses in early nineteenth-century Scotland

Movement	*Females*		*Males*	
	Suspects (%)	*Witnesses (%)*	*Suspects (%)*	*Witnesses (%)*
R-r	46	48	36	43
R-u	19	24	25	26
U-r	15	11	16	14
U-u	19	17	23	18
Total (N)	*368*	*238*	*1840*	*320*

Table 7.3 Inter-sectoral movements of Scots and Irish in early nineteenth-century Scotland

Movement	*Females*		*Males*	
	Irish (%)	*Scottish (%)*	*Irish (%)*	*Scottish (%)*
R-r	38	49	37	38
R-u	30	19	31	23
U-r	5	15	12	16
U-u	27	17	19	22
Total (N)	*66*	*534*	*455*	*1653*

Table 7.4 Inter-sectoral movements of occupational groups in nineteenth-century Scotland

Movement	*Females*			*Males*		
	Agriculture (%)	*Servants (%)*	*Textiles (%)*	*Agriculture (%)*	*Servants (%)*	*Textiles (%)*
R-r	72	67	24	61	55	38
R-u	16	16	25	21	21	26
U-r	10	10	18	11	15	16
U-u	1	7	33	6	8	20
Total (N)	*67*	*135*	*51*	*201*	*71*	*328*

necessarily indicate why people moved, but include simple connections (such as through family relationships or simple residence) and activities (such as paid labour, marriage, or crime). It should be stressed that these links are not exhaustive in the least but they do provide a look into the reference points which deponents and officials used to identify their ties to places. The main categories here include family, work, residence and temporary/other; the last includes a wide range of mostly temporary links from punishments and suspected crimes to visits and vagrancy.[9]

Females mentioned their family and simple residence to a far greater extent than did males, and this was even more so for female witnesses. This is not too surprising but it does raise important questions about gender and links to the wider world. Female labour, even before marriage, was not highly esteemed and this may simply reflect women's acknowledgement of this when faced with an official questioning them. That is, the categories of their actual work may have been beyond the ken of most officials making it easier to reference women to their families, particularly their parents. Alternatively, this may also support the idea that males viewed their world primarily through work, regarding their family connections as less important to officials.

In Table 7.5, the links of female suspects and witnesses differ in important ways. Suspects were less likely to mention either family or residential links and emphasised work, temporary or unknown links. Male suspects and witnesses, however, were much more similar, with the main differences being witnesses making more mention of residences and suspects providing more information about temporary stays. This implies, for both female and male suspects, a lifestyle with fewer constraints.

Despite these differences between suspects and witnesses there were few between the Irish and the Scots when separated by gender (Table 7.6). Occupational groups within each gender had greater differences, with females in textiles having the greatest proportion in 'temporary/other' (Table 7.7). The reasons behind this were predominantly related to criminal incidents, suggesting either that women in textiles were more independent or that they were under greater scrutiny. The first reason may tie in with

Table 7.5 Links of suspects and witnesses in nineteenth-century Scotland

	Females		*Males*	
	Suspects (%)	*Witnesses (%)*	*Suspects (%)*	*Witnesses (%)*
Family	30	38	22	20
Work	25	22	38	42
Residence	14	27	5	17
Temp./other	19	8	28	15
Unknown	12	5	7	7
Total (N)	*517*	*411*	*2582*	*541*

Table 7.6 Links of Scots and Irish in nineteenth-century Scotland

	Females		*Males*	
	Irish (%)	*Scottish (%)*	*Irish (%)*	*Scottish (%)*
Family	35	34	28	20
Work	24	24	38	39
Residence	17	20	4	8
Temp./other	13	14	22	26
Unknown	11	8	8	7
Total (N)	*96*	*820*	*622*	*2420*

Table 7.7 Links of occupational groups in nineteenth-century Scotland

	Females			*Males*		
	Agriculture (%)	*Servants (%)*	*Textiles (%)*	*Agriculture (%)*	*Servants (%)*	*Textiles (%)*
Family	29	33	26	16	21	25
Work	46	42	29	49	47	48
Residence	9	5	4	8	4	4
Temp./other	6	12	33	21	15	16
Unknown	10	8	7	5	14	6
Total (N)	*102*	*199*	*69*	*297*	*111*	*473*

their lower figure for family links; this is in contrast to males in textiles whose proportion of family links was higher than those of other male occupational groups. Finally, Table 7.8 shows the links of females and males whose occupation is known in rural and urban places. Work figures highest in all groups, though it is highest for females in urban places. Females in such situations with family links in urban places are much fewer, suggesting the strong rural links of the deponents. 'Other' reasons are highest in

Table 7.8 Links in rural and urban places (of those with known occupation) in nineteenth-century Scotland

	Rural places		*Urban places*	
	Females (%)	*Males (%)*	*Females (%)*	*Males (%)*
Family	33	25	20	16
Work	39	42	45	39
Residence	8	6	9	6
Temp./other	13	21	20	30
Unknown	8	6	6	9
Total (N)	*352*	*1653*	*148*	*1229*

urban places, following from the criminal incidents under investigation as well as the deponents' stays in towns and cities.

Case studies

Despite the fragmentary nature of the deponents' information about mobility, many of their statements touched on issues pertinent to the themes of gender, family and work. This section explores some of these, including temporary and permanent separations between spouses and other family members, how such periods involved support from other family members, and how mobility was used by individuals and households. These issues in particular have been raised by studies of migration and the life course, a framework particularly influenced by Elder and Hareven.[10] Everyday transitions such as leaving home, looking for work, marriage, separation and becoming unemployed affect individuals as well as their network of family and friends. Individuals can decide whether to draw on their network's support in such situations; alternatively, transitions and individuals' responses to them can end up damaging the network at a time when it is needed most. The deponents' stories illustrate the support given to family and friends, as well as the expectations placed on people by themselves and their networks. Gender in particular could play a large role not only in individuals' options and aspirations, but also in their supposed responsibilities. This in turn often had the effect of directing their geographical movements.

Women, children and families

Much of the information came from females who were conversely less likely than males to discuss their own lives in much depth. This may point to marriage having greater importance for women than men in Scottish society at this time, but it was not uncommon for some women to discuss exclusively their husbands' lives, often not raising their own work and family roles. As if to emphasise this, most men also stated their own work and actions, often to the exclusion of their wives' except to state that a marriage had occurred. Thus, much of the information about marital relations coming from both men and women concentrates on the role(s) of husbands.

As with most of the deponents' histories, isolating one action from another is difficult and not always desirable. Many of the married deponents discussed their mobility, work or family support, and often some combination of the three. One example of such a combination comes from a broken marriage in the north-east. Margaret Gordon and Alexander Dow were married in 1802 in a rural parish in Banffshire; she was raised in another parish some 30 km to the north-west in Aberdeenshire. At the time of the marriage both Margaret and Alexander served one farmer in that county and twelve months later they moved to another farm nearby. Seven years later in 1810 Alexander left Margaret with five children and in 1813 he became a bigamist by marrying the daughter of a nearby farmer. In the meantime, Margaret had moved back to her parish of origin with her children [446].[11]

Other cases regarding family relationships and work follow below, illustrating the ways in which females and males made a living, how they moved between jobs and how they supported (or rejected) one another. The stories of women and girls in particular shed light on their labour and gender roles, yet by no means were these uniform throughout the country except that they were generally more restricted than males. Occasionally, women broke out of their usual positions to the surprise of husbands, officials and contemporary commentators.[12] For example, some women entered farm service, or harvested with friends or their children while their husbands were temporarily away.

Children figured highly in many women's stories. Cases such as child murder and concealment of pregnancy particularly raise important questions about the links between mobility, gender and sexuality, both for the individual and the community.[13] Both crimes carried the possibility of capital punishment until 1809 when punishment for the latter was put at two years.[14] Many of these cases involved migrants and twelve of these contained detailed information about the women (and sometimes men) involved in the crimes. The occupations of the suspects included one bleacher while the rest were domestic or farm servants scattered throughout Scotland. A few were in their late thirties or forties, but most were in their early twenties.

Most of the women conceived, gave birth to and, in some cases, got rid of, their children away from their parents' homes. Mobility, particularly for service, was an important element in evading the law and the immediate moral judgements of their families. Movement from the parental home usually occurred before conception, and this is reinforced by the number of servants among these women, a finding in common with Mitchison and Leneman's (1989) work. Permanent movement before birth would seem an obvious strategy for women trying to keep their actions secret from their families, neighbours and churches, yet such movement was not found at all. Instead it seems that the family ties of most of the women continued throughout, or following, the period of their pregnancies: many returned to their families or home areas before or soon after giving birth. Agnes Johnstone [297], a servant at a farm in the Scottish Borders, was suspected of concealment of pregnancy. The farm was near the residence of two of her aunts, both witnesses in the case. Johnstone stayed with one of them between giving birth and returning to her father's house near Edinburgh. In another case Helen Law [937] gave birth at the 'Lying in Hospital' in Edinburgh; she stayed there for the two weeks allowed, and went back to her father, a labourer in Linlithgow, west of the capital.

These women used and furthered their family relations despite their 'crimes' and in the midst of extremely difficult periods. Yet, while most women seem to have been closer to their families or at least more aware of their family links than men were, there were other women who gave little indication of this. Janet Hannah [508], suspected of child murder, gave details about the places of her farm service and her family relations which covered a twenty-year period, but gave no information about her current family relations, her lover or even why she had abandoned her child. Catherine Falconer [935] was also suspected of child murder while she was a changekeeper's servant. She only stated her father's name and said nothing else about her family. Other information regarding her came from her employer and a former farm servant.

One woman who suffered ill health and had family nearby was Ann Baxter [497], who was 22 years old in 1818. Her father, a sailor and school teacher, had died when she was 6; her mother continued to reside in Bridgeton, Glasgow. Baxter had worked in the

> Cotton Mills of Oswald Stevenson and Company and Mr. William Dunn in Bridgeton since she was able to work but left them, on account of bad health, about four months ago [April 1818]. That about two months ago [June 1818] she went to work in the Bleachfield of Mr. Williamson of Carmyle, where she continued for about five weeks, and since that time she has not wrought at any work, and been in no regular Lodgings.

Such differences in the apparent levels of family ties may have depended just as much on the actual extent of communication and support as on an individual deponent's decision to disclose such links. Their decisions probably depended on the history of their families as they seem to cross boundaries of age, occupation and region.[15] In other types of cases, where deponents also withheld information, some eventually said it was because of their shame. Fear must also be acknowledged as a possible gag.

Weavers and wanderers

Males were more likely to discuss their movements between jobs, occasionally mentioning family relationships in passing. Male weavers and other artisans were probably more affected by economic downturns than were those in less-skilled work such as labourers and small traders. Weavers, for example, might have to move from a fairly stable workplace, often at home, and go into casual work, competing with those who had been doing it longer. The responses of weavers and their families to such crises is occasionally known, although those with a skilled spouse and children would have had more room to manoeuvre.[16]

After the Peace of 1815, the number of weavers increased substantially, yet wages were falling and the authorities gave up 'all attempts to control the absconding of apprentice weavers, prior to the completion of their contracts'.[17] A few weavers in the Precognitions indicated how they coped with the increasing competition as well as their difficulties with leaving their trade. James Nelson [1146], an apprentice weaver in Hamilton, had earlier worked in nearby Airdrie for two months; but with 'trade becoming then very dull' [c.1819] he put all his money into hardware to sell in the countryside. Other weavers went into agricultural work, such as Duncan McAllister [973]. At 21 years of age he had worked as both a weaver and labourer. In early 1819, 'when the weaving became dull', he left his native Beith in Ayrshire and went to England: 'That since that time he has been two or three times in England and in intervals returned to Scotland and wrought in different parts of Scotland at different jobs when he could get anything to do sometimes in the farming line but not at weaving.'

Former artisans, farm labourers and casual workers were prepared to go far afield for their work, wandering between villages and towns throughout the country. They shared a confidence (or possibly a desperation) that work opportunities would present themselves if they were in the right place at the right time. The 'wandering', primarily carried out by males, was not aimless so much as a way of trying their luck in one place after another. This approach to finding work is usually evident in the statements of labourers and other casual workers. This contrasts with the directed harvest migrations between the Highlands and Lowlands.[18]

Others went in and out of work with few commitments to their trade, easily entering and leaving it. Peter Macdonald [329] had worked as a servant until 1816 when he began to work 'with a horse and cart of his own' until the horse died during that same year's harvest. He next went to work as a labourer around Glasgow. Macdonald was not completely footloose, as he frequently visited his mother who lived near Perth and his brother who worked near Glasgow. He maintained family contacts by returning to his mother and going job-hunting with his brother.

Occasionally the statements provide a glimpse into the deponents' decisions regarding work and mobility. Roderick Boyd [1138], a 20-year-old native of Londonderry, Ireland, was a sailor and pedlar, and served five years in the British navy. He came to Aberdeen on a ship from London in late 1819, succumbed to a great fever and stayed there for some time. He was 'on his way through Perth towards Leith [the port town north of Edinburgh] with the view to get a place on a ship' when he met a pedlar and went to the west coast town of Oban with him instead. Another change of plan was made by Margaret Grieg [1169] who, in November 1820, went with her husband from their home in Argyll to Peterhead, a north-east fishing town. They went in order to get Ferguson employment 'on board some vessel'. They found no work but were told there was an opportunity in Inverness; they left Peterhead in early December in the company of a rope-spinner from Perthshire, who was also on his way to Inverness for employment. The ease with which both males and females accompanied new-found friends is striking, pointing to a culture of shared and flexible mobility.

Marriages

The marriages found in the Precognitions often coincided with both spouses being in stable jobs and in which they remained for at least a year after wedding. Such occupations usually included farm servants or artisans, though hawkers with a steady business also married and continued to ply their trade, often taking their spouses on as co-workers. The jobs of spouses were sometimes the same, such as in the case of weavers, hawkers and farm servants; such occupations were common to both genders throughout the Lowlands, though the overall incidence of female employment, especially after marriage or children, is unknown.

The financial circumstances of married couples in the Precognitions is occasionally known. There is no explicit mention of either women or men planning for marriage, but a few of the men seem to have saved money for a few years before marrying. Most people probably expected to get married and the lack of information may indicate that it was presumed to be the norm. Nevertheless, the low ratio of men to women in Scotland for the 20–30 age group would have lessened many women's chances for marriage.

Temporary separations between spouses arose for a number of reasons but were usually linked to the work of the husband. Only occasionally did deponents state details about financial support that came from husbands who were temporarily absent. The best example is of a couple who had not married but were regarded by his employer as husband and wife. John Wilson [324] and Douglas Forrester (a woman) [325] had a child together in 1798. John worked as a printer in Edinburgh at the time and visited Douglas occasionally there; for the most part they both stayed in Edinburgh but apparently did not live together. In 1816 John began work as a lighthouse keeper in the Firth of Forth, the estuary north of Edinburgh.

He took Douglas with him and 'she lived with him for some months' until he left in September for another lighthouse in south-west Scotland. After he left, the Superintendent of Lightkeepers for Northern Lighthouses sent money to Douglas as part of John's wages. Meanwhile John had married at Stranraer in February 1817 and, when charged with bigamy, said he 'never meant to acknowledge her [Douglas] as his wife. That while at Inchkeith he sent for her on one occasion, and upon another she came of her own accord.'

This story indicates that a mechanism was in place for some employed men to support their families and thus their own mobility. This was not likely to have been a common practice for most employers of men who were away from home. The families of itinerants such as sailors and some labourers would have had to supplement their incomes, partly because of the uncertainty of the husband's wage returning with him, but mostly because a labouring man's wages were usually too low to support his entire family in the first place. There is ample evidence in other studies as well as in the Precognitions of the importance of women's labour to the household, particularly in spinning and weaving.[19] In several instances in the Precognitions, women's work supported men's mobility, yet this may have been usually limited to low-skilled work. There is the case of Patrick Gavin [178], a weaver, who married Jean McManus in 1807 in Co. Tyrone. They had left there in 1809 and ended up in Carlisle in early 1812. In February 1813 he went 'to seek work about Edinburgh leaving both his Wife and children' in Carlisle. He 'heard the prices were better in Scotland' and felt that there was 'no harm as he left his wife, who can weave, to finish the Web.'

In the light of the marital difficulties of some couples who were temporarily separated, the marriages of hawkers seem remarkable in two ways. First, their separations were frequent and often long because of the nature of their work. Second, their marriages apparently lasted the longest of all the deponents'. This may in fact be a consequence of the work if those away from home, usually men travelling on their own, valued their families because of their long separations. Likewise there was an obvious mutual dependency resulting from the unknown level of income from any one trip. But this does not entirely explain the long-lasting ties between hawkers as the same situation arose for the families of sailors and soldiers. Hawkers gave no indication of extra-marital relationships and presented a picture of devotion to their families. The reasons for such loyalty are unknown, but there was a greater interdependence and possibly greater equality between male and female hawkers than was found in other working couples. This apparent fidelity is most evident when both husband and wife went on the road. Couples on the road endured the same hard conditions whether travelling together or apart, and staying on in such a line of work may have been a test of loyalty to one another. The main point here though is that women who hawked, unlike women in other forms of work, had a high degree of autonomy from their husbands in their decisions about where to travel and how to carry out their business. Such autonomy, combined with pooling resources, may have encouraged hawkers to stay together longer or permanently.

A few examples shed light on this. In 1815 two hawkers, William Coyle [232] and his wife, had returned to Glasgow with their children after a year in Liverpool. They had previously lived in Glasgow for twenty years. On their return his wife immediately went to sell goods in Edinburgh. Leaving their children with some neighbours Coyle set out a week later; on arriving in Edinburgh he was told his wife had returned to Glasgow. He then went on to several places in the Borders before returning home. Another couple, Jean Hunter [170] and William Tweedie [171], were based in Donaghadee, Ireland, and had been married for ten years. Tweedie had hawked for twelve years and also had some experience in keeping a public house. On their present trip they travelled together from Stranraer to Ayr and then split up, he going to Nottingham and she to Glasgow. Both of these couples illustrate the autonomy of both husbands and wives, the necessity of separating and the expectation of reuniting.

Permanent separations, bigamy and remarriage

Permanent separations are also in evidence in the Precognitions, especially in bigamy cases. Despite the legal availability of divorce, such separations were usually an easier option for those with few possessions, as well as for those in common-law marriages. In the bigamy cases deponents gave unusually thorough accounts of their marital and family histories, probably because of both the relationship's crisis and the officials' need to establish the identities of the parties involved. In addition, bigamy cases provide some of the strongest hints about the importance of immediate family, to women in particular. Almost all of the cases of bigamy involved a spouse or partner who moved geographically. Indeed, mobility was probably the most common characteristic of these cases since remarriage while a previous spouse was alive was illegal and nearly impossible if both husband and wife remained in the same area. Almost all of these cases arose from husbands' attempts to remarry and in only one had both a husband and wife earlier agreed to their separation. Thus, for men at least, bigamy may have been the only way out of a dissatisfying marriage. Within the twelve cases studied here the separations usually occurred after five years.

In the bigamy cases there was rarely any hint of reconciliation. Only seven of these cases have enough details to piece together the histories of all the people involved. Each situation was different from the others, in the events leading up to the husband's departure, the reactions of both wives and the known involvement of their families. Men suspected of bigamy gave a variety of reasons for leaving their spouses and families, from petty disagreements to serious threats.

The emotional and financial investments put into marriages make separations volatile events at any time. A severance could have been devastating for women, particularly if their husbands were the primary earner and if they were left to care for several children. The anger of some women, as their lives were turned upside down, is apparent in their statements and actions. Yet it is not possible to provide a blanket description of men and women's feelings about their marriages, particularly when expectations of fidelity and economic support may have differed geographically and socially, as did attitudes to illegitimacy.

Some of the bigamy cases provide a glimpse into men's reasons for leaving and women's responses to their husbands' departures and remarriages. James McCloy [164], a weaver and widower with seven children, married his second wife, Margaret Perry [165], in Northern Ireland, in 1808; they went to south-west Scotland, late in 1809. They remained together until the summer of 1813 when James left; he later complained that she had 'behaved ill'. (James makes no mention of where his children were after his departure, however.) He remained in the south-west and, at the start of the harvest that year, married Agnes Thomson whom he had met there. James then tramped and sold goods in the countryside until making his statement that December. Agnes had lived in the area for twenty years but had kept her 'certificate of character' from Ireland where she was raised. Margaret's anger at the situation was such that she burned both Agnes' certificate and marriage licence.

The statements of couples in bigamy cases provide insights not so much into people's actual experiences of marriage but more into what they deemed important about their relationships. Most of the stories go only so far, tantalising with fragments of information and emotion. At the same time several themes converge in such stories. James's transition from weaving at home to harvesting and hawking throughout the country involved several changes at once: he gave up his work, his marriage and home to take on informal tasks, a bigamous marriage, and an ever-changing residence. The willingness to change work, in this case taking on less prestigious jobs, enabled all of these to occur. Work was not, however, the driving force in McCloy's decisions to move. Rather, the desire for domestic change was enabled by the opportunities presented by casual and temporary work.

Throughout several of the bigamy cases family members of the couples were mentioned, either as active supporters of one of the spouses or merely as reference points. Catherine Falconer [1244] was from Caithness in the far north as were James Mackady [1243] and his first wife, Margaret Murray. Catherine had married a soldier from the same parish but, 'being a soldier', he had left soon after the wedding. James and Margaret had been married for seven years when in 1817, Margaret said, his 'affections seemed to be alienated from her to Catherine Falconer'. That year, James lost his job as a post runner, and soon he and Catherine went to Edinburgh.

They were married there, set up house and he soon became a brewer's servant. Three years later Catherine gave birth but within a month she 'repented her improper conduct with him and left him', returning to live with her mother in Caithness.

James had a brother in Edinburgh and an uncle in Leith. Neither Catherine nor any witnesses mentioned her as having relatives in the area. While there is not enough evidence to say that she had no acquaintances to support her in Edinburgh it seems that both her mother and home parish provided a place of security and repentance. Her actions were apparently so extreme that she had to be with one or the other, her mother or James, with little choice socially or financially to strike out on her own.

The widowed and deserted were likely to seek remarriage as a guard against poverty, but this could create problems for the children with implications for mobility. Little is known about children's reactions to remarriage from the statements but the two recorded show them opposed to it. When her mother decided to remarry, Elizabeth Jameson [645], aged 10, 'ran away from her'. She began to hawk goods which her brother made at Stirling and was later forced by her aunt to hawk with her. Janet Anderson [1200], a 27-year-old bleachfield worker, was the child of a widowed labourer in Angus. He had remarried but since Anderson 'could not agree with her stepmother she left her father's house'. She was then six months pregnant and went to Dundee where she found work. Such opposition was, however, unlikely to prevent remarriage in this period, but both of these cases point toward the recurrent, though not invariable, theme of movement to towns and cities in the face of difficulties. Indeed, other studies suggest such problems may just have easily led to vagabondage rather than rural–urban movement.[20]

Conclusions

In conclusion, this chapter suggests that mobility had as much to do with conventional social reasons as with economic ones; social reasons especially included the influence of the family and its supporting or debilitating role. Economic reasons can be seen both as presenting and allowing choices (awful as they may be) but throughout the deponents' statements there is a subtle interplay between the economic and the social. Second, most of the mobility described and analysed here is of an everyday sort, for temporary as well as more continuous purposes. As such, it provides a picture more of a society at work (in several meanings of the term) than of one single group of people or places. Third, the importance of gender differences and relations figures highly; the mobility of females and males differed in important ways though this was less in evidence when occupation was considered. The deponents' stories go further by revealing females and males in constant negotiation over finances, responsibilities and support. Interdependence was essential to many but it could also prove costly.

Notes

1 Important studies of Scottish migration include T.M. Devine, 'Social Stability and Agrarian Change in the Eastern Lowlands of Scotland, 1810–1840', *Social History*, 3, (1978): 331–346; *idem*, 'Social Responses to Agrarian "Improvement": the Highland and Lowland Clearances in Scotland', in R.A. Houston and I.D. Whyte (eds), *Scottish Society, 1500–1800*, Cambridge: Cambridge University Press, 1989, pp. 148–168; M. Gray, 'Scottish Emigration: the Social Impact of Agrarian Change in the Rural Lowlands, 1775–1875', *Perspectives in American History*, 7, (1973): 95–174; R.A. Houston, 'Geographical Mobility in Scotland, 1652–1811: the Evidence of Testimonials', *Journal of Historical Geography*, 11, (1985): 379–394; R.A. Houston and C.W.J. Withers, 'Population Mobility in Scotland and Europe, 1600–1900: a Comparative Perspective', *Annales de Demographie Historique*, 31, (1990): 285–308; I.D. Whyte, 'Migration in Early-Modern Scotland and England: a Comparative Perspective', in C.G. Pooley and I.D. Whyte (eds), *Migrants, Emigrants and Immigrants: a Social History of Migration*, London: Routledge, 1991, pp. 87–105; I.D. Whyte and K.A. Whyte, 'The Geographical Mobility of Women in Early Modern Scotland', in L. Leneman (ed.), *Perspectives in Scottish Social History: Essays in Honour of Rosalind Mitchison*, Aberdeen: Aberdeen University Press, 1988, pp. 83–106; C.W.J. Withers, 'Highland Migration to Dundee, Perth and Stirling, 1753–1891', *Journal of Historical Geography*, 11, (1985): 395–418; and *idem*, and A. J. Watson, 'Stepwise Migration and Highland Migration to Glasgow, 1852–1898', *Journal of Historical Geography*, 17, (1991): pp. 35–55.

2 Women's work and social experiences are discussed in E. Breitenbach and E. Gordon (eds), *Out of Bounds: Women in Scottish Society, 1800–1945*, Edinburgh, Edinburgh University Press, 1992; E. Gordon and E. Breitenbach (eds), *The World is Ill Divided: Women's Work in Scotland in the Nineteenth and Twentieth Centuries*, Edinburgh, Edinburgh University Press, 1990; R.A. Houston, 'Women in the Economy and Society of Scotland, 1500–1800', in Houston and Whyte, *Scottish Society*, pp. 118–147; E. King, *The Hidden History of Glasgow's Women: the Thenew Factor*, Edinburgh: Mainstream Publishing, 1993; L. Leneman, '"A Tyrant and Tormentor": Violence against Wives in Eighteenth- and Early Nineteenth-Century Scotland', *Continuity and Change*, 12, (1997): 31–54; D. A. Symonds, *Weep Not for Me: Women, Ballads and Infanticide in Early Modern Scotland*, University Park: Pennsylvania University Press, 1997; and C.A. Whatley, 'Women and the Economic Transformation of Scotland, *c.* 1740–1830', *Scottish Economic and Social History*, 14, (1994): 19–40.

3 M. Anderson, *Family Structure in Nineteenth-century Lancashire*, Cambridge: Cambridge University Press, 1971; A.G. Darroch, 'Migrants in the Nineteenth Century: Fugitives or Families in Motion?', *Journal of Family History*, 6, (1981): 257–277; T.K. Hareven (ed.), *Transitions: the Family and the Life Course in Historical Perspective*, New York: Academic Press, 1978; *idem*, 'Family History at the Crossroads', *Journal of Family History*, 12, (1987): ix–xxiii; K. Schurer, 'The Role of the Family in the Process of Migration', in Pooley and Whyte, *Migrants, Emigrants and Immigrants*, pp. 106–142; and L.A. Tilly, 'Individual Lives and Family Strategies in the French Proletariat', *Journal of Family History*, 4, (1979): 137–152.

4 R.D. Lobban, 'The Migration of Highlanders into Lowland Scotland, *c.* 1750–1850, with particular reference to Greenock', unpublished Ph.D. thesis, University of Edinburgh, 1970.

5 S. Chant (ed.), *Gender and Migration in Developing Countries*, London: Belhaven, 1992; L. Schenk-Sandbergen (ed.), *Women and Seasonal Labour Migration*, New Delhi:, Sage, 1995; and V.A. Lawson, 'Hierarchical Households and Gendered Migration in Latin America: Feminist Extensions to Migration Research', *Progress in Human Geography*, 22, (1998): 39–53.

6 Elder, G. H., Jr, 'Family History and the Life Course', in Hareven, *Transitions*, pp. 17–64; *idem*, 'Perspectives on the Life Course', in *idem* (ed.), *Life Course Dynamics: Trajectories and Transitions*, Ithaca, NY: Cornell University Press, 1985, pp. 23–49; *idem*, 'Families and Lives: Some Developments in Life-Course Studies', *Journal of Family History*, 12, (1987): 179–199.

7 AD14, West Register House, Scottish Record Office.

8 Rural (R) includes places with less than 5,000 inhabitants while urban (U) includes those with 5,000 or more. Population sizes come from the 1821 census and from calculations using later censuses. Rural also includes general areas (such as 'Ireland') which were mentioned by deponents.

9 There are parallels in King's discussion of motivations for moving (S. King, 'Migrants on the Margin? Mobility, Integration and Occupations in the West Riding, 1650–1820', *Journal of Historical Geography*, 23, (1997): 284–303).

10 See particularly Hareven, *Transitions* and Elder, *Life Course Dynamics*.

11 Numbers in brackets refer to the people selected for this study; their case numbers can be found in Appendix B of D. Tidswell, 'Geographical Mobility, Occupational Changes and Family Relationships in Early-Nineteenth Century Scotland', unpublished Ph.D. thesis, University of Edinburgh, 1993.

12 See Symonds, *Weep Not for Me*.

13 See T. C. Smout, 'Aspects of Sexual Behaviour in Nineteenth-Century Scotland', in A. A. Maclaren (ed.), *Social Class in Scotland: Past and Present*, Edinburgh: John Donald, 1976, pp. 55–85; and J. A. D. Blaikie, 'The Country and the City: Sexuality and Social Class in Victorian Scotland', in G. Kearns and C. W. J. Withers (eds), *Urbanising Britain: Essays on Class and Community in the Nineteenth Century*, Cambridge: Cambridge University Press, 1991, pp. 80–102.

14 R. Mitchison and L. Leneman, *Sexuality and Social Control: Scotland 1660–1780*, Oxford: Basil Blackwell, 1989, p. 212.

15 For English perspectives, see M. Berg, 'Women's Work, Mechanization and the Early Phases of Industrialization in England', in R. Pahl (ed.), *On Work: Historical, Comparative and Theoretical Approaches*, Oxford: Basil Blackwell, 1988, pp. 61–94; S. Horrell and J. Humphries, 'Women's Labour Force Participation and the Transition to the Male-Breadwinner Family, 1790–1865', *Economic History Review*, 48, (1995): 89–117; E. Jordon, 'The Exclusion of Women from Industry in Nineteenth-Century Britain', *Comparative Studies in Society and History*, 31, (1989): 273–296; and P. Sharpe, *Adapting to Capitalism: Working Women in the English Economy, 1700–1850*, London: Macmillan, 1996.

16 N. Murray, *The Scottish Hand Loom Weavers, 1790–1850: A Social History*, Edinburgh: John Donald, 1978, p. 28.

17 ibid., pp. 68–69.

18 See T. M. Devine, *The Great Highland Famine: Hunger, Emigration and the Scottish Highlands in the Nineteenth Century*, Edinburgh: John Donald, 1988.

19 See I. D. Whyte, 'Proto-industrialisation in Scotland', in P. Hudson (ed.), *Regions and Industries*, Cambridge: Cambridge University Press, 1989, pp. 228–251.

20 L. P. Moch, *Moving Europeans: Migration in Western Europe since 1650*, Bloomington: Indiana University Press, 1992, p. 88.

8 Wives or workers?

Single British female migration to colonial Australia

Jan Gothard

The image of the 'bride ship' is a provocative one. Particularly current in the North American context, there are a number of movies and books which focus on the theme of women who took passage from Britain, Scandinavia or northern Europe (it is essentially a white and Protestant image) to be delivered into the hands of unknown marriage partners, for better or worse. The corollary of the bride ship is an image of women arriving at the western frontier on trains. As Susan Jackel wrote of the Canadian West in the late nineteenth century, this was

> one of the most durable folk myths among British women of the period . . . the crowds of bride-hunting males who were said to congregate at prairie railway stations, ready to propose instant marriage before girls even had time to collect their baggage from the station-agent'.[1]

These sorts of images tap into the idea of the pioneering heroine, conquering hardship and usually her man – invariably a rough diamond beneath the grizzled and forbidding exterior, too long deprived of female company and washing facilities. Such women represented gentility and civilisation on the new frontier. It is a compelling theme that popular media have appropriated, promoted and popularised.

Less romantic than the 'bride ship' is the complementary notion of women bought and paid for, indeed of women selling themselves into sexual partnerships. Associated with this too is the idea of an organised trade, a mechanism whereby individual women originating from all over Europe were somehow assembled together and sent off *en masse*. Bride ships or, as Babette Smith puts it more prosaically, 'a cargo of women'.[2]

Nineteenth-century Australian colonial societies introduced women *en masse*, at government expense. These women came out both as convicts and as free and assisted immigrants. Between 1788 and 1852, 25,000 women convicts were sent out from Britain. Thereafter, the transportation of women convicts ceased entirely; when the British government commenced transporting convicts to Western Australia in 1850, women were not among them. Some government-assisted emigration of single British women to New South Wales and Van Diemen's Land took place from the 1830s but the large-scale process of female migration to Australia did not gain momentum until the 1850s and 1860s. The transportation of convict women to the Australian colonies has recently been accorded a great deal of interest and will not be the focus of this chapter;[3] rather, I will examine the voluntary or 'free' government-assisted migration of single women.

In the course of the 1850s, all the Australian colonies but Western Australia were granted self-government, and in 1859 Queensland came into existence independent of New South Wales. Western Australia attained self-government in 1890 and consequently its earlier immigration policy was determined by its political dependence on Britain. However, with the granting of self-government, the other colonies' dependence in immigration matters on the Colonial Land and Emigration Commissioners (CLEC) declined. The CLEC were part of the British colonial office which had dealt with colonial emigration and land policies from the 1840s. With self-government each colony gradually moved to appoint its own emigration agents and agents-general in Britain. Although the CLEC retained some of their former responsibility for despatching emigrants to the colonies, at colonial request, their powers of selection decreased on the appointment of colonial government representatives in London; this followed the shift to colonial legislatures of the responsibility for directing colonial policies.

Between 1860 and 1900 up to 90,000 single British women accepted an assisted passage to one of the six Australian colonies: 18,000 to New South Wales, 13,000 to Victoria, 9,100 to South Australia, 46,000 to Queensland, 1,700 to Western Australia and 1,600 to Tasmania. The periods when assistance was offered comprise, roughly, 1860 to 1886 in New South Wales, from the 1850s to 1873 in Victoria, 1850s to 1883 in South Australia, 1860 to 1900 in Queensland, from the 1850s to 1890 in Tasmania and from 1850 to 1900 in Western Australia. In all colonies, assistance operated intermittently between those dates.[4] Apart from the migration of single women to Western Australia in the 1850s and 1860s, which was funded by the British Treasury, all this female migration was paid for by colonial governments.

What occurred in the latter half of the nineteenth century was certainly a large-scale exercise in emigrating women, but were they intended as 'brides'? There is no doubt that most of the women eventually – and some very rapidly – married after arrival in the colonies. That will not be the focus of this chapter. My aim here is to examine the intentions of the colonial governments that funded single female migration. Though their motives are, I believe, quite transparent, they have been obscured by the currency of the idea that the value of women lay not in their productive but their reproductive capacities.

Single women wanted

The experience of arrival varied with time and circumstance. One military officer greeted a boatload of female convicts as 'damned whores', a phrase now infamous in Australian history but one which encapsulates colonial attitudes to those women. Convict women could anticipate a rowdy welcoming committee of single men, including dock workers and militia, eager to participate in the spectacle of assessing the prospective sexual talent. Over time the rabble was contained. In Western Australia almost a century later, police were employed to escort single immigrant women from the vessel to the depot and, though the wharf was crowded, male onlookers apparently restricted any expression of emotion to 'three cheers for Old England in good deep voice'.[5] Yet it remained a market in women. The subsequent hiring out of immigrant women from the depot still represented something part way between a spectator sport and an auction. In the 1880s, for example, when the wife of the governor of New South Wales wanted to watch the proceedings at the depot, the colony's immigration officer prevented her. '[S]he would be shocked by what she would witness', she was told; namely, a clamour of desperate Sydney employers, mostly middle-class and society women, competing for the limited and valuable services of newly arrived domestics.[6] At that period demand for domestic servants was so great that prospective employers had to have their credentials vetted and even to pay for the privilege of attending the hiring room.[7] A decade later, the *Western Mail* still described the hiring process at the Fremantle female immigrant depot in Western Australia as 'not altogether an elevating one', with its suggestion of 'the squatter picking out the best workers from a herd of two-year old cattle'.[8]

Many aspects of the drama of arrival and reception of working-class immigrant women remained familiar from the convict era. What had changed was the cast. The bidders were no longer single men seeking sexual partners but middle-class colonial women seeking domestic assistance.

The domestic servant problem

The constant and unmet demand for satisfactory domestic servants which characterised middle-class life in colonial Australia drew frequent comment from observers and visitors to the colonies.[9] The reasons for this shortage are not clear, although it was a problem the colonists shared with the British middle class. W.A. Sinclair referred to the rate of family formation, the size of colonial families and the middle-class status associated with servant-keeping as determinants of demand for domestic servants; and Bev Kingston has argued that the preference of colonial women for factory work also influenced the availability of domestics.[10] The 'problem' has also been discussed by such historians as Margaret Barbalet and Charlie Fox, though, as Fox correctly pointed out, '[g]iven the importance of domestic service in the nineteenth century it is surprising that there are so few analyses of it'.[11] Ann Curthoys has similarly called for a detailed study of domestic service in Australia.[12] To date, Paula Hamilton is the only Australian historian to have examined the experiences of immigrant domestics in colonial domestic service.[13] Yet the shortage of domestic servants is fundamental to understanding colonial Australia's policies of female migration.

Despite a good deal of contemporary debate in the colonial press echoing similar discussions in Britain, there were only two possible colonial responses to the domestic servant problem: train up local young women to enter domestic service or import servants ready made. The reluctance of local women to enter domestic service in the first place was a cause of the problem with no easy cure, and, in any case, '[i]n the colonies, it was well understood that reproducing the workforce through births was costly, and importing labour was cheap'.[14] So colonists and their governments, eager for immediate solutions, pursued the alternative. Domestic servants were the largest category of labour, male or female, given assistance with the cost of passage to the Australian colonies.

The historiography of female migration

Female migration has attracted increased attention over the last two decades from both historians and sociologists.[15] One writer, Mirjana Morokvasic, focusing primarily on Western Europe but drawing examples from Eastern Europe, North Africa, Asia and Latin America, has outlined a taxonomy of attitudinal shifts to be found in contemporary writings in the field.[16] Patterns of migration are gender-specific, she argued, but in writings as recent as the mid-1970s women have largely been excluded (the 'absent woman' approach) or depicted only as wives, mothers or members of families ('migrants and their wives').[17] These representations leave women either invisible or else dependent, and thus economically invisible, because of exclusion from the paid labour market. As Morokvasic wrote,

> [w]hile justifying the absence of migrant women from their research and categorising them as unproductive, [these] authors projected on to migrant women their own, only partially rejected image of women generally as invisible and socially (therefore sociologically) not important or not worth investigating.[18]

Although Morokvasic's work stemmed from analyses of twentieth-century migrations, her discussion has some relevance here. Historians writing of migration to Australia have found it difficult to overlook completely the existence of female immigrants. The raised historical profile of Caroline Chisholm, 'the immigrant's friend', is partly responsible for this.[19] Further,

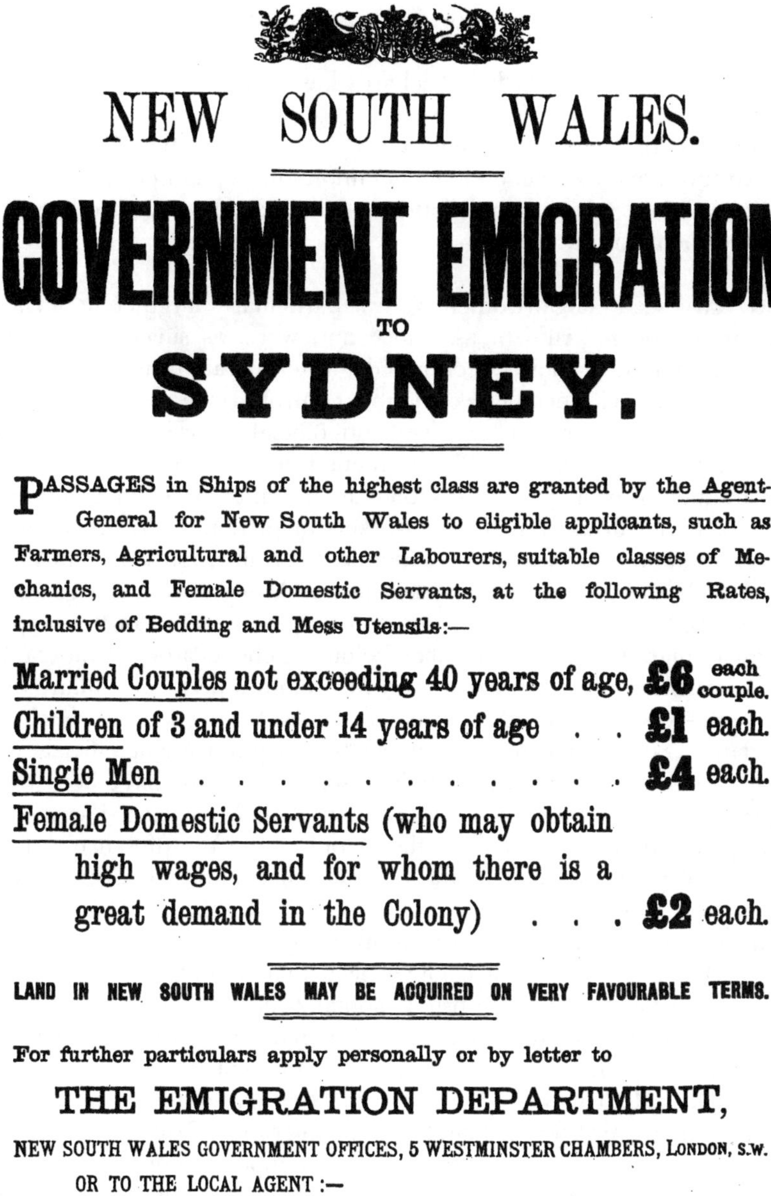

Plate 8.1 Poster advertising government emigration to Sydney, *c.*1880s

Source: Printed courtesy of State Records of New South Wales, Australia. SRNSW ref.: SR Document 102.

a feature common to Australian and New Zealand migration in the nineteenth century has also promoted recognition of female migration: the intervention of colonial governments and the availability of substantial government assistance. As Eric Richards has written,

> [i]t was, of course, precisely because Australian migration required extraordinary governmental intervention and human engineering that it was more selective and better documented than most other mass movements of the time.[20]

As we have seen, single women were a particularly large component of programmes of government assistance and were, as single women and assisted immigrants, 'doubly controlled' by immigration authorities.[21] As a result of this well-documented 'double control', single women are even *more* visible in government archives and official records than are male immigrants. Yet, in spite of this heightened visibility, female immigrants have frequently been presented either as migrants' wives or prospective wives, or caricatured as inefficient workers or prostitutes. In these modes of representation the women's economic role, although substantial, has been largely overlooked or trivialised, just as Morokvasic has argued.

There is, however, another factor distorting perceptions of the purpose of female migration to the Australian colonies. The idea of a demographic sexual imbalance in both Britain and the colonies permeates many mid-nineteenth-century historical sources and has been taken up freely by historians. Like the nineteenth-century British government officials who monitored colonial immigration policy, some historians have been over-influenced by awareness of what historian R.B. Madgwick described as the disproportion of the sexes in the colonies, and the presence of large numbers of young women in the agricultural counties of England who were unable to find employment and would be willing to emigrate.[22]

This explanation for colonial assistance policies always stemmed more from a British perception of colonial need than colonial readings of the same circumstances. The British Colonial Office's Colonial Land and Emigration Commissioners (CLEC), who managed colonial emigration and land policies from the 1840s, saw the apparent disproportion of the sexes in the colonies, with women significantly outnumbered by men, as a primary motivation for facilitating female migration. British concern with colonial sex ratios were also overlain with contemporary notions of Britain's own 'redundant' middle-class women. Despite the class differences, solving the 'problem' of England's redundant women by shipping off the excess to mate with working-class colonial men had an 'appealing symmetry' about it for British government policy makers, but the appeal was largely lost on both the colonists and prospective middle-class emigrants.[23]

Certainly the rhetoric of sexual, hence social, balance had served to justify British-directed and British-funded policies of assisting female migration. A poster from the 1830s was forthcoming about British government intentions, namely encouraging the emigration of

> SINGLE WOMEN to the AUSTRALIAN colonies with the view of reducing the great disparity which exists there between the sexes and of improving their social condition.[24]

We can see the same formula at work in female migration programmes to Western Australia in the 1850s and 1860s. British-funded female migration was part of the convict transportation package negotiated between that colony and Britain, and the British government administration understood the intended outcomes of this programme in the same way as they had understood the female migration programme they had funded in the 1830s: delivering marriage partners to the colony's single working-class men. But this emphasis on the disparity of the sexes largely evaporated once control of colonial emigration and responsibility for payment shifted to colonial hands.[25] From the 1850s and 1860s, as colonial governments one by one implemented their own policies of immigration, they specifically rejected such population-based arguments.

Wives or workers?

The colonists were as familiar with the ideology of the civilising feminine influence as were the British, and certainly the question of the disparity of the sexes and its social consequences was aired in the colonies. On a visit to the Victorian goldfields early in the 1850s, for example, the colony's governor Sir Charles Hotham reported that the diggers lacked 'that grand element of order . . . female society', and that view was shared by other colonial administrators.[26] Ellen Barlee, sister of a Western Australian colonial official and an advocate of female migration, also wrote in 1885 that, 'the Emigration question [had] a twofold purpose – That of obtaining *domestic servants*; the other, respectable wives and mothers for a future generation of Colonists'.[27] However, the message came more frequently from Britain. The CLEC, for example, until its demise in 1873, continued to observe that,

> [t]he small number of female immigrants as compared with male, and the disproportion of the sexes in the colony, is a matter much to be regretted, and deserves the serious attention of the local government.[28]

The message went unheeded, regardless of source. Once colonial governments assumed responsibility for immigration, assisted immigration policies were henceforth framed with all eyes on colonial conditions rather than on British exigencies, and the colonists remained sceptical about CLEC motives.[29] In 1860, for example, the Tasmanian Board of Immigration advised its selection committee in Britain to exercise great care in their selections, noting that

> [i]t is of great consequence that none but first class Immigrants should be engaged; great expense being incurred in introducing them, exceeding £21 a head, and if such a class as those from Reformatories are to be sent out, the Board here might as well at once avail themselves of the services of [the] Land + Emigration Commissioners.[30]

Hobart's *Mercury* similarly recorded, 'England has been accustomed from the first to make of her colonial empire . . . an outlet for more than one "social evil".'[31] Tasmania, as a former convict colony, may have held particularly jaundiced views about the intentions of the British government, but similar views circulated in other colonies.

Other British institutions and individuals also pressed the case, to the constant chagrin of the colonists' migration agents in Britain. When Henry Jordan set out to select single women for domestic service in Queensland in the 1860s he was plagued by well meaning offers from British interest groups, and responded tartly on one occasion,

> An idea prevails that the dearth of labor and of females makes almost anything acceptable, and this is too often encouraged by gentlemen who have been resident in Australia themselves, but have no idea of it as a home for themselves, or their families.[32]

Also in Queensland, a Select Committee inquiry in 1864 into the management of immigration explicitly rejected the demographic argument, on the grounds that female immigrants would not go to outer districts where the majority of male immigrants went, and questioned whether there was in fact any need to increase the number of females in proportion to the number of males.[33] But the argument did not go away. As late as 1892, in response to the London *Evening Standard*'s suggestion that 'surplus' single females should be shipped out to Australia, the *Bulletin* responded tiredly that

> when any country contains two women to every three men, it has as many as can be sufficiently provided for . . . There is no room in Australia for the superfluous women of England.[34]

Long used to acting as the 'dumping ground' for Britain's unwanted, colonists remained wary of any argument which seemed to place British interests before their own.

Part of the issue here was the 'character' or morality of the women the colonists feared the British wanted to ship out, and this concern with character remained paramount when the colonists themselves selected domestic servants for migration. The other question, though, was one of practical and financial management of migration. In the Australian colonial context, assisted female migration programmes operated on a paternalistic basis, with colonial governments assuming responsibility for women in transit and after they arrived in the colonies. Once women passed into their new employer's hands, the government could effectively relinquish this charge, but until that moment, the single women had to be housed, fed and protected, all at colonial government expense.[35] The colonists had neither the facilities nor the desire to introduce single women who could not support themselves immediately on arrival in the colony. Aside from being the only paid work opportunity open to women, domestic service enabled the government to introduce single women into employment which provided both board and lodging.

Nor were there significant employment openings for newly arrived women other than in domestic service. The experiences of middle-class British women who migrated to colonial Australia as governesses, many under the auspices of the Langham Place feminists behind the Female Middle Class Emigration Society, have been well documented.[36] Yet their number was fewer than 300 over several decades; openings were extremely limited. Thus, in 1863, in response to an inquiry from the CLEC, all the Australian colonial governments warned against the private emigration of governesses to the colonies, unless they came to pre-arranged situations.[37] The situation scarcely changed over the decades.

The availability of factory work has been cited as being partly responsible for the dearth of local domestic servants, but here again there were few if any opportunities available for single immigrant women. Colonial Australia was slow to develop any manufacturing industry, factory openings were limited and wages were generally lower than domestic wages. Indeed, they were barely adequate for subsistence. For single women arriving in the colonies without a family behind them (the situation of the very great majority of assisted female immigrants), factory work was an impossible option. According to labour historian T.A. Coghlan, an investigation into the circumstances of female factory workers in Sydney in 1891 indicated that 'the majority of the women workers had homes with their fathers or other relatives' while 'those not so circumstanced were usually compelled to hire cheap lodgings and stint themselves in food'.[38] On Coghlan's figures, a female factory worker earning less than average wages would have had no margin at all after paying for private board and lodging,[39] whereas domestic service offered room and board in addition to a wage. A single woman without a family home to fall back on could not contemplate going into factory work.

Other factors too, served to undercut the 'balance the sexes' justification for single female migration. The relative rates of re-migration of males and females, with women being more likely than men to remain in the colonies; the higher proportion of women amongst nominated immigrants

(immigrants coming out to their families); the distribution and ages of the males and females throughout the colony with a large proportion of females in the cities; and the real difficulties encountered by working men in rural areas who married and started families: all these factors made the issue of the colonial sex ratio less pressing than the British imagined. The inability of women other than domestic servants to find an immediate place in colonial society meant that the colonists' pressing need for domestic labour became the colonial governments' sole justification for assisting female immigration. In practice, the issue of the imbalance of the sexes was of limited relevance. It is unfortunate then that Madgwick's emphasis on the demographic sexual balance which underpinned British schemes in the 1830s has continued to shape understandings of colonially-funded immigration policies in the latter half of the century.

Of course many, even most, immigrant women married, and their marriages exacerbated the domestic service problem in two ways: leaching away the number of women available for hire and creating new families and potentially increasing demand. The immigration of single women as domestic servants had its own multiplier effect on demand, as colonial immigration officials were well aware.

> [F]emale domestic servants of every description . . . *must* be an increasing requirement from the fact of so many who yearly marry and become themselves employers.[40]

Although not all working-class families could aspire to employ a servant, some certainly did. Evidently the 'demands' of the sex ratio compounded the demand for paid domestic labour.

In marrying, female immigrants left the labour market and, it is clear, met the British criterion for desirable immigration by becoming marriage partners for the colonies' single men. Yet in some circumstances colonial governments actually impeded that process; they had paid for female domestic servants and that is what they wanted, regardless of the sexual needs of working-class men (and women). In Tasmania in the 1850s, the Catholic Bishop of Hobart, inquiring on behalf of a parishioner, was advised by the Attorney-General that a female immigrant who married before her employment contract expired was still bound to fulfil her term of service, though this might mean living apart from her husband.[41] Other colonies required immigrant women to repay a contribution towards their passage if they did not work as a domestic servant for a fixed period. Alice Wright and Elizabeth Hancock, who arrived in Western Australia in 1889, were both compelled to repay fifteen pounds passage money to the colonial government when they decided to leave the colony before they had spent twelve months there working as domestic servants.[42]

Working-class women who could not help fill the one existing gap in the female labour market were neither wanted nor needed in the colonies.

Gender alone was never sufficient justification for an assisted passage. Selection agents in Britain were given strict instructions about the age, health and character of single women applying for assisted passage, but ability to work in domestic service and the intention of doing so were equally important. In Western Australia in the 1890s, despite the worsening disparity of the sexes caused by the colony's gold rush that decade, the colonial government refused to permit the assisted immigration of women who did not meet their strict occupational policy. This applied even when women were coming out to family, or to other institutions which could offer them support. Henry Payton, a Perth tailor whose wife kept a few boarders, applied to nominate his sister Mabel, a 25-year-old single woman from Ealing, London, but colonial officials rejected the application, noting that '[w]e do not I should say want to import Governesses or Bookkeepers', Mabel Payton's two occupations.[43] And Bishop Gibney's request to introduce young women from Miss Corless's Nurses Training Institution in Dublin was also rejected that same decade.[44] Gibney's women were not trained exclusively as nurses, and were all of high character and useful in any capacity of household work, according to the Bishop. The official response was, however,

> [t]here is no doubt that the want of nurses is at times greatly felt in Perth, but it is questionable whether there is regular work all the year around that can be depended upon.[45]

So the application was rejected.

It is true colonists were often disappointed, in terms both of the morality of the women despatched and their lack of appropriate domestic experience and suitability for colonial employment. But the two complaints could often coincide. Of the allegedly disreputable women who migrated to Tasmania on the *Aurora Australis* and the *Isles of the South* in the early 1860s, Hobart city missionary J.H. Smales remarked that he would not hire a single one of them.[46] Single women, as mothers of the next generation of colonists, would ideally be women of good character. The more immediate concern, however, was the morality of women who would be living and working as domestics in colonial homes.

Assumptions about the importance of the sex ratio to colonial assistance schemes, shared by British government agencies and historians alike, take the motives of single emigrant women for granted.[47] The complement to the argument that colonial governments introduced women to marry them off is the view that women emigrated *in order* to be married off. This caricature was common in both Britain and the colonies. Yet others writing outside the colonial and imperial context also suggest that employment, not the availability of single men, was a key factor in stimulating the mobility of single working women. Work on domestic service in nineteenth-century France and Britain confirms this view of women workers, with domestics a particularly migratory group.[48] This view is reinforced by personal accounts. The life story of domestic servant Hannah Cullwick, extraordinary not least because it is documented, is none the less typical in its depiction of domestic service as an occupation involving a series of relocations throughout a working life.[49]

Such analyses reveal that 'the history of domestic service in the nineteenth century is the story of urban migration'.[50] It should come as no surprise then, that women emigrating to the Australian colonies chose to stay in the larger towns and cities where employment in domestic service was readily available, rather than heading for rural locations where far more single men, prospective marriage partners, were available. Married country women desperate for servants were well aware of that, and passed their message of complaint on to immigration authorities. In some cases they were listened to, and new arrivals were denied the option of staying in town. Despite the 'lure' of single men, compulsion was sometimes the only way to get immigrant domestic servants to move inland. As Patrick O'Farrell has remarked of the distribution of Irish immigrants in Australia, '[i]n the cities Irish women tended to stay, not merely for social preference, but because these were the locations of their employment in domestic service'.[51]

Conclusion

Single female migration was fundamental to the broader process of nineteenth-century labour migration, and future studies of labour migration should take account of the experiences of the immigrant domestic servant and the general structure of female immigration. Such a process necessitates greater understanding of the value of paid domestic labour in the colonial context. My own earlier comparative work on the six Australian colonies has suggested relative homogeneity on this matter over the period 1860 to 1900, but even a cursory comparison with different periods within Australian history, such as Katrina Alford's discussion of the early colonial period, indicates differences.[52]

Further, the relationship between paid and unpaid domestic labour must underpin any future studies of the value of paid domestic labour. An examination of work undertaken on female migration elsewhere clearly suggests that the emphasis on paid domestic labour identified in the Australian context was not always so marked in other countries. In Canada, for example, Susan Jackel has suggested the importance of what she referred to as 'matrimonial colonization' as the motive behind the introduction of middle-class female immigrants to the Canadian west between 1880 and 1914.[53] Norma Milton has also highlighted the emphasis placed on the availability of husbands in advertising designed to attract single women emigrants to Canada.[54] While single British women were implored to try the Canadian frontier where they would quickly find themselves husbands,

URGENT!

Thousands of nice girls are wanted in THE CANADIAN WEST.

Over 20,000 Men are sighing for what they cannot get–**WIVES** ! *Shame !*

Don't hesitate–COME AT ONCE. If you cannot come, send your sisters.

So great is the demand that anything in skirts stands a chance.

No reasonable offer refused
They are all shy but willing.
All Prizes ! No Blanks.

Hustle up now Girls and don't miss this chance. Some of you will never get another.

Special Application Card from

Plate 8.2 Poster recruiting young women to Canada

that style of entreaty was completely absent from the advertising circulated by Australian colonial governments. Australian advertising from the 1860s focused on high colonial wages and the demand for domestic servants. Men contemplating emigration to New Zealand in the nineteenth century were advised of the value of a '*really useful* woman as a wife', a commodity said to exceed the value even of a thoroughbred horse in the settler's baggage and kit.[55] By contrast, married men in the Australian colonies frequently found their wives and children to be encumbrances when seeking rural employment.[56] Of course, class differences between New Zealand settlers and Australian agricultural labourers should not be overlooked, but this kind of difference also suggests a need to reassess the role played by domestic servants and wives in different regional circumstances.

Work undertaken on female emigration to South Africa suggests other factors still. Cecillie Swaisland has identified four different waves of female emigration across the nineteenth and twentieth centuries, with the demand for single female migrants as domestic servants undercut by the availability of black domestic workers. In this context employment openings for British women, particularly in the twentieth century, lay in the professional arena.[57] On the other hand, Jean Jacques Van-Helten and Keith Williams have argued persuasively that the intention behind planned schemes to facilitate the migration of single British women to the Transvaal in the early twentieth century was to get black men out of domestic service and into the mines; white British women were brought in to take their jobs.[58] The distribution of the population, the degree of urbanisation and the family-based or labour intensive nature of agricultural and rural production, and colonial and imperial race relations are all factors which serve to explain regional differences in the nature of demand for single female immigrants.

Drawing on the Australian context, this chapter has argued the need to reconsider patterns of colonial immigration and of immigrant experience in terms of gender. It calls for a reassessment of the nature of labour migration and a recognition that the ninety thousand or more single working-class women who migrated to the Australian colonies under government assistance schemes in the second half of the nineteenth century did so as paid domestic workers. This intention was pursued single mindedly by the colonial governments which funded the schemes and it ultimately shaped the lives which single immigrant women led. Not bride ships, then, but transports of labour.

Notes

1 S. Jackel (ed.), *A Flannel Shirt and Liberty: British Emigrant Gentlewomen in the Canadian West, 1880–1914*, Vancouver and London, University of British Columbia Press, 1982, p. xxiv.

2 B. Smith, *A Cargo of Women: Susannah Watson and the Convicts of the Princess Royal*, Kensington, NSW, New South Wales University Press, 1988.

3 D. Oxley, *Convict Maids: the Forced Migration of Women to Australia*, Cambridge, Cambridge University Press, 1996; J. Damousi, *Depraved and Disorderly: Female Convicts, Sexuality and Gender in Colonial Australia*, Melbourne, Cambridge University Press, 1997; K. Daniels, *Convict Women*, Sydney, Allen & Unwin, 1998.

4 These figures are based on statistics gathered for my doctoral thesis, J.S. Gothard, 'Government-assisted Migration of Single Women from Britain to Australia, 1860–1900', unpublished Ph.D. thesis, Murdoch University, 1991. It is possible that the number of government-assisted single immigrant women arriving in the Australian colonies between 1850 and 1900 could have been as high as one hundred thousand.

5 D. E. Darbyshire, *In Time for Lunch: the Personal Diary and the Official Journal of Douglas E. Darbyshire, Surgeon-in-charge of the Young Women Emigrants Sailing in the S.S. Cornwall from England to Australia, 1898*, Fremantle, Fremantle Arts Centre Press, 1991, p. 91.

6 'Immigration (Report of the agent for immigration on complaints as to manner of hiring immigrants per S.S. "Parthia")', New South Wales, *Votes and Proceedings of the Legislative Assembly*, 1885–6, vol. 2, pp. 867–868; *Sydney Morning Herald*, 21 January 1886.

7 G. F. Wise to principal under secretary, 30 January 1886, 4/4662, Archives Office of New South Wales.

8 *Western Mail*, September 1897; press collection, Fawcett Library, London.

9 For example, R.E.N. Twopeny, *Town Life in Australia*, Harmondsworth, Penguin, 1973, first published 1883; C.J. Rowe, 'Housekeeping Troubles in the Australian Colonies', *Westminster Review*, vol. 134, 1890, pp. 509–514; M. Sanger Evans, 'Domestic Servants in Australia: a Rejoinder', *Westminster Review*, vol. 136, 1891, pp. 46–53.

10 W. A. Sinclair, 'Women at Work in Melbourne and Adelaide since 1871', *Economic Record*, vol. 57, no. 159, December 1981, p. 351; B. Kingston, *My Wife, My Daughter and Poor Mary Ann*, Melbourne, Nelson, 1975, chapter 4.

11 Kingston, *My Wife*, especially chapter 3, 'The Servant Problem'; B. Kingston, 'Poor Mary Ann: Domestic Service as a Career for Girls in Australia in the Late Nineteenth Century', *Refractory Girl*, no. 7, November 1974, pp. 4–9; M. Barbalet, *Far From a Low Gutter Girl: the Forgotten World of State Wards South Australia 1887–1940*, Melbourne, Oxford University Press, 1983; W. A. Sinclair, 'Women at Work in Melbourne and Adelaide since 1871', *Economic Record*, vol. 57, no. 159, December 1981, pp. 344–353; W. A. Sinclair, 'Women and Economic Change in Melbourne 1871–1921', *Historical Studies*, vol. 20, no. 79, October 1982, pp. 278–291; C. Fox, *Working Australia*, North Sydney, Allen & Unwin, 1991, pp. 66–72, 190.

12 A. Curthoys, 'History in a Vacuum: a review of Katrina Alford, *Production or Reproduction? An Economic History of Women in Australia, 1788–1850*, Oxford University Press, 1984', *Hecate*, vol. 10, no. 1, 1984, p. 77.

13 P. Hamilton, *'No Irish Need Apply': Aspects of the Employer–Employee Relationship in Australian Domestic Service 1860–1900*, London, Working Papers in Australian Studies, 1985.

14 Shirley Fisher, 'The Pastoral Interest and Sydney's Public Health', *Historical Studies*, vol. 20, no. 78, April 1982, p. 75.

15 See A. Phizacklea (ed.), *One Way Ticket: Migration and Female Labour*, London and Melbourne, Routledge & Kegan Paul, 1983; *International Migration Review*, Special Issue: *Women in Migration*, vol. 18, no. 4, Winter 1984. See also J.T. Fawcett, Siew-Ean Khoo and P. C. Smith (eds), *Women in the Cities of Asia: Migration and Urban Adaption*, Boulder, CO, Westview Press, 1984.

16 M. Morokvasic, 'Women in Migration: Beyond the Reductionist Outlook', in Phizacklea, *One Way Ticket*, pp. 13–31.

17 Morokvasic, 'Women in Migration', pp. 13–15. See also V. N. Thadani and M. P. Todaro, 'Female Migration: a Conceptual Framework', in Fawcett, Khoo and Smith, *Women in the Cities of Asia*, p. 36.
18 Morokvasic, 'Women in Migration', p. 18.
19 Caroline Chisholm has been the subject of two book-length biographies. See M. Kiddle, *Caroline Chisholm*, Melbourne, Melbourne University Press, 1950; M. Hoban, *Fifty-one Pieces of Wedding Cake: a Biography of Caroline Chisholm*, Melbourne, Polding Press, 1984.
20 E. Richards, 'Annals of the Australian Immigrant', in E. Richards, R. Reid and D. Fitzpatrick, *Visible Immigrants: Neglected Sources for the History of Australian Immigration*, Canberra, Research School of Social Sciences, 1989, p. 13.
21 C. McConville, 'Peopling the Place Again', in V. Burgmann and J. Lee (eds), *A Most Valuable Acquisition: a People's History of Australia Since 1788*, Melbourne, McPhee Gribble/Penguin, 1988, p. 78.
22 R. B. Madgwick, *Immigration into Eastern Australia 1788–1851*, Sydney, Sydney University Press, 1969, p. 92 (first published 1937).
23 The phrase comes from C. Macdonald, *A Woman of Good Character: Single Women as Immigrant Settlers in Nineteenth-century New Zealand*, Wellington, Allen & Unwin/ Historical Branch, 1990, p. 8.
24 Public Record Office (London) CO 384/35 (10), cited in P. Sharpe, 'Female Emigration Schemes to Australia in the 1830s', *Essex Journal*, Spring 1994, p. 16.
25 This oversimplifies forty years of complex policies in six colonies. Victoria and Western Australia are particularly complicated. The intricacies of policy are beyond the scope of this paper but have been analysed in detail in Gothard, 'Government-assisted migration'.
26 G. Serle, *The Golden Age: a History of the Colony of Victoria, 1851–1861*, Melbourne, Melbourne University Press, 1963, p. 157.
27 Miss Barlee to crown agents, 26 March 1885, 'Letters Advocating the Establishment of a Training Home for Girls with the Object of Supplying the Demand for Female Servants', Western Australia, *Votes and Proceedings of the Legislative Council*, 1885, p. 622 (emphasis in original).
28 '29th General Report of the Emigration Commissioners' (hereafter, '29th report of the CLEC'), *British Parliamentary Papers* (hereafter *BPP*), 1868–1869, XVII, 119, p. 29.
29 See J. Gothard, '"Pity the Poor Immigrant": Assisted Single Female Migration to Colonial Australia', in E. Richards (ed.), *Poor Australian Immigrants in the Nineteenth Century*, Canberra, Research School of Social Sciences, 1991, pp. 97–116, for a discussion of the impact of the emigration priorities of the CLEC, and of private philanthropic emigrationists, on colonial government attitudes to female immigration after the 1850s.
30 Board of Immigration to Committee Members, 14 February 1860, CB 7/5/2, Archives Office of Tasmania (hereafter AOT).
31 *Mercury*, 28 December 1860.
32 Henry Jordan to Colonial Secretary, 27 October 1862, COL/12, Queensland State Archives.
33 Evidence of Henry Jordan, 'Minutes of Evidence before the Select Committee into the Resignation and Return of the Emigration Commissioner, 1864', Queensland, *Votes and Proceedings of the Legislative Assembly*, second session, pp. 1048, 1049.
34 *Bulletin*, 12 March 1892, p. 6, quoted in N. Hicks, *'This Sin and Scandal': Australia's Population Debate 1891–1911*, Canberra, Australian National University Press, 1978, pp. 104–105.

35 Further elaboration is beyond the scope of this chapter. It is dealt with more fully in J. Gothard, *Blue China: Single Female Migration to Colonial Australia,* Melbourne, Melbourne University Press, 2001.
36 A. J. Hammerton, *Emigrant Gentlewomen: Genteel Poverty and Female Migration 1830–1914*, Canberra, Australian National University Press, 1979; P. Clarke, *The Governesses: Letters from the Colonies 1862–1882*, Hawthorn, Vic., Hutchinson, 1985.
37 '23rd Report of the CLEC', *BPP*, 1863, XV, 247, pp. 13–14. See also *The Times*, 26 April 1862.
38 T.A. Coghlan, *Labour and Industry in Australia: From the First Settlement of 1788 to the Establishment of the Commonwealth in 1901*, London and Melbourne, Oxford University Press, 1918, vol. 3, pp. 1589–1590.
39 Coghlan, *Labour and Industry*, p. 1589.
40 'Report of the Immigration Agent for 1858', Victoria, *Papers Presented to Parliament*, 1859–1860, vol. 3, no.6, p. 9 (emphasis in original).
41 Gothard, 'Government-assisted Migration'; R.W. Willson to Colonial Secretary, Tasmania, 23 July 1855; Colonial Secretary's Office to Rt Revd Bishop Willson, 7 August 1855, CSD 1/56/1192, AOT.
42 Board of Immigration Meeting, 30 December 1889, ACC.489/5, Public Records Office of Western Australia (hereafter PROWA).
43 Application by Henry J. Payton, Form A, notes on form, colonial secretary to under secretary, 12 August 1895, box 5, ACC.553, PROWA.
44 Bishop Parry to Colonel Forbes, secretary, immigration board, 24 August 1891, box 5, ACC.553, PROWA.
45 Correspondence from Miss Corless's Nurses Training Institution, May 1894, notes on file, Octavius Burt to colonial secretary, 24 July 1894, 1243/94, ACC.527, PROWA.
46 Evidence of J.H. Smales, 'Select Committee into Immigration for 1861', Tasmania, *House of Assembly Journals*, 1861, vol. 7, no. 150, p. 10.
47 See, for example, K. Alford, *Production or Reproduction? An Economic History of Women in Australia, 1788–1850*, Melbourne, Oxford University Press, 1984, p. 98.
48 T. M. McBride, *The Domestic Revolution: the Modernisation of Household Service in England and France 1820–1920,* London, Holmes & Meier, 1976, p. 47. See also A. W. Worthington, 'On the Unequal Proportion between the Male and Female Population of some Manufacturing and Other Towns', *Journal of the Statistical Society of London*, vol. 30, 1867, pp. 68–79; E. G. Ravenstein, 'The Laws of Migration', *Journal of the Statistical Society*, vol. 48, 1885, pp. 167–235; and 'The Laws of Migration' (second paper), *Journal of the Statistical Society*, vol. 52, 1889, pp. 241–305.
49 L. Stanley (ed.), *The Diaries of Hannah Cullwick, Victorian Maidservant*, London, Virago Press, 1984.
50 McBride, *The Domestic Revolution*, p. 34.
51 P. O'Farrell, *The Irish in Australia*, Kensington, NSW, New South Wales University Press, 1986, p. 85.
52 Gothard, 'Government-assisted Migration'; J. S. Gothard, '"Radically Unsound and Mischievous": Female Migration to Tasmania, 1856–1863', *Australian Historical Studies*, vol. 23, 1989; Alford, *Production or Reproduction?*, p. 87.
53 Jackel, *A Flannel Shirt and Liberty*, p. xvii.
54 N. Milton, 'Essential Servants: Immigrant Domestics on the Canadian Prairies, 1885–1930', in S. Armitage and E. Jameson (eds), *The Women's West*, Norman and London, University of Oklahoma Press, 1987, pp. 208–209.
55 C. Macdonald, 'Ellen Silk and her Sisters: Female Emigration to the New World', in London Feminist History Group, *The Sexual Dynamics of History: Men's Power, Women's Resistance*, London and Leichhardt, NSW, Pluto Press, 1983, p. 72 (emphasis in original).

56 Alford, *Production or Reproduction?*, pp. 185, 188.
57 C. Swaisland, *Servants and Gentlewomen to the Golden Land: the Emigration of Single Women from Britain to Southern Africa, 1820–1939*, Oxford and Pietermaritzburg, Berg Publishers/University of Natal Press, 1993, pp. 7–8.
58 J. J. Van-Helten and K. Williams, '"The Crying Need of South Africa": the Emigration of Single British Women to the Transvaal, 1901–10', *Journal of Southern African Studies*, vol. 10, 1983.

9 A historical perspective on female migrants

Motivations and strategies of nineteenth-century Hessians

Simone A. Wegge

Introduction: nineteenth-century female migrants from Europe

In many well-known studies of nineteenth-century European emigration, especially those focusing on quantitative analysis, historians have paid less attention to female migrants than to male migrants.[1] We know, for instance, very little about such observable characteristics as their age, occupation and destination. As a consequence we can infer very little about their motivation for leaving home or the strategies they used to achieve their migration goals. We know much more about the men who left Europe, partly because men dominated the international migration flows in the nineteenth century and until the 1920s. Most emigrant populations were well over 50 per cent men,[2] which differs quite remarkably from many contemporary migrant populations.[3]

In addition, existing data sources have done little to reverse our lack of knowledge about female emigrants. Most immigration statistics available to historians are in the form of flow data, not individual-level data. Thus, the standard reference on historical immigration statistics for the nineteenth century, Ferenczi and Willcox (1929), refers to men and women only in passing, providing very little information specifically about either gender.[4] Where data on individuals are available, such as in the case of the US passenger records, information on occupation does indeed exist for women but not for all of the adult women travelling.[5] Similarly, other types of micro data, such as local emigration statistics or European port statistics, describe many married women merely as wives and attribute occupation and property to the male heads of household, even in the case of a family enterprise such as a farm.[6] Fortunately, women migrating by themselves are recorded in most of these micro data sources in some more detail. Of course, very practical reasons can exist for the lack of more studies on women. The study of immigrant assimilation, for instance, involves following individuals through time. This is more difficult in the case of women, since many would marry and change their surnames. It is thus not surprising that the most sophisticated study to date of nineteenth-century US immigrant wealth and occupational mobility concerns men exclusively.[7]

Migration data effectively underrepresent women's economic contribution in the same way as many types of historical labour statistics do, given that most historic societies defined women in terms of their husbands or fathers.[8] The net effect is that many of the studies on the largest emigrant groups of the nineteenth century, such as the English, the Irish, the Germans and the Italians, do not address the role women played in any significant way. For the purposes of studying migration behaviour, the underreporting of occupational information for women is unfortunate, since occupational statistics are often used to infer motive. As scholars we must be careful not to assume too readily that women usually migrated within a family or played only a minor role in the actual decision to move.

Existing qualitative studies of the female migration experience tend to focus on women's lives after the move, as immigrants.[9] Most of this research is based on isolated case studies. Although case studies illustrate human phenomena one cannot retrieve from data, such work does not usually provide a guide to the possible degree of representation of each experience. My work here is based on a new source of micro data on German emigrants covering over 50,000 individuals who left their homeland between 1832 and 1857, mostly for the United States. Using large data samples I address how women pursued their migration goals in a region of heavy emigration in the nineteenth century, the principality of Hesse-Cassel. I have used these data to study other issues related to migration behaviour.[10]

What we do know about women is that they typically migrated with their families and less often alone in the nineteenth century.[11] Among German emigrants, families tended to establish themselves permanently in the New World, as suggested by the gender imbalance of returnees, in which men were even more overrepresented than the emigrant populations themselves.[12] A similar relationship between the propensity for permanent settlement and family and female migration exists among other national migrant groups, namely the Italians.[13] Even though women were much less likely to return to their homelands than men, female return migration rates fluctuated in a similar fashion to the return migration rates of men. This pattern is evident for American immigrants in the latter half of the nineteenth century and the early part of the twentieth century.[14] Differential return rates provided a counterweight to the gender imbalance in emigration rates, so that after the mid-nineteenth century the foreign-born population in the United States was always more equally divided between men and women. Between 1850 and 1930, foreign-born women made up 43 to 46 per cent of the foreign-born population in the United States, a higher proportion than they represented in the annual immigrant populations throughout this period.[15]

In the nineteenth century, women may have been slightly more likely than men to move within their homelands. Women's preference for staying within their country's borders served as the basis for one of Ravenstein's famous migration laws, which states that women dominate internal migration.[16] Ravenstein's laws or, more aptly, hypotheses, are based on statistical observations and do not originate from any fully developed model of human behaviour.[17] The veracity of Ravenstein's laws notwithstanding, several works on migration have shown that female internal migration rates were indeed higher than for males. In parts of Germany, for instance, Hochstadt shows that internal migration rates for women were higher than those for men.[18] The evidence for another large migrant donor, England, lends weaker support to Ravenstein's internal migration hypothesis, as Baines demonstrates that internal migration rates were often equal or only slightly higher for women.[19] Not all studies on British emigration concur, however.[20] Irish migration patterns serve as a counter-example to Ravenstein's idea, as they exhibited very little internal migration and much overseas migration. Overseas moves for Irish women were about equal to those of men, and in some decades even higher.[21]

Still, much of what we know about female migrants is based on aggregate statistics on migration flows or on case studies of individual movers, but not on large micro data samples. Micro data on migrants have the advantage of providing detailed information about individual migrants from which one can address issues regarding their demographic characteristics and their possible motivations to leave. A larger data sample makes one's findings more precise. This chapter extends the literature on nineteenth-century female migration by examining a new large source of micro data on emigrants, collected at the level of the individual. The data studied in this chapter concern over 50,000 different emigrants who left the German principality of Hesse-Cassel between 1832 and 1857. Of these, 14,900 can be identified as women. As an important source of emigrant data gathered in the home country of the emigrants, it illustrates for women the link between family role and economic identity as well as the male-orientation typical of many existing primary sources on historical migrations. I compare women migrating alone to women migrating with family, examining individual characteristics and the use of family networks to explore the motivations of female migrants. From these unique data, one can explain better women's reasons for abandoning their homelands and the particular strategies they may have used.

The focus on German emigration is relevant for the study of mass emigration from Europe between 1815 and 1930, during which time over 60 per cent of European migrants settled in the United States. After 1853 and until the mid-1890s, German emigrants constituted the largest group of emigrants arriving annually in the US.[22] Thus, in absolute numbers, German migrants dominated the American immigration flows for many decades. Before the 1880s, Germans came primarily from Baden,

Württemberg, the Palatinate and the various Hessian states. Some of the highest regional emigration rates in Germany were those of the principality of Hesse-Cassel. For the other large national groups during the age of mass migration, the Irish, the British, the Italians, the Russians and the Spaniards, very little micro data exist in the homelands of these many millions of migrants.[23] Women, moreover, made up approximately 40 per cent of German emigrants, a higher proportion than for most emigrant populations.[24] This means that samples of German emigrant populations provide a good represention of women, enough to study many of the interesting patterns and characteristics of female migration behaviour. In this chapter I first describe the data on female migrants from the principality of Hesse-Cassel. I then discuss what we can and we cannot learn from these data about the motivations and strategies of European women to leave their homeland in the mid-nineteenth century.

Female emigrants from Hesse-Cassel: the data

The principality or electorate of Hesse-Cassel occupied the northern and eastern areas of the present-day state of Hesse in Germany. Map 9.1 shows the area in relation to the rest of Germany. This area of Europe shared many of the same problems that prevented other countries from experiencing economic growth, particularly a heavy reliance on agricultural production and a series of rulers and governments that did little to promote the needs of their subjects.[25] Many historical accounts describe Hesse-Cassel as poor and backward, especially Auerbach (1993), Bovensiepen (1909), Möker (1977), and Kukowski (1995), who offers the most in-depth study of Hessian poverty. The principality contained only a handful of urban centres with populations greater than 5,000, but it bordered on the free city of Frankfurt, which exerted a positive economic force on the Hessian economy. Over three-quarters of the population was involved in agriculture.[26] Many who wanted to work as artisans were constrained by the antiquated guild laws, which permitted most artisan professions to be practised only in the few towns which were officially designated as a city or *Städt*. The many hundreds of remaining communities were permitted only a few types of less-skilled craftsmen, such as blacksmiths and carpenters.[27] Hessians may have been poor, but levels of illiteracy were very low in Hesse-Cassel as a result of Hessian rulers' emulation of progressive Prussian education policies.[28]

Female emigrants from this area have been studied in previous work, specifically Auerbach (1993) and Assion (1991). Auerbach's work discusses in very interesting detail the many different types of migrations that took place from Hesse-Cassel in the eighteenth and nineteenth centuries. Her study is based on the extensive archival holdings of the Hessian *Staatsarchiv*, from which she recounts the actual migration experiences of hundreds of individuals and families, and in the process describes the goals of many

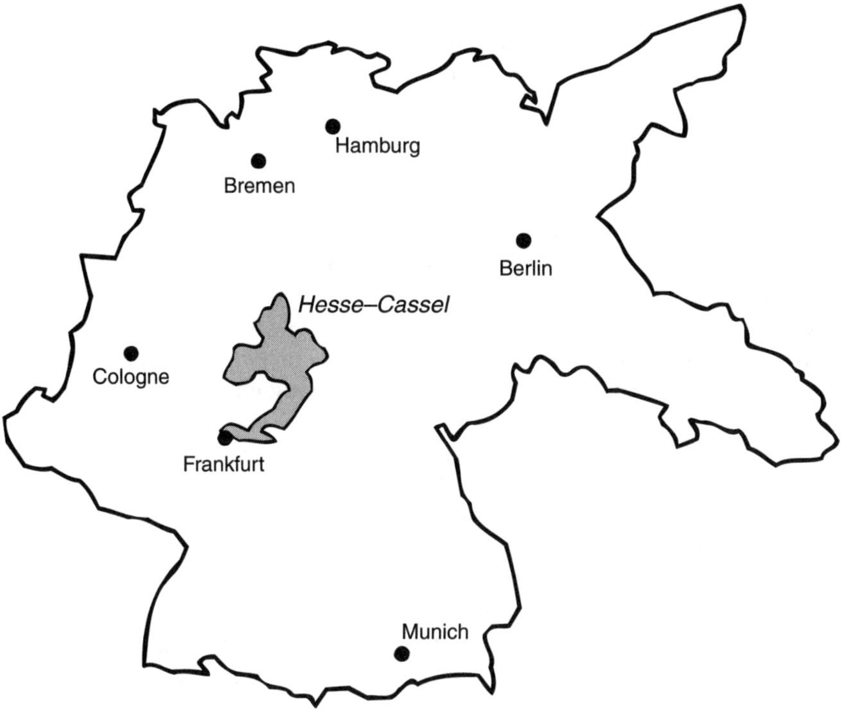

Map 9.1 The German Confederation exclusive of Austria, 1815

migrants and the economic and social circumstances they faced.[29] In contrast, Assion (1991) is a more quantitative study of Hessian passengers who left from the port of Hamburg for overseas destinations between 1855 and 1866.[30] The Assion study offers a convenient comparison for my study of Hesse-Cassel emigrants, especially since the majority of the emigrants in that sample were from the principality of Hesse-Cassel. The Hamburg emigrants should share important similarities with the emigrants in the emigrant permit lists of Hesse-Cassel.[31]

The Hesse-Cassel emigrant permit lists

The emigrant permit lists I use in this chapter serve as a unique source of micro data on nineteenth-century European emigrants who left mostly for the United States. The lists exist as a result of the concerns of government officials, who wanted to have some way to monitor how much currency emigrants departed with and to deter emigration of those with outstanding debts or incomplete military service.[32] Above all, authorities were concerned with preventing men in their late teens and early twenties from leaving without having served their requisite time in the military. Women did not have to serve in the military. As a result, very few men in their early twenties but many women of the same age left the principality.

The existing permit lists for the years 1832 to 1857 cover over 50,000 different emigrants and provide the following variables of observation: surname and first name (or relationship to head of household); year and sometimes month of departure; village of origin; country of destination; travelling status (alone or with family); age; occupation; cash being taken (including in some cases a future inheritance). Through the use of archival codes that exist for each emigrant record and extensive data manipulation, I have determined other characteristics, including: gender and the legal status of the emigrant.[33] By the 1850s, many emigrants were leaving without filing an emigrant permit, prompting Hessian authorities to keep records on the illegal emigrants as well. Among the different subsets of women, a large variance exists in the percentage of those who left legally, which seems to be partially a problem of how information on women was or was not recorded, making the analysis of why different women were more prone to leaving legally or illegally rather unfruitful.[34]

Several of the variables, such as surname, year of departure, village and country of destination, are known for all emigrants. The other variables, month of departure, age, occupation and exported cash, are not provided for each emigrant. In many cases this is just a matter of missing data. Information on cash assets and occupation, however, existed primarily for the male heads of the household. So even for the individuals travelling alone, records tend to be more complete for the men than for the women.

Examples of these data, a family and two women and a widow, are shown in Table 9.1. One can see the possible ways that women show up in the records, as a wife or daughter of the head of household travelling within a family group, as a widow taking three family members with her, and as a woman migrating by herself on the journey to a foreign destination. Clearly the data provide most information on adult men. In comparison to women moving with husbands or fathers, however, the records are more complete when a woman was emigrating alone or served as a head of household for a departing emigrant group. As one can see from the example in Table 9.1, married women were recorded by nineteenth-century authorities in two ways, as a wife or by their first name. Unfortunately, they were sometimes not recorded at all, but it is difficult to distinguish in each case whether the women who were wives actually went and are truly missing from the data or whether they stayed at home or were deceased.[35]

Approximately 14,900 women emigrated from Hesse-Cassel. Table 9.2 lists all the various ways in which women were described by name in the data. Women were referred to most frequently by their own first name,

Table 9.1 Examples of records in the emigrant permit lists, Hesse-Cassel, 1832–1857

Travel group	*Village/Kreis*	*Surname*	*First name*	*Date*	*Goal*	*Age*	*Job*	*Cash*	*Family*
1	Wehrda/MR	Becker	Christine	1852	AN	44			99
1	Wehrda/MR	Becker	Wife of Johann Peter	1852	AN				99
1	Wehrda/MR	Becker	Johann Peter	1852	AN	44	TI	T 40	99
1	Wehrda/MR	Becker	Son of Johann Peter	1852	AN	1			99
1	Wehrda/MR	Becker	Daughter of Johann Peter	1852	AN	2			99
2	Floh/SM	Brill	Widow of Heinrich	1853	AN			T 170	3
3	Allmus/FD	Druecker	Christina	1856	AN		AR	T 5	
4	Albungen/ESW	Berg	Helene	1856MR	ANY		TG	T 0	

Source: Hessiches Staatsarchiv Marburg, HESAUS data, 1832–1857.

Notes
Kreis This stands for district or county. There were 21 *Kreise* in Hesse-Cassel.
Date 'MR' stands for March.
Goal 'AN' is North America; in almost all cases, USA. 'ANY' is New York City.
Job 'TI' stands for cabinet maker or carpenter. 'AR' stands for factory worker. 'TG' stands for labourer.
Cash Given in Thaler (a Thaler was worth US$0.70).
Family '99' indicates that the emigrants are travelling with family. '3' indicates this person took three others with her. (The only emigrants travelling alone are Christina Druecker and Helene Berg in Groups 3 and 4 respectively.)

Table 9.2 The recording of women in the Hesse-Cassel emigrant permit lists, 1832–1857

Reference style	*Frequency*	*Travelling with family*	*Travelling alone*
Own first name	8,500	2,662	5,838
Wife	3,192	3,119	73
Daughter of an adult	2,788	2,763	25
Illegitimate daughter	1	1	0
Daughter of a widow	25	24	1
Widow	366	254	112
Mother	4	4	0
Sister	19	19	0
Mother-in-law	4	3	1
Stepdaughter	2	2	0
Total (N)	*14,901*	*8,851*	*6,050*

Source: Hessiches Staatsarchiv Marburg, HESAUS data, 1832–1857.

followed by the association of wife of a particular man, then daughter of a particular adult, and then as a widow. The familial associations cited reflected by and large an existing relationship with another male person emigrating at the same point in time. The recording of children transcends gender, as a high percentage of young men travelling with fathers were likewise referred to as sons of a particular departing adult. But men were never listed as a husband or widower of a particular woman. Describing so many adult women in terms of their relationship to a man reflects at the very least the perspective of nineteenth-century Hessian authorities in addition to other cultural and economic norms of this place and time. In addition, much of what these bureaucrats cared about, the evasion of military service or outstanding debts and the export of cash, concerned men very centrally. Implicitly it reflects also one society's view on property rights, a set of economic and social benefits that could easily be assigned unequally across gender. Interestingly enough, the Hamburg port lists, in contrast, record female emigrants by their first names, regardless of age or marital status, but these lists were kept for different reasons and did not keep track of emigrant assets. They still manage to record most married women's occupations as 'wife'.

In the case that a woman travelled alone or as the sole head of household, she would be referred to most commonly by her first name. Essentially, a woman travelling alone was listed very differently in the data: only 30 per cent of those travelling with family were referred to by their first names, but of those travelling alone over 96 per cent are listed in the records under their first names, in essence like a head of household. Occupational information for women travelling alone is also more complete, partly because these women were more likely to be formally employed. In contrast, occupational information is rarely available for wives travelling with husbands.

The emigrant records show a high incidence of emigrant families headed by men without wives, suggesting that some wives may have been left off the lists.[36] Still, it is difficult to ascertain exactly how many, since some wives were referred to by their first name without an age and are thus indistinguishable from daughters. Further, some wives migrated later, once their husbands had set themselves up in the new homeland.[37]

To obtain a rough estimate of how many women are missing one can compare these data with those of the Assion study on Hamburg passengers. Assion (1991) has argued that the Hamburg lists have the advantage of recording all of the women who emigrated, unlike the sources in the home regions. The average percentage of women in the Hamburg data between 1855 and 1866 was 40.2; in addition, there is no upward trend in this percentage, as 41.3 per cent of the emigrants in 1855 and 42.5 per cent in 1856 were women. Of the Hesse-Cassel emigrant permit lists, women comprised a slightly lower percentage of the total: 35.1 per cent in 1852, 25.3 per cent in 1853, 34.5 per cent in 1854, 35.7 per cent in 1855, 37.9 per cent in 1856, and 38.4 per cent in 1857. While the percentage of women emigrants increases over time, it is slightly lower than the figures for the emigrants who left from Hamburg. This indicates a possible undercounting of 14 per cent for 1855 and 11 per cent for 1856 in the Hesse-Cassel data.[38] It is unclear how many of these were wives.

One can easily speak of a feminisation of the Hessian emigrant population. Women became an increasingly larger proportion of the total group of emigrants in the 1850s, an upward trend that had started in the 1840s. The change occurred not only on the basis of gender but also in terms of family composition. Before the 1850s it was rare for women to leave on their own, but the number doing so in 1857 constituted almost a threefold increase from ten years earlier. The feminisation of American immigrant populations has been described in similar but broader terms.[39] Newly established ethnic migrations tended to be dominated by men, with higher percentages of women arriving in later decades, once a migration tradition had been established.[40]

Female emigrants from Hesse-Cassel: possible family strategies of women emigrants

The most important motives for these German emigrants, as for most nineteenth-century European emigrants, were economic, and in the case of young men, there was the added objective of evading military service. In comparison, the yearning for greater religious freedom was a secondary concern. Emigrants left with the idea that they would enjoy a higher standard of living and possibly greater chances of upward mobility in the new country than they could expect at home. Constraints were very important as well in predicting who might go and who might stay home. Those without the financial assets and savings to pay for the move stayed home, unless they could acquire assistance from their communities or from relatives at home or in their destination. Hessian labourers, for instance, left in droves but were underrepresented in terms of their total number in the general population. They were thus less likely to leave, which I explain partly on the basis of their inability to afford the move.[41] Some families and individuals may have been interested in starting a new life elsewhere but faced challenges in adapting to a new economy. Hessian farmers, like labourers, were less likely to leave. The farmers who left, unlike the labourers, could easily afford it, as they were taking relatively large amounts of cash with them.[42] Artisans, in comparison with farmers and labourers, were more likely to migrate and could easily transport their most important asset – their skills.[43] Such factors, the expected economic return on migration or one's prospects in the new homeland, financial constraints and possible difficulties in converting one's physical capital into a portable form, all influenced the relative propensities of different individuals to leave, no matter what their occupation or social standing. There were other important socioeconomic factors that influenced the decision to leave or stay. The incentive to migrate differed across inheritance regime, and previous migrants from the same village were also very influential in encouraging more friends and relatives to move overseas.[44]

For the most part women had access to a higher standard of living through their relations and through marriage. The majority of female emigrants, about 60 per cent, moved with male family members, just like many other Europeans.[45] These men and women then together faced migration decisions influenced by the hard economic realities described above. The other 40 per cent left unaccompanied, with a plan to join previous migrants or await subsequent migrants from the homeland. About half of these solo travellers can be linked to a relative with the same last name and from the same village who left in a different year. Many of these women were not as alone as might first appear, and with the identification of matrilineal relationships many more would have been found to be part of a family migration network. A more precise definition of a family migration network is provided later in this chapter. Still, many of the women travelling alone were taking on particular risks. Women for the most part did not have access to higher-paying skilled professions at home. Guild ordinances, for instance, forbade women to be employed in most lines of artisan work.[46] But they still had to worry about how to pay for the passage and whether the pay-off to migrating would be positive in the sense of a new job or a husband or both. For unmarried female migrants chances for marriage served as an important vehicle towards economic prosperity and were most likely a key motive in leaving their homeland.[47] As in other German regions, Hessian marriage laws prohibited

Table 9.3 Characteristics of male and female emigrants, Hesse-Cassel, 1832–1857

Category by family and/or travel mode	*Networked (%)*	*Network groups: Group 1 – Group 2 – Group 3*	*Going to US (%)*	*Legal status, % legal*
Women, with family	40.1	32 – 47 – 14	92.9	56.1
Sample size	8,851	3,312	8,784	4,749
Women, alone	48.2	30 – 45 – 16	97.5	2.6
Sample size	6,050	2,654	6,001	4,558
Wives, with family	39.2	27 – 50 – 16	92.6	65
Sample size	3,118	1,143	3,105	2,171
Wives, alone	50.7	27 – 49 – 16	94.5	16
Sample size	73	34	73	57
Daughters, w/family	40.8	28 – 49 – 15	93.3	59.6
Sample size	2,784	1,036	2,771	1,878
Daughters, alone	46.2	–	92.3	50.0
Sample size	26	–	26	16
Widows, w/family	49.8	22 – 53 – 16	97.8	29.7
Sample size	279	125	276	202
Widows, alone	42.0	13 – 53 – 21	96.4	2.0
Sample size	112	41	112	98
Men, alone	47.0	42 – 39 – 13	80.2	62.5
Sample size	18,086	8,500	17,834	9,729
Sons, w/family	39.1	27 – 49 – 15	92.2	67.3
Sample size	2,764	989	2,756	1,861

Source: Hessiches Staatsarchiv Marburg, HESAUS data, 1832–1857.

couples from legally marrying if they could not provide evidence that they could support themselves financially. Given the limited employment options open to women, the search for a marriage partner was based, at least partially, on economic concerns.

As mentioned above, the records are more complete in regards to the women who were employed and migrated alone, which included both those who never married or were widowed.[48] These are the women one suspects were more likely to have acted independently; their migration behaviour is thus of great interest. Understanding female migration is best done by classifying the women in the types of groups they left in and in their respective roles within those groups. Below I analyse each group separately: wives, widows, daughters and women travelling alone (typically unmarried). Although I identified 60 per cent of the women as travelling with family members, I suspect that more women left with relatives but were missed by the data collectors. In any case the sample sizes are very large for each group and can provide significant clues about either population.[49] My findings reflect primarily what I have found for women who left in the 1850s, since few women left in the 1830s or 1840s. Unfortunately, this dearth of information on women emigrants in the earlier decades means less can be said about changes over time.

Women travelling with family

Wives and mothers

My discussion of wives is limited to those who were identified as 'Wife of . . .' with the blank filled in with their husband's name. Many wives were referred to by their first names, but these women are not easily identified as wives. Still, my sample of wives includes 3,119 different women, of whom 98 per cent travelled with family. The majority of wives travelling in 1852 or later were classified as legal emigrants. This is very different from the men and women travelling alone, who constituted the bulk of the illegal population, perhaps because they could leave in a less noticeable way.

The modal age group for wives was 36 to 40, and very few wives were younger than 27 (Table 9.4).[50] A cursory glance at the Hamburg lists in Assion (1991) shows quite similarly several wives in their early twenties but many married women in their thirties and forties. Women may have been slightly more likely to emigrate at an age when their families had saved up or inherited enough to afford the migration costs or when they expected to welcome few additional children into the family. It may also reflect a late age at marriage.

Many of the interesting family details, especially those related to social status and wealth, were ascribed to their husbands. For the most part wives who left with their husbands did not report that they were leaving with cash assets, since any cash the family owned was recorded with the male head of household. Wives leaving without the company of husbands, on the other hand, were some of the poorest emigrants, with the exception of those women who travelled with family members, as Tables 9.5–9.6 show. But wives leaving by themselves were usually joining family members at the destination and did not need much in cash except for the travel costs.

Married women undoubtedly worked alongside their husbands, especially in the case of farm households, but one would never gather this from the Hessian emigrant permit lists. Over 3,000 women were identified as wives, and occupations were identified for only 33 of these women. Such a small sample size warrants our examining the types of occupations that show up. Wives were listed as farmers, labourers, midwives and seamstresses, with labourer as the modal job, as one can see in Table 9.7. 'Labourer' was a catch-all label for various job descriptions including servant, farm labourer, maid, manual worker (*Handarbeiter*) and even seamstress. Unfortunately, the Hesse-Cassel data do not distinguish between these different jobs.

In several instances, wives were listed with the same occupation as their husbands, and such cases included tailors, painters, labourers, goldsmiths and shoemakers. Wives with occupations different from their husbands

Table 9.4 Age distribution of Hesse-Cassel emigrants, 1832–1857

Age groups	*All women travelling with family, under 19 (%)*	*All women travelling with family, over 18 (%)*	*All women travelling alone (%)*	*Wives travelling with family (%)*	*Widows travelling with family (%)*	*Daughters travelling with family (%)*	*Men travelling alone (%)*	*Sons travelling with family (%)*
0–1	16.5	–	1.5	–	–	25.2	0.2	21.4
2–3	13.8	–	3.6	–	–	14.6	0.1	18.3
4–5	12.7	–	0.7	–	–	12.0	0.1	10.2
6–9	21.1	–	2.2	–	–	18.1	0.4	19.8
10–13	20.9	–	1.4	–	–	14.4	0.6	13.9
14–18	15.2	–	18.2	–	–	9.9	20.6	10.6
19–22	–	25.0	32.2	3.0	–	3.6	32.0	3.7
23–26	–	15.9	19.7	–	–	1.6	12.5	1.4
27–30	–	10.5	10.2	16.0	–	0.2	14.7	0.6
31–35	–	10.3	5.1	16.0	–	0.2	10.7	–
36–40	–	10.9	1.5	25.0	16.7	–	3.7	–
41–45	–	8.1	0.7	16.0	16.7	–	1.9	–
46–50	–	8.2	–	6.2	29.2	–	1.0	–
51–55	–	6.2	–	6.2	29.2	–	0.3	–
56–60	–	2.3	0.7	9.4	4.2	–	0.2	–
61–65	–	1.5	–	3.1	4.2	–	0.1	–
65+	–	1.1	2.1	–	–	–	0.1	–
Sample size	1,553	533	137	32	24	465	4,960	481

Source: Hessiches Staatsarchiv Marburg, HESAUS data, 1832–1857.

Table 9.5 Cash statistics of Hesse-Cassel emigrants (in Thaler)

Percentile	*All women going with family*	*All women going alone*	*Wives leaving alone*	*Widows going with family*	*Widows leaving alone*	*Men leaving alone*
20th	0	0	0	0	0	0
40th	0	0	0	0	0	0
Median	0	40	0	30	0	30
60th	0	50	0	100	30	50
80th	0	60	40	300	60	100
90th	0	100	120	486	110	200
95th	80	114	200	857	150	400
98th	200	200	300	1,300	400	900
Sample size	8,851	6,049	73	279	112	18,085

Source: Hessiches Staatsarchiv Marburg HESAUS data, 1832–1857.

Notes:
1 The sample sizes for wives leaving with family and both types of daughters are all very small.
2 One Thaler was worth approximately US$0.70.
3 These cash assets did not always include the funds emigrants had with them for travel costs.

Table 9.6 Cash statistics of Hesse-Cassel emigrants (in Thaler, no zeros)

Percentile	*All women going with family*	*All women going alone*	*Wives going with family*	*Wives leaving alone*	*Widows going with family*	*Widows leaving alone*	*Men leaving alone*	*Men going with family*
20th	50	40	50	50	100	40	50	100
40th	80	50	100	75	150	60	58	200
Median	100	50	120	120	200	60	70	225
60th	140	58	170	150	270	80	100	300
80th	257	86	300	200	486	114	200	571
90th	400	101	300	300	857	170	364	1,000
95th	700	150	500	500	1,200	400	650	1,400
98th	1,200	236	800	500	1,500	500	1,800	2,300
Sample size	707	3,462	67	15	142	47	9,646	4,368

Source: Hessiches Staatsarchiv Marburg, HESAUS data, 1832–1857.

Notes
1 The sample sizes for wives leaving with family and both types of daughters are all very small.
2 One Thaler was worth approximately US$0.70.
3 These cash assets did not always include the funds emigrants had with them for travel costs.

Table 9.7 Common occupation of female emigrants in Hesse-Cassel

Occupation	*All women travelling with family (%)*	*All women travelling alone (%)*	*Wives travelling with family (%)*	*Daughters travelling with family (%)*	*Widows travelling with family (%)*	*Men travelling alone (%)*
Factory worker	0.4	0.8	–	–	3.7	0.5
Midwife	1.7	–	6.1	–	3.7	–
Hats, caps, glove maker	–	0.7	–	–	–	0.1
Farmer	3.9	–	3.0	6.3	11.1	9.9
Seamstress	8.2	3.7	9.1	12.5	11.1	7.3
Shoemaker	1.7	–	–	6.3	–	7.4
Labourer	70.1	91.3	45.5	62.5	59.3	19.4
Restaurant owner	1.7	–	–	–	3.7	0.2
Sample size	231	1,607	33	16	27	11,210

Source: Hessiches Staatsarchiv Marburg, HESAUS data, 1832–1857.

Notes

1 Only the most common occupations are listed, meaning that the percentages do not add up to 100.

2 'Labourer' includes occupations such as maid, servant and various types of manual worker.

included the following pairs in terms of female/male job identification: a labourer/painter, miller/mill builder, professor/pharmacist, midwife/ farmer, awl smith/labourer and wallpaper hanger/locksmith. In this tiny sample, wives and husbands essentially share the same relative social class. For the vast majority of married women, social status and wealth must be derived from the occupational identity and cash assets of their husbands: for those men with occupational listings, 24 per cent were farmers, 14 per cent were labourers and over 40 per cent were artisans. Labourers in general tended to be unmarried men or women.

Through much of the first half of the nineteenth century, illegitimacy rates rose in the principality of Hesse-Cassel and most likely had an effect on emigration patterns. Not all emigrant mothers travelling with children were married. There is little mention in the records, however, of mothers leaving with children born out of wedlock. Only one child is specifically mentioned as illegitimate. Still, one can find several cases of women who travelled with children but without a husband, and who cannot be traced to an adult male of the same surname who left earlier or later from the same village. Some of these women were married to men who escaped detection in the official documents or to a man emigrating from another town or region. It is also quite probable that some of the women were unmarried and emigrating with their illegitimate children, but such women cannot be positively identified in these data.

Widows

Widows in general are an interesting group, and for the sake of sample sizes I focus on the widows who travelled with family members. Although information on ages is scant, most widows were between the ages of 46 and 55, old enough to be at an age when women become widows but not so old as to be physically unable to emigrate. Auerbach (1993) believes that many of these women had few chances to marry again, which one might attribute partially to their age. Many, however, did not need men for economic reasons. Widows travelling with family, usually their children, were some of the wealthiest emigrants departing from Hesse-Cassel. Table 9.6 provides cash statistics. These women were taking a median amount of cash of 200 Thaler, compared to a comparable figure of 70 Thaler for men leaving alone.[51] Men leaving with families, for the most part heads of households, still took more cash than widows. The medians are close, however, with widows taking 200 Thaler and family men 225 Thaler. In terms of financial wealth, the widows look more like male heads of households than men leaving alone. Given some of the amounts involved, many of these widows may have been liquidating their estates before migrating.[52] In spite of their relative wealth, widows were some of the biggest users of family networks and were very likely to migrate after someone from their family had done so. This would lead one to think that widows migrated in higher numbers in the 1850s than other female emigrant groups. On the contrary, widows leaving with family were more likely to leave in the 1840s than widows leaving without family members and women in general leaving on their own. Departure figures are shown in Table 9.8. For these widows, a migrant network offered more than just economic assistance but also other benefits such as protection and companionship.

The occupational distribution of widows shows both a greater variety of occupations than for other women and a higher incidence of jobs indicating some amount of wealth, specifically farmers and restaurant/pub owners. Widowhood was one way to acquire economic responsibilities normally left to men. Most of the widows travelling with family and almost all of the widows travelling alone left illegally. The relatively wealthy widows may have wanted to hide assets to avoid the small exit tax or abscond without paying debts in the community, either of which would have required a rather hasty and unannounced departure. One could not be successful at either strategy under the normal procedures of issuing an emigrant permit. Money thus provides a possible explanation as to why this wealthier subset of women was more likely to be classified as illegal.

Table 9.8 Year of departure for Hesse-Cassel emigrants, by per cent of total (cumulative)

Year	*All women going with family (%)*	*All women going alone (%)*	*Wives leaving alone (%)*	*Wives going with family (%)*	*Daughters going with family (%)*	*Widows going alone (%)*	*Widows leaving with family (%)*	*Men leaving alone (%)*	*Sons going with family (%)*
1836	0.1	0.0	0.0	0.1	0.0	0.0	0.0	0.3	0.0
1840	2.3	1.9	1.4	0.5	0.5	0.0	2.2	4.9	1.1
1845	8.6	3.5	4.1	3.3	6.3	1.8	5.7	13.1	6.8
1847	21.3	6.7	9.6	9.2	13.9	3.6	12.9	19.7	4.4
1851	28.5	9.3	11.0	14.7	18.1	3.6	15.4	30.0	14.7
1852	46.9	22.8	23.3	37.5	38.9	14.3	29.0	42.0	40.2
1853	53.7	37.8	39.7	44.4	44.4	30.4	41.2	55.0	46.1
1854	71.6	59.6	63.0	65.8	65.7	55.4	62.7	73.0	65.3
1855	78.8	69.1	78.1	74.8	74.4	78.6	72.0	80.3	74.4
1856	87.9	80.9	84.9	85.3	85.0	83.9	84.2	88.5	84.9
1857	100.0	100.0	100.0	100.0	100.0	100.0	100.0	100.0	100.0
Sample size	8,851	6,050	73	3,118	2,784	112	279	18,086	2,764

Source: Hessiches Staatsarchiv Marburg, HESAUS data, 1832–1857.

Daughters

My discussion of daughters is limited to the 2,788 young women who were specifically described as a daughter of an adult man or woman. Most of these children are referred to as a daughter of a male parent, as one can see in Table 9.2. In addition, one daughter was described as an illegitimate daughter, and twenty-four young women were named as daughters of specific widows.

As members rather than heads of a household, very little is known about these female children. Information on ages exists for only 465 different daughters. A quarter of them were listed as under the age of 2, while 14 per cent were of the age of 2 or 3, and another 12 per cent were of the age of 4 or 5 (Table 9.4). This uneven age distribution information may indicate in part the effect of high infant mortality.[53] With the modal age of wives at 36–40 and a high probability of wives following family members (often husbands) in a later year, mothers may also have timed their emigration until after the birth of a child. A few records also exist on job classifications, with the most common occupation for daughters being 'labourers', which included various types of labourers as well as servants. In addition, daughters leaving with family members were more likely to leave in the 1840s than those leaving alone, and daughters were more likely to be leaving on a legal basis than on an illegal basis (Table 9.3).

Did parents treat sons differently from daughters? Not really, as far as the data show. It does not seem that parents favoured taking one over the other, as almost an equal number of young men were identified as sons emigrating with a family member. Sons are equally likely to have been networked, i.e., to have followed family members who had emigrated before them, and emigrated to the US compared to daughters, but they were slightly more likely to have left on a legal basis.

Women travelling alone

Over 6,000 women travelled alone, that is, unaccompanied by a direct family member – about 41 per cent of all the women recorded. Many of the emigrants travelling alone were unmarried women, something we can infer from their ages in Table 9.4. The age distributions for single women and married women are vastly different: roughly 80 per cent of women travelling by themselves were younger than 27, but only 3 per cent of the married women (at least of those for whom age information exists) were younger than 27. The relative youthfulness of the women travelling alone suggests that many were probably unmarried. What is quite remarkable are the extraordinarily low numbers of women over the age of 35 who left home alone. The women who did leave later in life tended to be married or widowed.

Women travelling alone were also more likely to be formally employed. The vast majority of occupational information on women concerns women who left alone. From these data we know the occupations for over 1,600 of them. Overwhelmingly, at over 90 per cent, these women were classified as being labourers, or servants, manual labourers, maids and farm labourers. Not surprisingly, these women were segregated into a few types of jobs, as was typical of women all over the world in the nineteenth century.[54]

The Hesse-Cassel data on emigrant occupations are an improvement over what can be found in the later Hamburg passenger lists. For the female emigrants, the Hamburg lists combine occupational information with marital status, and thereby list one or the other, but not both. Hence, almost 50 per cent of the women in the Hamburg lists are classified as 'unmarried' and are probably also labourers, but we do not know for sure their exact occupations.

Women leaving on their own, interestingly, have the highest median cash figures of all the various groups of women. Part of this reflects the purely practical matter that these women were bearing the emigration costs by themselves. Among these lone emigrants are a few wives and widows leaving on their own, both of which groups tended to take less than women leaving alone in general (Table 9.5). The group is thus comprised mostly of young and single women, and the higher median cash value for these women reflects also their higher propensity to have been formally employed in their home villages, even if only as a servant or labourer of some sort. At the very least, employment as a labourer may have implied better access to or more control of cash. Certainly many of the women leaving with their families were better off, but cash and property were listed in the records under their spouses' or fathers' names.

An interesting comparison is that of young men to young women. Did men leaving on their own have similar or different characteristics to women travelling by themselves? Men leaving on their own were also comparatively young, mainly between the ages of 14 and 35. Given that over 66 per cent of the men were 26 or younger, many were probably unmarried, similar to the women. But proportionately more men over the age of 30 left on their own, and some of these men may have been married. One of the most interesting characteristics of this group of men is their lower preference for migrating to the United States.[55] While 98 per cent of the women travelling on their own went to the US, only 80 per cent of the single-travelling men settled in the US (Table 9.3). For the men other German regions remained attractive, particularly regions like Westphalia, which could offer employment in growing industrial sectors. Unmarried Hessian men were thus more likely than their fellow womenfolk to participate in one type of internal migration, that between German states. Women may still have migrated at higher rates between *Kreise* or between villages. Lastly, the occupations of men were multiple, with over 300 different job classifications present in the data. The heterogeneity in the male labour market emphasises further just how segregated a labour market women faced.

The use of family networks by women

Women were more likely to leave in the 1850s than in the 1840s partly because they were prone to following others, namely family and friends who had migrated earlier. There were many reasons to leave as a networked migrant besides the social benefits. Migrating as part of a chain lowered the costs of migration, especially if previous migrants helped later ones by sending updated information about the new country, and prepaid tickets. If new migrants joined family at the destination, the established migrant could provide room and board, help secure employment and show the new arrival around. This assistance helped new migrants to smooth the transition to a new way of life and thereby lowered the chance of failing at the beginning. With few financial resources, women had good reasons to make the best use of family and other personal contacts overseas.

To measure family networks I divided up migrants into non-networked and networked subsets. I defined a network as a tie between migrants leaving in different years coming from the same family and village. For instance, if I observed a member of the Feldmann family leaving the village of Giesel in 1842, and another Feldmann member leaving Giesel in 1849, I classified these migrants as networked, with the 1842 individual belonging to 'Group 1' and the 1849 Giesel family members belonging to 'Group 2.' If I observed family members of the Hausmann family leaving the village of Dudenrode solely in the year of 1853, I classified these migrants as non-networked. This classification mechanism isolates primarily patrilineal ties, ignoring the remaining family ties between individuals who are related but have different surnames. It also ignores ties between friends. On balance it is probably a conservative assessment of the number of actual social networks. Still, the patterns found may very well understate the real differences between networked and non-networked migrants, and an improved classification scheme would strengthen any interesting differences found with the current breakdown.[56]

Women migrating alone were more likely than women travelling with family members to migrate as part of a chain than emigrants in general; about half of these women could be identified as being related to another individual who had migrated at an earlier or later point in time (Table 9.3). Seventy per cent of these networked women were following a relative who had migrated earlier, leading one to question how many of them really possessed a large degree of economic independence. Of all networked women in general, most migrated as part of Group 2, and thus moved only after other members of their family had established some kind of life in the new country. In many cases, women were following husbands or fathers, meaning that these networks represented rather complicated family strategies. Men moving on their own were just as likely to use family networks, but they were more likely than women to start a migrant network as a part of a Group 1. This explains in part why men were more likely than women to leave in the 1840s. Widows especially shunned moving as part of Group 1 and were the subset most likely to be a part of Group 2.

Conclusions

Emigration in Hesse-Cassel was an interesting demographic event. Given its special nature, authorities attempted to keep track of entire annual emigration populations and prepared records on individuals from all different age cohorts. Certainly bureaucrats recorded what was most interesting to the governing authorities, focusing on those individuals with more earning opportunities and thus a greater effect on state income sources, and on those who might evade either military service or personal debts. Thereby the emigrant permit lists have more to say about men than about women. Nevertheless, the records have relevance in terms of society's perceptions of women's economic and social identities in their communities. While many adult women were recorded by their first names in the data, many were referred to more anonymously as a wife of a particular man. Assets were attributed to the head of household, typically male. Usually only in the case that a woman was travelling by herself (often unmarried), or as a widow, were her job and assets considered seriously and written down.

Women tended to travel with family. And even among those who travelled alone, almost half of them were travelling as part of a migration network. Thus, the vast majority of women, 79 per cent, were somehow tied, financially and/or emotionally, to their families. Here it is unclear to what degree women avoided travelling alone for safety reasons.[57] In comparison to men, women moved in much greater proportions in the 1850s than in the 1840s. This fact further indicates that women were probably more likely to move once they had a family member (husband or fiancé in many cases) or a friend at the destination. My measure of networks isolated only the patrilineal relationships and undercounted the number of actual networks women used; thus even more women may have been part of a family migration network.

Almost all women went to the United States. This was true not only of adult women and daughters moving with family members, but also of women leaving alone. The second favourite choices of Hessian emigrants after the US were other German states, to which some men (mostly young) moved but not very many women or families. For husbands, fiancés, or fathers in nearby German states, return migration was a real possibility, and perhaps a deterrent for the family members at home to follow.[58]

Some women acted independently in seeking their own happiness and fortune.[59] Women migrating alone, most presumed to be young and unmarried, probably had some control over their own decisions, as did widows. Still, these women chose to travel to the US and not to other areas in the world, and particularly not to other German states. Actually, women travelling alone had the highest rates of migration to the United States at 97.5 per cent. Surely many could have been joining spouses or future spouses, since almost half of those leaving alone were involved in a family migration network, but what were the others planning to do? The opportunity to marry was likely an important motive and was easier in the US than in Hesse-Cassel or in other areas of Germany where one had to prove the economic viability of a household.[60] And if one could not marry, one could find work easily enough.[61] Economic incentives were likely quite important, but they were not the only motivation, as documentation also exists in a few cases of women escaping from abuse at home.[62] It is difficult to measure how frequently this or other personal circumstances occurred which strongly encouraged women to leave the homeland.[63]

A number of the women emigrating were quite well off, including many widows. The majority, however, took few financial assets with them. Fifty per cent of the women leaving on their own reported taking at least 50 Thaler with them (Table 9.6), an amount equal to almost three-quarters of what men moving alone reported. In addition, a quarter of the women travelling alone reported being employed, usually as a maid, servant or some type of labourer. Were these women joining family overseas? Were they searching for something in addition to economic prosperity, perhaps a kind of societal freedom? Further research into emigrants' lives at the destination through tracing could provide some answers to such questions. Those who never married and kept their maiden names can be traced in the US census.

The Hesse-Cassel experience shows that women at all stages of the life-cycle emigrated. The results I have presented suggest that these women faced a variety of economic and social circumstances that were related at the very least to their respective ages, marital status and wealth. It is only with a large dataset of information at the level of the individual that one can fully demonstrate the complexities of female migration behaviour. Aggregated data, which characterise many historical and contemporary migration statistics, cannot provide the same insights. More such studies at the micro level would help our understanding of female migration behaviour, especially since women dominate many contemporary migrations. The long-distance movement of women, moreover, is related to other relevant themes in social history, such as economic opportunity, the right to property, and the changing nature and prospect of marriage and family.

Acknowledgements

This chapter was written while the author was a visiting scholar during the 1999/2000 academic year at the Hoover Institution of Stanford University, at the Agricultural History Center of UC Davis and at the Institute for European Studies at UC Berkeley. This work has benefited from comments made by Christiane Harzig, Mary-Louise Nagata, Pam Sharpe and David Surdam. The author recognises the generous support of grants from the German Marshall Fund and the Economic History Association.

Notes

1 S. S. Weinberg, 'The Treatment of Women in Immigration History: a Call for Change', *Journal of American Ethnic History* II (1992): 25–46 laments in general the dearth of studies on the assimilation process of women immigrants.

2 I. Ferenczi. and W. Wilcox, *International Migrations, Vol. I, Statistics*, New York: National Bureau for Economic Research, 1929.

3 Contemporary immigrant populations, especially those in the United States, look starkly different and are more heavily constituted by women and by family migrations. See E. Kofman, 'Female Birds of Passage – a Decade Later: Gender and Immigration in the European Union', *International Migration Review* 33 (1999): 269–299.

4 The same can be said about the second volume, W. F. Willcox, *International Migrations, Vol. II, Interpretations*, New York: National Bureau for Economic Research, 1931.

5 R. Cohn, 'A Comparative Analysis of European Immigrant Streams to the United States during the Early Mass Migration', *Social Science History* 19, 1 (1995): 63–89.

6 The Hamburg port statistics serve as one example. For a sample of Hessian emigrants in the 1850s and 1860s, married women are described in terms of occupation as a 'wife'. See P. Assion (ed.), *Über Hamburg nach Amerika: Hessisiche Auswandernde in den Hamburger Schiffslisten 1855 bis 1866*, Marburg, Germany: Institut für Europäische Ethnologie und Kulturforschung der Universität Marburg, 1991.

7 J. P. Ferrie, *Yankeys Now: Immigrants in the Antebellum United States, 1840–1860*, New York: Oxford University Press, 1999.

8 This is a recurring theme in the journal *Historical Methods*. See articles by E. Herr, 'The Census, Estimation Biases, and Female Labor-force Participation Rates in 1880 Colorado', *Historical Methods* 28 (1995): 167–182 and M. Abel and N. Folbre, 'A Method for Revising Estimates: Female Participation in the U.S. Before 1940', *Historical Methods* 23 (1990): 167–176 on their concerns about US government statistics on female labour-force participation.

9 Just one example in this literature is C. Harzig *et al.* (eds) *Peasant Maids, City Women: from the European Countryside to Urban America*, Ithaca, NY: Cornell University Press, 1997, which provides a careful analysis of European women and their experience of adapting from the European countryside to urban America. A helpful guide to this literature, at least for works prior to 1990, is D. Gabaccia (ed.), *Immigrant Women in the United States: A Selectively Annotated Multidisciplinary Bibliography*, Westport, CT: Greenwood Press, 1989, a bibliography on migration articles and books devoted to the female experience. An interdisciplinary perspective about women in the immigration literature is provided by D. Gabaccia (ed.), *Seeking Common Ground: Multidisciplinary Studies of Immigrant Women in the United States*, Westport, CT: Greenwood Press, 1992.

10 S. A. Wegge, 'Chain Migration and Information Networks: Evidence From Nineteenth-century Hesse-Cassel', *The Journal of Economic History* 58 (1998): 957–986; S. A. Wegge, 'Network Strategies of Nineteenth-century Hesse-Cassel Emigrants', mimeo, 1999; S. A. Wegge, 'Self-selection of Nineteenth-century

German Emigrants: Evidence from the Principality of Hesse-Cassel', mimeo, revised May 2000.

11 D. Gabaccia, *From the Other Side: Women, Gender, and Immigrant Life in the U.S., 1820–1990*, Bloomington: Indiana University Press, 1994; W. D. Kamphoefner, W. Helbich and U. Sommer (eds), *News from the Land of Freedom: German Immigrants Write Home*, Ithaca, NY: Cornell University Press, 1991; Cohn, 'Comparative Analysis'.

12 W. D. Kamphoefner, 'German–American Return Migration', in R.J. Vecoli and S. Sinke (eds), *A Century of European Migrations, 1830–1930*, Urbana: University of Illinois Press, 1991; Cohn, 'Comparative Analysis'.

13 For Italian emigrants, the higher the degree of return migration, the smaller the percentage of women in the initial wave of migration, see S.L. Baily, *Immigrants in the Lands of Promise: Italians in Buenos Aires and New York City, 1870–1914*, Ithaca, NY: Cornell University Press, 1999. In a comparison of Italians who settled in New York City with those who settled in Buenos Aires, Baily finds that emigrants who went to Buenos Aires were more likely to be female, part of a family migration and a permanent settlement process.

14 D. Gabaccia, 'Women of the Mass Migrations: from Minority to Majority, 1820–1930', in D. Hoerder and L. P. Moch (eds), *European Migrants: Global and Local Perspectives*, Boston: Northeastern Press, 1996, pp. 90–111; L. G. Tedebrand, 'Sources for the history of Swedish immigration', in H. Runblom and H. Norman (eds), *From Sweden to America: a History of the Migration*, Minneapolis: University of Minnesota Press, 1976, pp. 76–93.

15 Bureau of the Census, 1975, p. 14.

16 E. G. Ravenstein, 'The Laws of Migration', *Journal of the Statistical Society* 48 (1885): 167–235.

17 The migration scholar must tread very carefully in assuming any of his hypotheses to be true, especially since empirical findings often do not lend support to his hypotheses.

18 S. Hochstadt, *Mobility and Modernity: Migration in Germany 1820–1989*, Ann Arbor: University of Michigan Press, 1999, p. 78.

19 D. Baines, *Migration from a Mature Economy: Emigration and Internal Migration in England and Wales, 1861–1900*, Cambridge: Cambridge University Press, 1985, p. 238.

20 C. Pooley and J. Turnbull, *Migration and Mobility in Britain Since the 18th Century*, London: UCL Press, 1998, p. 67, another more recent study on English migrants does not find evidence to support Ravenstein's conclusion and shows that men and women had comparable rates of internal migration between 1840 and 1920.

21 A most striking characteristic of Irish migration patterns is the low internal migration rate over much of the nineteenth century, a function of low Irish urbanization rates. T. W. Guinnane, *The Vanishing Irish: Households, Migration, and the Rural Economy in Ireland, 1850–1914*, Princeton, NJ: Princeton University Press, 1997, pp. 105, 122; P. Travers, 'There Was Nothing for Me There': Irish Female Migration, 1922–71', in P. O'Sullivan (ed.), *Irish Women and Irish Migration*, London: Leicester University Press, 1995, p. 148.

22 Bureau of the Census, 1975, pp. 105–6.

23 The main source of micro data for these individuals consists of the American passenger ship records, which have their own data quality problems. See Ferenczi and Willcox, *International Migrations*.

24 Ferenczi and Willcox, *International Migrations*, pp. 401–422.

25 The electorate of Hesse-Cassel had a long tradition as one of the few smaller European states to maintain a sizeable standing army (C. Ingrao, *The Hessian Mercenary State*, Cambridge: Cambridge University Press, 1987, p. 7). In the eighteenth century, this led to a profitable mercenary business with England, and

in the post-Napoleonic age it spurred many young men to emigrate surreptitiously in order to avoid military service.

26 B. Hildebrand, *Die Statistische Mittheilungen über die Volkswirtschaftlichen Zustände Kurhessens*, Berlin: Trautweinschen, 1853, pp. 53, 99.

27 These included such artisans as general blacksmiths, wheelwrights, weavers, carpenters, masons, shoemakers, etc. See R. Bovensiepen, *Die kurhessische Gewerbepolitik und die wirtschaftliche Lage des zünftigen Handwerks in Kurhessen von 1816–1867*, Marburg: Elwert, 1909, p. 17.

28 Hildebrand, *Die Statistische Mittheilungen*; Ingrao, *The Hessian Mercenary State*, p. 7.

29 Individual immigrants ended up for various reasons in governmental documents of the state of Hesse-Cassel including the following: inheritance disputes between a migrant and a family member, a controversial emigrant permit application, a village contesting funds to be handed over to an impoverished returning migrant, and so forth. The archives for this principality also contain many documents describing local and state officials' assessment of the impact of migration on their homeland.

30 The Hamburg port lists serve as a rich source of data on nineteenth-century European emigrants. Assion *et al.* assembled this data set by culling the voluminous Hamburg passenger lists for those stemming from Hessian states, most of whom moved to the US. These Hessian regions and nearby cities included the Electorate of Hesse-Cassel, Grand Duchy of Hesse-Darmstadt, the Duchy of Nassau, the principality of Waldeck, the Landgrave of Hesse-Homburg, the free city of Frankfurt, and the area of Wetzlar (belonging to the kingdom of Prussia).

31 I limit my comparisons to the Hesse-Cassel emigrants who left between 1852 when the recording of illegal emigrants commenced and 1857, where my data end. In this way, my data overlap a bit with the 1855–1866 Hamburg study.

32 I. Auerbach, *Auswanderung aus Kurhessen: Nach Osten oder Westen?*, Marburg: Hessisches Staatsarchiv Marburg, 1993.

33 In terms of gender, I was able to identify the gender for 95 per cent of the emigrants. Information on legal status exists for the years 1852–1857.

34 Women were not required to serve in the military. For this reason, and for others, government data collectors may have been less concerned with their departure and less concerned with properly recording it. More importantly, Auerbach (*Auswanderung aus Kurhessen*, p. 18) comments on the lack of documentation for some subsets of women, which makes the figures on percentages of legal emigrants in Table 9.3 suspect.

35 If the woman left at a time prior to or later than the family migration in question, then I can identify this demographic event.

36 Auerbach, *Auswanderung aus Kurhessen*, pp. 18, 145.

37 ibid., p. 145; Wegge, 'Network Strategies'.

38 The best way to assess possible missing data is to compare the proportions of women versus men of the respective totals for the various family identities. The Hamburg data mix occupational identification with family identity, while the Hesse-Cassel data add family identity to the first name and in less than half the cases. Thus the two data sources do not permit a more detailed comparison.

39 Gabaccia, 'Women of the Mass Migrations'.

40 The percentage of women as a total of all immigrants arriving in the United States increased slowly from 31 per cent in the 1820s to over 50 per cent in the 1970s. Within specific ethnic migrant groups, however, the increase was faster, which is not discernible from the data Gabaccia used since they are an average of female representation for newer emigrant groups and older ones combined. By ethnicity, in the century after 1820, the emigrant populations with largest percentages of women were Canadians, some northern and central

European groups, and individuals of African descent arriving from the Caribbean (Gabaccia, 'Women of the Mass Migrations', pp. 91–92). Irish emigrant populations had the highest absolute proportion of women at 48 per cent.

41 Wegge, 'Self-selection'. Labourers left in large numbers but in low propensities relative to their portion of the working population. The labourers who did leave left with little cash, inferring that those who stayed home had similar portfolios and were cash-constrained.

42 The returns to farming were not necessarily that great given the large set-up costs and the acquisition of foreign agricultural practices. Possible large liquidity costs in converting their property to cash, or a large debt burden, would have made migration further unattractive.

43 Wegge, 'Self-selection'.

44 Wegge, 'Network Strategies'; Wegge, 'Chain Migration'.

45 Gabaccia, *From the Other Side*, p. 30; Kamphoefner *et al.*, *News from the Land of Freedom*, p. 523; Cohn, 'Comparative Analysis', pp. 63–89.

46 Assion, *Über Hamburg nach Amerika*, p. 151.

47 Auerbach, *Auswanderung aus Kurhessen*, refers often to marriage restrictions; see also Assion, *Über Hamburg nach Amerika*, p. 153 for a more specific description of Hessian marriage law; S. Sinke, with S. Gross, 'The International Marriage Market and the Sphere of Social Reproduction: a German Case Study', in D. Gabaccia (ed.), *Seeking Common Ground: Multidisciplinary Studies of Immigrant Women in the United States*, Westport, CT: Greenwood Press, 1992, argue that marriage was an important motivation for many German women migrating to the US in the nineteenth century.

48 There are certainly cases of divorced or separated women, but this is not immediately apparent from the emigrant records. Some of the women travelling on their own were also married, joining their husbands or preceding them (or perhaps in a few cases escaping them). These various cases are difficult to identify from the emigrant permit lists and must be further investigated in the more detailed archival records.

49 Specifically the sample sizes for women who travelled with family members and without family members are 8,851 and 6,050 respectively.

50 Information on ages and occupations is based on very small sample sizes.

51 A Thaler was worth approximately $0.70 US.

52 In a few cases, cash figures were estimates of future estates coming upon the death of relatives.

53 Assion, *Über Hamburg nach Amerika*, p. 70, emphasises this point since the proportion of children under one year is equivalent to the proportion found in the general population.

54 Gabaccia, 'Women of the Mass Migrations', p. 94.

55 Auerbach also comments that the US was an attractive goal for unmarried women with illegitimate children. See Auerbach, *Auswanderung aus Kurhessen*, p. 20.

56 The scheme is further discussed in Wegge, 'Chain Migration' and Wegge, 'Network Strategies'.

57 Auerbach, *Auswanderung aus Kurhessen*, p. 126.

58 In addition, more men probably left for the US but left illegally before 1852, escaping detection in the official records.

59 In thinking about family migrations, it is not necessarily the case that the head of household made the decision to move. Still, it is difficult to gauge what role each family member played in deciding that a family would emigrate. Parents emigrating may have decided to do so for the own welfare or for that of their children, or for both. Identifying the decision-maker(s) is difficult without the knowledge of personal histories.

60 Auerbach, *Auswanderung aus Kurhessen*, argues that many were leaving home because their dowries were insufficient to guarantee them a successful marriage match at home.

61 See Assion, *Über Hamburg nach Amerika*, p. 154, and the discussion of reports from the Deutsche Gesellschaft in New Orleans regarding employment conditions for women in the US in the 1850s.

62 Auerbach, *Auswanderung aus Kurhessen*, pp. 168, 171, 173–174.

63 Auerbach discusses various personal reasons that provided important motivations for some for 'escaping' from Germany. For instance, cases existed in which adults fled from respective spouses, illegitimate children or other social responsibilities (Auerbach, *Auswanderung aus Kurhessen*, pp. 18, 145). To what degree these were common factors is unclear.

10 When the migrants are men

Italy's women and transnationalism as a working-class way of life

Donna Gabaccia

During the long era of international migration that shaped the world between the Napoleonic Wars and the First World War (1815–1914), 60 per cent or more of all global migrants were men. The earliest students and theorists of migration saw this as a natural phenomenon, determined by biology.[1] Yet even in the nineteenth century and (more noticeably) today, gender ratios vary considerably, and in some shorter-distance migrations, women outnumber men.[2]

This chapter focuses on gender relations in Italy's mass migrations. The 16 million migrants who left Italy between 1870 and 1914 formed one of the most significant migrations of the modern world. About a third went to the US and Canada, a quarter to Argentina and Brazil, and almost half to other European countries, notably Switzerland, France, Austria and Germany. Migration from Italy was otherwise typical of the nineteenth century in that most migrants were men – those whom one scholar has termed 'the men without women'.[3] Overall, two-thirds of the migrants who left Italy between 1870 and 1920 were men of rural backgrounds.[4] Not surprisingly, many of Italy's migrants were sojourners who returned to Italy or migrated repeatedly over the course of their working lives. The 'women who waited' – contemporaries, and their historians in Italy have called them 'white widows' – have also attracted some scholarly attention.[5]

Italy's men and women thus provide us with an early example of transnational lives, or lives shaped by time in more than one nation. Recent attention to transnationalism has changed the way we think about migration in the contemporary world by emphasising the degree to which migrants continue to live in two places.[6] Yet transnational lives, and transnationalism itself, are by no means new phenomena, nor are they characteristic only of the contemporary world. Unlike today's migrants, however, most of whom are literate, with some urban experience prior to migration, Italy's men and women in the nineteenth century were generally illiterate, rural people. They had no telephones with which to communicate. Even writing or reading a letter was a challenge. They could not hop onto jet planes for short visits to distant relatives. It is therefore hard not to wonder why, when faced with such obstacles, so many of Italy's families opted for transnational lives. Certainly, they lived at a time when transnational life was more disruptive to the lives of migrants than it is today.

Gendered divisions of labour and of labour markets, culturally patterned family preferences and definitions of appropriate male and female behaviour all influence migration. They help determine whether men and women migrate or remain immobile together, or whether they instead separate as one leaves the other behind. Many readers in the English-speaking world will assume that male-dominated migrations from countries like Italy simply reflect the peculiarities of Latin patriarchy. It is true that Latins, like many other Europeans in the nineteenth century, believed that women were best kept within the family circle. Unlike other Europeans they also feared the power of women's sexuality when released from male control. Yet the migration of sons also threatened a father's control over his family. Furthermore, Mediterranean societies have generally assigned control of women's sexuality to other women, whose day-to-day surveillance of each other was unaffected by male migration. Distinctive characteristics of Latin patriarchy are probably not the most convincing explanations for Italy's gendered patterns of migration.

Changes in local and global job markets in the nineteenth century had considerably more influence on migrants' decisions during the era of mass, international migration. After 1830, the abolition of slavery worldwide threatened the stability of European empires dependent on raw materials from their colonies, and generated new, largely Asian and male, migrations of semi-free labourers into colonial agriculture and mining. Italian men, and somewhat fewer women, participated in these migrations. At the same time, anti-imperial revolutions in the Americas created huge and new, but sparsely populated, national states that believed, along with the Argentine Juan Bautista Alberdi, that 'to govern is to populate'.[7] These nations sought new settlers and citizens, preferably in fertile and hard-working family groups with balanced sex ratios. Family migrations from Italy were much more important in the settlement of Argentina and Brazil than of the US, Canada or Australia. Finally, industrial capital spread from its earlier concentration in a few cities in northern Europe and Great Britain to other parts of Europe and the Americas and, to a lesser extent, Africa and Asia. The migratory workers – many of them Italian – who built cities and factories in Europe and the Americas, were men working in seasonal construction jobs. The Italian migrants who later migrated to work in factories included a significant female component in the Americas (but not in Europe). Factory employment in women's industries – not the demand of expanding urban middle classes for domestic servants – most often motivated women to leave Italy.[8] The majority, however, remained at home, in large part because they did much more there than merely 'wait' for men to return. Transnationalism was common among Italy's residents mainly because it so often made economic sense for both men and women.

Gender and migration from Italy

By almost any measure, migration from Italy in the nineteenth century was on an impressive scale. Overall, no other people migrated in so many directions and in such impressive numbers – relatively and absolutely – as from Italy. Furthermore, few showed such firm attachments to their home regions or returned in such large proportions – 50 per cent or more.[9] Still, migration varied considerably across Italy's regions, as did women's representation, and these variations provide clues to the complex interaction of gender, labour and migration.

Scholars have always known, but rarely attempted to explain, why migrations varied so much from region to region in Italy. These variations provide at least a few clues to why men and women more often separated than migrated together. While students of culture note differing attitudes toward gender and women's sexuality in northern and central Italy and in the south, migration patterns do not fall neatly into central, northern or southern patterns. Table 10.1 shows that some of the more prosperous and supposedly less patriarchal northern regions of Italy actually had very high rates of migration both before and after 1900. Migration developed somewhat more belatedly in the southern part of the country but there, too, a few regions had very high rates of migration while migration from others was negligible. Overall, 45 per cent of Italy's migrants came from the north, and only a third from the south of the country. Table 10.2 shows that destinations even more than emigration rates varied with regional origin. Southern Italians generally, Sicilians in particular, and – in the north of Italy – Ligurians, showed a special preference for migration to the United States. Europe attracted mainly Italians from the north and the centre, while Latin America was equally attractive to those of northern and southern origins.

As Table 10.3 shows, the supposedly more modern, less patriarchal and Europeanised north of Italy actually had lower rates of female migration – with the notable exception of Liguria – than most of the supposedly more patriarchal south. By tracing gendered work opportunities at home and abroad, we can better understand this outcome and its meaning. Work opportunities for men and women in Italy's north and south were sharply different. In much of mountainous northwest Italy, where peasant families maintained fairly firm access to their own lands, older women's work on the land freed younger women to migrate to textile factory jobs in nearby cities, such as Biella, Turin and Milan, or in foreign cities. Also freed to migrate were men, whose wages supplemented the work of older women as food-producers. Many took seasonal jobs as construction workers or seasonal agricultural labourers across the Alps.[10] In Sicily, by contrast,

Table 10.1 Annual rates of Italian emigration, by region, 1876–1914

Region	*Province*	*1876–1894 (%)*	*1895–1914 (%)**
North	Piedmont	1.0	10.3
	Lombardy	0.6	0.9
	Veneto	20.6	30.3
	Liguria	0.5	0.5
	Emilia	0.3	10.0
Centre	Tuscany	0.5	10.0
	The Marches	0.1	10.6
	Umbria	–	10.3
	Lazio	–	0.6
	Abruzzi-Molise	0.6	20.5
South	Campania	0.6	10.9
	Apulia	0.1	0.8
	Basilicata	0.2	20.6
	Calabria	0.7	20.3
	Sicily	0.2	10.6
	Sardegna	0.1	0.5

Source: *Annuario statistico della emigrazione italiana* (Roma, 1926), Table III.

Note
* Migrants as percentage of total regional population in 1881 (for 1876–1894) or 1911 (for 1895–1914).

Table 10.2 Percentage of all Italian emigrants going to the US, by regional origin, 1876–1914

Region	*Province*	*Percentage*
North	Piedmont	10
	Lombardy	6
	Veneto	3
	Liguria	23
	Emilia	12
Centre	Tuscany	17
	The Marches	20
	Umbria	19
	Lazio	71
	Abruzzi-Molise	59
South	Campania	64
	Apulia	57
	Basilicata	53
	Calabria	48
	Sicily	72
	Sardegna	12

Source: *Annuario statistico della emigrazione italiana* (Rome, 1926), Table III.

Table 10.3 Percentage female of all Italian emigrants, by province, 1876–1925

Region	*Province*	*Percentage*
North	Piedmont	22
	Liguria	29
	Lombardy	17
	Veneto	16
Centre	Emilia	19
	Tuscany	21
	The Marches	21
	Umbria	18
	Lazio	14
South	Abruzzi/Molise	19
	Campania	27
	Apulia	21
	Basilicata	30
	Calabria	19
	Sicily	29
	Sardegna	15

Source: *Annuario statistico della emigrazione italiana* (Roma, 1926).

fewer peasants owned or controlled stable plots of land near their villages. Men travelled long distances in order to work, and they effectively excluded the competition of women wage-earners on large landowners' commercial estates by 1880. Women could not so easily feed their families, thus freeing men for migration, in southern regions like Sicily.[11]

Industrial jobs in the Americas (along with the empty lands of Brazil and Argentina) also seemed to offer southerners (and Ligurians) and women from both places far better opportunities for employment than transalpine Europe, where northern Italians were most likely to migrate and where gender ratios were heavily unbalanced. In Europe, construction jobs, and unskilled and semi-skilled positions in a few male industries were open to Italian men. The employment of foreign females in Germany, France and Switzerland's textile industries was far more limited. By contrast, Argentina and Brazil welcomed Italians as both settler families and in their new industries. In fact, earlier Italian merchants and craftsmen developed much of the urban industry in these two Latin countries, and Italian employers seemed to prefer workers, both male and female, from their homeland. In the US and Canada, construction was the main sector of male Italian employment, but predominantly female industries like garments, cigars, textiles and shoes also employed large numbers of Italian women.[12] Thus, a combination of good opportunities to work at home and poor options abroad, may have limited female migration from Italy's north. At the same time, poor options at home and relatively good options abroad may explain the higher rates of female migration from many parts of the south, especially from Sicily.

We know less about how rates of return varied from region to region. Local studies suggest that the heavily male transalpine migrants from the north were most likely to return. Returning men were 80 per cent of those leaving from the Veneto and more than 90 per cent of those departing Friuli in the 1890s.[13] But since the Italian government did not systematically count returners from the Americas until 1905, or from Europe until 1921, even tentative conclusions are impossible. The proportion of returners from the Americas – 49 per cent between 1905 and 1920 – seems impressive at a time when travel across the Atlantic took one to three weeks and cost more than half the yearly income of an average peasant.[14] Samuel Baily has estimated rates of return from 44 to 53 per cent from Buenos Aires and New York around 1900.[15] Betty Boyd Caroli cites a contemporary study that found 54 per cent of southerners, 50 per cent of central Italians and 40 per cent of northerners returning from the United States.[16] Temporary male migration was not exclusively a northern pattern, nor were gender-balanced migrations of family groups limited to the south. Transnationalism thus became a way of life throughout Italy during the mass migrations.

Transnational family economies

Separations during migration were most consistently characteristic of migration from Italy's north and from southern regions during the onset of migration. Culture certainly shaped migration patterns in both cases, and ties of family, sexual desire and sentiment all lured the men without women home to northern and southern villages. More important, whether in the north or in the south, the separation of men from women during migration proved not only economically feasible but in many cases more advantageous than transplantation in family groups. Separation seemed the most dependable strategy in a family's search for security, especially in Italy's north.[17]

Family security meant many things, of course – money, a dowry, house or land, a trade or profession, increased consumption of modern goods, the comforts of a familiar dialect, cuisine or religious rite, and the respect of friends and relatives. A description of family budgets – earnings and consumption – in both Italy and abroad uncovers the complex decision-making that underlay transnationalism during this era of male migration. Unfortunately, we cannot easily compare southern and northern patterns of transnationalism. Italians saw emigration mainly as a problem of the south, directed to the US, and the nations of the Americas – which attracted disproportionate numbers of southerners – also focused more attention on immigrant workers than the nations of Europe. Consequently, we still have little good evidence on earnings and expenditures among migrants in Europe. My analysis focuses on transnationalism among American-bound migrants, most (although not all) of them southerners.

Transnationalism during the era of mass male migrations meant the creation of family economies transcending national borders. In these family economies, flows of cash remittances complemented the comings and goings of men.[18] Initially, family economies linked work camps populated by wage-earning Italian men and rural Italian villages housing disproportionate numbers of women and children awaiting their return. Families accepted separations to keep family members as fully employed as possible. But men and women also schemed how and when to reunite or (in the case of the unmarried) to marry. Whether to locate a family's 'home base'[19] in Italy or abroad was a complex decision, emerging from a gradual process of learning about wages and prices in several places. While we cannot trace the learning process itself with any precision, the factors influencing Italians' decisions are clear enough.

Migration required families to learn what levels of security and material wellbeing they obtained by combining cash earned in Italy and abroad with food-raising and cloth production at home. Families also assessed the moral worth of differing work for men, women and children at home and abroad. The most important challenge was to learn the real value of cash earnings. Letters home and returning men reported on earnings abroad, and explained what those earnings meant once transformed into the moneta, scudi or lire of Italy. In Europe and in North America, unskilled sojourners from Italy typically earned wages a third lower than the wages of natives. In the US that meant $1.50 a day at the turn of the century or – given seasonal unemployment – a bit less than $300 per year.[20] When translated into lire, these wages seemed generous. In the Abruzzi in the 1870s, for example, agricultural workers earned 1–2 lire a day (except during harvests, when wages rose to 15 lire). Peasant men averaged 25 to 50 lire in income monthly but worked only nine or ten months each year. By contrast, in the Americas, a male sojourner working in construction earned 117 lire a month in the spring and 170 in autumn. Even if a migrant man borrowed 100 lire to pay his passage, and paid interest of 80 to 100 additional lire to a *padrone* (labour recruiter), or suffered two or three months unemployment, foreign wages were clearly higher than in Italy.[21] A man's annual income of $300 was more than five times that of a prosperous peasant family in Italy's north, and even larger when compared to family cash incomes in the south.

Unfortunately for male sojourners, living costs abroad were also much higher than in Italy. American observers who found appalling conditions in all-male boarding houses always noted (but rarely praised) the thriftiness of the men without women. Most men struggled to keep expenses below $200 a year. Sojourners denied themselves food, sex and pleasure in order to generate a surplus, while natives fumed over migrants' unAmerican living standards. They recognised that Italian workers could live on their low wages because they ate little more than rice, pasta, bread and vegetables, while native workers wanted meat. In fact, native workers needed high wages in order to pay for the higher costs of meat, housing, reproduction and family security in developing economies.[22] Italian men, too, had dependants, but they chose to spend their wages on reproduction where prices were low – in Italy.[23]

Men from the Abruzzi later claimed that they could save 1000 to 1500 lire during a year's work in the US. A year of work in Europe generated about 600 lire in savings, and six months' work in Germany produced a surplus of 300 to 500 lire. Even that more modest sum equalled the cash income of a peasant family.[24] When combined with women's production of food and cloth men's cash incomes easily sustained life and the reproduction of the next generation. Although peasants lived poorly, died young, and complained of '*la miseria*' (misery), they rarely starved. New sources of cash from abroad opened possibilities for greater security, comfort and pleasure in Italy. In 1880, a postal clerk in Picinisco saw almost 130,000 lire cross his counter – or about 150 lire for each of the 850 Europe-bound migrants from his small town.[25] Remittances to Italy soared with migration to the Americas, from 13 million lire in 1861 to 127 million lire in 1880, and then to 254 million a year after 1890 and 846 million a year after 1906. So large was the cash inflow that it ended Italy's negative balance of foreign trade by 1912.[26] American savings in particular struck peasants as extraordinary windfalls.

Still, men's remittances purchased security and comfort only if women and children at home continued to produce food and clothing. Analyses of migrant men and their wages often ignore their connection to the work of the women who waited for them at home. These women were also workers, albeit subsistence producers of food and clothing, working without wages for a family's consumption. Visitors from Europe and America noted with disgust the heavy and exhausting work of peasant women in Italy. In the north, they found women ploughing, mowing, carrying heavy loads of hay, wood, stone and water, grinding their own grains on hand mills, making their own bread, raising small animals, harvesting, gleaning, and processing food.[27] In the Val D'Aosta, a mountainous area of northwestern Italy where most men migrated seasonally to France, the investigator for a governmental inquest reported women were 'the true beasts of burden' of the region.[28]

In the centre and south, too, observers noted 'the women work like slaves', carrying as many as 70 kg of produce on their heads, often only eight days after giving birth.[29] Emma Ciccotosto, the daughter of a peasant family in the Abruzzi, whose father was absent for most of her childhood reported:

> Everything my mother knew she learned from her mother, and that included a lot of farm work . . . everything was done by hand. Our farm grew corn, wheat, olives, and flax, as well as vegetables and poultry. We had two sheep which my mother milked . . . Occasionally

> we raised a pig which my mother would sell . . . all the animals were stabled at the far end of the house and their manure was thrown out of a small door into the yard where it piled up until we had time to collect it to spread on the ground for the next season's planting.[30]

'We', meant this woman and her young children, aided by groups of neighbours working communally at harvest times.

Spinning and weaving were other chores on Emma Ciccotosto's mother's long list of tasks. In the northern regions of Lombardy and Piedmont, women's domestic production of cloth continued alongside both silk- or wool-spinning cottage industries, and the development of modern spinning and weaving mills after 1880.[31] In Italy's south, by contrast, women had begun to put aside their spindles and looms already in the 1870s, as cheap imported cloth rendered their labours unprofitable.[32]

Although women's work rates had declined from over 50 per cent over the previous thirty years, especially in the south, census takers in 1901 still listed one in three Italian women as active, wage-earning workers outside their homes. (This was a higher rate of female employment than in the United States, for example.) From Naples in 1909, Oreste Bordiga reported that female day labourers actually outnumbered men in one region of heavy male emigration.[33] The working women were the lucky ones: desperate women in Sicily, with its limited options for female work, instead reasserted feudal rights to collect snails and greens on uncultivated lands.[34] 'They graze like animals', a middle-class observer of women foragers noted with horror. The luckier white widows in southern areas turned to their parents, in-laws and female neighbours for support when necessary. They raised small household animals to eat or sell and they opened tiny shops to earn a few extra cents as 'penny capitalists'.[35] Although the culture increasingly condemned women who worked in the fields as immoral, it also harshly criticised women who did not work. They were the female 'brooms' that swept away family resources through their idleness.[36] The occasional woman who lived in idleness on remittances – as some clearly did – easily fell victim to gossips' charges of '*ozio*' (laziness).[37]

The desire to establish a family on a more secure footing within existing village hierarchies – as landed peasants, rentiers, or small artisans and shopkeepers – motivated male migration, scholars agree. These represented the occupations most respected in much of rural Italy in the nineteenth century, and they defined a more comfortable and civilised way of life within reach of Italy's peasants.[38] Few scholars have systematically measured upward mobility of returners.[39] But existing evidence suggests that occupational mobility was limited, occurring largely within the peasant class, as wage-earning *braccianti* (labourers) and peasants' sons acquired leases or small plots of land. Few returners became wealthy landowners because remittances too quickly inflated the value of local land.[40] Land hunger in Italy remained intense and produced a new wave of land occupations after the First World War.[41]

By contrast, many returners purchased new housing or improved the houses they owned, guaranteeing a healthier, more comfortable and more secure if modest life.[42] Houses signalled their improved social status too, since the very poorest had no homes, and sometimes still lived as mendicants or in caves. Investment in housing was especially common where sojourners returned from the Americas. In the area around Salerno in the first decade of the century, peasants paid 1000 lire (one to three years' savings) for houses government investigators found to be 'substantial'. These were freestanding, two-storey dwellings, quite unlike the older one- and two-storey attached houses of most villages. With plastered walls, and floors of brick, they had proper windows, a separate kitchen, an internal staircase and two upstairs rooms. Some had balconies and shutters, sturdy wooden doors, and a tiled roof.[43] In some villages, returners introduced acetylene lighting or made enquiries about obtaining an electricity supply in towns without piped water or sewage. The contrast of the homes of migrants to the 'old black homes, piled on top of each other and separated only by torturous, dark little streets' impressed even moralising middle-class observers.[44]

Cash earned abroad further transformed consumption habits among rural Italians, allowing many to enjoy a considerable sense of material improvement. Already in the 1870s and early 1880s, investigators had noticed with displeasure peasants' new-found fascination with purchasing from the local *pizzicagnolo*, or small shopkeeper who sold cheap trinkets, cloth, household equipment and pipes.[45] In many regions of the north, and a few of the larger cities of the south, poor men and women had already abandoned traditional costumes before migration. Bourgeois observers complained that 'homewoven cloth does not sufficiently satisfy [women's] vanity', so that the 'mania for dressing up' increased daily.[46] Mass migration accelerated a transformation in consumption already underway. Poor Italians abandoned sandals and wooden clogs for shoes; men purchased suits of wool and velvet, hats, and watches. By 1910, traditional women's costumes had disappeared in the coastal areas around Naples, and even in isolated mountain villages, women no longer wore traditional costume but donned only distinctive scarves, shawls or headwear.

Cash also allowed poorer migrants to eat well, which made it possible that their children could eventually grow as tall and robust as urbanites. Nineteenth-century investigations had established that Italian peasants consumed sufficient food to survive while working hard but that many men nevertheless failed to achieve draft requirements for height. They also concluded that peasant diets – regardless of region – were monotonous, largely vegetarian and probably nutritionally insufficient.[47] Northern peasants ate as much as a kilo of cornmeal polenta daily; their evening meal was a thick soup (*minestra*) of grains, legumes and vegetables, along with a little wine and occasional cheese. The poor rarely ate wheat bread, except in Sicily and Apulia, and even southerners rarely consumed pasta, except on holidays. Southerners ate more greens, fruits and vegetables, but their only seasoning was oil and they rarely ate cheese or meat. Even on holidays, they drank wine mixed with water (*vinello*).[48]

Twenty-five years later governmental investigators found sweeping changes in the diet of southern peasants. Wheat bread increasingly replaced other grains. Peasants more often kept a pig, and they used its meat to season pasta dishes weekly rather than twice a year. From the Molise, a member of the local elite complained about inflated food prices as 'the wives of the Americans arrive at the marketplace and buy up all the fresh fish newly arrived from Temoli, regardless of price'.[49]

The decision to send men abroad to earn wages, and to have them send remittances or return with their savings to Italy appears even more rational when we consider the costs of transplantation abroad. At least in the Americas, male sojourners could not easily support a transplanted family on their own earnings. In New York, where the typical Italian man earned from $250–$350 a year in the early twentieth century, Robert Chapin estimated that a family of four to six required about $800 a year to live adequately.[50] In Buenos Aires, the discrepancy between an unskilled labourer's earnings and estimated costs of family living was equally large.[51] Settlement abroad became financially feasible only when a man could find year-round or better-paid work, when a family could count on additional sources of cash income or when it could produce its own food.

Women and children had to become wage-earners for most families to survive the move to the Americas. According to Samuel Baily, 38 per cent of married Italian women in selected districts in Buenos Aires in 1895 worked for wages outside the home, while 60 to 80 per cent of unmarried women did so. In New York, ten years later, about 7 per cent of married women worked outside the home, and almost half of unmarried women did so. Women in Buenos Aires may have been more willing to leave home to work because they found employment in small-scale shops owned by fellow Italians, or because more were from Italy's north. Southern Italian women in New York, by contrast, had to move well beyond family circles to work for wages in garment factories owned by Jewish, German, or American employers.[52]

In New York, however, married women found industrial work to do at home. As homeworkers, they sewed trousers, cracked nuts and made artificial flowers, effectively combining wage earning with domestic chores.[53] Only a few New York census takers counted homeworkers as wage earners, but those who did found rates of wage earning among married and unmarried Italian women comparable to, or surpassing, those of Buenos Aires.[54] Although less well-studied, Italian families in France also seemed to expect some form of wage earning from married women and children alike.[55]

In Buenos Aires and in New York, immigrant women transformed domestic work into cash by taking into their homes sojourning men separated from their families. Family-based boarding was a new social relationship, and a source of income without precedent, in Italy. (This explains the use of the term 'bordante' for the men who became boarders – a term used throughout the Italian diaspora.) About a third of New York's Italian wives kept boarders at any one time; in Buenos Aires, the percentage was even higher, over 40 per cent. Boarders included relatives as well as friends and neighbours who paid small fees in exchange for meals, a bed and clean laundry. Boarders' contributions to family incomes were relatively small – scarcely a third of female wages earned outside the home – but (like home industrial work) they allowed many married women to continue working within the family circle and to fulfil domestic obligations too.[56]

Even with women and children working, and with boarders making their contributions, families of unskilled workers in New York and Buenos Aires struggled to pay high housing, food and clothing costs. In New York, in 1909, Robert Chapin estimated that three-quarters of Italian immigrant families in the city earned less than the $800 needed for a family of four to six to live securely. He reported Italians spending a fifth of their income on rent, almost half on food and 12 per cent on clothing. Yet, surprisingly, 58 per cent of the Italian families he surveyed also reported a budgetary surplus and some savings.[57] In Buenos Aires, where information about family budgets is scantier, Italian incomes were also well below those reformers found necessary to maintain minimum standards, yet over half of all working-class families there too reported some savings.[58] Many immigrant families obviously began saving at relatively low incomes. They did so by forgoing some of the pleasures of consumption in the modern, and industrialising cities of the Americas.

In neither New York nor Buenos Aires did immigrant families stint on food. Immigrant families in New York ate more eggs, meat, cheese and milk than returners to Italy. Many reported the satisfaction they felt in eating great quantities. 'Don't you remember how our *paesani* here in America ate to their heart's delight till they were belching like pigs and how they dumped mountains of uneaten food out of the window?', one woman in New York reminisced with pleasurable exaggeration.[59] In Buenos Aires, too, where beef was an important product of the nearby pampas, immigrants remembered eating well.[60] More than any other consumer choice, plentiful food and drink symbolised well-being for transplanted Italians in both North and South America.

Evidence from New York suggests that families more often skimped on clothing, housing, recreation and entertainment. Married women (and their youngest children) sometimes still went barefoot, made their own clothes and remodelled cast-offs. Men claimed only very small pleasures for themselves – notably tobacco, a coffee or a beer at a nearby café. Like their children, husbands and sons turned over their paychecks to their wives and mothers, who were the budget managers in most families.[61] Adolescent children proved the least willing to forgo the pleasures of urban consumerism. Some openly resented having to turn over 'every cent'; others quietly 'borrowed from mother'. One girl in Rhode Island reported 'I'll never forget the time I got my first pay . . . I went downtown, first, and I spent a lot, more than half of my money . . . I just went hog wild'. More complied and 'handed our pays in'. Girls desired modern clothing, urban shoes and hats. Boys wanted to enjoy sports, shows, dancehalls or other commercial entertainments.[62] Somewhat reluctantly, mothers in New York relinquished control over their sons' wages, but having already accepted that their daughters left the family circle to work for wages, mothers seemed less willing to allow adolescent girls control over their own wages.

In both densely settled New York and lower-density Buenos Aires, immigrant mothers ruthlessly limited the amount they spent on rent in order to facilitate saving. In New York, families moved frequently in search of the cheapest quarters. Many families also willingly lived in very close proximity, with families of five or more in two rooms. In New York's downtown Little Italy the youngest of families with one or two children doubled up and lived in one room each, or three families to a three-room apartment. They shared a kitchen, and often housed additional boarders in what census takers called 'partner households'.[63] Because so many Italian immigrants crowded into small, old tenement dwellings, social reformers like Robert Chapin despaired of their ever learning or accepting American housing standards.[64]

Home ownership was even more important, for migrants had left a homeland where home ownership had been relatively common, even among quite poor peasants. Returners could purchase houses with savings from a year or two of work by one successful male migrant. In the Americas, by contrast, home ownership required a long-term struggle, and one in which the wages of growing children were crucial – but disputed – elements. Few Italians in high-density New York became home owners before the 1920s; a government investigation in 1909 found home ownership rates of only 1 per cent. By contrast, in Buenos Aires, with its lower-scale housing, and its higher proportions of skilled and white collar immigrants, 16 per cent of Italian families in 1904 already lived in houses they owned. Compared to returners, however, these were shabby results.[65]

Thus, it is not at all clear that transplantation of men and women together to the Americas was the best choice for family groups pursuing short-term security. The parsimony of mother budget managers, like that of the men without women, originated in part in a desire to assist family members in Italy. But it also reflected persisting feelings of insecurity about the financial future, and a desire to hold open the possibility of return to the home village. While family solidarity clearly facilitated migration, transplantation abroad also demanded changes at the centre of family life. Families who relocated abroad were peasants and artisans who had only recently severed their ties to subsistence production. In doing so, they relinquished their ideal of families working together under the leadership of the husband and father in order to benefit from women and children's cash contributions to a consumer family economy. They faced as well the growing independence of their own children as wage-earners and consumers. Faced with complex trade-offs like these, the long-term commitment of many Italians to transnationalism is easier to understand, and to see as a sensible choice, no matter what its hardships.

Conclusion

International family economies developed out of rational, shrewd choices, but we cannot easily know whether to credit that shrewdness to the men without women or the women who waited for them. Transnationalism as a way of working-class life allowed men to earn where wages were relatively high and to spend where prices were relatively low. Prices in Italy remained low, furthermore, because so many women and children continued to be enmeshed in subsistence production and remained outside the consumer marketplace. Studies of Italy's migrations often comment on the importance of foreign labour markets in driving male migration. One male emigrant summarised his feelings about work, 'My job was my *via crucia*, my misery, my hatred, and yet I lived in continuous fear of losing the bloody thing. THE JOB that damnable affair, THE JOB . . . this blood-sucking thing.'[66]

'THE JOB . . . this blood-sucking thing' loomed large in decisions about the location of a family home base, and in women's and children's migrations, too. Only the pampas of Argentina and the plantations of Brazil and Australia offered migrants possibilities to work together as families, and to combine wage-earning and subsistence production in familiar ways. Cities offered women better wage-earning opportunities – in domestic service and in industry – but only if women worked away from their families. The lure of female jobs was strongest when women's opportunities to work in Italy were also most limited – as they were, for example, in Sicily. Families reached different conclusions when faced with such choices. Sicily had the highest rates of female migration in part because women could better contribute to family economies abroad than at home.

At the same time, maintaining a home base in Italy typically required either repeated male migrations or very long separations of fathers and sons from their families. In the north, contract labourers might go seasonally to Europe for many years. In the south, too, Emma Ciccotosto's father left her Abruzzi home twice for short sojourns in the US before emigrating again to Australia in the 1920s. Only after fifteen years of circulatory migrations to two continents did he call for his wife and children to reestablish their home base in Australia. In the lives of the Ciccotosto family one senses uncertainty, false starts and mixed reactions, not only to the hardships of separation but to prospects for achieving family security in Italy, America or Australia.

Whether they reunited in Italy or abroad, Italy's men and women generally desired security for themselves as part of family groups. Most women, and migrated men, needed to work – the question was where and under what conditions. Migrants' lives responded as much to the reproduction of families in Italy as to the exigencies of wage earning abroad. Working in different locations and at quite diverse tasks, Italian men and women seemed almost to occupy different class positions within the global economy, even as their family lives intimately entwined them. Wage-earning and subsistence production proved surprisingly compatible for both Italy's supposedly more economically and culturally advanced northerners and its supposedly more 'economically backward' and patriarchal southerners alike. For surprising numbers of Italian men and women, transnationalism and male emigration provided a surer foundation for family security than female emigration and family transplantation, even to the distant magnets of the economically booming United States and Argentina.

Notes

1 E. G. Ravenstein, 'The Laws of Migration', *Journal of the Royal Statistical Society* 48 (1885): 167–235.

2 D. Gabaccia, 'Women of the Mass Migrations: from Minority to Majority, 1820–1930', in D. Hoerder and L.P. Moch (eds), *European Migrants: Global and Local Perspectives* (Boston: Northeastern University Press, 1996), pp. 90–111; M. F. Houstoun *et al.*, 'Female Predominance of Immigration to the United States since 1930: a First Look', *International Migration Review* 28 (Winter 1984): 908–963.

3 R. F. Harney, 'Men Without Women: Italian Migrants in Canada, 1885–1930', in Betty Boyd Caroli, Robert F. Harney and Lydio F. Tomasi (eds), *The Italian Immigrant Woman in North America* (Toronto: The Multicultural History Society of Ontario, 1978), pp. 79–101.

4 *Annuario statistico italiano* (Roma: Commissariato dell'Emigrazione, 1926), pp. 241–242; S. L. Baily, *Immigrants in the Lands of Promise: Italians in Buenos Aires and New York City, 1870–1914* (Ithaca, NY: Cornell University Press, 1999), Table 2.3.

5 C. B. Brettell, *The Men Who Migrate and the Women Who Wait: Population and History in a Portuguese Parish* (Princeton, NJ: Princeton University Press, 1986); L.S. Reeder, 'Widows in White: Sicilian Women and Mass Migration, 1880–1930', unpublished Ph.D. thesis, Rutgers University, 1995. A useful study of women who waited in Italy's north is P. Audenino, 'Le custodi della montanga: donne e migrazioni stagionali in una comunità alpina', in P. Corti (ed.), 'Società rurale e ruoli femminili in Italia tra Ottocento e Novecento', *Annali dell'Istituto 'Alcide Cervi'* 12 (1990): 265–288. See also V. Teti, 'Noti sui comportamenti delle donne sole degli "americani" durante la prima emigrazione in Calabria', *Studi emigrazione* 24 (1987): 13–46; P. Corti, 'Societés sans hommes et intégrations des femmes à l'étranger; Le cas de l'Italie', *Revue européenne des migrations internationales* 9, 2 (1993): 113–128.

6 N. Glick-Schiller, L. Basch and C. Blanc-Szanton (eds), *Towards a Transnational Perspective on Migration: Race, Class, Ethnicity, and Nationalism Reconsidered* (New York: Academic Press, 1992); L. G. Basch, N. Glick-Schiller and C. Szanton Blanc, *Nations Unbound: Transnational Projects, Postcolonial Predicaments, and Deterritorialized Nation-States* (Langhorne, PA: Gordon and Breach, 1994).

7 Quoted in J. C. Moya, *Cousins and Strangers: Spanish Immigrants in Buenos Aires, 1850–1930* (Berkeley: University of California Press, 1998), p. 49. See also Walter Nugent, 'Frontiers and Empires in the Late Nineteenth Century', *Western Historical Quarterly* 20 (November 1989): 393–408.

8 For worldwide migrations, see Lydia Potts, *The World Labour Market: a History of Migration* (London: Zed Books, 1990); Robin Cohen (ed.), *The Cambridge Survey of World Migration* (Cambridge: Cambridge University Press, 1995); Robin Cohen, *Global Diasporas: an Introduction* (Seattle: University of Washington Press, 1997). See also Dirk Hoerder, *Global Migrations* (Durham, NC: Duke University Press, forthcoming).

9 R. J. Vecoli, 'The Italian Diaspora', in R. Cohen (ed.), *The Cambridge Survey of World Migration* (Cambridge: Cambridge University Press, 1995), p. 114; R. Foerster, *The Italian Emigration of our Times* (New York: Russell and Russell, 1968), pp. 3–4; see also Mark Wyman, *Round-Trip to America: the Immigrants Return to Europe, 1880–1930* (Ithaca, NY: Cornell University Press, 1993) and J.D. Gould, 'Emigration, the Road Home: Return Migration from the U.S.A.', *Journal of European Economic History* 9 (Spring 1980): 41–112.

10 F. Ramella, *Terra e telai: sistemi di parentela e manifattura nel Biellese dell'Ottocento* (Torino: Einaudi, 1984).

11 D. Gabaccia, 'In the Shadows of the Periphery: Italian Women in the Nineteenth Century', in M. J. Boxer and J. H. Quataert (eds), *Connecting Spheres: Women in the Western World, 1500 to the Present* (New York: Oxford University Press, 1987), pp. 166–175.

12 D. Gabaccia, *Italy's Many Diasporas* (London: University College of London Press, 2000), p. 78.

13 R. del Fabbro, *Transalpini: Italienische Arbeitswanderung nach Süddeutschland im Kaiserreich 1870–1918* (Osnabrück: Universitätsverlag Rasch, 1996), p. 4.

14 G. Rosoli (ed.), *Un secolo di emigrazione italiana, 1876–1976* (Rome: Centro Studi Emigrazione, 1978), Table 5.

15 Baily, *Immigrants in the Lands of Promise*, Table 3.4.

16 B. Boyd Caroli, *Italian Repatriation from the United States, 1900–1914* (New York: Center for Migration Studies, 1973), pp. 49–50.

17 A large scholarly literature has long debated the supposed familism of Italians, but it has focused almost exclusively on the south. See, e.g. the work of Edward Banfield, *The Moral Basis of a Backward Society* (Glencoe, IL.: The Free Press, 1958). His many critics included S. F. Silverman, 'Agricultural Organization, Social Structure and Values in Italy: Amoral Familism Reconsidered', *American Anthropologist* 70 (1968): 1–20; W. Muraskin, 'The Moral Basis of a Backward Sociologist: Edward Banfield, the Italians and the Italian-Americans,' *American Journal of Sociology* 79 (1974): 1484–1496. For general historical introductions to the issues of Italian family history, see P. Macry, 'Rethinking a Stereotype: Territorial Differences and Family Models in the Modernization of Italy', *Journal of Modern Italian Studies* 2, 2 (1997): 188–214; D. I. Kertzer and R. P. Saller (eds), *The Family in Italy: from Antiquity to the Present* (New Haven, CT: Yale University Press, 1991).

18 There is a large, and contentious, scholarly literature on family economies. For the evolution of the argument, particularly about the relationship of patriarchy, gender and family solidarity and decision-making, see L.A. Tilly and J. Scott,

Women, Work and Family (New York: Holt, Rinehart & Winston, 1978); P. Hilden, 'Family History vs. Women in History: a Critique of Tilly and Scott,' *International Labor and Working Class History* 16 (Fall 1979): 1–11; L. Tilly, 'After Family Strategies, What?' *Historical Methods* 20 (Summer 1987): 123–125.

19 Basch, Glick-Schiller and Szanton Blanc, *Nations Unbound*, p. 240.

20 On wages, see Foerster, *The Italian Emigration of Our Times*, pp. 143–144, 166, 200, 378–379.

21 *Atti della Giunta parlamentare per l'inchiesta agraria e sulle condizioni della classe agricola* (Rome: Forzani Tip. Del Senato, 1883–1886), vol. XII, fasc. I, p. 486.

22 R. Harney, 'Men Without Women: Italian Migrants in Canada, 1885–1930', in B.B. Caroli, R.F. Harney and L.F. Tomasi (eds), *The Italian Immigrant Woman in North America* (Toronto: Multicultural History Society of Ontario, 1978): 79–101.

23 M. Burawoy, 'The Functions and Reproduction of Migrant Labor: Comparative Material from Southern Africa and the United States', *American Journal of Sociology* 81 (March 1976): 1076–1087. There is a sizeable and useful scholarly literature, inspired by feminist socialist theorists, on the reproduction of labour power. See K. Young *et al.*., *Of Marriage and the Market: Women's Subordination in International Perspective* (London: CSE Books, 1981); A. Kuhn and A. Wolpe, *Feminism and Materialism: Women and Modes of Production* (London: Routledge & Kegan Paul, 1978); C. Meillassoux, *Maidens, Meal, and Money: Capitalism and the Domestic Economy* (Cambridge: Cambridge University Press, 1981). See also J. Smith, I. Wallerstein and H. Evers (eds), *Households and the World Economy* (Beverly Hills, CA: Sage Publications, 1984).

24 *Inchiesta parlamentare sulle condizioni dei contadini nelle provincie meridionali e nella Sicilia* (Rome: Tip. Naz di Giovanni Bertero, 1910), vol. 2, p. 258.

25 *Atti della Giunta parlamentare per l'inchiesta agraria*, vol. VII, fasc. II, p. 347.

26 On remittances, see *Annuario statistico italiana*, pp. 1637–1645; D. Cinel, *The National Integration of Italian Return Migration, 1870–1929* (Cambridge: Cambridge University Press, 1991), pp. 141–144.

27 Besides E. Zappi, *If Eight Hours Seem Too Few: Mobilization of Women Workers in the Italian Rice Fields* (Albany: State University of New York Press, 1991), and del Fabbro, *Transalpini*, pp. 264–265; see *Atti della Giunta parlamentare per l'inchiesta agraria*, vol. IV, fasc. I, pp. 8–17 (on the Veneto) and vol. VIII, tomo I, fasc. II, pp. 628–632 (on various regions of Piedmont).

28 *Atti della Giunta parlamentare per l'inchiesta agraria*, vol. VIII, tomo II, fasc. I, p. 126.

29 ibid., vol. IV, p. 259.

30 E. Ciccotosto and M. Bosworth, *Emma: a Translated Life* (Fremantle, Australia: Fremantle Press, 1990), pp. 22–25.

31 Besides Ramella, *Terra e telai*, see L.A. Tilly, *Politics and Class in Milan, 1881–1901* (New York: Oxford University Press, 1992), pp. 71–72.

32 Gabaccia, 'In the Shadows of the Periphery'.

33 *Inchiesta parlamentare sulle condizione dei contadini*, vol. IV, p. 257.

34 D. Gabaccia, *From Sicily to Elizabeth Street: Housing and Social Change Among Italian Immigrants, 1880–1930* (Albany: State University of New York Press, 1984), ch. 3; see Reeder, 'Widows in White'.

35 See L. Reeder, 'When the Men Left Sutera: Sicilian Women and Mass Migration 1880–1920', in D. Gabaccia and F. Iacovetta (eds), *Foreign, Female and Fighting Back* (Toronto: University of Toronto Press, forthcoming 2002).

36 Giuseppe Pitrè, *Proverbi siciliani* (Palermo: 'Il Vespro', 1978), orig. published 1870–1913, vol. II, p. 92.

37 *Inchiesta parlamentare sulle condizioni dei contadini*, vol. 4, 'Caserta'.

38 On class relations in rural Italy, see Renzo Del Carria, *Proletaria senza rivoluzione* [4 vols](Roma: Sanelli, 1975); F. Della Peruta, *Società e classi popolari nell'Italia dell'Ottocento* (Siracusa: Ediprint, 1985).

39 Besides Cinel, *National Integration of Italian Return Migration*, and Caroli, *Italian Repatriation from the United States*, see the work of Francesco Paolo Cerase, 'Su una tipologia di emigrati ritornati: il ritorno di investimento', *Studi emigrazione* 4, 10 (1967): 327–344; 'Expectations and Reality: a Case Study of Return Migration from the United States to Southern Italy', *International Migration Review* 8 (1974): 245–262; *L'emigrazione di ritorno: Innovazione o reazione? L'esperienza dell'emigrazione di ritorno dagli Stati Uniti d'America* (Rome: Istituto Gini, 1971); G. Gilkey, 'The United States and Italy: Migration and Repatriation', *Journal of Developing Areas* 2 (1967): 23–35.

40 Cinel, *National Integration of Italian Return Migration*, pp. 164–168.

41 A. Papa, 'Guerra e terra', *Studi storici* 10 (1969): 3–45.

42 J. Davis, *Land and Family in Pisticci*, London School of Economics Monographs on Social Anthropology, 48 (New York: Humanities Press, 1973); Gabaccia, *From Sicily to Elizabeth Street*, pp. 32–33.

43 *Inchiesta parlamentare sulle condizioni dei contadini*, vol. V, p. 504.

44 ibid., vol. 2, pp. 186–187.

45 *Atti della Giunta parlamentare per l'inchiesta agraria*, vol. V, tomo II, p. 154.

46 ibid., vol. I, p. 236.

47 For an overview, S. Somogyi, 'L'alimentazione nell'Italia unita', in R. Romano and C. Vivanti (eds), *Storia d'Italia*, vol. V: *I Documenti* (Torino: Giulio Einaudi, 1973), pp. 841–887.

48 *Atti della Giunta parlamentare per l'inchiesta agraria* contains detailed notes on the diet of peasants in all of Italy's regions in the 1870s and 1880s.

49 *Inchiesta parlamentare sulle condizioni dei contadini*, vol. II, p. 159.

50 R. C. Chapin, *The Standard of Living Among Workingmen's Families in New York City* (New York: Charities Publication Committee, 1909); see also L.B. More, *Wage Earners' Budgets*, Greenwich House Series of Social Studies, 1 (New York: Henry Holt, 1907).

51 Baily, *Immigrants in the Lands of Promise*, pp. 108–113.

52 Baily, *Immigrants in the Lands of Promise*, Table 7.7; M. Cohen, *Workshop to Office: Two Generations of Italian Women in New York City, 1900–1950* (Ithaca, NY: Cornell University Press, 1993); E. Ewen, *Immigrant Women in the Land of Dollars: Life and Culture on the Lower East Side, 1890–1925* (New York: Monthly Review Press, 1985), ch. 6; N. L. Green, *Ready-to-Wear; Ready-to-Work: a Century of Industry and Immigrants in Paris and New York* (Durham, NC: Duke University Press, 1997), ch. 6.

53 For a contemporary's report, see M.H. Willett, *The Employment of Women in the Clothing Trade*, Columbia University Studies in History, Economics and Public Law, 16 (New York: Columbia University Press, 1902); for a recent assessment, C. R. Daniels, 'Between Home and Factory: Homeworkers and the State', in E. Boris and C. R. Daniels (eds), *Homework: Historical and Contemporary Perspectives on Paid Labor at Home* (Urbana: University of Illinois Press, 1989).

54 L. Betts, 'Italian Peasants in a New Law Tenement', *Harper's Bazaar* 38 (1904): 804; Gabaccia, *From Sicily to Elizabeth Street*, p. 64; see also T. Kessner and B. B. Caroli, 'New Immigrant Women at Work: Italians and Jews in New York City, 1880–1905', *Journal of Ethnic Studies* 5 (1978): 19–32. Louise C. Odencrantz, *Italian Women in Industry: a Study of Conditions in New York City* (New York: Russell Sage Foundation, 1919), pp. 16, 21, also found 24 per cent of married Italian women working outside the home.

55 Foerster, *Italian Emigration of Our Times*, pp. 144–147.

56 Baily, *Immigrants in the Lands of Promise*, Tables 7.5, 7.6. See also R. F. Harney, 'Boarding and Belonging: Thoughts on Sojourner Institutions', *Urban History Review* 2 (1978): 8–37. For general patterns in the US, see J. Modell and T. K. Hareven, 'Urbanization and the Malleable Household: an Examination of

Boarding and Lodging in American Families', *Journal of Marriage and the Family* 35 (1973): 467–479.

57 Chapin, *The Standard of Living Among Workingmen's Families*, pp. 245–250. See also State of New York, *Factory Commission Report* (1915), Vol. 4, pp. 1608–1609, 1619–1620, 1668.

58 Baily, *Immigrants in the Lands of Promise*, Tables 5.5, 5.6.

59 Gabaccia, *From Sicily to Elizabeth Street*, p. 92.

60 On Argentina, see P. Corti, 'Circuiti migratori e consuetudini alimentari nella rappresentazione autobiografica degli emigranti piemontesi', in A. Capatti, A. De Bernardi, and A. Varni (eds), *L'alimentazione nella storia dell'Italia contemporanea, Storia d'Italia, Annali* (Torino: Einaudi, 1997); P. Ortoleva, 'La tradizione e l'abbondanza; Riflessioni sulla cucina degli italiani d'America', *Altreitalie* 7 (1992): 31–52; A. Schneider, 'L'etnicità, il cambiamento dei paradigmi e le variazioni nel consumo di cibi tra gli italiani a Buenos Aires', *Altreitalie* 7 (January–June 1992): 71–83. On the US, more generally, D. Gabaccia, *We Are What We Eat: Ethnic Food and the Making of Americans* (Cambridge, MA: Harvard University Press, 1998), pp. 51–55; D. Gabaccia, 'Italian-American Cookbooks: from Oral to Print Culture', *Italian Americana* 16, 1 (1998):15–23 and C. Helstosky, 'The Tradition of Invention: Reading History through "La Cucina Casareccia Napoletana"', in *Italian Americana* 16, 1 (1998): 7–23.

61 Gabaccia, *From Sicily to Elizabeth Street*, pp. 101–102.

62 Direct quotes are from J. E. Smith, *Family Connections: a History of Italian and Jewish Immigrant Lives in Providence, Rhode Island, 1900–1940* (Albany: State University of New York Press, 1985), p. 75.

63 Gabaccia, *From Sicily to Elizabeth Street*, pp. 75–77.

64 Baily, *Immigrants in the Lands of Promise*, ch. 6.

65 Baily, *Immigrants in the Lands of Promise*, Table 5.7; see also S.L. Baily, 'Patrones de residencia de los italianos en Buenos Aires y Nueva York: 1880–1914', *Estudios Migratorios Latinoamericanos* 1 (1985): 8–47.

66 M. LaSorte, *La Merica: Images of Italian Greenhorn Experience* (Philadelphia, PA: Temple University Press, 1985), p. 61.

11 Gender and twentieth-century Irish migration, 1921–1971

Enda Delaney

Introduction

Migration has been a persistent feature of Irish population change since the seventeenth century and numerous studies have been published dealing with Irish emigration in the modern era.[1] From 1815 until 1845, in total approximately one million people migrated from Ireland to North America, somewhere in the region of half that number left for Britain and roughly 30,000 people went to the other significant destination for Irish migrants, Australia.[2] During the great Irish famine (1845–1850), the rate of migration accelerated considerably to an annual gross figure of approximately 200,000 persons, and the years immediately after the famine were marked by continuing migration, which reached its highest point in 1851 when 250,000 migrants left Ireland.[3] Post-famine Ireland was characterised by a social structure in which emigration played a pivotal role, albeit with varying intensity depending on the economic situation both in Ireland and in the receiving countries, principally the United States and Britain (see Table 11.1).

Migration from nineteenth-century Ireland was unusual in one key respect: the high proportion of single females who travelled to the United States and Britain. This was a relatively unique feature of the European migration flow in the nineteenth and early twentieth centuries.[4] This aspect of nineteenth-century Irish migration has been the subject of fairly extensive investigation, with a particular focus on the relationship between female migration, education and the social structure of post-famine rural Ireland.[5] However, for the twentieth century and more especially for the period after Irish independence in 1921, few historians have examined the relationship between gender and Irish migration.[6] The impetus for a gender-orientated analysis of migration within a global context has come from such cognate social science disciplines as sociology and geography rather than history.[7] Similarly, in relation to gender and twentieth-century Irish migration, only one historian has tackled this important subject and for the most part his analysis deals with the political reaction to female migration.[8] The aims of this chapter are first to outline

Table 11.1 Irish emigration, 1852–1921

Period	*Females*	*Males*	*Total*
1852–1860[1]	494,101	518,257	1,012,358
1861–1870	380,019	469,817	849,836
1871–1880	281,616	342,317	623,933
1881–1890	375,408	395,298	770,706
1891–1900	231,956	201,570	433,526
1901–1910	173,727	172,297	346,024
1911–1921[2]	83,204	81,187	164,391

Source: Commission on Emigration and Other Population Problems, 1948–1954, *Reports*, Dublin, Stationery Office [1955], Pr. 2541, Table 28, pp. 318–319.

Notes
1 9-year period.
2 11-year period.

the patterns of Irish migration between 1921 and 1971, with a special focus on the gender profile of the Irish migrant flow, and second, to examine the policy of the Irish state in relation to migration, but more especially significant differences in terms of views expressed with regard to female emigration. The final section of the chapter is devoted to the complex issue of explaining gender differentials in migration, with a particular emphasis on a range of explanations which might be regarded as being economic in nature.

Before turning to the profile of the Irish migrant flow between 1921 and 1971, three important contextual points should be made. First, migration was, of course, not unique to twentieth-century Ireland but the one key difference is that Irish people travelled from rural Ireland to British cities rather than to Irish cities: in effect, a form of urbanisation across national boundaries. The available evidence suggests a low level of migration within Ireland throughout the entire period. Second, migration from Ireland in the twentieth century was predominantly a movement of population out of rural and small-town Ireland owing to the distribution of the total population. In 1926 roughly one-third of the Irish population lived in towns with a population of 1,500 persons or over.[9] By 1971 the picture had changed somewhat with over 50 per cent of the Irish population residing in towns of 1,500 persons or over.[10] Regional migration data indicate that whilst a significant proportion of the migrants came from urban areas, especially the capital city of Dublin, the majority of migrants came from rural areas, particularly in the west, north-west and south-west of Ireland.[11] Lastly, Britain rather than the United States became the principal destination for Irish migrants in the twentieth century. Prior to the onset of the Depression in 1929, the United States was the preferred destination for most Irish migrants with a smaller but substantial flow travelling to Britain. However with the gradual lifting of the Depression in the mid-1930s, Irish migrants opted to travel to Britain with increasing regularity.

Estimates indicate that over 80 per cent of Irish migrants travelled to Britain in the postwar period until 1971: thereafter the choice of destinations became more varied.[12]

Patterns and profile

In 1921–1922 the twenty-six counties of the Irish Free State became an independent state. Whilst annual migration statistics had been published under the British regime, no such data were collected by the Irish authorities and therefore we have to rely on intercensal estimates of net migration.[13] Whilst these estimates provide rather static snapshots, they are useful in gauging the scale of migration from twentieth-century Ireland (see Table 11.2). In general terms, Irish migration registered peaks in the mid-1930s, in the war years and late 1940s, and throughout the 1950s (see Table 11.2).[14] In the mid-1930s, Irish emigration increased as opportunities for employment became available in Britain, particularly in the 'new' industries located in the south-east of England. The outbreak of war in September 1939 resulted in restrictions being imposed on Irish citizens wishing to travel to Britain, but during the war, the Irish and British authorities concluded an informal labour transfer arrangement whereby Irish citizens were for the first time officially recruited for employment in Britain. Some 150,000 Irish citizens travelled to Britain during the war under these arrangements and this migrant labour played an important role in wartime civilian industries.[15] In the postwar period as in the interwar years, Irish citizens continued to enjoy free access to the British labour market. During the immediate postwar period, a surge in migration is evident and the 1950s marked the peak of Irish migration when roughly 40,000 people migrated from the country annually, reflecting the sorry state of the Irish economy at this time. By the close of our period, a decreased level of migration and indeed substantial return flow from Britain was apparent which can be explained by the relative economic prosperity in Ireland during the 1960s.

Table 11.2 Average annual Irish net migration, by gender, 1926–1971

Period	*Females*	*Males*	*Total*	*Females per 1,000 males*
1926–1936	9,420	7,255	16,675	1,298
1936–1946	7,454	11,258	18,712	662
1946–1951	14,075	10,309	24,384	1,365
1951–1956	17,696	21,657	39,353	817
1956–1961	20,486	21,915	42,401	935
1961–1966	8,598	7,523	16,121	1,143
1966–1971	5,831	4,950	10,781	1,178

Source: *Census of Population*, 1971, I: *Population of District Electoral Divisions . . .*, Dublin, Stationery Office, 1972, Table x, p. xxi and Table xi, p. xxii.

The profile of the migrant flow sheds some light on the reasons for Irish migration. The typical migrant was young, and Fitzpatrick's aphorism relating to nineteenth-century Irish migrants, that they 'claimed neither status or skill' applied equally to the majority of migrants from twentieth-century Ireland.[16] For example, data derived from applications for travel permits between 1943 and 1951 indicate that over half of the males who received travel permits were aged under 25 years, with nearly 70 per cent of females being less than 25 years of age.[17] Detailed analysis of the admittedly fragmentary evidence available concerning the occupational background of migrants indicates that they were invariably recorded as 'agricultural labourers', 'domestic servants' or 'relatives assisting' (both male and female) on family farms.[18] However, these labels were applied indiscriminately to young men and women who had not yet entered the labour market and therefore definitive statements on the occupational profile are precluded. Unfortunately, the evidence does not allow for an analysis of social class but it can be stated with some certainty that those confined to the bottom rungs of the economic ladder were more likely to migrate. Notwithstanding the fact that the great majority of migrants were unskilled workers with an agricultural background, a skilled and professional element constituted a constant if numerically small proportion of the flow.[19]

Our principal concern here is with the relationship between gender and Irish migration, and it can be seen that in four intercensal periods (1926–1936; 1946–1951; 1961–1966 and 1966–1971) more females than males migrated from Ireland (see Table 11.2). Taking the long-range view from 1926 until 1971, there is little overall difference between the total numbers of females and males who migrated (973 females per 1,000 males).[20] Using cohort depletion techniques the scale of this exodus and its impact on both sexes can be illustrated (see Table 11.3). Roughly one in three of the population aged under 30 years in 1946 had left Ireland by 1971, highlighting the sheer enormousness of migration from postwar

Table 11.3 Estimated percentage of each age cohort 'lost' from the Republic of Ireland as a result of net migration up to 1971

	1926		*1936*		*1946*	
	Females	*Males*	*Females*	*Males*	*Females*	*Males*
0–4	31.4	34.1	37.6	37.9	38.2	38.6
5–9	31.0	32.5	36.3	37.8	40.7	40.6
10–14	31.5	31.4	34.2	36.9	39.6	40.0
15–19	33.9	31.2	28.5	31.4	33.8	35.6
20–24	23.9	25.6	21.5	26.6	22.6	26.4
25–29	10.7	5.9	16.9	16.8	15.5	13.8

Source: After Donal Garvey, 'The history of migration flows in the Republic of Ireland', *Population Trends*, 1985, no. 39: Table 3, p. 24.

Ireland, and it is equally significant that this exodus affected both sexes alike. This relative parity in terms of gender is an unusual feature of twentieth-century European migration flows and we shall return to possible explanations for this pattern at a later stage.

Migration, gender and state policy

Recent writings rightly stress the crucial role of the state in 'shaping the history of international migration'.[21] In the case of Ireland, the policy of the state in relation to migration, in so far as a distinct policy existed, will be outlined paying particular attention to the differences in policy and administrative discourse over time as they relate to gender. A central element of the ideology which was developed and articulated in pre-independence Ireland was that self-government would in turn lead to the cessation of migration out of the country. Such an optimistic aim was perhaps more a rhetorical aspiration rather than a concrete policy objective. Nevertheless, this sentiment conditioned subsequent attitudes in respect of migration over the course of the period considered here. In brief, 'emigration' was viewed as harmful to national morale and well-being, and in many ways the failure 'to stem the haemorrhage' was seen as an embarrassing failure on the part of Irish policymakers.[22] Successive governments condemned migration out of Ireland as an 'evil' whilst at the same time reaping the benefits arising from such vast numbers leaving the country, principally reduced unemployment and the deflated potential for social unrest. However, in terms of gender, the Irish state on a number of occasions displayed sustained interest in female migration and the welfare of females living in Britain.

Much of the impetus for the Irish state's active interest in female migration was the result of representations made by Roman Catholic clergy. Statements issued by Irish Roman Catholic prelates rarely, if ever, stemmed the flow of migrants, but pressure applied to the government was a significant factor in instigating the formulation of official policy, particularly regarding female migration. The recurrent theme of many of the public statements (and private representations) by members of the Irish Catholic hierarchy was that young Irish women in particular were susceptible to moral 'dangers' in 'godless' Britain. In the late 1930s Roman Catholic bishops in Ireland and Britain urged the Irish state to regulate female migration and to take responsibility for ensuring the welfare of female migrants (both physical and moral) through the appointment of a welfare officer to be based in London. The response of the government of the day was not to interfere with the free movement of labour and to suggest that the welfare of Irish migrants in Britain more properly fell within the remit of Catholic clergy in Britain rather than the Irish state.[23]

For the first time the Irish state was involved in the control and regulation of migration with the onset of war in September 1939. By necessity the Second World War resulted in the regulation of labour migration between Ireland and Britain owing to security considerations. A complicated set of measures was implemented by authorities on both sides of the Irish Sea which regulated and monitored labour migration.[24] In July 1941 a scheme was put in place whereby Irish citizens wishing to travel to Britain for employment were facilitated by the Irish state. The only restriction imposed was that all applicants for work in Britain be over 22 years, although the available evidence suggests that in practice this regulation was not adhered to for the most part.[25]

The machinery which was established to regulate and monitor migration out of Ireland during the Second World War was gradually dismantled in the immediate postwar period, although a travel identity card was still required to enter Britain until April 1952.[26] Throughout 1946 and 1947 the number of applications for travel identity cards for females increased significantly. As a result of this development the Irish state seriously considered imposing a prohibition on the migration of females for employment in Britain. Since this flow was no longer regulated, many women under the age of 21 years were leaving for work in domestic service in Britain owing to the better conditions of work and pay.[27] According to Irish officials this movement of population had consequences which could only be limited by refusing permits to females under a specified age such as 21 or 22 years:

> The moral and social dangers of emigration are obviously the greater the younger and more inexperienced the emigrant and the most effective method of protecting the interests of young female emigrants is the imposition of an age limit below which girls would not be allowed to emigrate. This method would have the additional advantage of going some way to protect our own population from an alarming loss of women of marriageable and child bearing age.[28]

It is of particular significance that females were perceived to be unable to protect their own 'interests' and what was required was direct state intervention to ensure that only female migrants aged over 21 years would be allowed to leave the country. In the event, the government of the day did not embark upon this drastic course of action, presumably because of the practical difficulties involved and the fear of the negative perception that such a ban on female migration would create.[29]

In the postwar period the hierarchy of the Roman Catholic Church in Ireland became increasingly involved in making representations to successive Irish governments with regard to female migration to Britain. For example, at their meeting in October 1947, the bishops passed a resolution which expressed their 'alarm' at the continuing high level of female emigration, and deplored the activities of 'foreign agents' who were involved in recruitment of female labour for work in Britain.[30] Eamon de

Valera, the taoiseach (prime minister) at that time, requested that the issues raised by the Catholic bishops be investigated by the various government departments concerned. His reply to the bishops acknowledged that female migration was 'causing the government particular anxiety', and outlined the policy of his government on migration for employment in Britain:

> Among the principal objects of the government's policy are the development of the national resources to the maximum extent and the encouragement of increased production in agriculture and manufacturing industry. There would seem to be the most effective means available to the state for dealing with the problem of emigration.[31]

In addition, he ruled out the possibility of a prohibition on migration of females which would constitute 'the restriction of a fundamental human right which could only be justified in circumstances of great national emergency'.[32] Thus, even though a distinction was made on occasions between male and female migration by the Irish state and its policymakers, and in some senses, female migration was perceived to be inherently deleterious both to the individuals themselves and the country as a whole, state intervention in the flow of labour to Britain remained minimal, with the exception of the period of the Second World War. What is perhaps most revealing is that similar anxieties were rarely expressed in relation to male migrants by clerics or policymakers, which is a reflection of the views prevalent at the time. In other words, it was perceived that young women were more likely to 'fall by the wayside', despite the fact that evidence to substantiate this unscientific conjecture was rarely cited. Irish politicians and civil servants therefore viewed female emigration to Britain as posing a greater threat to national well-being than the movement of males. In the minds of policymakers, male migration could be rationalised with relative ease on the basis of the steady well-paid employment available in Britain. On the other hand, analysis of official discourse would indicate that female emigration was regarded as less comprehensible and altogether more harmful to the country as a whole.

Gender, socioeconomic change and migration

Numerous studies have outlined the principal explanation for Irish migration, namely, economic underdevelopment, a feature common to highly migratory European societies in the postwar period such as Italy, Portugal, Spain and Greece. Until the 1960s, when innovative economic planning initiatives together with wider developments in the international economy resulted in a degree of relative prosperity, the Irish economy experienced a number of severe crises, particularly in the 1950s.[33] Clearly the lack of sustained economic development which was reflected in the low level of industrial employment is a fairly convincing all-encompassing explanation for the high rates of Irish migration. However, in order to understand why females migrated from Ireland at much the same rate as males, and to assess if females left for different reasons than males, we must turn our attention to the nature of socioeconomic change in twentieth-century Ireland.

The Irish rural economy underwent momentous changes between 1921 and 1971, and more especially in the postwar period.[34] Declining incomes and a sharp decrease in the numbers employed in agriculture resulted in a large surplus of labour. In other societies this labour surplus was absorbed by manufacturing, service or industrial employment but this was not the case in Ireland. Non-agricultural employment opportunities were limited and were geographically biased towards urban centres such as Dublin and Cork. The areas with the highest rates of migration were counties in the west, north-west and south-west of Ireland where there were few opportunities for non-agricultural employment.[35] For women the situation was particularly acute in the postwar period in that the limited alternative employment available favoured males rather than females.[36] This may well be a reflection of the ethos of the governing elite: for example, the government-appointed Commission on Emigration and Other Population Problems stated in 1955 that 'the provision of work for men would be more advantageous, from the demographic point of view, than the provision of work for women'.[37]

In the postwar period it can be argued that a change in attitudes towards employment is evident. Sporadic employment in low-status occupations such as domestic service or temporary labouring or local authority roadwork was rejected in favour of the steady well-paid employment available in Britain. This applied equally to males and females, but the imperative to migrate was especially strong for females in that there were very limited opportunities for paid employment open to them in an agricultural economy. Hannan's analysis succinctly underlines this disparity in terms of the relationship between the rural economy and female migration.

> The greater the proportion of farmers in the community, the greater this excess [in the number of females seeking non-agricultural employment] will be. And, unless the local non-farm demand for labour is biased toward female employment, the greater will be the sex differences in migration.[38]

Whereas in other agricultural societies the traditional mores or customs ensured that the female role on the family farm was essentially that of an unpaid helper, in rural Ireland an emphasis was placed on females securing an occupation which would provide a source of independent income. Factory and clerical work which would provide females with non-agricultural employment were extremely difficult to secure in rural

Ireland.[39] In addition, as Daly has posited, there is also some indication of a distinct change in mentality:

> The rising emigration of young women meant that they were placing their personal interest above those of family and society: a change from a family-based system to one which gave greater weight to the woman as an individual.[40]

Of course, it could be argued, on the other hand, that migrants were placing the family's interest above their own in that in order for uneconomic farming units to survive, the non-inheriting children, both male and female, had little option but to leave the family holding.[41] Nevertheless, Daly is surely correct in pointing to the changing priorities of women in rural Ireland: the bleak future which was mapped out for many young females was rejected in favour of paid employment in Britain and a stark contrast in terms of status and remuneration.

The principal finding which emerges from a detailed analysis of a range of detailed case studies undertaken in the postwar period is that for the most part the fundamental cause of migration for both females and males was economic in nature.[42] It was not so much a case of migrating to subsist, since clearly temporary employment working in agriculture or staying on the family holding would enable an individual to eke out an existence, albeit an impecunious one. The absence of non-agricultural employment in migration-prone areas of Ireland, such as the west and north-west, left individuals with little choice but to migrate if they wished to secure steady, reasonably well-paid employment. This was particularly the case for females and, since females tended to stay longer in education, especially farmers' daughters, this ensured that their income and occupational aspirations could rarely be satisfied locally or indeed within Ireland.

But this is not the complete picture as a range of factors which could be broadly classified as 'sociocultural' must also be considered. Quite apart from the availability of employment in Britain, it is clear that the lifestyle and standard of living available in Britain was also a significant determinant. The Commission on Emigration found that the conditions in rural Ireland were being contrasted with those in the cities of Britain.

> Poor material standards of life are to be found in many parts of the country, but particularly in rural areas, where the exacting demands of agricultural activities are aggravated in a great many cases, by the inadequacy of such amenities for houses and farms as power, light, water and sanitation. Through the cinema and the radio, and above all by direct experience, either personal or through relatives, people in such conditions are, more than ever before, becoming aware of the contrast between their way of life and that in other countries,

> especially in urban centres, though their impressions in these matters are often more favourable than the facts warrant. They are gradually becoming less willing to accept the relatively frugal standards of previous generations.[43]

The social life in small rural communities was perceived to be dreary, and there were indeed few amenities for recreation. As one female migrant interviewed in 1948 explained, she had 'a better life in Croydon than [in] Sligo'.[44] However, whilst it is relatively straightforward to identify these elements of sociocultural change, it is quite another matter to provide detailed evidence to actually establish the importance of this factor. There is no doubt that life in Britain was portrayed as a great deal more attractive than in rural Ireland, but oral testimony from migrants living in Britain would seem to suggest that this factor was of little significance in the decision to leave Ireland.[45]

Related to this factor is the whole question of the status associated with unskilled work in Ireland. Retrospectively ascribing status to a specific occupation is a vexed question, although clearly agricultural labouring and domestic service were low-status occupations in rural Ireland and the same stigma was not associated with similarly unskilled work in Britain, at the very least in the minds of some Irish migrants. It should be remembered that migration to large British urban centres provided a form of anonymity when compared to rural or small-town Ireland with its rigid social structure and few avenues for social mobility. The low status of traditional forms of female employment such as domestic service and farm work, either as wife or daughter, resulted in many young women travelling to Britain for other forms of employment not readily available in Ireland. As Daly has argued, the small numbers entering domestic service in Ireland or opting to share the drudgery of farm life in the postwar period suggest 'that many women no longer found traditional Irish living conditions and the status which they afforded tolerable'.[46] Organisations such as the Irish Women Workers' Union and the Irish Housewives' Association underlined the point that domestic service was not subject to the same low status in Britain as in Ireland in evidence presented to the Commission on Emigration in 1948.[47] Somewhat curiously contemporaries associated this factor of the low status associated with certain employment as solely concerning female migrants, even though agricultural labourers were viewed in very much the same light as domestic servants in rural Ireland.[48]

Some accounts of twentieth-century Irish female migration place an undue emphasis on the role that marriage prospects played in the decision to migrate. For one historian, 'the high rate of female emigration is undoubtedly related to the low rate and late age of marriage'.[49] In some senses, migration was viewed as a means of finding a marriage partner, since these partners were either in short supply or unwilling to marry owing to the rather arcane inheritance practices that were such a distinctive feature of rural Ireland. But the relationship between migration and marriage is not nearly so cut and dried. First, there is little evidence to support the contention that females left Ireland in order to secure a marriage partner, even though numerous accounts, both contemporary and historical, would have us believe that this was the case.[50] Second, the fact that female migrants left at a younger age than their male counterparts may well suggest that securing employment rather than a husband was the overriding concern. However, the absence of detailed studies of the marriage patterns of Irish female migrants in twentieth-century Britain taken together with similar studies of females living in Ireland would preclude any definitive statements on this matter. The construction of migration life-histories would seem a suitable method by which evidence could be gathered and recent research on Irish female migrants living in Leicester underlines the value of this approach.[51]

Finally, one factor which is frequently neglected in studies of twentieth-century Irish migration should be mentioned briefly. With the exception of the Second World War when entry was controlled, Irish citizens enjoyed the benefit of free access to the British labour market. When legislation was introduced to restrict immigration from the Commonwealth in the 1960s, Irish citizens were exempted from any form of control, ostensibly owing to the 'special' historical relationship between Ireland and Britain, but clearly the fact that Irish citizens were white was a crucial factor in these considerations.[52] Of equal consequence is that a continuous demand existed in Britain from the 1930s onwards for unskilled labour. Irish female migrants were strongly represented in the services sector, especially domestic service and in the nursing profession, although by the 1960s, Irish female migrants can be found across a broad range of occupations.[53] Similarly, the demand for heavy unskilled male labour, particularly in the postwar period, ensured an abundance of opportunities for male migrants willing to work in construction, transport and civil engineering and a whole host of other types of employment.[54] This factor must be taken into account in any consideration of the relationship between gender and Irish migration, since it could be reasonably argued in a counterfactual sense that without the demand for example of unskilled male labour, the gender profile of the Irish migrant flow may well have been considerably different.

Conclusion

Twentieth-century Ireland provides a relatively unique case study for an examination of the relationship between gender and migration in that a relative parity in terms of gender was a feature of the Irish migrant flow between 1921 and 1971. Data drawn from a variety of sources indicate that for the most part the Irish migrant, male or female, was young, single and unskilled and probably from the west, south-west or north-west of

Ireland. Whilst the Irish state, and in particular Irish politicians, invariably condemned migration, the state in terms of the provision of social welfare for the unemployed without doubt benefited from the exodus to Britain. Research on Irish government records demonstrates that the Irish state was especially concerned with female migration, mainly as a result of representations from Roman Catholic clergy. The Irish state very seriously considered imposing a prohibition on female migration in the late 1940s on the dubious grounds that young women were unable to cope with the difficulties of urban life in Britain. However, practical and political considerations ensured that this drastic step though contemplated was not implemented. The overarching conclusion which emerges is that females left twentieth-century Ireland for much the same reasons as males: to secure steady employment and to fulfil occupational and income aspirations. This chapter has also highlighted the desirability of examining determinants other than those which could be classified as economic in nature. Sociocultural change, be it in the form of rising expectations or changing attitudes towards employment, marriage or status, was clearly as important in determining migration flows. In explaining migration, therefore, we should bring into the analysis not only those determinants that could be regarded as economic in nature, but also social and cultural variables.

Within the wider European context during the postwar period, the Irish migrant flow differed significantly in terms of the gender profile. Mass migration from southern Europe to the advanced economies of western Europe throughout the 1950s and 1960s was dominated by males, although the proportion of females in the migrant flows from Portugal, Greece and Italy increased throughout the 1960s.[55] For example, in the case of Portugal in 1960 29 per cent of migrants were female but by 1968 this had risen to 52 per cent.[56] Explanations as to why Ireland diverged from the general trend in twentieth-century European migration centre on two features of the Irish experience of emigration. In the first instance, there was a long-established tradition of female emigration since at least the mid-nineteenth century. Second, the demand for female workers in Britain ensured that plenty of opportunities existed for Irish female migrants. Both tradition and contemporary circumstances therefore shaped the history of gender and migration from twentieth-century Ireland.

Notes

1 The most useful short account is D. Fitzpatrick, *Irish emigration, 1801–1921*, Dublin, Economic and Social History Society of Ireland, 1984. Other more detailed studies include D. H. Akenson, *The Irish diaspora: a primer*, Belfast, Institute of Irish Studies, 1994; P. Blessing, 'Irish emigration to the United States, 1800–1920: an overview', in P. J. Drudy (ed.) *The Irish in America: emigration, assimilation and impact*, Cambridge, Cambridge University Press, 1985, pp. 11–37; D. Fitzpatrick, 'Emigration, 1801–70', in W. E. Vaughan (ed.) *A new history of Ireland,*

V: Ireland under the union, I (1801–70), Oxford, Clarendon Press, 1989, pp. 562–622; *idem*, 'Emigration, 1871–1921', in W.E. Vaughan (ed.) *A new history of Ireland, VI: Ireland under the union, II (1871–1921)*, Oxford, Clarendon Press, 1996, pp. 606–652; J. H. Johnson, 'The context of migration: the example of Ireland in the nineteenth century', *Transactions of the Institute of British Geographers*, 1990, vol. 15, pp. 259–276; K. A. Miller, *Emigrants and exiles: Ireland and the Irish exodus to North America*, Oxford, Oxford University Press, 1985; W. J. Smyth, 'Irish emigration, 1700–1920', in P. C. Emmer and Magnus Mörner (eds) *European expansion and migration*, Oxford, Berg, 1992, pp. 49–78.

2 Fitzpatrick, 'Emigration, 1801–70', p. 565.

3 L. Kennedy and L. A. Clarkson, 'Birth, death and exile: Irish population history, 1700–1921', in B. J. Graham and L. J. Proudfoot (eds) *An historical geography of Ireland*, London, Academic Press, 1993, p. 175.

4 D. Baines, *Emigration from Europe, 1815–1930*, London, Macmillan, 1991, p. 43.

5 D. Fitzpatrick, '"A share of the honeycomb": education, emigration and Irishwomen', *Continuity and Change*, 1986, vol. 1, pp. 217–234; *idem*, 'The modernisation of the Irish female', in P. O'Flanagan, P. Ferguson and K. Whelan (eds) *Rural Ireland, 1600–1900: modernisation and change*, Cork, Cork University Press, 1987, pp. 162–180; P. Jackson, 'Women in nineteenth-century Irish emigration', *International Migration Review*, 1984, vol. 18, pp. 1004–1020; K. Miller with D. N. Doyle and P. Kelleher, '"For love and liberty": Irish women, migration and domesticity in Ireland and America, 1815–1920', in P. O'Sullivan (ed.) *Irish women and Irish migration*, London: Leicester University Press, 1995, pp. 41–65; J. Nolan, *Ourselves alone: women's emigration from Ireland, 1885–1920*, Lexington, The University Press of Kentucky, 1989.

6 For sociological and geographical accounts see J. Rudd, 'The emigration of Irish women', *Social Studies*, 1987, vol. 9, pp. 3–11; *idem*, 'Invisible exports: the emigration of Irish women this century', *Women's Studies International Forum*, 1988, vol. 11, pp. 307–311; B. Walter, *Gender and Irish migration to Britain*, Cambridge, Geography Working Paper No. 4, Anglia Higher Education College, 1989; *idem*, 'Gender and recent Irish migration to Britain', in Russell King (ed.) *Contemporary Irish migration*, Dublin, Geographical Society of Ireland, 1991, pp. 11–20.

7 See, for example, S. Pedraza, 'Women and migration: the social consequences of gender', *Annual Review of Sociology*, 1991, vol. 17, pp. 302–325; A. Phizacklea (ed.) *One way ticket? Migration and female labour*, London and Melbourne, Routledge & Kegan Paul, 1983.

8 P. Travers, 'Emigration and gender: the case of Ireland, 1922–60', in M. O'Dowd and S. Wichert (eds) *Chattel, servant or citizen: women's status in church, state and society*, Belfast, Institute of Irish Studies, 1995, pp. 187–199; *idem*, '"There was nothing for me there": Irish female emigration, 1922–71', in P. O'Sullivan (ed.) *Irish women and Irish migration*, London, Leicester University Press, 1995, pp. 146–167.

9 W. E. Vaughan and A. J. Fitzpatrick (eds) *Irish historical statistics: population, 1821–1971*, Dublin, Royal Irish Academy, 1978, p. 27.

10 ibid.

11 E. Delaney, *Demography, state and society: Irish migration to Britain, 1921–71*, Liverpool and Kingston/Montreal, Liverpool University Press and McGill-Queen's University Press, 2000, pp. 50, 131–132, 166–167, 233–240.

12 B. M. Walsh, 'Expectations, information and human migration: specifying an econometric model of Irish migration to Britain', *Journal of Regional Science*, 1974, vol. 14, p. 108.

13 The remaining six counties remained within the United Kingdom and became Northern Ireland. This chapter is only concerned with the 26 county political unit, the Irish Free State (Irish Republic from 1949 onwards).

14 For useful accounts of the trends in Irish migration, see P. J. Drudy, 'Irish population change and emigration since independence', in *idem* (ed.) *The Irish in America: emigration, assimilation and impact*, Cambridge, Cambridge University Press, 1985, pp. 63–85, and C. Ó Gráda and B. M. Walsh, 'The economic effects of emigration: Ireland', in B. J. Asch (ed.) *Emigration and its effects on the sending country*, Santa Monica, Rand, 1994, pp. 97–152.
15 Delaney, *Demography, state and society*, pp. 112–159, 135–137, 179–182.
16 Fitzpatrick, 'Emigration, 1801–70', p. 575.
17 Commission on Emigration and Other Population Problems, 1948–54, *Reports*, Dublin, Stationery Office, [1955], Pr. 2541, p. 129.
18 Delaney, *Demography, state and society*, pp. 49–50.
19 For more details, see R. Lynn, *The Irish brain drain*, Dublin, Economic and Social Research Institute, 1968.
20 *Census of population, 1971, I: population of district electoral divisions*, Dublin, Stationery Office, 1972, Prl. 2564, p. xxii.
21 A. R. Zolberg, 'The great wall against China: responses to the first immigration crisis, 1885–1925', in J. Lucassen and L. Lucassen (eds) *Migration, migration history, history: old paradigms and new perspectives*, Bern, Peter Lang, 1997, p. 291; see also *idem*, 'The next waves: migration theory for a changing world', *International Migration Review*, 1989, vol. 22, pp. 405–406.
22 For a fuller assessment of this issue, see E. Delaney, 'State, politics and demography: the case of Irish emigration, 1921–71', *Irish Political Studies*, 1998, vol. 13, pp. 25–49.
23 Delaney, *Demography, state and society*, pp. 65–69.
24 Good overviews of the range of measures introduced can be found in Commission on Emigration, *Reports*, pp. 268–270, and in a valuable unpublished history of the Irish in Britain completed under the auspices of the series of official histories of the Second World War, PRO LAB 8/1528, A. V. Judges, 'Irish labour in Great Britain, 1939–45', pp. 1–7.
25 Delaney, *Demography, state and society*, p. 132.
26 Commission on Emigration, *Reports*, p. 268.
27 National Archives of Ireland (hereafter N.A.I.), DT S 11582 B, Department of External Affairs: memorandum for the government [on female emigration], 30 Aug. 1947, pp. 4–5.
28 ibid., p. 8.
29 See Delaney, *Demography, state and society*, pp. 187–189, for a discussion of these issues.
30 N.A.I., DT S 15398 A, copy of letter from Dr James Staunton to Eamon de Valera, 13 Oct. 1947.
31 ibid., copy of a letter from Eamon de Valera to Dr James Staunton, 16 Feb. 1948.
32 ibid.
33 For useful accounts, see D. Johnson, *The interwar economy in Ireland*, Dublin, Economic and Social History Society of Ireland, 1985; K. A. Kennedy, T. Giblin and D. McHugh, *The economic development of Ireland in the twentieth century*, London, Routledge, 1988; L. Kennedy, *The modern industrialisation of Ireland, 1940–1988*, Dublin, Economic and Social History Society of Ireland, 1989.
34 See, for more details, D. A. Gillmor, *Economic activities in the Republic of Ireland: a geographical perspective*, Dublin, Gill and Macmillan, 1985, pp. 170–172.
35 Delaney, *Demography, state and society*, pp. 166–167, 233–234.
36 D. Hannan, 'Irish emigration since the war', unpub. Thomas Davis Lecture, 1973, p. 3; on female employment more generally, see M. E. Daly, *Women and work in Ireland*, Dublin, Economic and Social History Society of Ireland, 1997, pp. 41–6.

37 Commission on Emigration, *Reports*, p. 171.
38 D. Hannan, 'Migration motives and migration differentials among Irish rural youth', *Sociologia Ruralis*, 1969, vol. 9, p. 210.
39 Commission on Emigration, *Reports*, p. 142.
40 M. E. Daly, 'Women in the Irish workforce from pre-industrial to modern times', *Saothar*, 1987, vol. 7, pp. 80–1.
41 For a fascinating comparative example of this pattern of female migration *mutatis mutandis*, see J. Luby and O. Stark, 'Individual migration as a family strategy: young women in the Philippines', *Population Studies*, 1988, vol. 42, pp. 473–486.
42 See Delaney, *Demography, state and society*, p. 289.
43 Commission on Emigration, *Reports*, p. 174.
44 Trinity College Dublin, Manuscripts Department (hereafter TCD), MS 8306, rural surveys: S.4, Leitrim and Donegal, p. 2. Although the respondent was interviewed in Leitrim, she was actually from county Sligo.
45 R. King and H. O'Connor, 'Migration and gender: Irish women in Leicester', *Geography*, 1996, vol. 81, pp. 316–317.
46 Daly, 'Women in the Irish workforce', p. 80.
47 TCD, MS 8307, transcripts of evidence: Irish Housewives' Association, pp. 3, 9; Irish Women Workers' Union, p. 4.
48 Commission on Emigration, *Reports*, p. 138.
49 Travers, '"There was nothing for me there"', p. 151.
50 See, for example, Commission on Emigration, *Reports*, p. 79; P. Moser, 'Rural economy and female emigration in [sic] the west of Ireland, 1936–56', *UCG Women's Studies Review*, 1993, vol. 2, p. 45; Travers, 'Emigration and gender', pp. 195–197.
51 King and O'Connor, 'Migration and gender'.
52 C. Holmes, *John Bull's island: immigration and British society, 1871–1971*, Basingstoke, Macmillan, 1988, pp. 216–217; 252–253; for a detailed assessment of the legislative issues, see K. Paul, 'A case of mistaken identity: the Irish in postwar Britain', *International Labour and Working-Class History*, 1996, vol. 49, pp. 116–142.
53 J. A. Jackson, 'The Irish in Britain', in P. J. Drudy (ed.) *Ireland and Britain since 1922*, Cambridge, Cambridge University Press, 1986, pp. 129–131; Walter, 'Gender and recent Irish migration to Britain', pp. 16–18.
54 Jackson, 'The Irish in Britain', pp. 129–131.
55 Massimo Livi Bacci, 'The countries of emigration', in *idem* (ed.) *The demographic and social pattern of emigration from the southern European countries*, Florence, Dipartimento Statistico-Matematic dell'Università di Firenze, 1972, pp. 33–34.
56 ibid., p. 34.

12 Maids on the move

Images of femininity and European women's labour migration during the interwar years[1]

Barbara Henkes

At the end of the nineteenth century, industrialisation, urbanisation, and the rapid development of means of transportation offered new possibilities for European women to participate in the labour market. Young women left the country to make their fortune in the city, often at first as live-in domestic servants. Factories, sweatshops and department stores also provided alternatives to domestic work in urban settings. Although the transition to the city gave girls and women new perspectives, it also required strategies for survival. In particular, women's organisations were concerned about protecting 'innocent' young women from dangers threatening them in an unfamiliar and anonymous urban environment.[2] All the same, the city remained attractive as the dynamic centre of economic, social and cultural life, ensuring that this form of female migration inland continued.

The mobility of single European women was not limited by national borders, however. Not only did they find their way to North and South America, Australia or South Africa,[3] but the migration of young women seeking work in neighbouring countries also took place within Europe[4] – for example, between Germany and the Netherlands. The character of women's migration drastically changed under the influence of the First World War. During the interwar years tens of thousands of German women left their war-torn native soil to try their luck in undamaged neighbouring countries. Most of them found work and lodging as live-in domestic servants. While in 1920, only 9,100 female foreign workers were registered in the Netherlands, three years later the number had increased fivefold. The foreigners' registers indicate that the number of German maids in 1923 must have been about 40,000. Following a brief decline, this number increased in the early 1930s again to about 40,000 in 1934. It is worth noting that this was a fluctuating group whereby the young women involved generally stayed in service for about two years before they returned to their country of origin, married or changed jobs. From 1934, the number of foreign maids decreased once again: at the end of 1936 the number of German maidservants was estimated at 22,000. By the time Germany invaded the Netherlands in May 1940, there were only about 3,500 German maids left.[5]

The ties between Germany and the Netherlands that had existed from earlier days were helpful in getting this migration started. The Dreesmans, Kloppenburgs, Hirschs and other established families of German origin from the business community were – like their Dutch counterparts – in need of cheap, conscientious domestic servants. Since Dutch working-class girls were able to find work outside the domestic sphere, there was a so-called shortage of housemaids in the Netherlands, a problem which could be alleviated by the arrival of German girls. Much like the migration of single women to the cities, the transition of German girls across the Dutch border evoked concern about the potential dangers their mass mobility to another country might involve.

In this chapter, I want to explore the images of femininity that emerged in this process of mass female migration between Germany and the Netherlands during the interwar years. To what extent did the perspective that migrating women were potentially vulnerable victims of male lust dominate public debates? Was there also space for a perspective which treated migrants as self-confident, enterprising young women?

In order to answer these questions, I deal with the three parties involved in this migration project: the German girls themselves, the German and Dutch governmental agencies, and the German and Dutch religious organisations concerned with the protection of girls. Attention will be paid to how each group defined the problems associated with the arrival of German girls in the Netherlands and how each distinguished between girls that were considered suitable or unsuitable for migration. By looking at whether female migrants were viewed as virtuous or not, I will show which images of femininity were linked to young women's migration and how these images intersected with other class, regional or social categories. I will be drawing on documents from government and private organisations as well as the life stories of the German maids themselves.[6] In this way I hope to delineate the interaction between more articulated discourses on femininity, at an institutional level, and the less articulated images of femininity, at an individual level.

Young women's aspirations

> I went to Holland with the idea that Holland was a paradise. At least according to the stories told by a friend, you could do 'miracles' in Germany with every guilder earned in Holland.[7]

This is how Mrs Akkerman justifies her decision to go to the Netherlands. Many of her fellow-travellers also mention the rapidly deteriorating situation in Germany, with the runaway inflation and mass unemployment, and the good prospects for making a life in the Netherlands. The mere possibility of better earnings, however, does not explain why so many German girls left their homeland as many others preferred to stay, despite the poor circumstances in which they and their relatives lived. The desire to see more of the world, in combination with a degree of self-confidence and self-esteem, were indispensable for the young women who migrated. According to Mrs Stark who came from the border-town of Gronau to the industrial town of Enschede and later moved on to The Hague:

> We had to earn money and I wanted to get out of it, out of the uniformity here, I wanted to see something, to broaden my horizon . . . I'm different from my sister. My sister was like: 'well, I feel fine at home'. Not me: I always wanted to know what was beyond. I was thirsty for knowledge. And I must say, it did a lot for me.[8]

Mrs Van Vliet's autobiographical accounts also show a combination of material need and a longing for cultural expansion, when it came to leaving for the Netherlands. Born in 1899 as the eldest of three daughters, she grew up in the grand duchy of Oldenburg. The family lived on a small farm, which was mainly run by her mother while her father worked in the nearby shipyard. 'Not poor and not rich', is how Mrs Anna Van Vliet describes the circumstances in which the family lived during her younger years.[9] To Anna, at least, this meant that there was not enough money to allow her to continue her education after primary school. As a housewife's helper (*Stütze der Hausfrau*) she was taken into a farmer's household and given board and lodging for a training period:

> In the evening . . . we sat in the living-room with some mending or a piece of fancy-work. Embroidering complex monograms on linen for one's trousseau . . . For the whole training was based on a future marriage, wasn't it! I didn't fancy this prospect at all. A girl who married a small farmer could expect nothing but toiling on the land for the rest of her life. Well-to-do farmers' sons liked having their eyes on the pretty daughters from . . . farmers beneath their own station; but marrying them was another thing.[10]

Looking back on this episode in her life, Mrs Van Vliet shows an awareness of her limited prospects within the agrarian community. This must have reinforced her clear aversion to farm work:

> If you had to work in summer, you couldn't help perspiring terribly. There was an awful lot of dust and you got horribly dirty; I never liked that. I could do any kind of work I wanted, but I disliked getting dirty. Ruining my finger nails, having my hair all knots and tangles, and getting a colour, such a farmer's colour, well, I just didn't like that at all.[11]

An advertisement by a well-to-do lady in the small city of Oldenburg offered her a way out. City life brought 'culture' and variety, and rescued her from 'that dirty agricultural labour', as Mrs Van Vliet puts it.[12] In this way, she expresses a familiar modernist opposition between 'civilised' city life and 'primitive' country life, that was common at that time in Western Europe as (female) migration from the country to the city became more widespread.

An unfortunate love affair, combined with the deteriorating economic situation in Germany, gave Anna the impulse she needed to explore other possibilities. After her successful move to the city, the migration to the Netherlands did not seem such a radical step. She successfully answered an advertisement by a German professor's family in Utrecht (a large city in the centre of the Netherlands). With the 'feeling of sensational expectation' she crossed the border in 1920.

International protection of girls

The promising perception of the Netherlands as 'the land of milk and honey' provided an important 'pull'-factor in the process of migration of German women. Their departure to the 'Guilder Paradise' (*Guldenparadies*), however, evoked opposition as well. Since the end of the nineteenth century, young women's wanderlust was accompanied by warnings against the 'increased moral and physical dangers' that the girls' stay away from home entailed. The dangers involved in moving across national borders were equal to the dangers of moving from the country to the city. The ignorant young women were said to be in imminent danger of falling into the wrong hands through unverifiable newspaper advertisements or shady intermediaries. During the journey, they ran the risk of encountering ruthless white slave-traders. Once they had arrived at the place of destination, misfortune still lay in wait, according to the media and especially the Catholic and Protestant Women's Organisations for the Protection of Girls that had been active in Western Europe since the last decades of the nineteenth century.[13]

Protecting girls entailed numerous activities. Warnings against travelling unprepared were issued in newspaper articles and pamphlets as well as by local clergymen and other authorities. This preventative care was combined with information about reliable mediation agencies and girls' societies at the place of destination. Once young women had embarked on the train, it was important that they be chaperoned during their journey. The female travellers were met at the big stations or at the border by a 'station worker' – a lady recognisable by the white armband – who stood by ready to help as trains pulled in. If the newcomers didn't yet have a position, they could stay in hostels for women only. Others, who had already arranged a place of employment, were invited to attend the weekly meetings in local girls' societies.[14] From the end of the nineteenth century on, these kinds of measures were taken on behalf of girls and women who travelled on their own to the city and who, 'because of the new freedoms of these times, became increasingly unprotected'.[15]

In Germany, the care for travelling women was halted during the First World War when women working in the train stations, along with the Red Cross, were kept busy helping soldiers, refugees and the wounded. But directly after the war, the renewed mobility of young women brought the dangers of moral decay and 'white slave trade' to the forefront of their interests again. The Protestant, Catholic and Jewish Societies for the Protection of Girls all saw the possibility of taking up denominational station work in the old mode again and expanding it across the border with the help of their international contacts. In the Netherlands, the Protestant Union, the Catholic Society for the Protection of Girls (*Vereeniging ter Bescherming van Meisjes*) and the liberal Women's League (Vrouwenbond) all had departments devoted to the care of young women. Station workers in cities like Arnhem, Utrecht and Amsterdam were confronted from 1920 onward with girls from Germany who arrived in the Netherlands looking for work. At the station in Utrecht alone, as many as fifty to sixty German girls might arrive at the same time. The ladies had their hands full trying to prevent the newly arrived from getting on the wrong train or allowing themselves to be side-tracked by characters with questionable intentions. Countless examples were cited of intrusive, unreliable or even 'unsavoury looking' gentlemen who bothered the girls, as well – according to the station workers' reports – as equally numerous expressions of gratitude from the German travellers for the help which was offered to them.[16]

The suspicion against men hanging around the girls was linked to the prevailing anxiety concerning uncontrolled sex drives – in particular, of men – and the inability of young girls to offer sufficient resistance against them. In particular, girls outside the realm of parental surveillance were considered to be continually subject to temptations which not only brought danger to them personally but also constituted a threat both to public morality and to the reputation of German women abroad. Morality and patriotism became irrevocably intertwined in the discussion about the international migration of unmarried women.[17]

In order to supervise the female travellers as well as possible, the Dutch station workers maintained intensive contact with German sister organisations. Together, they conferred about expanding the girls' care at the border because it was here that they could halt young, unsuitable or unprepared girls before they entered foreign territory.[18] With the support of the Dutch government, a hostel was established at the German border town of Emmerich, where stranded travellers could spend the night. During the first five months of her employment in 1922, a station worker in Emmerich registered a total of 2,314 girls returning to Germany as well as 10,344 German girls on their way to the Netherlands.[19]

The Dutch and German women's organisations in the place of destination also collaborated intensively. The Dutch Society for the Protection

Plate 12.1 German station worker (*Bahnhofsmissionarin*) in action, *c.*1930

Source: Reproduced with permission of Archiv des Diakonischen Werkes der EKD, Berlin.

of Girls was extremely busy. According to the annual report of the Catholic Society for the Protection of Girls in 1922,

> Due to the increased stream of foreign girls, especially German girls, a large number of local departments were required to organize . . . special meetings for these girls and in many cases to employ German personnel so that these girls, torn from their families and family life, could find support in the organization for maintaining their honour, innocence, and virtue.

These societies offered young German women a safe home base (*ein Stück Heimat*) in the unfamiliar Dutch surroundings, where they could meet once or twice a week under the leadership of a German or German speaking sister or a laywoman (*Fürsorgerin*). The numbers of participants varied from 200 in the big cities to 10 or 15 girls in the smaller towns. Often the societies also served as an employment agency in order to secure 'reliable' situations for 'decent' girls.[20] Nevertheless, these precautions did not prevent many German maids from getting into trouble. The anxious *Fürsorgerin* Johanna Schwer, responsible for the German Catholic girls' society in Amsterdam, wrote in 1925:

> Many of them have lost their faith and good morals, have spent their money on worthless trash and cinema, and have lost their fancy and love for their work. How many girls are not here nowadays, who not only have to look after themselves, but also after their child![21]

Other German and Dutch agencies in the Netherlands also expressed their anxiety about 'the religious, moral and social distress in which a large part of the girls find themselves almost daily'. Holland was not only the land of the solid guilder for the hard-working German girl; it was also the land of moral threat to the innocent single German girl.

However, the warnings against moral decay could not deter many young German women from leaving their homeland. Once the necessity or desire to leave had absorbed their attention, they didn't pay much heed to possible objections to their departure. Moral decay was still an abstract notion which didn't concern the potential leave-taker particularly. Paradoxically, the Societies for the Protection of Girls facilitated the conditions of girls' migration through their activities, while, at the same time, creating a climate of deterrence with their warnings about moral danger.

Push and pull in the 1920s

In the Netherlands, concern for the fate of German girls was initially subordinate to the enthusiasm with which the German maids were hailed. This was due to the scarcity of good, cheap domestic help. The newspapers and periodicals of women's organisations praised the qualities of the German maids, presenting them as 'subservient' and 'experienced' in domestic activities. The underlying feeling of admiration for the Prussian culture emerged in idyllic reports about the arrival of 'disciplined young working daughters displaying the image of the German people during the days of and following Bismarck'. In contrast, the 'strong sense of freedom expressed by our Dutch girls' appeared to be considerably less popular.[22]

Moreover, the German girls who had suffered hardships in the previous years were supposedly 'less likely to make demands'. It was unlikely to be worse for them than at home and, in view of the exchange rate, the guilders they earned would be worth their weight in gold in Germany. In short, the solution to the pressing scarcity of domestic help which had plagued the Dutch housewife since the end of the last century, seemed to be lurking just around the corner.

The hymns of praise for the German maid did not continue, however. The eager way that German girls made use of the opportunities Dutch households offered them also caused some alarm. Moreover, the realisation dawned that this migration would not remain temporary in the case of all German girls. As the unemployment in the Dutch labour market increased during the first half of the 1920s, voices of dissent emerged, calling for a ban on German maids in the Netherlands.

The negative publicity in the Netherlands about unemployment and the decreasing demand for foreign maids was taken up by German media and the authorities in an attempt to keep girls from migrating to the neighbouring country. The warning was issued that many German girls had been 'seduced with salaries in guilders' to seek their fortune in Holland. They had been successful for a while, but now times were changing. The *Kölnische Volkszeitung* reported in June 1922:

> Most of them don't find jobs, are confused and helpless, ashamed of returning home without success. Often they lack resources, become degenerate, and take to the streets or the public houses. In large cities, for example, the Hague, the situation is already desperate: 90 per cent would be infected with venereal diseases.

This alarming news spread through all of Germany. In the same period, an identical warning could be found in southern Germany in the *Freiburger Tageszeitung*, and the ominous predictions even reached as far as Berlin. By way of the ambassador in the German capital, the Dutch government was confronted with this negative publicity. This led the Ministry of Labour in 1923 to commission a serious inquiry about the influence of German maids on unemployment among Dutch domestic servants as well as the threat of German maids to public morality in the Netherlands. The conclusion of this investigation was that the demand and the supply of domestics were more or less in balance. The conclusion was drawn that it was, therefore, unnecessary to recruit more German girls, although it was also not necessary to prevent them from coming to the Netherlands. With respect to the dangers they presented to public morality, the governmental report saw little reason for concern: it occurred only very sporadically that German maids had to be deported due to bad behaviour (usually minor thefts performed while in service). For the Dutch government, these results provided no reason for intervention.[23]

While in 1923 it was still considered an option to curtail the arrival of German maids, a year later, they took the initiative themselves to return. The introduction of the *Rentemark* in the autumn of 1923 brought the rampant inflation to a halt, and with it such an improvement in circumstances in Germany came about that many German girls turned their backs on the Netherlands of their own accord. But despite the stabilisation of the German currency and the improved living situation, Germany continued to struggle with considerable unemployment, while the Dutch labour market developed more auspiciously. Once again, poverty and unemployment brought German girls over the border, particularly girls from the industrialized Ruhr area. Their contribution to the total number of migrants rose noticeably after 1924.

Financial need versus desire for adventure

The German girls who came to the Netherlands after 1924 formed a second 'generation'. If the reports about their predecessors had been full of alarming news, these new arrivals caused even more unease. The first generation contained quite a few girls from the middle classes who had become impoverished through inflation. They, at least initially, felt insecure and out of place in their subservient position as maid.[24] They did not go out much as they did not know yet where to go and their expectations were primarily directed towards returning home as quickly as possible. Those who came after this first generation were mostly the daughters of the industrial working class. They were more accustomed to having to negotiate the position of maid and probably felt more at home in their new circumstances, particularly as the path had already been trodden by their predecessors. This may have accounted for the impression that the first group was both smaller and more 'civilised' in their behaviour. As German girls began to act with less timidity and entered the Dutch street scene as a group, they took on the reputation of being 'common', 'loud' and 'immoral'.[25]

They then came to be regarded as a different breed of women: young girls who, because they had grown up during the war and the turmoil of revolutionary movements afterwards, had lost touch with the Christian virtues. The girls from the Ruhr were thought to be 'loose' and too much concerned about their 'freedom'. While these girls could have used the patronage of the church, they preferred to go to cinemas or dance halls rather than frequenting the girls' societies which had been especially organised for them. They not only shortchanged themselves with their careless behaviour, however; they also damaged the reputation of other German girls and of Germanness in general, according to the warning issued from German (Christian) authorities.

In this way, a negative image emerged whereby city life, industrial areas, working-class, revolutionary movements, the desire for freedom, secularism, immorality and lack of patriotism were linked in one long, associative chain. This image was also adopted and articulated by Dutch authorities. For example, the director of the Dutch Labour Exchange in the German city of Oberhausen was given the mandate in 1928 not to hire German maids from the industrial areas, but to look for domestic servants from the outlying rural districts. In a report written in January 1929, the police of Amsterdam made note of the large number of girls from the mining region (Bottrop, Hamborn, Gladbach and surroundings) who behaved 'less appropriately'. According to the police, they frequently left their service without notice. 'If they have got the freedom they desire, it will soon become evident that this is not in their best interest, as they might begin to roam or may fall in with less desirable company', was the hypothetical conclusion of this report.

'Freedom' – which in this case meant the withdrawal of parental supervision or any form of patronage – would bring young, female migrants in constant danger of falling into disrepute. The National Bureau for Trade in Women, Children and Immoral Documents was also of this opinion. In its annual report of 1929 the Bureau warned about the increase in the number of complaints about German women and girls behaving immorally in the Netherlands:

> In contrast to a few years ago, when many German women came here out of financial necessity and knew how to roll up their sleeves and work, lately countless young girls have left Germany, many of whom are of frivolous nature and would only too gladly withdraw themselves from parental supervision.

In this way, a contradiction was built up between the acceptable and unacceptable migration of women: between those who went to foreign countries 'out of necessity' and those who were driven by a 'desire for freedom' or 'lust for adventure'. And it shows how this opposition was nurtured by other contradictions, for example, between industrial and rural regions, working and middle classes, and between 'uncontrollable' and 'dependent' women.

These discourses resonate in the stories of the German maids themselves. 'When I left, there were only a few girls, and they were proper girls: the daughters of doctors and ministers.' This is the emphatic opinion of Mrs Van Vliet, who had come to the Netherlands in 1920 from the North German town Oldenburg and, therefore, belonged to the first generation. She continues:

> Afterwards, girls arrived who were just simple children from working-class neighbourhoods. And then they went out on Sundays, they were free, and they went to bed with boys and that kind of thing. But we were . . . not just me, there were others, we didn't go along with that, that just wasn't done. We had learned at home that we weren't supposed to do that. And it didn't appeal to us.[26]

Mrs Van Vliet's aspiration for upward mobility and feminine respectability contributed towards her detachment from her fellow countrywomen, whom she identified as 'quite common girls from the working-class quarters' in big cities, while she was from the country. Like the German and Dutch migration authorities, she draws a distinction between 'respectable' (middle-class) girls from the country and the more 'common' working-class girls from industrial areas. In this respect, her migration account shows how the opposition between the 'primitive' country and the 'civilised' city, as it was first introduced to support her choice to retreat from the country, is reversed when she needs to ally herself with the migration of respectable women. From that perspective, the city no longer stands for culture and civilisation, but is the synonym for immorality and decadence, while the country stands for innocence and authenticity.

Like Mrs Van Vliet, Mrs Jaswetz differentiates between 'the first' (to which she counts herself) and those German girls who came 'later'. The first group came to the Netherlands out of the necessity to earn money, while the latter went for more 'freedom'. In her view, the girls of the second generation were 'thirsty for pleasure'; 'they went dancing and so on'. They were for the most part 'Bottroper girls' (*Bottroper Mädel*), as Mrs Jaswetz called the girls from the industrial regions. Although she herself was from Bottrop, she did not consider herself part of this group which was known for being 'free' and 'cheap': 'They went around in gangs, those German girls were . . . wild, and so, so vulgar and loud in the shops. We didn't like that at all. We were a different breed. We were as quiet as mice.'[27]

Just as Director Knischewitsy of the Bureau for Advice for Emigrants (*Auswandererberatungsstelle*) in Düsseldorf complained that the girls from Bottrop 'could damage the reputation of the German girl',[28] Mrs Jaswetz talks about 'Bottroper girls' and Mrs Holz – who was also from Oberhausen – speaks of 'that Krupp scum'[29] (referring to the steel factories in the Ruhr region) when trying to distance themselves from other German girls in the Netherlands. In constructing a difference between 'proper' and 'improper' women's migration, the actual or assumed differences in social origin were magnified. If no clear-cut differences in social background could be found – as was the case with Mrs. Jaswetz – then differences in girls' motives for leaving Germany were constructed. In this way, the *necessity* to earn money of the first generation was linked to modesty and decency, while the *wish* of the second generation to earn money was connected to their 'addiction to adventure', promiscuity, and, ultimately, their ruin.

Combating immorality

As complaints about the 'quality' of the German girls began to multiply toward the end of the 1920s, the call for more control prior to their departure arose. It was essential to prevent 'immature elements' from crossing the border and becoming a burden to the Dutch populace and disgracing the German nation. Käthe Kuhlenbäumer of the National Union of Catholic German Societies for the Protection of Girls (*Nationalverband der Katholischen Mädchenschutzvereine*) wondered, after her visit to a German–Dutch conference in 1929 on the care of German girls in the Netherlands:

> Is it not a threat to the prestige of our German civilisation abroad, if, for example, 132 German girls were expelled by the Dutch police from The Hague only during the past year, 55 of them for immoral

> behaviour, 55 of them for theft and the rest of them because they were without means of support or without papers?[30]

Under the motto 'prevention is better than cure', the German and the Dutch Societies for the Protection of Girls waged a common battle for stricter measures in order to prevent the departure of women below the age of 18. Moreover, they saw an important task for themselves in controlling the 'quality' of both the migrant maid as well as her future mistress. The contact of the girls' protection societies with the German Bureaus for Advice for Emigrants and the Employment Offices initially consisted of occasional requests to find out whether a particular maid or mistress was suitable. However, in the second half of the 1920s, their cooperation took on a more structural character.

When a girl reported her intention to leave to the Bureau for Advice for Emigrants, she had to fill in a special inventory with questions about her background and about her future position in the Netherlands. Women who were engaged with the Dutch Societies for the Protection of Girls gathered information about the future work situation. Was the employer's family known to be decent (*einwandfrei*)? Would the girl be able to fulfil her religious duties? Was there separate sleeping accommodation for the maid, and would the workload not be too heavy?

The emigration consultants in Germany or women from the German Societies for the Protection of Girls made enquiries about the girl who wanted to leave as well. Was her behaviour really beyond reproach? Did she come from a stable background? Was she not too young to cope with the work? Teachers, pastors or doctors were approached for an answer to such questions. 'Nice, diligent, and pious' (*Brav, fleißig* and *fromm)* were the terms for girls who were considered suitable for emigration. In addition, if they were 'well brought up, reasonably healthy and strong' (*gut erzogen, recht gesund* and *kräftig*), nothing stood in the way of their departure, even if they were not yet 18. However, should a girl leave a 'superficial, breezy impression' (*oberflächlichen, windigen Eindruck*) on her judges then much would be done to prevent her from leaving. As long as young women were driven by financial necessity, their trip across the border could be justified. However, the motivation of an enterprising spirit, particularly in the guise of a 'fine and noticeably attired female body' was disqualified as 'lust for adventure'. One feared that any tendency toward adventurousness would irrevocably bring a girl unhappiness.[31]

Growing efforts on the part of the alien police, the military police, the railroad officials and various private organisations demonstrated just how much value broad layers of society placed upon the fight against 'immoral' behaviour. Fear that proper morals would be disturbed was not limited to bourgeois circles engaged in girls' protection and other fighters against immorality, however. Fear – and fascination – concerning 'promiscuity' and unrestricted interaction with the opposite sex existed among the

German girls themselves too. 'I was always afraid that boys would do something crazy to me. You heard such awful things about German girls who were harassed by Dutch boys', tells Mrs Rijsbaarman, who 'was lucky' – as she calls it – that she met a 'well-mannered boy' whom she later married.[32] Fear of the unknown and of not being able to exercise control over unexpected events, along with a vague notion of 'unruly', 'animal' sexual drives in men, were recurrent themes in the reminiscences of former German maids. In addition to the lack of information and the puzzling warnings which they received from home – along the lines of 'don't go with men or you'll have a child' or 'come back the way you were when you left' – this fear was exacerbated by many upsetting reports about damsels in distress who came to 'wrack and ruin'.

That this fear was not without basis, is evidenced by the records of the Catholic Martha Society in the city of Haarlem. They describe dramatic experiences of German girls who were 'taken by surprise' by the consequences of their encounters with males. In the autumn of 1922, the board went into considerable detail about a German girl who 'has been knocked up' and became an unwed mother. The pastoral advisor felt that she should be sent back as soon as possible, 'as this will teach the others a lesson'.[33]

Just what this lesson was and how girls could protect themselves from such dramatic consequences remained unclear. For, despite the taboo concerning encounters with the opposite sex, it was still expected that they would marry sooner or later. This clearly made contact with men unavoidable. It was possible to ignore this dilemma by assuming that the German maids stayed temporary and would return sooner or later 'undamaged' to their fatherland.

Preserving young women for the German fatherland

From the beginning, morality, religion and patriotism formed the initially somewhat abstract cornerstones of the approach taken by German denominational organisations in the Netherlands toward German maids. Young, single countrywomen were to be guarded against moral ruin by binding them to the church in order to prevent them from disgracing their fatherland. The nationalist sentiments which went along with these practices did not present a barrier between the German and Dutch protectors of girls. On the contrary, the Dutch found it equally important to save their fatherland from immorality.

Efforts to protect German girls in the Netherlands continued unabated. Catholic and Protestant circles wholeheartedly agreed that this work had top priority, especially in view of the steady increase in the number of German maids crossing the border to the Netherlands in the beginning of the 1930s. In the wake of the stock market crash in 1929, the American loans which had to a large degree kept the German industry afloat were withdrawn. Countless companies went bankrupt, salaries sank and millions of people lost their jobs. In the Netherlands, the immediate consequences of the crash were lessened because the Dutch business world was not as dependent on the American situation as was Germany. Between 1929 and 1931, the German Federal Bureau of Emigration (*Reichsstelle für das Auswanderungswesen*) registered more than a threefold increase in the number of maids who left Prussia for the Netherlands.[34] In 1929, The Hague displayed a comparable increase from approximately 3,000 to 4,000 German Catholic maids to nearly 10,000 in 1931.[35] This development continued through 1933. However, during this period, the Land of the Solid Guilder was also sorely affected by the diminishing labour market and increasing unemployment.

The pressure of the economic crisis threw a new light on the shortage of housemaids in the Netherlands. Initially, the need for good, cheap domestic help had primacy and welcome use was made of the potential services of foreign maids. However, with the rapid increase in unemployment, other interests began to prevail. In December 1932, an article on 'Unemployment and the need for maidservants' in a local newspaper, raised the question that would occupy people's minds for the next few years: 'What are we doing here in Holland with these German, Austrian, Czech and other foreign girls, while there are so many unemployed (girls) in need of our support?' 'Foreign intruders' was the name given to the maids from abroad who not only allowed valuable Dutch currency flow over the borders, but took up with Dutch lovers who would 'otherwise have been reserved for a Dutch maiden'.[36]

Notions about competition from non-Dutch domestics occupying the positions of Dutch girls were not limited to the labour market. The marriage market was also at stake. This not only gave the discussions about foreign domestic servants an extra boost in newspaper columns of the day, but it also emerged more than half a century later in the reactions I encountered to my call for former German maids, and other people involved, to respond to my research proposal. Maria Without-A-Name, 'an unmarried woman', as she called herself, in an anonymous letter written in June 1987 to me, notes:

> The German maids, destitute and in search of men and money, arrived by the thousands. They stole our boys with coquetterie and subservient manners. They were scabs, working for rich ladies to whom no self-respecting Dutch woman would lend her services. Many Dutch girls and married women were robbed of their lovers and men back then by those sweet seducers.

These words show how notions about women's migration were shaped by national and gender relations. Governmental policy was limited to the presumed competition on the labour market, but the support for this policy was provided by women who felt threatened by the German maids in other areas of social life as well.

While new measures were being developed in the Netherlands to keep German maids out, the flow had already begun to change, just as it had ten years earlier. From 1934 onwards, fewer German girls came to the Netherlands and an increase in the young women returning to Germany was noted. Residence in the Netherlands had lost much of its appeal since the economic crisis had affected incomes. At the same time, Hitler's rise to power made their stay in another country less necessary for economic reasons.

Those who remained in the Netherlands after 1936, had good situations, serious lovers or had become anchored in Dutch society in some other way. Most of them had not the slightest intention of returning to the German *Reich*. If the German maids had not exchanged their German nationalities for Dutch ones by marrying Dutchmen, they were confronted in December 1938 with a summons by the German government to come back to their homeland. The fatherland, represented by the National Socialist authorities, needed its daughters and made a collective appeal to the German girls to return. If they refused, they would lose their citizenship.

The Action for the Collective Return of German Maids, or the *Hausmädchenheimschaffungsaktion*, as it was called in German official jargon, aimed at recruiting more women for the German labour market. But there were other motives as well. As was emphasised from different directions, the Netherlands was 'poison' for the young, politically unformed German girls. At this time, the usual warnings about the moral dangers which invariably accompanied the migration of unmarried German women, became saturated by a virulent nationalism, whereby anti-semitic ideas found a resonance as well. Many German girls were thought to occupy a 'morally or economically improper' position. In this way, they became a 'target for Jewish lads and Dutch persons of a certain type' (*Freiwild für Judenjungs und bestimmte Holländer*). The image of the Netherlands which had already been diminished by the economic crisis, was now further devalued by National Socialist pronouncements concerning 'hostility towards Germany' and the 'semitisation' of the Netherlands. German women were told to stop being 'a servant people for other states' (*ein Dienstbotenvolk für andere Staaten*), when they were so much better off in their own country. Here – and only here – they could remain the future mothers of the German People.[37]

The large number of written requests from German maids and Dutch mistresses for dispensation, as well as the news in the Dutch press about the 'run on the town halls' indicate that there was not much enthusiasm among German maids for returning. German girls who were still in the Netherlands in 1939, were apparently seldom touched by the appeal to their position as future 'mothers of the fatherland'. This action did, however, mark the end of the intensive migration of young, unmarried women from Germany to the Netherlands during the Interbellum.

Conclusion

The discourses on femininity which accompanied the large-scale migration of young, single German women to the Netherlands, needs to be viewed against the backdrop of a society strongly in flux since the second half of the nineteenth century. Urbanisation and geographic mobility went hand in hand with high expectations and intense fears of the unknown. In particular, the city embodied the unknown with all its opportunities and its dangers. In contrast to the stable circumstances of rural life, city life entailed transient contacts and uncontrollable seductions to which young women, in particular, were prey. Their sexual integrity was at stake.

In this process, we can see how the perception of women as 'pure', modest and 'unspoiled' became interwoven with rural settings. The image of city girls as 'cheeky' and 'spoiled' provided a contrast. However, as a dynamic centre of economic and cultural life, the city continued to be attractive, while the country seemed, in contrast, staid and 'primitive'. Such opposition played an important role in the migration of young, unmarried women from the end of the last century onward, and they gained renewed strength in the years between the two world wars as the migration of young women across the border from a wartorn Germany emerged. At that moment, however, a new element was introduced. In addition to the opposition between country and city, the opposition between an impoverished but respectable German fatherland – the Heimat – and the rich, but morally dubious country abroad was constructed.

Attempts from both German and Dutch societies for the Protection of Girls to prevent mishap by meeting girls at the stations and setting up special girls' clubs, were accompanied by the articulation of a discourse of femininity where a high premium was placed on virtue and modesty. In contrast, curiosity and a sense of enterprise were disqualified as a risky 'desire for adventure'. In this way, a contradiction was constructed between 'reliable' and 'unreliable' female migrants, whereby the former deserved full support, while the latter had to be sent home as soon as possible in order to prevent them from contaminating the others with their bold behaviour.

Young women were viewed at first glance as the dependent, vulnerable party: in theory, they were regarded as 'good' unless city life or living abroad had exerted a corrupting influence on them. Whether this image was emphasised or not, depended on the economic circumstances and the political climate in the country of origin as well as in the country of destination. Since the image was based on actual dangers confronting young women, it could develop at any moment into a 'moral panic' which would then have to be curtailed by governmental measures.

This occurred for the first time in 1923, when growing unemployment in the Netherlands provided the justification for an investigation into the influence of German maids on unemployment and morality. Although the results of this inquiry were negligible, the German government, under pressure from concerned women's organisations, decided to issue measures for limiting the migration of young women under 18 years.

Such measures were expanded and intensified by the Dutch government throughout the 1930s, when it became clear that the malaise was not going to pass the Netherlands by. Then too, these measures were supported by warnings concerning the dangers threatening single women abroad. Finally the limitations to the admittance of foreign domestic help further evolved into the forced expulsion of German maids to their fatherland at the end of the 1930s – this time with the German government appealing to the German maids as women and future mothers of the nation whose innocence and morals were being threatened in the morally dubious Netherlands.

The stories of the women migrants themselves also refer to this dominant discourse, whereby first the city and later the foreign country are linked to immorality. But they often present a multi-faceted narrative about their migration. On the one hand they emphasise the new possibilities city life in the foreign country offered them, while on the other hand they mention how they dealt with the dangers that accompanied their arrival in unknown surroundings. The former German maids present themselves as individual agents who were able to make their own decisions and act independently, often stressing – not unlike the dominant discourse of the organisations for the protection of girls – their own innocence and sexual integrity by distancing themselves from other German girls, city girls from the working classes, who were 'loud' and 'noticeably roaming around the streets' and who had, in fact, already lost their innocence before they came to the Netherlands.

In this way, the migrants themselves managed to construct a migration narrative in which they combined a romantic opposition between the innocent country girl and the spoiled city girl with the modernist opposition between the 'primitive' country (or the impoverished homeland) and more cultivated or rich surroundings which offered them new perspectives. When the 'father'land called back its young daughters, it became clear, however, just how vulnerable and dependent these young, single women living abroad were. Only marriage with a Dutch man could save them from the National Socialist appeal to German women as future mothers of the German nation. At that moment, it was evident how limited the 'protection' offered by the Societies for the Protection of Girls actually was. With their focus on moral dangers and their support for measures to prevent the uncontrolled migration of women, they ignored the necessary civil rights which could have given German migrant women a substantial basis for protection, independent of an alliance with a Dutch man.

Thus, the migration of young, single women remained a risky undertaking and it was in the interests of all concerned to draw upon dominant images of femininity as modest and vulnerable, of woman as a potential victim. The life stories of German maids, however, display niches where we can discover an unmistakable pride in their self-sufficiency and the entrepreneurial spirit with which they undertook their migration and dealt with the dangers involved.

Notes

1 I would like to thank Hélène Vossen and Petra de Vries for their stimulating comments. Kathy Davis did a wonderful job by translating this article from Dutch – and some German – into English.

2 See for example, J. R. Walkowitz, *City of Dreadful Delight: Narratives of Sexual Danger in Late Victorian London*, London, Virago, 1992.

3 See for example M. Blaschke and C. Harzig (ed.), *Frauen wandern aus: deutsche Migrantinnen im 19. und 20. Jahrhundert*, Bremen, Universität Bremen, 1990; G. Buijs (ed.), *Migrant Women: Crossing Boundaries and Changing Identities*, Oxford, Berg, 1993; H. R. Diner, *Erin's Daughters in America: Irish Immigrant Women in the 19th Century*, Baltimore, MD, Johns Hopkins University Press, 1983; A.J. Hammerton, *Emigrant Gentlewomen: Genteel Poverty and Female Emigration, 1830–1914*, London, Croom Helm, 1979.

4 See for example, L. P. Moch, *Moving Europeans: Migration in Western Europe since 1650*, Bloomington, Indiana University Press, 1992.

5 Based on the statistics from the Dutch Central Statistic Office (Centraal Bureau voor de Statistiek), cited by B. Henkes, 'Changing Images of German Maids during the Inter-war Period in the Netherlands: from Trusted Help to Traitor in the Nest', in P. Thompson and R. Samuel (eds), *The Myths We Live By*, London, Routledge, 1990, p. 234. Additional information and corrections were published in G. van der Harst and L. Lucassen, *Nieuw in Leiden. Plaats en betekenis van Vreemdelingen in een Hollandse stad (1918–1955)*, Leiden, Primavera Pers, 1998, p. 66. Needless to say that these registration figures can only be an indication of the actual foreign domestic maidservants present at the time.

6 This article is primarily based on the material I collected during the research for my book *Heimat in Holland. Duitse dienstmeisjes 1920–1950*, Amsterdam, Babylon/De Geus, 1995 – that was translated in German as *Heimat in Holland. Deutsche Dienstmädchen 1920–1950*, Straelen, Straelener Manuskripte Verlag, 1998. During the research 104 former German and several Austrian maids filled in a lengthy questionnaire, while I spoke with 37 women about their temporary or permanent migration to the Netherlands.

7 Questionnaire Mrs Akkerman-Heuten, 1987.

8 Biographical interview with Mrs Stark-Blömers, 9 October 1989.

9 Mrs Van Vliet told me her life story during four meetings in September, November and December 1986 and May 1993. At the end of our first meeting she presented me with the manuscript of an unpublished autobiography she wrote in 1974, 1977 and 1979.

10 Mrs A. Van Vliet-Haye, *De jonge jaren van een Plattelandsmeisje in het Groothertogdom Oldenburg* (A country girl's youth in the grand duchy of Oldenburg), unpublished autobiographical account, Amsterdam, 1977, p. 54.

11 Biographical interview with Mrs Van Vliet-Haye, 14 December 1986.

12 Biographical interview with Mrs Van Vliet-Haye, 1 November 1986.

13 See for example 1895–1955: *Katholischer Mädchenschutz. Festschrift.* Freiburg, 1955; J.D. Van Romondt Vis-Quarles de Quarles (ed.), *Vijftig jaar vrouwenwerk 1882–1932. Gedenkboek van de Nederlandsche Vereeniging ter Behartiging van de Belangen der Jonge Meisjes*, Amsterdam, 1932.

14 See for example *25 Jahre Deutsche Bahnhofsmission, 1897–1922. Jubiläumsjahresbericht*, w.p., 1922; A. J. Gruber and F. Muysken, 'Het stationswerk', in Van Romondt Vis-Quarles de Quarles (ed.), *Vijftig jaar vrouwenwerk*, pp. 81–89.

15 J. I. D. A. J. Engelberts and J. J. Mackay, 'De Union van 1914 tot 1918', in Van Romondt Vis-Quarles de Quarles (ed.), *Vijftig jaar vrouwenwerk*, p. 64.

16 Annual reports of the Dutch denominational stations work, cited by Henkes, *Heimat in Holland*, pp. 42–46.

17 See also B. Henkes, 'German Maids in the Prosperous Guilderland and the Land of Moral Threats: Nation-Images and National Identity during the Interwar Period', in A. Galema, B. Henkes and H. Te Velde (eds), *Images of the Nation: Different Meanings of Dutchness, 1870–1940*, Amsterdam, Rodopi, 1993, pp. 133–159.

18 In addition to the already existing station care in the large cities, this led to the establishment of new station work centres at the border between Germany and the Netherlands, namely in Nieuwe-Schans (March 1921), Oldenzaal (March 1922), Bentheim (April 1922), Gronau (April 1922) and Elten-Emmerik (April 1922).

19 *Rundschreiben der Evangelischen Deutschen Bahnhofsmission*, 29, November 1922.

20 The data of the first Annual Report (1927) of the St Elizabeth Foundation for Catholic German girls in The Hague may serve as an illustration of the extent the activities of some of these societies could assume: the visitors totalled 15,000. Sometimes more than 150 girls came in one evening during the winter months. Their own agency succeeded in finding 240 situations.

21 *Mädchenschutz*, vol. 1, September 1925.

22 'Nederlandsche en Duitsche dienstboden', *Drentsch en Asser Dagblad*, 1 August 1924.

23 Coverage in *De Nieuw Rotterdamse Courant* of 14 March 1924 and other newspapers.

24 See, for example, E.J. Hammerton, *Emigrant Gentlewomen* and C. Swaisland, 'Female Migration and Social Mobility: British Female Domestic Servants to South Africa, 1860–1914', in G. Buijs (ed.), *Migrant Women: Crossing Boundaries and Changing Identities*, Oxford and Pietermaritzburg, Berg/University of Natal Press, 1993, pp. 161–179 for similar problems with the decreasing status of middle-class migrant women and, therefore, the intersection of class and gender in women's migration.

25 See M. J. Piore, *Birds of Passage: Migrants and Industrial Societies*, Cambridge, Cambridge University Press, 1979, p. 62 and E. N. Glenn, *Issei, Nisei, War Bride: Three Generations of Japanese American Women in Domestic Service*, Philadelphia, PA, Temple University Press, 1986, p. 10 on the behaviour of 'pioneers' in the migrations movement which could be characterised by a strong sense of individualism. In the long run single migrants were more likely to build communities and became, thus, more visible. This evoked mixed reactions from the receiving society and also among the migrants themselves, as it was often linked to negative notions about moral conduct.

26 Biographical interview with Mrs Van Vliet-Haye, 26 September 1986.

27 Biographical interview with Mrs Jaswetz-Rakowski, 13 September 1989.

28 Report from the Bureau for Advice for Emigrants in Düsseldorf of 1 January 1927 until 31 March 1927.

29 Biographical interview with Mrs Holz-Nitka, 12 September 1989.

30 *Mädchenschutz*, 1929, vol. 5, nr. 11/12.

31 This information is based on the archives of the Bureau for Advice for Emigrants in Münster. The results of a sample of registration forms and the accompanying correspondence shows that 15 per cent of the registrations involved girls who were thought to be too young; in 5 per cent of the cases the rejection was justified with reference to the dishonest or immoral behaviour of the girl.

32 Biographical interviews with Mrs Rijsbaarman-Fitsch, 7 November 1987 and 4 March 1988.

33 Minutes of the meeting of the board of the Martha Society of November 1926.

34 *Nachrichtenblatt der Reichsstelle für das Auswanderungswesen*, 1 January 1935, cited by W. Sahner, *Katholische und evangelische Seelsorge des Deutschtums in Holland. Kirchliche und kulturelle Gliederung. Eine kirchenmissions-geschichtliche und pastoral-theologische Studie.* Emsdetten, 1950.

35 According to the annual reports of the German Catholic St Elizabeth foundation in The Hague of 1929 and 1930/31.

36 *Nieuwe Tilburgsche Courant*, 30 November 1932.

37 Based on reports and correspondence between German representatives in the Netherlands and National Socialist authorities in Berlin, cited by Henkes, *Heimat in Holland*, pp. 155–165. German maids in Belgium, France, Great Britain, Switzerland and other European countries were confronted with this action for forced repatriation too. See for example R. Bochsler and S. Gisiger, *Dienen in der Fremde. Dienstmädchen und ihre Herrschaften in der Schweiz des 20. Jahrhunderts*, Zürich, Chronos, 1989, pp. 14–15.

13 Female migration and the farm family economy in interwar Japan

Janet Hunter

The late nineteenth and early twentieth centuries witnessed the migration of substantial numbers of young men and women within Japan, many of whom moved to take up employment in the nation's growing modern manufacturing sector. Conspicuous in this migration was the role of those – mainly women – who worked in the textile sector, which by the end of the First World War employed around two million Japanese. The largest branches of textile production – silk reeling, cotton spinning and weaving – made particular use of young women. These women often travelled long distances to take up textile employment, and were in large part the daughters of farming families.[1] Physically separated from their homes and families for the duration of their employment, they were accommodated in dormitories at the mill. They, and other migrants from rural areas, were one manifestation of the links between agriculture and manufacturing which have been at the heart of debates on Japan's pattern of industrialisation.

Textile migration was part of what has been referred to as *dekasegi* (temporary migration for the purpose of finding work), a term denoting workers who absented themselves from their families either for seasonal employment or for some limited period of time. Texts on *dekasegi* in Japan highlight the fact that the majority of female textile employees worked at the most for a few years and usually returned to their home villages afterwards, often marrying in their home neighbourhoods.[2] Some writers have cast doubt on this well-used stereotype, however, and it is often difficult to identify workers' experiences after leaving the factories, but there is no doubt that many workers retained strong links with their families during their time of work, and often afterwards as well.[3]

The purpose of this chapter is to comment on the significance of female textile migration for the village communities themselves, and in particular for the farm family economy. It will be shown that the economic contribution of textile migrants to the village and family economies was very significant through the interwar years and a high proportion of these female textile migrants continued to be regarded – and regarded themselves – as ongoing members of multifunctional farm families, notwithstanding their geographical separation from their home base. This migration was thus an important source of income for rural communities, and sustained the economic existence of what have been called 'pluriactive' farm families in Japan, that is, families that remained on the land, but demonstrated an ongoing flexibility in the face of shifting income earning opportunities.

The first section of the chapter will briefly outline the significance of textile production in Japanese manufacturing in the interwar years, and provide some outline statistical data on the composition of the textile workforce. In particular it will indicate the gender, age and marital status profiles of that workforce, and the significance in it of migrant workers who came from farm families. The second half of the chapter will outline the economic significance of workers' wages and remittances for local economies. While it is difficult to obtain accurate figures, it is apparent that this migrant labour offered economic support on a very substantial scale. The conclusion will briefly outline the pressures acting both to undermine and to sustain this link, and suggest its importance in the longer-term development of Japan.

Textile production and textile migration

In Japan both silk reeling and cotton spinning – two of the largest sectors of textile production – had already undergone extensive expansion and mechanisation prior to the First World War. During the 1920s they were joined by the third major area of production, the weaving of cotton cloth, as manufacturers in the traditional production areas (*sanchi*) expanded mechanised production, and large cotton spinning companies set up integrated spinning and weaving mills.[4] These three branches of activity accounted for a large proportion of total textile employment throughout the interwar years (see Table 13.1). They were also of crucial importance to Japan's export trade, as shown in Table 13.2.

These different branches of textile production were in many respects very diverse. The silk industry relied on domestically produced cocoons, while cotton production was dependent on imported raw material. This in turn impacted on their location, cost structures and business interests. They varied in such factors as scale of operation, concentration of capital and ownership, and sophistication of technology. Nevertheless, in the interwar years the key three branches identified above had one major feature in common: they all drew primarily on the same source of labour, that is, young female members of the population, a high proportion of them from rural areas. Their growth was thus a major factor in stimulating internal migration in prewar Japan.

The composition of the textile labour force by gender and age in 1920–1940 is shown in Tables 13.3 and 13.4. It is apparent that between 1920 and 1940 women constituted a substantial majority of workers in this industry, and also that the female workforce in these larger, more

Table 13.1 Number of workers employed in Japanese textile manufacturing, by process, 1920–1940 (% in parentheses)

	1920		*1930*		*1940*	
Silk reeling	438,900	(20.9)	480,700	(29.0)	234,000	(14.0)
Cotton spinning	250,100	(11.9)	151,900	(9.2)	141,900	(8.5)
Weaving	701,800	(33.4)	424,300	(25.6)	480,500	(28.7)
Dyeing, finishing	300,000	(14.3)	202,300	(12.2)	211,200	(12.6)
Sewing, tailoring	213,200	(10.6)	232,900	(14.0)	384,400	(22.9)
Other	196,200	(9.3)	165,700	(10.0)	223,000	(13.3)
Total	2,100,200		1,657,800		1,675,000	

Sources: Calculated from Naikaku Tōkeikyoku, *Taishō 9-nen Kokusei Chōsa Hōkoku Zenkoku no Bu*, vol.2, *Shokugyō*, Tokyo, Naikaku Tōkeikyoku, 1929; Naikaku Tōkeikyoku, *Shōwa 5-nen Kokusei Chōsa Hōkoku*, vol.2, *Shokugyō oyobi Sangyō*, Tokyo, Naikaku Tōkeikyoku, 1935; Sōrifu Tōkeikyoku, *Shōwa 15-nen Kokusei Chōsa Hōkoku*, vol. 2, *Sangyō.Jigyōjō no Chii*, Tokyo, Sōrifu, 1962. Hereafter 1920, 1930 and 1940 censuses, respectively.

Notes

1 Figures to nearest 100, percentage figures rounded to nearest 0.1%, hence do not total 100.

2 'Textiles' is here taken to include all processes from initial processing of raw materials to making of garments. Artificial fibres excluded.

Table 13.2 Value of textiles as a percentage of total Japanese exports, 1920–1940

	1920	*1930*	*1940*
Cotton thread	7.8	1.0	1.6
Cotton textiles	17.2	18.5	10.9
Silk thread	19.6	28.4	12.2
Silk textiles	8.1	4.5	1.0

Source: T. Nakamura, *Economic Growth in Prewar Japan*, New Haven, CT, Yale University Press, 1971, p. 36.

Table 13.3 Gender distribution (by per cent) of workers in silk reeling, cotton spinning and weaving, 1920–1940

Year	*Silk reeling*		*Cotton spinning*		*Weaving*	
	Men	*Women*	*Men*	*Women*	*Men*	*Women*
1920	17.2	82.8	29.3	70.5	28.2	71.8
1930	14.0	86.0	31.3	68.7	31.0	69.0
1940	16.1	83.9	22.2	77.8	27.0	73.0

Source: Interwar Censuses, see Table 13.1 for details.

Table 13.4 Percentage of female workforce under 20 years of age, 1920–1940

	Silk reeling	*Spinning*	*Weaving*
1920	64.0	66.4	49.0
1930	64.4	67.0	48.9
1940	61.8	72.3	53.0

Source: As Table 13.1.

mechanised branches of production was primarily young – mostly under the age of 20. Given this age profile, it is not surprising that a very high proportion of all female textile workers were also unmarried – around 80 per cent in silk reeling and spinning, and over 60 per cent in weaving.[5] In family terms they were essentially daughters rather than wives and mothers.

Identifying the family backgrounds of workers is more difficult. Contemporary employers assumed a 'rural connection', and set wage levels and articulated labour policies by explicit reference to it. Many commentators at the time shared this assumption, but cited little more than anecdotal evidence. National census data gives little indication of parental occupation, but during the interwar period national and local government authorities, as well as public and private organisations, undertook relatively detailed cross-sectional surveys showing the origins, family background and destinations of migrant workers. These provide adequate evidence to support the statement that the rural connection – invariably taken as the norm for all textile workers – was true of at least a large part of the textile workforce. Extensive analysis of migration patterns has shown very clearly the patterns of movement between different prefectures in Japan, and helped to identify the movement of female migrants from predominantly rural prefectures into those prefectures where the expanding textile industries were primarily located.[6] The findings of systematic statistical surveys undertaken at national and regional level are supported by lower-level surveys based on sample populations and questionnaires. Table 13.5 shows the findings of one of these surveys.

The movement of farm family daughters into textile work thus constituted a significant element in the extensive internal migration in Japan from the late nineteenth century. Since we know that turnover rates in these industries were high, the data suggest that by the late 1930s in large areas of the Japanese countryside a majority of women would at some time have worked in textile production, either locally or at a distance. Textile migration was thus of ongoing importance, not only to the growth of these industries, but to workers' families and village communities.

Table 13.5 Family origins of spinning workers in Osaka, 1927

	Number	*Percentage*
Agriculture	13,474	61.66
Fishing	1,180	5.40
Commerce	1,463	6.70
Labourers/workers	1,384	6.33
Crafts/artisan	875	4.00
Other	2,228	9.28
Unknown	1,248	6.7
Total (N)	*21,852*	*100.00*

Source: Chūō Shokugyō Shōkai Jimukyoku, *Bōseki Rōdō Fujin Chōsa*, Tokyo, Chūō Shokugyō Shōkai Jimukyoku, 1929, pp. 23–25.

Note
This survey was based on questionnaires distributed to around 45,000 workers in 49 factories. Responses were returned by nearly 22,000 workers in 34 factories. Except for two, all the factories approached were cotton spinning mills.

Migration and the village economy: savings and remittances of textile workers

The impact of this migration on the communities from which migrants came was social, cultural and political, as well as economic, but it is the economic aspect that has aroused particular controversy. As noted, the relationship between the rural and manufacturing sectors has constituted one of the most contentious areas of debate in modern Japanese historiography, and the contribution of migrant workers to both the industrial and agricultural economies has been a key element in these debates. Marxist-Leninist-influenced historians in particular have argued variously that the low-wage employment of farmers' daughters enabled tenants to pay excessive rents to landlords who dominated the agricultural sector, sustaining semi-feudal production relations, and facilitated capital accumulation by making cheap labour available to industrialists. Under these scenarios the gender of the migrant labour force and the poverty of the agricultural sector combined to make textile workers stereotypical objects of exploitation.[7] Recent scholarship has posed a strongly revisionist view, seeking to refute the image of the rural population as passive and exploited,[8] but the role of the migrant labour force has remained a topic of controversy. In the light of these debates the question of remittances and savings takes on a particular significance. We therefore need to explore two main issues: the significance of the farm family economy rather than individual wage levels in the decision to migrate to textile work, and the extent of the remittances sent back to families and their importance to the local economy.

There is no doubt that individual wage levels played a role in the migration of farmers' daughters into textile work. Average figures for textile workers' daily wages show that in cotton spinning and weaving they were consistently higher than the wages of female daily contract workers in agriculture. The same was true for silk reeling, except in the trough of the interwar depression, 1931–1934.[9] Staying at home, of course, assumed availability of agricultural or other local employment, which was not always the case. It thus appears that by moving further afield the earning capacity of the individual daughter could be that much greater. However, wage levels were far from being the sole determinant of this migration. Contemporary statements by employers and the authorities suggest that they viewed textile employment in non-local factories in the interwar years as analogous to more traditional forms of by-employment (subsidiary income earning activities, usually cash crop production or manufacturing activity within the household). Evidence also indicates that this perception of textile migration as an integral part of family income-earning strategy was shared by many workers and their families. That household needs rather than individual wage levels were a key factor in this migration is supported by the fact that right through the 1930s workers' responses to questionnaires aimed at ascertaining why they had taken up employment were dominated by statements such as 'to help the family economy' or 'because my parents wanted me to'. The same 1927 survey of spinning workers referred to above showed 69 per cent of respondents giving as their reason for taking up spinning employment 'to help the family finances', followed by 17 per cent giving the reason 'to support myself and obtain a dowry'.[10] Statements from all strata of Japanese society show that wage work of this kind for women was seen in economic terms as an extension of the family economy, a perception reflected in the far from unique assumption that these workers' wages should be set at a 'supplementary' level, since they did not need to support a partner or a family. In the early years of manufacturing development the families of textile workers had also received lump sum advances on their daughters' wages on signing a contract. Although this practice diminished during the interwar years, in some areas, particularly in smaller-scale weaving operations, it persisted.[11]

By the interwar period it was legally and practically possible for the individual worker to keep her own wages, rather than contributing some part of them to the family budget. Nevertheless, all the evidence that we have suggests that the majority of textile workers remitted much of their earnings to their families, and often saved, perhaps with a view to a dowry, money which would otherwise have had to be found by the family from other sources. For example, a 1918 survey of women silk workers in part of Gifu Prefecture (in central Japan) showed their average income to be ¥70 per annum, of which some 78 per cent was sent home for use by the family, or put by for savings.[12] Later surveys showed a huge variation in remittances, but suggested average figures of ¥14–33 per month, and up to ¥200–300 per annum.[13] Given current wage levels this suggests that anything from 50 to 90 per cent of workers' wages were reaching their families.[14] Promises of substantial remittances were made by recruiters to persuade farm families to send their daughters away to work. Remittance maximisation was also encouraged by employers, since it helped their recruitment base. During the interwar years many companies still took on the responsibility of sending a part of workers' earnings at regular intervals back to their families,[15] helping to ensure a high level of remittances. This process took place monthly, half-yearly or yearly. One senior Post Office official was reported as saying that the high level of remittances was a condition for the continued existence of branch post offices in remoter parts of the countryside.[16]

Quantifying the importance of workers' wages to the village and family economy is more difficult, but the available evidence suggests that there were many villages throughout rural Japan whose income depended to a considerable extent on income flow from absent workers, both male and female. There were so many female textile migrants that their remittances were a significant part of this flow. The extent of textile migration from certain regions has been noted already, and surveys and commentators in the interwar years identified some villages where a third or more of young females were away working at any one time, or where one out of every two or three households had a migrant female member.[17] Even though the amounts sent by individuals may have been small, remittances on this scale collectively reached substantial proportions.

Comprehensive figures for the total volume of contributions are unavailable, and assessing the significance of income to villages is problematic. One academic in the early 1930s noted that few materials on the importance of *dekasegi* earnings to farm villages existed. In farm surveys, he commented, the amounts given tended to be vague, and were almost certainly an underestimation. His own view was that the amounts were critical (*ketteiteki*) to village income.[18] However, some sample figures can give some indication of the importance that this remitted income might assume in the household and village economy, and in the local economy as a whole. One 1927 survey suggested that 15 to 20 per cent of the total income of a 453 household village in Niigata Prefecture on the Japan Sea coast – the largest outflow area for female textile workers – came from migrant women in silk reeling, commenting that 'without this income, there would not be enough in the village's kitchens'.[19] Elsewhere in the same region migrant workers were said to account for 30 per cent of village income, while a village in Shizuoka, south-west of Tokyo, claimed to receive ¥120,000 per annum from about 700 girls.[20] In 1936 the village of Ikazawa in Niigata Prefecture had a population of 4,816 in 773 households. Of this population some 386 migrant female textile workers remitted on average ¥50–60, a total of *c.*¥20,000, and amounting to around a quarter of the village's total cash income.[21] Studies of the Kōfu Basin in Yamanashi Prefecture, west of Tokyo, suggested that in 1931–1935 farm families were earning a quarter of their income from non-agricultural sources, in which silk filature work was a major part.[22]

Support for the significance of non-agricultural, cash income of this kind for the farm household is found in the surveys on farm family economies (*nōka keizai chōsa*) undertaken during the interwar years at the behest of the Ministry of Agriculture and Forestry. These surveys showed that on average farming families were dependent on non-agricultural sources for around 20–25 per cent of total household income throughout the interwar years, and in most years agricultural income alone was inadequate to support the household's expenditure. This was true of farmers almost regardless of whether they owned all the land they farmed, rented it all, or operated on a mixture of owned and tenanted land.[23] Umemura Mataji, in his seminal study of the relationship between wage levels, employment and the agricultural sector, suggested that in the interwar years income from waged work amounted to 40–50 per cent of the net income from agricultural production.[24]

Remittances to agricultural families remained significant throughout the interwar years. Certainly, the ability of farm family daughters to generate textile income fluctuated. Problems in the silk industry in the late 1920s, and its catastrophic collapse after 1929, proved extremely grave for many rural localities and families. New employment opportunities in silk reeling diminished, and many existing workers were made redundant, with the result that one Gifu village which had earlier been dispatching 300 migrant silk workers, by 1932 had only fifty-six.[25] The financial difficulties faced by many silk producers had a knock-on effect on their workers and their families. Many silk employers failed to pay wages due to those workers who remained in employment. In Nagano Prefecture, the centre of the mechanised silk reeling industry, the prefectural authorities took out a ¥1million loan to support producers, but during 1930–1931 around one-eighth of due wages remained unpaid. Even after prefectural help some ¥500,000 was still outstanding.[26]

Employment opportunities in other branches of textiles also suffered. Constrained markets and finances through much of the 1920s, and an impending ban on nightwork (implemented in 1929)[27] pushed cotton spinning firms towards the introduction of new technology and labour rationalisation. Labour productivity improved dramatically in the late 1920s, and this was accompanied by reduction in demand for workers. For a brief while the Depression also inflicted suffering on the cotton industry. Within a short space of time the heavy devaluation of the yen contributed to the recovery of the cotton industry on the back of export demand, and labour opportunities again increased, but the recovery of cotton spinning and weaving, and the rise of new branches of textile production, such as artificial fibres, were not sufficient to compensate for lost silk employment. In 1940 textile employment stood at a level little higher than that of the depths of the recession in 1930. Moreover, the relative decline in employment opportunities for young women as the male-dominated heavy and chemical industries expanded contributed to a weakening of women's position in the labour market. Notwithstanding the buoyancy and expansion of large parts of textile production, it became more difficult for female migrant workers to secure this kind of employment. Nevertheless, textile migration remained very significant. This was an industry which in 1940 was still employing nearly 1.7 million workers, a very high proportion of whom were migrant females.

The income that such workers were able to send to their families thus fluctuated, and in most cases is likely to have declined substantially during the trough of the Depression. Money wages in all branches of textiles declined substantially after 1928, and only began to recover in the later 1930s. Moreover, female industrial wages reflected more closely changes in farm income and farm wage levels than did male industrial wages. With the agricultural sector worst hit by depression, the wages of female migrants fell further than those of men, and were slower to recover. However, given the catastrophic declines in the prices of agricultural products, notably cocoons and rice, between 1929 and 1933, the relative significance of migrants' earnings in total village cash income may in some cases have increased, as female manufacturing wages for those who were employed did not decline quite so far as agricultural prices.[28] Farm economy surveys show that, notwithstanding declines in some cases, cash remittances and non-agricultural income remained crucial to the farm economy throughout the interwar years.[29] Indeed, Kaoru Sugihara has argued persuasively that a relatively rapid recovery in farm family income after the early 1930s enabled the agricultural sector to play a significant role in overall recovery, both through expenditure on household and farm inputs, and through the provision of cheap labour.[30] We can say with some confidence that right through the interwar years migrant female workers in the textile industry were continuing to make a major contribution to village and family income, and hence to both spending power and labour supply.

Since decisions relating to consumption and expenditure within the farm family tended to be made on the basis of the needs of the household, rather than the needs of the individuals within it, it is very difficult to know how much of a migrant worker's wages may have been allocated to her personal consumption. Certainly most workers by the interwar period were using a small part of their earnings to acquire personal comforts, such as, for example, entertainment, clothing and make-up. Dowry savings were, in a sense, individual, as they enhanced marriage prospects and future position, but in times of need these would have been forfeited to the survival of the household. However, the remittances which, as we have seen, constituted the largest part of their earnings, became an integral part of the farm household's income. As such, they went towards the necessities for production and consumption for the household as a whole. The penetration of the market economy over decades had meant that farmers progressively purchased more commodities from outside, and this kind of cash income clearly assisted in that process. Most of the information that we have from, for example, farm family budgets, suggests that the prime allocation of such funds was to sustain daily life and the agricultural production process, particularly during the middle years of the interwar decades when agricultural incomes declined considerably. The main items consumed by the agricultural sector were basic necessities, such as foodstuffs like soya beans, or clothing, or else industrial inputs for agriculture, like fertiliser. Interviews with migrant textile workers from the interwar years, for example, suggest that it was not uncommon for remittances to be sent at particular times of year to enable the purchase of fertiliser or other inputs.[31] Where money remained to the family after this kind of expenditure on basic needs, it might be saved (usually in the local savings bank, or post office), used for the repayment of debt, put towards the purchase or rent of additional land, or expended on the education of the sons of the house. Workers' reminiscences suggest, however, that in most cases remittances went into the household pool, and became part of a total amount whose allocation was determined by the household head.[32] In this respect these spending patterns suggest that farm family members tended to view this kind of migrant textile work as just one more form of the by-employment in which farm families had long engaged.[33]

Conclusion: forces for change

It was not to be expected that migrant workers would not on some occasions break free of their family connection. Indeed, the gradual industrialisation of the Japanese economy, the growth of permanent rather than temporary migration, and the socioeconomic changes that accompanied this accelerating transformation in the interwar years, clearly eroded the links that tied migrant workers of this kind to their families. Available evidence shows that by the interwar period there were a growing number of workers for whom family links were becoming progressively weaker. Some continued to send part of their wages home, but rarely returned to visit their families, let alone stay permanently. A substantial number detached themselves from their families, and led independent lives as part of the growing industrial proletariat. These workers often moved between jobs, within the textile industry, and between textiles and other employment. By the interwar years it had become more common for female workers in general to shift between alternative non-agricultural employments. There were more such employment opportunities open to them, and information regarding the availability of opportunities was far more widespread. Improvements in transport networks also facilitated mobility. A member of the Saitama Factory Inspectorate surveying 126 girls leaving Saitama weaving mills in 1930–31 noted how they were often lost to their families, moving to other factories, or becoming maids, barmaids and even prostitutes.

Moreover, although every effort was made to set wages at 'supplementary' level, this did not preclude some workers' wages being sufficiently high to allow them to sustain an independent existence. While average textile wages were low, the structure of wage payment was such that it was possible for a highly skilled and experienced worker to earn well in excess of the average wage.[34] Where there were competing opportunities for employment in the vicinity, wages were likely to be pushed up further. Notwithstanding the complexity of methods of wage calculation in much of the textile industry,[35] it is not unrealistic to suppose that at least a minority of these workers were capable of supporting themselves independently.

It cannot be denied, therefore, that changes in the interwar decades enhanced the opportunity for girls to become independent of their families, a shift clearly facilitated by the fact that most workers were geographically separated from their families. This physical separation weakened workers' position as an integral part of the household, however much they might try to maintain it. Textile migration was thus a means of separating at least some workers from the environment of the household and the rural community. Indeed, Takafusa Nakamura has gone so far as to assert that from before the First World War members of the population who left farms in search of higher income tended not to return even in depressions, and after leaving spinning factories 'the women became – and almost necessarily so – wives of urban workers'.[36] For all the pressures weakening migrants' relationship with their families, however, there were at least as many acting to reinforce it, and, as has already been shown, a substantial number of textile migrants retained a strong economic relationship with the farm family from which they came. Even in the Saitama survey mentioned above, whose author bemoaned the separation of girls from their families, the fact that nine of the sample returned home to marry, and twenty-five moved back to work in farming, suggests that even for this group some links remained strong.[37]

These pressures sustaining the status quo were diverse in nature. Some were economic; while the evidence on workers' average incomes conceals the ability of some workers to earn considerably above that average, it also hides the fact that a very large number of migrant textile workers earned considerably below it. Basic wage levels for women were far lower than those of men, and, while there was a huge variation, textile workers as a whole were relatively poorly paid. In addition, the majority of migrant workers were accommodated at the mill, with deductions made from their wages to help cover the cost of board and lodging. Provision of these facilities was invariably subsidised to some degree by the employer.[38] There may well have been many workers whose income levels were such as to discourage thoughts of a greater degree of independence.

Even more important, perhaps, was the fact that socially, politically and legally most textile migrants continued to be identified as members of the farming household, and this position had a fundamental impact on the institutional framework of textile migration. Discussion of this institutional context lies beyond the scope of this chapter, but it was crucial to the link with families remaining pivotal for many workers. In this context it may be suggested that the economic transformation of the interwar years offered new opportunities for farm family daughters to further diversify their economic activities *within* the context of the family, rather than outside it, and this is what many migrant workers appear to have done. For much of the pre-Second World War period much textile migration, like migration to many other forms of employment, thus continued to be undertaken within the context of the farm family economy.

Further analysis is needed on this, but this ongoing significance of the farm family economy suggests two provisional conclusions for longer-term development patterns in Japan. One is that in the process of migration to textile work gender differences in migration patterns and family relations became more apparent. Male migrants tended to be older. They were freer of social and legal restraints on their independence. They were less fettered by a 'life cycle' view of employment. They were less able than women to find a living back in agriculture and could often obtain better-paid work in the expanding heavy industrial sector. It was in general easier, and more practical, for them to break free of the family constraint. This does not mean that fewer women than men migrated out of rural areas on a more permanent basis. By the interwar years there were almost as many female as male migrants in Japan's conurbations.[39] Many of these women, however, were rural wives migrating to be with their husbands. Having perhaps earlier migrated as daughters on a temporary basis, they now migrated as wives and mothers on a more permanent one. In both cases it suggests that family relations had a more decisive influence in determining female migration than tended to be the case for men.

Second, although the geographical separation of workers from their families and changing economic and social circumstances all acted to promote greater autonomy on the part of workers, a very large number, as we have seen, continued to be tied to the interests of their families. Textile employment thus continued to be identified as part of the changing opportunity set facing farm households in certain areas of the country, and the physical separation of workers from their families did not fundamentally alter that fact. The remittances of migrant workers helped to sustain the significance of the farm family unit in Japanese industrialisation, both as an economic unit and as a cohesive social entity.

Notes

1 Agriculture remained the largest sector by occupation in the Japanese economy, and although the sector's contribution to GNP progressively declined over the interwar years, by 1940 agriculture, forestry and fishing still accounted for over 36 per cent of the total occupied population (calculated from 1940 national

census, Sōrifu Tōkeikyoku, *Shōwa 15-nen Kokusei Chōsa Hōkoku*, vol.2, *Sangyō-Jigyōjō no Chii*, Tokyo, Sōrifu Tōkeikyoku, 1962, pp. 102–104).

2 See e.g. M. Nakamura, *Rōdōsha to Nōmin*, vol.29 of *Nihon no Rekishi*, Tokyo, Shōgakkan, 1976, pp. 90ff.

3 Both Takafusa Nakamura and Richard Smethurst have suggested that a majority of urban female factory workers became permanent urban residents, while Barbara Molony has demonstrated through the use of oral history that many workers did not return home, but moved from one employment to the next (T. Nakamura, *Economic Growth in Prewar Japan*, New Haven, CT, Yale University Press, 1981, p. 128; R. J. Smethurst, *Agricultural Development and Tenancy Disputes in Japan, 1870–1940*, Princeton, NJ, Princeton University Press, 1986, p. 100; B. Molony, 'Activism Among Women in the Taishō Cotton Textile Industry', in G. L. Bernstein (ed.), *Recreating Japanese Women, 1600–1945*, Berkeley, University of California Press, 1991, pp. 217–238).

4 For the development of cotton weaving, see T. Abe, *Nihon ni okeru Sanchi Men'orimonogyō no Tenkai*, Tokyo, Tokyo University Press, 1989. A broader overview of the development of the cotton industry can be found in T. Ushijima and T. Abe, 'Mengyō', in S. Nishikawa *et al.* (eds), *Nihon Keizai no 200 Nen*, Tokyo, Nihon Hyōronsha, 1996. G. Federico's *An Economic History of the Silk Industry, 1830–1930*, Cambridge, Cambridge University Press, 1997 and M. Nakamura and C. Molteni, 'Silk-reeling Technology and Female Labour', in M. Nakamura (ed.), *Technology Change and Female Labour in Japan*, Tokyo, United Nations University Press, 1994, pp. 25–58 both contain substantial information on the development of silk reeling in Japan, as does Smethurst, *Agricultural Development and Tenancy Disputes in Japan*, pp. 184ff.

5 These estimates are based on figures in the interwar censuses. For full references see those for Tables 13.1–13.4.

6 For information on the geographical patterns of textile worker migration see my 'Continuity and Change in the Japanese Labour Market: Rural Impoverishment and the Geographical Origins of Female Textile Workers', in S. Metzger-Court and W. Pascha (eds), *Japan's Socio-Economic Evolution: Continuity and Change*, Folkestone, Kent, Japan Library, 1996, pp. 76–90.

7 See e.g. M. Yamada, *Nihon Shihonshugi Bunseki*, Tokyo, Iwanami Shoten, 1934; K. Ōkōchi and H. Matsuo, *Nihon Rōdō Kumiai Monogatari – Shōwa*, Tokyo, Chikuma Shobō, 1976; M. Sumiya, *Nihon Chinrōdō no Shiteki Kenkyū*, Tokyo, Ochanomizu Shobō, 1976; M. Nakamura, *Rōdōsha to Nōmin*. There are strong resonances of this scholarship, but with a feminist perspective, in E. P. Tsurumi, *Factory Girls: Women in the Thread Mills of Meiji Japan*, Princeton, NJ, Princeton University Press, 1990.

8 See e.g. Smethurst, *Agricultural Development and Tenancy Disputes in Japan*; P. G. Francks, 'Peasantry, Proletariat or Private Enterprise? The Japanese Farmer in the Industrialisation Process', *Japan Forum* 1990, vol. 2, no. 1, pp. 91–104; K. Sugihara, 'Japan's Industrial Recovery, 1931–6', in I. Brown (ed.), *The Economies of Africa and Asia in the Inter-war Depression*, London, Routledge, 1989.

9 Data on average wages for female textile workers can be found in Tables 38, 40 and 47 of S. Fujino *et al.*, *Sen'i Sangyō*, vol. 11 of *Chōki Keizai Tōkei: Suikei to Bunseki*, Tōyō Keizai Shinpōsha, Tokyo, 1979. Those for agricultural workers can be found in vol. 9 of the same series (*Nōringyō*, Tokyo, Tōyō Keizai Shinpōsha, 1966, Table 34, pp. 220–221).

10 Chūō Shokugyō Shōkai Jimukyoku, *Bōseki Rōdō Fujin Chōsa*, Tokyo, 1929, p. 25. This finding was supported by other surveys, e.g. Kirisutokyō Joshi Seinenkai Nihon Dōmei Rōdō Chōsabu, 'Jokō ni kansuru Chōsa', *Sangyō Fukuri* 1932, vol. 7, no. 12, pp. 11–12.

11 The persistence of advance payments in weaving is noted in Y. Watanabe, 'Saitama-ken ni okeru Kigyō Jokō no Kisū Chōsa', *Sangyō Fukuri* 1934, vol. 9, no. 1, pp. 19–20.
12 S. Harada, *Labour Conditions in Japan*, New York, Columbia University Press, 1928, repr. 1968, p. 119.
13 Chūō Shokugyō Shōkai Jimukyoku, *Bōseki Rōdō Fujin Chōsa*, p. 70; Fukuoka Chihō Shokugyō Shōkai Jimukyoku, *Dekasegi Jokō ni kansuru Chōsa*, Fukuoka, Fukuoka Chihō Shokugyō Shōkai Jimukyoku, 1928, p. 49.
14 Levels of textile wages are shown in S. Fujino *et al.*, *Sen'i Sangyō*, Tables 38, 40 and 47.
15 Tsunanmachi Shi Henshū Iinkai, *(Jokō) Dekasegi Kankei Shiryō oyobi Kikitori*, vol. 8 of *Tsunanmachi Shi Henshū Shiryō*, Tsunanmachi, Niigata Pref., Tsunanmachi Shi Henshū Iinkai, 1982, pp. 150ff. Almost all the women interviewed said that the sending of remittances had been entrusted to the company.
16 Fukuoka Chihō Shokugyō Shōkai Jimukyoku, *Dekasegi Jokō ni kansuru Chōsa*, pp. 48–49.
17 T. Katsura, 'Honpō Seishigyō Rōdō Jijō', *Shakai Seisaku Jihō* 1924, nos 40–42, p. 90; Fukuoka Chihō Shokugyō Shōkai Jimukyoku, *Dekasegi Jokō ni kansuru Chōsa*, p. 22; T. Minoguchi, 'Nihon Menpu Shinshutsu no Haikei', *Shakai Seisaku Jihō* 1936, vol. 194, p. 62.
18 S. Watanabe, 'Nōka Keizai to Rōdō Shijō to no Kanren o Chūshin to suru Jakkan no Shiryō', *Keizaigaku Ronshū* 1933, vol. 3, nos 8–9, p. 89.
19 Cited in K. Takagi, 'Suwa Seishigyō ni okeru Jokō Hogo Kumiai no Seisei to Hatten', *Yamagata Daigaku Kiyō (Shakai Kagaku)* 1971, vol. 3, no. 4, p. 513.
20 Watanabe, 'Nōka Keizai to Rōdō Shijō to no Kanren o Chūshin to suru Jakkan no Shiryō', pp. 90, 95.
21 Minoguchi, 'Nihon Menpu Shinshutsu no Haikei', p. 62. This example has been taken up by other scholars, notably K.Takahashi, *Nihon Sangyō Rōdō Ron*, Tokyo, Chikuma Shobō, 1937, pp. 237–238.
22 Smethurst, *Agricultural Development and Tenancy Disputes in Japan*, p. 170.
23 Tables summarising the findings of the *nōka keizai chōsa* can be found in Nōsei Chōsa Iinkai (ed.), *Kaitei Nihon Nōgyō Kiso Tōkei*, Tokyo, Nōrin Tōkei Kyōkai, 1977, Tables M-a-1, M-a-2, Trends in the Farm Family Economy by Ownership Status, 1921–1975, pp. 494–501. Averages exclude Hokkaido, the northernmost island.
24 *Chingin – Koyō – Nōgyō*, Tokyo, Ōmeidō, 1961, pp. 82–85.
25 Watanabe, 'Nōka Keizai to Rōdō Shijō to no Kanren o Chūshin to suru Jakkan no Shiryō', p. 92. The dramatic drop in silk reeling employment between 1930 and 1940 is apparent from Table 13.1.
26 ibid., p. 96.
27 Up to 1929 most cotton spinning mills had twenty-four-hour operation, on the basis of two twelve-hour shifts. International and domestic pressures led to legislation banning this being passed in 1923.
28 Watanabe, 'Nōka Keizai', p. 90. Indices for wage levels and agricultural prices are given in Nakamura, *Economic Growth in Prewar Japan*, pp. 216–217.
29 Nōsei Chōsa Iinkai (ed.), *Kaitei Nihon Nōgyō Kiso Tōkei*, pp. 494–501.
30 Sugihara, 'Japan's Industrial Recovery, 1931–6'.
31 Tsunanmachi Shi Henshū Iinkai, *(Jokō) Dekasegi Kankei Shiryō oyobi Kikitori*, p. 213.
32 ibid., pp. 150ff.
33 For a discussion of by-employment in earlier times see O. Saito, 'The Rural Economy: Commercial Agriculture, By-employment and Wage Work', in M. B. Jansen and G. Rozman (eds), *Japan in Transition: from Tokugawa to Meiji*, Princeton, NJ, Princeton University Press, 1986, pp. 400–420.

34 This is clearly shown in Y. Kiyokawa, 'The Transformation of Young Rural Women into Disciplined Labour under Competitive-oriented Management: the Experience of the Silk Reeling Industry in Japan', paper presented at the 10th International Congress of Economic History, Leuven, August, 1990.

35 See e.g. H. Takizawa, 'Meiji Makki Suwa Seishigyō ni okeru Kuriito Kōjo no Chingin Taikei', *Kōnan Keizaigaku Ronshū* 1974, vol. 15, no. 3, pp. 67–92.

36 Nakamura, *Economic Growth in Prewar Japan*, pp. 28, 128.

37 Watanabe, 'Saitama Chihō ni okeru Kigyō Jokō no Kisū Chōsa', p. 20.

38 One report from Gifu Prefecture in the late 1920s showed a silk mill charging female workers 15 sen for three meals per day, with a real cost of 25.2 sen (Harada, *Labour Conditions in Japan*, p. 125).

39 I. B. Taeuber, 'Population and Labour Force in the Industrialisation of Japan, 1850–1950', in S. Kuznets *et al.*, *Economic Growth: Brazil, India, Japan*, Durham, NC, Duke University Press, 1955, pp. 326–341.

14 Migrancy, marriage and family in the Ciskei reserve of South Africa, 1945–1959

Anne Mager

Gendered histories of migrant labour in Southern Africa have considerably deepened our understanding of migrancy in the region in recent years. Studies have problematised why it was predominantly men rather than women who migrated. They have established that patriarchal controls in pre-capitalist societies tied women to rural production processes and released young men for migrant labour. Some have shown that women's migrancy was shaped by gender dynamics within domestic units. Others have pointed out that emigrant women are frequently stereotyped as amoral, fiercely independent absconders. Scholars have questioned the meaning of 'family' and 'household' and interrogated linkages between domestic units and rural poverty.[1]

Much of this literature accepted the notions of 'family breakdown', and 'the decay of traditional structures of security and support' as coterminous with female (and male) migrancy. In this we echoed the view of contemporary liberals and the African male elite who lamented the destruction of pre-colonial family forms and modes of control over women and girls.[2] In contrast, Moore and Vaughan's work on Zambia sees women's migrancy as a range of strategies through which women seek to solve problems in their lives. Following their approach, this chapter questions the usefulness of the discourse of 'family breakdown' for understanding women's (and men's) migration and opts rather for the view that migrancy is a means to problem solving. This approach differs from the idea of migrancy as a household survival strategy in that it focuses on individuals within households rather than on household units.[3] It allows for a consideration of sexuality and domestic power relations as critical factors in female migrancy and it recognises that the effects of migrancy are so pervasive as to result in a 'profoundly altered world view'.[4]

This chapter focuses on female migrancy in the Ciskei reserve of the Eastern Cape of South Africa from the mid-1940s, when the number of women moving to town increased dramatically, to 1959, the year in which the apartheid regime successfully imposed influx control regulations on African women.[5] It raises questions about women's agency and invites exploration of the links between migrancy and gender relations. It

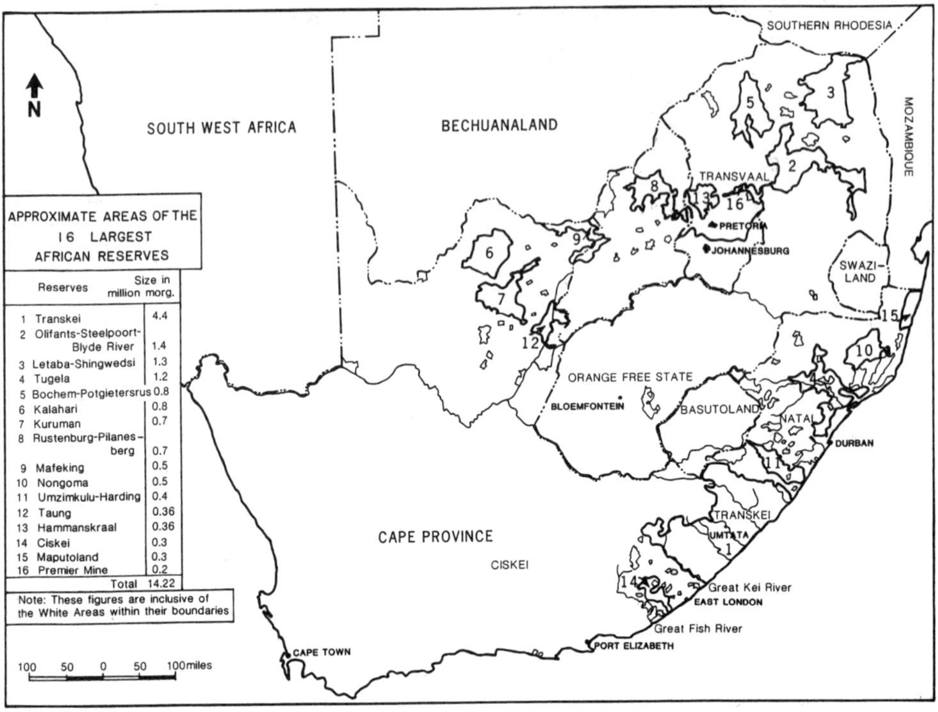

Map 14.1 South Africa: sites of African reserves, 1954

Source: Atlas for the Report of the Inquiry into the Socio-Economic conditions of the Native Reserves within the boundaries of South Africa 1951–1954 (Pretoria: Government Printer, 1955).

problematises the impact of migrancy on sexuality and meanings of marriage, caring and sex. It suggests that female migrancy can be read not as breakdown but as forging new pathways in an increasingly complex and rapidly changing social landscape.

The Ciskei reserve in the mid-1940s comprised the sprawling 'locations' between the Great Fish and Kei rivers in the Eastern Cape. A network of well-worn pathways linked these dispersed rural locations. In the east, along the railway line leading north from the white port city of East London, reserve areas were tightly squeezed between white-owned farms. Periodically ravaged by droughts throughout the 1940s and 1950s, the barren soil yielded little and women's labour went largely unrewarded. There was little prospect of households eking out a livelihood on the land. The overstocked and congested landscape could support neither people nor livestock. The possibility of men accumulating cattle and making *lobola* (bridewealth) payments and of women acquiring arable land on marriage was increasingly difficult for all and impossible for many.[6] The Native

Affairs Department (NAD), the missionaries and a few white traders were the only wage employers in the reserve. For both illiterate and missionary educated men and women, migration had become a necessity. The vast majority of people depended on the remittances of migrant workers.

Migrancy was by no means new to the Ciskei, the most overcrowded reserve in the country. However, with escalating population density in the mid-1940s – some 300,000 crammed into a mere 3,388 square miles – migrancy escalated. The state estimated that between 1946 and 1951, more than a quarter of men and a sixth of women over the age of 20 were absent from the Ciskei reserves.[7] Put another way, five people from every domestic unit were away at work. These figures belied the variability of migrancy across the region, age groups and genders. In some magisterial districts, the percentage of absent men had reached 70 per cent a decade or more earlier.[8] What was different about the 1940s and 1950s, was the increasing numbers of young women under 20 who were leaving rural locations.[9] Anthropologists observed that the 'occasional runaways' were now being joined by 'hordes of young girls' arriving in East London from the Ciskei locations.[10] Most of these young women were educated, their ability to speak English as marketable as their missionary training in domesticity.

Unlike male migrants, women did not enjoy patriarchal sanction for leaving home.[11] Neither blessing nor ceremony accompanied women's departure, even when it was deemed necessary within a household. Rather, ritual celebration of women's place in society continued to reflect past rather than present economic realities.[12] The absence of formal sanction for female migrants reflected a denial of women's migratory possibility within the patriarchal order. It also indicated a lack of support. Paradoxically, this lack of prescription afforded female migrants greater autonomy in the strategies they might adopt. With men refusing to acknowledge women's presence in town, they had few strategies for controlling urbanising women. In turn, female migrants developed a more individual and diverse set of strategies for coping with the demands of city life. While young men sought out 'home boys' with whom to form associations, young women avoided 'home patriarchs'. Even association with 'home girls' was rendered difficult by the isolation of domestic work.

Women's ability to move to town was facilitated by the juxtaposition of town and countryside in the Ciskei and Border region. It was encouraged by the industrial boom in the port city of East London following the Second World War. Not all women migrated to major urban centres, however. Women who had qualified as teachers found work at faraway rural schools or in the peri-urban townships of the Border.[13] Dozens of less-schooled women opted for weekly migration to the pineapple farms in the vicinity. Still others made their way to the smaller towns.[14] But the preference for East London as a destination for migrating women continued throughout the 1940s and 1950s. East London's proximity to rural villages entailed cheaper transport costs and enabled regular contact with home. The size of the city meant significant job opportunities, reasonable marriage prospects and the anonymity of a complex urban environment.

Young women migrated for a host of reasons. Many were propelled by rural poverty, some went to escape the tedium of rural life, others in the hope of pursuing their education and still others to assert their independence. Often, intra-household gender dynamics affected which women stayed and which migrated. Those who might attract *lobola* were carefully guarded; those 'spoiled' enjoyed greater freedom of movement. Girls ran away when they got wind of arranged marriages and demanded to live a modern life signified by 'school clothes'. Once in town, very few avoided sex or escaped at least one unwanted pregnancy. Many would not return to live in the rural areas. Many others sent regular remittances which supported rural households.[15]

Women who migrated to the city of East London

Women and men from rural Ciskei made up over three-fifths of East London's African population in the mid-1940s.[16] At least half of these were women. They hailed predominantly from the southern districts of the Ciskei, those closest to the city and with the oldest relationship to missionary education.[17] Live-in domestic work in the suburbs of white East London was the starting point for most young female migrants. In time, some gave up the loneliness and isolation of servants' quarters to take up lodgings in the townships of Duncan Village and the West Bank.

Accommodation options in the townships were partly defined by the outcomes of earlier patterns of in-migration evident in the social composition and economic activities of specific localities. Most single women over 30 lived in Duncan Village, where men tended to be older, poorer earners and in greater need of women to cook and wash for them. It was here that landladies who had settled permanently in town a decade earlier ran lodging houses for a living.[18] The West Bank remained a relatively 'respectable' location where many men in stable employment were able to keep 'regular' women.[19]

With limited formal employment opportunities, many urbanised and urbanising women took up occupations that rendered services to men. Many others, however, turned to informal commodity production as a means of livelihood in the interstices of industrial life. They kept 'their own economic and social footing, not by virtue of their relations to men, but in their own right'.[20] Self-employment activities encompassed brewing, hawking, dagga (cannabis) dealing and laundry work. Often the move from domestic work to self-employment followed the birth of a child as evidenced by the many economically independent women who were single mothers.[21] Their fertility not controlled by men and their children born of 'women not cattle', these women transgressed the boundaries of a male-dominated order.[22] Independent women wielded considerable social power, derived in part from their control of resources but also from the necessity of holding their own in the context of illicit liquor brewing, drunken brawls and police raids.[23]

The social power of independent women was recognised and drawn on by the Youth League of the African National Congress (ANC) in 1951. Recently radicalised, the Youth League and other organisations sought to put pressure on the East London City Council to improve conditions in the African townships.[24] They complained that council housing amounted to less than a quarter of the accommodation for the over 60,000 residents of *iMonti*.[25] Africans lived in dilapidated wood and iron shacks on to which were tacked as many as eight small rooms, holding up to forty-five occupants. Most of the lodgers were migrant men who paid rents of 25 to 30 shillings per month to extortionist site-owners and wrack-renting landladies. The latter comprised 70 per cent of all site and private house owners. TB was rife, with four times as many cases in the shanty areas as in the council houses. Infant mortality rates were horrifying; every second child died before the age of 1. Eighty public toilets served more than 20,000 residents in Duncan Village, where the streets were fouled with 'human detritus'.[26] School opportunities were limited to eight primary and one council high school, the latter accommodating a mere 350 pupils.

The Council's response to demands for improvement was to tighten controls over women and to ensure that Africans themselves paid for upgrading living conditions. To this end, the Council introduced two measures. First came the requirement that domestic workers register and apply for service contracts. This regulation reflected the Council's belief that the influx of women into the urban areas was the cause of social disorder in the townships. The second measure was the imposition of a 2-shilling levy on all lodgers in the African townships. Its purpose was to raise revenue for housing and upgrading infrastructure. Both measures would impact hardest on African women. Landladies would have to consider levy payments when determining rentals; live-out domestic workers would be burdened with extra costs; all women would run the gauntlet of permit inspectors.

Seething discontent over the 2-shilling levy and the registration of domestic servants came to a head in April 1951. The ANC Youth League amassed the support of young domestic workers and older landladies. Organised by the League's young men, 4,000 Africans converged on the white city centre, marching in orderly procession along the officially sanctioned seven-mile route from Duncan Village to the centre of East London. The grievances of the lodgers, landladies and domestic workers were displayed on banners carried by leaders of the procession. 'Stop further taxation', 'Down with lodgers fees', 'Our children need bread', they declared. A banner carried by women domestic workers stated plainly, 'We earn the least'.[27] The protesters marched silently past the hospital.

Outside the City Hall, they began singing the African nationalist anthem, Nkosi Sikelel' i-Afrika.

In the ensuing meetings with the city councillors, Africans demanded the removal of the levy, or alternatively, its payment by employers. The East London Council would not budge, however, and the ANC Youth League opted to test the legality of the Council's action. But the test case was lost. Thirty-four year old Lillian Zweni was fined 10 shillings or five days with hard labour for refusing to pay the lodgers' fee.[28] Nevertheless, for hundreds of wives, independent mothers and single women, the campaign against the lodgers' levy and registration of domestic service contracts transformed their private and domestic lives, albeit momentarily, as they entered the public arena of politics. Their political action impacted on male authority in both urban and rural contexts, generating considerable consternation. When rural traditionalists requested stricter controls on women and juveniles running away to town, a government official who had witnessed the march, warned them not to make themselves 'unpopular with women'.[29]

The question of how we read the actions of the independent women of East London persists. One contemporary African reading was that of Xhosa novelist J.D. Jongilanga. The novel *Ukuqawuka kwembeleko* (the breaking of the umbilical cord) represents the independent women in the city of East London as devoid of dignity, values and respect.[30] They are portrayed as the victims of the white man's education and commoditised economic system. Their independent action breaks the ties with tradition, literally snaps the umbilical cord. In contrast, Noni Jabavu, daughter of the renowned Fort Hare professor D.D.T. Jabavu, offers a more sympathetic reading.[31] Jabavu perceived that for these 'modern women' seeking solutions to real problems, the normative ideals for appropriate female behaviour were no longer adequate for the realities of their lives. In Jabavu's rationalist discourse, women's agency was not so much 'breaking down' as generating viable life strategies.

Significantly, there is more than a hint in both Jongilanga and Jabavu's work that women's independent action represented a challenge to men. Women were forging new ways in a world for which rural men had not yet devised rituals and rules. They imply that the tragedy was not so much women's actions as men's inability to acknowledge their initiative. Both writers identify families that were destroyed by men who denied the modern aspirations of young women and repeatedly reasserted patriarchal controls. These observations resonate with the central argument of this chapter.

The next section examines the incompatibility of official discourses of family and normative meanings of marriage with the lives of rural women. It points to the complex ways in which women sought to make sense of their lives.

Family, migrancy and marriage in rural Ciskei

The state no less than African patriarchs, sought to control the movements of African women. In their attempts to devise new means of control, government officials were endlessly redefining 'the African family'. An attempt to pin down this category in a 1955 Commission rendered a clumsy definition:

> an economy [*sic*] unit comprised of male family head and wife or wives and their children still living with them, some of whom are at home and others temporarily absent as migrant workers plus other adults who constitute part of the economic unit plus dependants (elderly mother or father and minor children) plus other family members.[32]

The official report attempted to conjure up a single definition from a set of complex and rapidly changing domestic arrangements. It did acknowledge the instability of families as a result of male migrancy, noting that men's absence often resulted in wives and children relocating within the reserve to live 'temporarily' with relatives.[33] Such arrangements often continued for decades. In the state's definition, 'the African family' had no fixed place of domicile. This perspective enabled the administration to ignore the impact of deterioriating conditions in the reserves on African families. Conditions in the overcrowded Ciskei led to increasing numbers of people roaming about endlessly in search of grazing; landlessness drove others to build temporary shelters on commonages. Yet others moved from place to place in the hope of acquiring a field through bribing a headman or inducing the South African Native Trust to allow settlement on land designated for other purposes.[34]

It is probable that neither 'family' nor 'household' had comprised a fixed entity for over a century in the Ciskei reserves. A census conducted in one Ciskei district from 1948 to 1950 found that 'the composition of the families had changed almost out of recognition from one census to another'.[35] In another district, 87 per cent of the domestic units had formally recognised or *de facto* female heads. Domestic units were in a state of flux as individuals moved in and out, supported or received support from others.

The instability of the categories 'household' and 'family' raises a host of questions pertaining to the meaning of marriage. How did people establish and maintain relationships of mutual affection and trust in the context of unstable domestic units? How did they organise domestic production and consumption? How did they perceive and cope with sexual desire? These questions are approached below through deconstructing normative meanings and interrogating practices.

Formal meanings of marriage were inscribed in customary law and the practices that flowed from it. Thus, *lobola* marriage payments continued to be 'the accepted guarantee of good faith and good conduct', despite limitations on the accumulation of cattle in the mid-1940s.[36] The legal discourse fixed *lobola* as a means of perpetuating gendered, asymmetrical power relations, giving men power over women. Stafford's 'Principles of Native Law' stated that 'a woman for whom *lobola* has not been paid has no status in her husband's family and her children may be taken from her by her guardian, her father or eldest brother'.[37] In tying marriage relationships to the interests of cattle-owning patriarchs, customary law had failed to adjust to the pressures of urbanisation, the demise in cattle and the increasing individualism of educated daughters.[38]

Changing practices in everyday life did not often fit the normative template. One of the most basic and visible changes was in the value and composition of *ikhazi* (*lobola* payments). While eight to ten head of cattle was the formal payment requirement in most areas, men were 'finding it almost impossible' to pay the full *ikhazi* in cattle. Despite the preference for cattle, *lobola* packages might comprise sheep, goats, a horse, cash or cattle in various combinations.[39] In some areas, cash had almost completely replaced livestock payments. Some fathers negotiated for *lobola* values to be tied to the market value of cattle, rather than to those fixed periodically under customary law.[40] *Lobola* transactions were fraught with conflict. Unstable domestic relations contributed to this conflict. In particular, *lobola* held by younger brothers in the absence of their seniors or by grandfathers in the absence of their juniors not infrequently led to mistrust, litigation and even annulment of marriage.[41]

Nor could meanings of marriage be assumed. Multiple factors, including economic status, Christianity and the degree of dependence on cattle profoundly affected the meaning of *lobola* in marriage. For some, romantic love was more significant than the status of *lobola* marrriage.[42] But for many men and women, *lobola* signified a special kind of womanhood or femininity – that most valued within the patriarchal gender regime. Women raised for exchange against cattle were carefully protected from influences which might lead to independent action. They were often denied access to white-men's schools and churches. In conservative patriarchal discourse, education was perceived as delaying marriage, increasing the risk of seduction and even leading to daughters becoming unwanted 'old maids'.[43] Church marriages were constructed as conferring too much power on women. Christian wives were represented as dangerous, 'a second man in the household' and accused of coming 'between a man and his ancestors'.[44] Nor did conservative women stand outside this patriarchal discourse. For these women, patriarchy was a law of nature; the church and its teachings 'did not change men'.[45]

For most couples marrying in the 1950s, the scarcity of resources and the shortage of cattle meant that few could afford a wedding feast and *lobola* payments might take a lifetime to fulfil.[46] Not surprisingly, many men preferred the informal *thwala* practice where a man carried off his bride secretly, usually without the woman's or her father's consent. *Thwala* brides were held under guard while arrangements were made for *lobola*. Ceremony in these instances was confined to a ritual show of resistance on the part of the bride, allegedly preserving her 'maidenly dignity'.[47] The custom of 'mock' resistance deliberately constructed an ambiguity, obscuring the feelings of the abducted bride. Let us consider a fairly ordinary case. A male suitor came up to a young woman while she was weeding her mother's sorghum field and asked her to accompany him as he was about to *thwala* her. As her suitor pulled her, the woman screamed and grabbed at some bushes. Overpowered, she followed him to his homestead where she remained under guard and carried out the ritual fetching of water from the river. In this instance, as in many others, *lobola* payments were finally settled through the courts.[48] It was immaterial for the customary courts whether the woman was 'taken with her own consent, or at her own suggestion or against her will, or whether she is decoyed or enticed away'.[49] The court records, then, cannot tell us what the woman felt about her marriage.

While many established marriages were under severe stress from economic hardship in the 1950s, extra-marital relations often exacerbated material strains. The male prerogative to enter into extra-marital relations was seldom questioned by men or women.[50] If women were prey to men, they also acted in their own self-interest. Economic considerations were often central. Wives who enjoyed regular remittances were less likely to seek lovers. Unfaithful wives took great risks. They were almost surely beaten and occasionally even stabbed to death.[51] However, adultery was not often a cause for divorce. If a woman confessed the name of her lover, she enabled her husband to charge the man with adultery, extract 'damages' from him and so regain his dignity.[52] Thus, adultery often precipitated fierce battles between men, including litigation.[53] The offender was deemed to have violated another man's property; for this he was required to pay compensation. Damages, fixed periodically by the courts, varied between three and five head of cattle between 1946 and 1959.

Absent men who wished to avoid returning to find their wives engaged in an adulterous relationship, took steps to prevent it. But it was not only fear of adultery that prompted the practice of arranging for men to 'look after' the sexual needs of wives whose husbands were away. Rather, several interlocking sets of beliefs came to shape this practice. Women, like men, were acknowledged to have sexual desires that required fulfilment.[54] Some husbands wished to control their wives' sexual activity, even if this meant nominating a male substitute. Others wished to control their wives' fertility. By insisting on external intercourse and holding the substitute responsible for pregnancy, husbands could achieve some degree of control. If this entailed some risk, for many men it was preferable to the risk of a woman acting autonomously. The woman herself was not consulted, her husband's representative simply arriving and stating his purpose.

Women who perceived themselves as having no choice, accepted the arrangement. 'This was agreed between the man who was going to Jo'burg and the other man. She [the migrant's wife] would be told that someone is going to look after her while he is away', one man explained. He also claimed that 'It was rare that a child be born out of that because this man would be careful enough not to make a child'. Not only were they able to avoid pregnancy but they knew that 'the man was supposed to leave when the owner was back'.[55] Some women were critical of such attempts to control their sexual activity. One claimed that wives of the 1950s generation 'hated to marry men who worked in Jo'burg'. Men who worked in Eastern Cape towns were able to come home more regularly and did not resort to arranging substitutes.[56]

How then do we account for the persistence of women's and men's belief in the social value of *lobola* and customary marriage? Many women in the Ciskei reserves held onto a normative vision of customary marriage, a homestead and children as rites of passage to adulthood and social acceptability. Part of the explanation for tight adherence to normative ideals may be gleaned from the idea that women's identities were symbolically mediated and constructed in a complex of 'culturally learned forms of interaction' in which *lobola* was the means to dignity, security and status for women.[57] Put differently, *lobola* was central to the way in which people made sense of themselves. There were material elements to this system of meaning making. For many women, adherence to normative meanings made sense in the context of a patriarchal regime which controlled women's access to resources. While cash remittances from a husband in stable employ was the most valuable of these, land and labour were next in importance. Women who defied convention in the rural locations were unlikely to have access to any of these resources.[58]

Not all women were in marriages. Well over 40 per cent of women in the Ciskei were *amankazana*, 'loose' or single women. Dozens of young women were widowed as a result of vast age differences between spouses; some wives were abandoned by migrant husbands; others never married and became *inkazana* by default rather than choice often following 'a fall' or 'a disappointment'.[59] *Amankazana* occupied a tenuous position in patriarchal society. Cattle and land shortages meant that they could not rely on their father's homestead for support. Moreover, customary law made no provision for the problems of unmarried mothers, deserted wives, widows and divorcees since they were assumed to be the responsibility of male guardians.[60]

While migrancy exacerbated the insecurity of most rural women, the absence of men in general made those already abandoned by husbands even more vulnerable. Resources within the reserves were highly inadequate. Some widows and abandoned wives had access to land but were short of labour. At least a third of the domestic units in one district had no men to assist in ploughing. Women who drew on the help of neighbours or kin in the ploughing season did so in return for long hours of labour. Unmarried women without land relied on providing labour – often for payment in kind – to those with greater resources.[61]

Women without men invariably exercised their limited options in sharply strategic ways. Many entered into sexual relationships with married men at some stage. Not all were motivated by economic survival, however.[62] Some stressed the 'emotional strain' of women abandoned by absconding husbands; court cases suggest that those who took up with former 'sweethearts', acted out of emotional desire and the recognition that arranged marriages were emotionally unsatisfactory.[63] Nevertheless, the unwritten code which allowed *amankazana* open relations with men favoured established patriarchal society rather than single women. It was accepted that male support for lovers should not extend beyond occasional gifts of money, food or labour for fear of diminishing resources needed for the *umzi* (home). On the margins of patriarchal society, *amankazana* had little choice but to put up with the status quo.

Relations between wives of the *umzi* and *amankazana* were not necessarily strained, however. Where mistresses were associated with the suppression of an individual woman's fertility and the celebration of male sexual desire, relations might be mutually beneficial. Breast-feeding mothers sometimes sought the support of a mistress to observe the taboos on sex. Their own abstinence was a sure means of birth control and, many believed, was necessary for the raising of healthy children.[64] Thus arrangements might be made by men themselves for the gratification of their desire and by wives as a means of regulating their own fertility while still holding onto their husbands.[65] Mistresses were often as integral to child rearing and fertility control as they were to sexual gratification.

However, difficulties arose through the reluctance of married men to engage in external intercourse. Consequently, parallel families were sometimes spawned.[66] Not only did this place an additional economic burden on the mother, but also upset the discretionary arrangement, impinging on the married woman's dignity. Occasionally, offended wives were driven to assault their husbands' mistresses or their illegitimate offspring.[67] But it was the *amankazana* who suffered greatest hardship.

Most often, mistresses were abandoned to raise illegitimate children with little or no support.[68] While the mother's 'family' took in the child, these households were often impoverished and headed by widows or unmarried mothers. Child maintenance might be secured through the courts, but for many mistresses the process was too cumbersome to cope with. An unmarried woman's case had to be brought to court by her guardian who might be away at work. Mistresses seldom pressed charges. The knowledge that success was unlikely without the backing of a senior man was all too often confirmed. Moreover, a clutch of myths or informal taboos militated against pressing for maintenance – 'your child died if you went to court', 'men took your child away' and 'you would get bad luck and sickness'. The myths clearly protected fathers and their legal families.[69] Meanwhile, men who refused to maintain their children but had paid *isondlo* (damages) frequently re-emerged to claim paternal rights, particularly of daughters about to marry. However, if the father had failed to pay damages, he was regarded as having forfeited his claim to paternal rights.[70]

The result was that some women raised seven or more children without support.[71] They leaned on both their mothers and their older offspring. This pattern was often repeated by the next generation in the family. Who would demand *lobola* for the girls? How would the men accumulate sufficient stock? Not surprisingly, *amankazana* often complained that their children had 'disappeared in Johannesburg'.[72] If their lives were fraught with hardship and difficulty, single women defended informal liaisons as a means of establishing their own domestic units, albeit in the shadow of formally sanctioned homesteads.

A closer look at male behaviour suggests that these unions had different meanings for men. If men held onto a vision of cattle, homestead, wives and children, it was only to suppress the knowledge that few could attain this dream. With *lobola* beyond their means, with wives wholly dependent on husbands and children a considerable financial burden, maintaining a marriage and homestead necessitated a lifetime of absence as a 'bachelor' migrant. Moreover, everyday practices suggest that attempts to regulate gender relations reflected an increasing concern with sex.[73] Control over sexual behaviour centred less on protecting the place of fertility in the reproduction of social relations than on understanding sex as an experience of the flesh, as providing sensual and physical satisfaction. If this view of sexuality implied greater individualism, it was exercised both within a context of continued male domination but against the grain of customary law. If some represented contemporary sexuality as 'degenerate', destructive of family life and leading to social decay, others saw their behaviour as a means of making practical sense of lives lived in the uncertainties of a massively congested rural reserve, rapid industrialisation and an uncertain future.

Conclusion

This chapter has viewed women's migrancy as a means of devising practical solutions to problems and as a response to the effects of capitalisation and commoditisation in South Africa in the decades following the end of the Second World War. Since men did not formally sanction female migrancy, male discourse constructed women who went to town as subversive. In this conservative patriarchal discourse, legitimated both by the apartheid state and African men, migrant women were held responsible for the breakdown of the African family. It has been argued that the patriarchal discourse of 'family breakdown' is unable to explain female agency. In reflecting the limits of precolonial discourses on relations between women and men, it closed off alternative ways of viewing social relations that may have been more sympathetic to women's real problems. Scholars failing to question this discourse fall into the same trap. In contrast, analysis of women's practices in urban and rural environments reveals that female migrancy stemmed from the increased viability of independent livelihoods for women and women's ability to develop strategic responses to social change. It has been suggested that the normative cultural template in the 1950s was increasingly out of synch with the choices that women had to make in their daily lives.

Notes

1 J. Guy, 'Gender Oppression in Southern Africa's Precapitalist Societies', in C. Walker (ed.), *Women and Gender in Southern Africa to 1945* (Cape Town and London: David Philip and James Currey, 1990), 33–47; B. Bozzoli with M. Nkotsoe, *Women of Phokeng* (Johannesburg: Ravan Press, 1991); A. Spiegel, 'Rural Differentiation and the Diffusion of Migrant Labour Remittances in Lesotho', in P. Mayer (ed.), *Black Villagers in Industrial Society* (Cape Town: Oxford University Press, 1980), 109–169; A. Mager and G. Minkley, 'Reaping the Whirlwind: the East London Riots of 1952', in P. Bonner, P. Delius and D. Posel (eds), *Apartheid's Genesis: 1935–1962* (Johannesburg: Ravan Press, 1993), p. 231; D. Hobart Houghton and E. M. Walton, *The Economy of a Native Reserve: Keiskammahoek Rural Survey*, vol. 11 (Pietermaritzburg: Shuter and Shooter, 1952), p. 111.

2 See Margaret Ballinger, House of Assembly, *Debates*, 1948, Vol. 64, Col. 170; for magistrates' opinions, see CA. 1/KHA, Case no. 7 of 1947, *Forward Mjusa vs. Reggie Mpusula*; CA. 1/KHA, Case no. 28 of 1951, *Ridini Mfanta vs. Sofece Yenani*; for a fictional account, see J. D. Jongilanga, *Ukuqawuka kwembeleko* (Lovedale: Lovedale Press, 1982).

3 See K. Crehan, 'Rural Households: Survival and Change', in H. Bernstein, B. Crow and H. Johnson (eds), *Rural Livelihoods: Crises and Responses* (Oxford: Oxford University Press and Open University, 1992), pp. 87–110.

4 H. Moore and M. Vaughan, *Cutting Down Trees* (Portsmouth and London: Heinemann and James Currey, 1994), p. 157.

5 The Native Labour Regulations Act of 1959 extended passes to African women. See D. Hindson, *Pass Controls and the Urban African Proletariat in South Africa* (Johannesburg: Ravan Press, 1987), pp. 64–68 for discussion of influx control legislation in the 1950s.

6 A. Mager, *Gender and the Making of a South African Bantustan: a Social History of the Ciskei, 1945–1959* (Portsmouth, London, Cape Town: Heinemann, James Currey, David Philip, 1999), pp. 72–80; P. Mayer and I. Mayer, 'Report on the Self Organisation by Youth among the Xhosa-speaking Peoples of the Ciskei and Transkei' (Rhodes University, Institute of Social and Economic Research, 1972), Part 2, pp. 29–30; Houghton, *Economy*, p. 109.

7 UG 61/1955. *Verslag van die Kommissie vir die Sosio-Ekonomiese Ontwikkeling van die Bantoegebiede binne die Unie van Suid Afrika 1951–1954* (Chairman: Tomlinson) (Pretoria: Government Printer, 1955), hereafter Tomlinson Commission Report, Chap. 13, p. 9, Table 6. The absentee percentages are given as follows: in 1946, out of a population of 314,000, 24.8 per cent of men and 14.6 per cent women were away; in 1951, of a population of 308,000, 23.3 per cent men and 14 per cent of women were away. Ch. 23, p. 32 of the same report gives the average percentage of men absent for five magisterial districts in 1946 in the Ciskei as 42.8 per cent. See also Houghton, *Economy*, p. 111.

8 Walker, *Women and Gender*, p. 176.
9 Houghton's calculations indicate 20 per cent of women between the ages of 15 and 24 leaving the Keiskammahoek district in the mid-1940s with 41 per cent of these choosing East London as their destination; Houghton, *Economy*, pp. 130, 133.
10 P. and I. Mayer, *Townsmen or Tribesmen* (Cape Town: Oxford University Press, 1974), p. 240, Table 1, n. 6; M. Wilson, S. Kaplan, T. Maki, E. M. Walton (eds), *Social Structure: Keiskammahoek Rural Survey*, vol. 111 (Pietermaritzburg: Oxford University Press, 1952), p. 147.
11 P. McAllister, 'Work, Homestead and the Shades: the Ritual Interpretation of Labour Migration among the Gcaleka', in Mayer, *Black Villagers*, pp. 205–254.
12 Guy, 'Gender Oppression', p. 46.
13 C. W. Manona, 'Marriage, Family Life and Migrancy in a Ciskei Village', in Mayer, *Black Villagers*, p. 84.
14 Mayer, 'Report', Part 2, p. 100; Houghton, *Economy*, pp. 131–132.
15 Mayer, *Townsmen*, pp. 239, 256; Houghton, *Economy*, pp. 129, 148–149.
16 63.5 per cent of East London's population originated in the Ciskei, with the number of women and men roughly equal. See D. Reader, *The Black Man's Portion: History, Demography and Living Conditions of East London* (Oxford: Oxford University Press, 1961), p. 47.
17 Mayer, *Townsmen*, pp. 233–234.
18 C. Bundy and W. Beinart, 'The Union the Nation and the Talking Crow', in *Hidden Struggles in Rural South Africa* (Johannesburg: Ravan Press, 1987), pp. 274–275.
19 Reader, *Black Man's Portion*, p. 45.
20 Mayer, *Townsmen*, p. 234.
21 In 1946, 64.5 per cent of recorded African births in East London were illegitimate (880 out of 1,364 births). Evidence of Rev. R. J. Moore on behalf of the Ministers Fraternal to East London Municipal Native Commission of Inquiry, 1949, Chairman A.S. Welsch (hereafter, Welsch Commission), *Daily Dispatch*, 19 July 1949.
22 See W. Jansen, *Women Without Men* (Leiden: E. J. Brill, 1987), for discussion of the notion of 'contradictory qualities' of masculinity and femininity.
23 In the first six months of 1949, there were over 1,400 convictions for the brewing of *qedeviki* – a potent brew sold for 3d per condensed milk tin. 70 per cent of those convicted were women. Evidence of Sergeant F. H. J. Coetzee to Welsch Commission, *Daily Dispatch*, 28 July 1949; 12 February 1953.
24 The middle-class Vigilance Association, in particular, was pressing for reform.
25 The 1951 census figure for Africans in East London was 39,727 while the Border Regional Survey figure for 1955 was 78,000, the census figure representing a 'considerable under numeration'. See Reader, *Black Man's Portion*, p. 42.
26 Annual Report of Medical Officer of Health, Dr Sinclair Smith, East London, 1948/9; Evidence of B.A. Steer, Vice-Chairman of Joint European and African Council, East London, to Welsch Commission, *Daily Dispatch*, 9 August 1949. Steer warned the Commission of an impending 'catastrophic crisis' in the locations.
27 *Daily Dispatch*, 16 April 1951.
28 *Daily Dispatch*, 30 August 1951.
29 Ciskeian General Council, *Proceedings of Ciskeian General Council*, 20 October 1950. The Native Commissioner of East London warned that thousands of women had recently staged a march against precisely such controls.
30 Jongilanga, *Ukuqawuka*. This view is echoed by the novelist R.L. Peteni, *Hill of Fools: a Novel of the Ciskei* (Cape Town: David Philip, 1979).
31 N. Jabavu, *The Ochre People* (Johannesburg: Ravan Press, 1982).

32 Tomlinson Commission Report, Ch. 24, p. 12.
33 Houghton, *Economy*, p. 117.
34 Mager, *Gender and the Making of a South African Bantustan*, pp. 87–91.
35 Houghton, *Economy*, pp. 51, 53.
36 SAB. K.20. Archives of the Secretary of the Commission of Inquiry into the Socio-Economic Development of the Bantu areas within the Borders of South Africa (1950–1954), hereafter Evidence to Tomlinson Commission; vol. 24. Questionnaire submitted by Magistrate for Keiskammahoek, A. L. Schaffer.
37 Quoted in Tomlinson Commission Report, Ch.19, p. 13.
38 See Simons, *African Women*, p. 95.
39 SAB. K.20. Evidence to Tomlinson Commission, vol.23. In the Herschel district, sheep, goats and horses might substitute for cattle at the rate of ten sheep to one beast or one horse in lieu of two head of cattle.
40 SAB. K.20. Evidence to Tomlinson Commission, vols 23–24, Questionnaires to Native Commissioners.
41 See CA. 1/KHA, Case no. 21 of 1948, *Nimrod Lungile Somta vs. John Menyiwa and Nkosiyane Meyiwa* where *lobola* cattle paid to a younger brother were not recognised by the court; CA. 1/KHA, Case no. 2 of 1954, *Nhandi Gqandu vs. Stwayi James* where a grandfather claimed *lobola* cattle were *sondlo* cattle, after the death of his son, the *lobola* holder.
42 See CA. 1/CAT (NAC SD), Case no. 15 of 1959, *Gladys Ramncwana vs. Tom Matuntuta*: a nurse fell in love with a ballroom dancing teacher. In CA. 1/CAT, Case no. 3 of 1948, *Jane Tembani vs. Howard Mabengeza*, Howard wrote, 'When I think of you, tears run down my cheeks'. See CA. 1/CAT, Case no.7 of 1953, *Mkenke Mastiki vs. Mqantongo Menziwe* for an account of a married woman who eloped with her lover.
43 Rev. J. J. R. Jolobe, Address to Ciskeian Missionary Council, 7 September 1949 (Lovedale Press, 1949).
44 O. F. Raum and E.J. de Jager, *Transition and Change in a Rural Community* (Fort Hare: Fort Hare University Press, 1972), p. 55.
45 Interview, A. Mager with Yaliwe Skatsha, Peelton, 27 October 1993.
46 See CA. 1/CAT, Case no. 10 of 1951, *Slinga Mame vs. Kekana Makaleni*; the trousseau included blankets, skirts, braids, scarves and blouses.
47 G. Machanik, *Native Appeal and Divorce Court, 1929 and 1930, Cape and O.F.S. Division* (Cape Town: Juta, 1930), vol. 1, p. 44; S. M. Seymour, *Native Law in South Africa* (Cape Town and Johannesburg: Juta, 1960), p. 66.
48 *Daily Dispatch*, 7 May 1947; *King William's Town Mercury*, 7 August 1948.
49 Simons, *African Women*, p. 117, p. 120, n. 41.
50 P. Mayer, 'Migrant Labour: Some Perspectives from Anthropology', vol. 3, 'Wives of Migrant Workers' (Rhodes University, Grahamstown, 1978), p. 125.
51 Wilson, *Social Structure*, p. 105; Case against Jim Kondile, quoted in *King William's Town Mercury*, 23 August 1947.
52 CA. 1/CAT, Case no. 6 of 1950, *Charlie Fata vs. Ceshana Mjonono*.
53 See CA. 1/KHA (NAC SD), Case no. 35 of 1956, *Marack Matengjane vs. Nxatu Ngowa*; CA. 1/KHA, Case no. 20 of 1955, *Nhanha Tyolweni vs. Zilumkele Sotewu*; CA. 1/KHA, Case no. 2 of 1956, *Jabavu Wele vs. Goli Sonkotyana*; CA. 1/KHA, Case no. 3 of 1956, *Mqondisi Jim Pitolisi vs. Koti Tutani and Tutani Peter*; CA. 1/LDF, Case no. 9 of 1956, *Willie Mgoma vs. Sipho Kulati and Sergeant Kulati*; CA. 1/LDF (NAC SD), Case no. 25 of 1958, *Newton Nolengane vs. Sipo Present*; CA. 1/CAT, Case no. 15 of 1947, *Jackson Pony vs. Raladiya Madala*.
54 This followed on sexual play in adolescence. Anthropologist Philip Mayer suggests that women as well as men regarded sexual gratification as axiomatic. See Mayer, *Townsmen*, pp. 252–253.
55 Interview, A. Mager with F. Mpande, Peddie, 23 October 1993.

56 Interview, A. Mager with Mrs Matomela, Peddie, 24 October 1993.
57 See C. Poynton, 'The Privileging of Representation', in T. Threadgold and A. Cranny Francis (eds), *Feminine, Masculine and Representation* (Sydney: Allen and Unwin, 1990), pp. 231–255.
58 Women's duties are described in Houghton, *Economy*, p. 140.
59 Houghton, *Economy*, pp. 90–91; Manona, 'Marriage', p. 198.
60 Simons, *African Women*, p. 211.
61 Houghton, *Economy*, pp. 142, 143; interview, A. Mager with Phyllis Nokoyi, Keiskammahoek, 17 July 1989; interview, A. Mager with group of single women, Tyefu's location, 25 May 1989.
62 Wilson, *Social Structure*, p. 91.
63 Houghton, *Economy*, pp. 111–112. Interview, Mrs Matomela; CA. 1/PDE (NAC SD), Case no. 43 of 1955, *Skade Fosi vs. Vizinto Lumkwana*; CA. 1/KWT, Case no. 39 of 1950, *Mhlontlo Magaga vs. Lungile Mashiqa*; CA. 1/LDF (NAC SD), Case no. 2 of 1951, *Fidyoli Nkoduso vs. Tutu Yawa* for wives who took up with their old *metsha* partners.
64 Mayer, *Townsmen*, pp. 98–99, 217.
65 Interview, A. Mager with Sister Peter, Bisho, 19 October 1993; interview, F. Mpande. See also CA. 1/KHA, Case no. 16 of 1954, *Ncediso Sityata vs. Jack Ntuma Gxanyana*; CA. 1/KHA, Case no. 14 of 1946, *Tom Matshoba vs. Mtshekexe Mbawana* for instances of wives acting as go-betweens for husbands and their lovers.
66 Interviews, A. Mager with Sister Peter, retired midwife, Duncan Village, 19 and 21 October 1993.
67 *King William's Town Mercury*, 23 May 1950. CA. GSC, Case no. 594 of 1954, *Rex vs. Constance Ntlange.*
68 Interview, group of single women.
69 Wilson, *Social Structure*, pp. 104–105.
70 CA. NAC SD, Case no. 219 of 1950, *Mkanzela vs. Rona*, quoted in Simons, *African Women*, pp. 224, 227.
71 Seven was the average number of births for women in the Keiskammahoek district; Houghton, *Economy*, p. 140.
72 Interview, group of single women. Wilson, *Social Structure*, p. 100, confirms this trend.
73 This is hinted at by Peteni in his novel, *Hill of Fools.*

15 Women and migrants

Continuity and change in patterns of female migration in Latin America

Paulina de los Reyes

Introduction

Traditionally, women have made up a majority of the internal migration in Latin America. During the 1950s and 1960s, the period of import-substitution, migratory flows to the big cities were mostly composed of women, which suggests that both transformations in the agriculture and pull factors in the cities had a selective impact on the female labour force. This trend has been followed by a new pattern connected with the globalisation process and the implementation of export-oriented economic strategies in most Latin American countries. New labour markets have been opened for women both in rural and urban areas creating in turn particular migratory flows. Interurban migration, temporary, rural–rural migration and the increased use of female labour in export oriented agricultural production as well as the predominance of women workers in the assembly industry illustrates this trend. At the same time, recent research shows that women workers in the cities have gone through a process of informalisation and growing job instability.

This chapter focuses on recent changes in patterns of female migration in Latin America and examines similarities and differences between current trends and traditional models. By doing so, the analysis sheds light on demographic, economic and ideological transformations in the region in order to present a new institutional framework for understanding the participation of women in society. Despite variations between the Latin American countries, and even within national boundaries, a regional approach is relevant and necessary. This is due not only to the inheritance of a common colonial past, but also to the current globalisation process which, deepening the differences between Latin America and other Third World regions, reconfirms the role of the region within the economic world order.

Migration as a gendered process

Historically, migration has been a means of improving the life chances of women and men. Demographic pressures, labour shortages and economic expansion have traditionally been considered as crucial factors behind the spatial redistribution of labour and mobility of the labour force. The focus on the economic aspects of migration and the male norm in the economy and working life have resulted in many analyses of contemporary migration flows explicitly or implicitly resting on the assumption of the migrants as male workers and of migration as a gender-neutral process.[1] From this perspective, the situation of women is addressed either as 'dependants' of male migrants or as members of the family left behind. Thus, research focusing on the situation of migrant women tends to underline social and cultural patterns in the societies of origin as well as their subordination to patriarchy. In this context migration is often understood as an emancipatory project aiming to improve the status of women, and therefore status changes are also conceptualised as a transition from tradition to modernity.[2]

Independently of the underlying values behind current understandings of migration, there is a growing awareness of the gender determinants of this process. The impact of gender, though hardly uniform, varies in different historical and cultural contexts and also in relation to other structures of power. Therefore the viability of migration for women must be related to obstacles and facilitators linked to their position *vis à vis* men in their societies of origin and fundamentally to the range of options their status allows. Conversely, the status of migrant women in host societies is shaped not only by their position as migrants but also by the dynamics derived from their being subjected to two gender orders; that of the society of origin and that of the host community. Conversely, patriarchal structures may form part of the push mechanisms compelling women to migrate and yet they can also be determinants of gender-segregated inclusion/exclusion models in host societies.

According to Lin, the character of women's migration depends on three sets of circumstances: the macro-structural context, the structure and function of the family, and women's own characteristics over the life cycle. These circumstances influence whether migration depends on a process of decision making on a family basis or on individual bases.[3] This model emphasises the relevance of marital status, life cycle and education to the propensity to migrate. Other authors underline, however, that migration can also be a response to a marginal position in the society of origin, and as such involves women who have transgressed the limits of accepted female behaviour. This is, for instance, the case of single mothers who may experience pressures to leave due either to the economic responsibility they bear for their children or in order to avoid social sanctions.[4]

The role of gender in migratory processes appears connected to a set of complex relations both in the origin society and the host community. Recent research and empirical figures show, however, the quantitative importance of women in migratory processes on both a national and international level. Moreover, in many cases we find that the women make the decision to migrate without their male relatives, and also that they are a key factor in the integration process of their families to the host society. In a recent report from the United Nations the significance, diversity and complexity of female migration is analysed and exemplified through studies in different regions and in various countries. Despite difficulties in measuring the extent of female migration, most available data indicates the increasing importance of female migration.[5] Therefore, the focus on the role of women in migratory processes calls for a discussion of the specificity of women's migration and the factors that, in different historical contexts, turn women into a special category of migrants. To the extent that gender is a socially constructed category, historical perspectives on female migration would be helpful to understand how the mobility of women influences the construction of different and changing conceptions of gender.

In the present chapter, female migration in Latin America is analysed within the framework of the transformations of the gender order during the post-war period. The gender order is basically understood as historically determined representations of, and norms and values for, the rights and duties involved in the definition of femininity and masculinity. Within this perspective, the changes of the pattern of female migration and the evolution of a labour market for women, as well as the demographic changes affecting women in the region, must be understood within a normative and institutionalised framework. This is a framework that assigns separate roles to women and men and offers differentiated access to social status and economic resources. A closer examination of the dynamics of change and continuity of different patterns of female migration would thus help to identify not only the mechanisms that reproduce and legitimise the gender order but also the conditions required for its transformation.

The traditional model, 1950–1970: import substitution, urbanisation and demographic transition

The gendered division of labour has undergone important changes in Latin American society during the post-war period. These changes appear to be closely linked to the economic strategies implemented by the Latin American governments and also to the demographic development of the region. Since the colonial period, Latin America had been integrated into the world system as an exporter of raw materials. A growing deterioration of the terms of trade, inflation and macro-economic unbalances during the 1950s bore witness to the extreme vulnerability of the Latin American economies and also increased the risks of political instability and social conflicts in the region. A stagnant agricultural sector and a rapid population growth contributed to the deepening of social and economic problems. Despite important variations between the countries of the region, most of the population lived in the countryside and depended on agriculture for their subsistence.[6]

According to current analyses, the problems in agriculture were to a great extent linked to the extreme concentration of land in big estates, *latifundios*. In contrast with the *latifundios*, were the tiny subsistence plots or *minifundios*. With little in between, the system generated almost feudal working relations, and was prone to structural inequalities and backwardness.[7] This tenure pattern resulted in inefficient agricultural production due to underutilisation of both land and labour force. Moreover, though unemployment was relatively uncommon, an important share of the agricultural population was underemployed and lived in poverty or extreme poverty.[8] Most of the agricultural population was tied to the small tenancies and formed part of the underemployed and surplus labour who occasionally worked in the big estates.

In this context the work of women has often been invisible and reduced to the domestic sphere. In economic analysis and statistical figures women were defined as housewives and household work as a reproductive activity rather than work. Accordingly, women have been seen as tied to the reproductive work within the household while men have been assumed to contribute to the monetary income of the household through either their salaried work or marketable production. This conceptual separation of productive and reproductive work or household and market activities has contributed to preserving an image whereby women are defined as outside the active population. This is also a factor in the polarising of the economic and social roles of women and men.

Fertility patterns and the reproductive conduct of women corresponded to this model. High fertility levels reaching a regional average rate of 5.9 children per woman in fertile age tied women to their family and reproductive responsibilities.[9] There are, however, important international and national variations. While Bolivian and Mexican women gave birth to an average of 6.8 children, women in Uruguay and Argentina had rates of 2.7 and 3.2 respectively. Additionally, though there is some uncertainty of figures regarding fertility in rural areas, it is possible to assume that rural women had the highest levels of fertility. According to the records of the FLACSO (The Latin American Faculty of Social Sciences), rural women had an average of two more children than women in urban areas.[10] On the whole, the profound rural–urban gaps appeared to be deeper than national variations. Accordingly, differences between countries are less pronounced if rural–urban variations are considered.

Closely connected to the high fertility level, mortality rates, and particularly child mortality, showed a high but decreasing level, indicating that Latin America in the 1950s was at the beginning of a demographic transition. This transition, which, in the countries of the Southern Cone, had already been stabilised in low fertility and mortality rates, was completed in most of the countries in the region during the 1960s and

1970s. The reproductive burden of women is also expressed in long fertility periods and early marriages. Another aspect is the high marriage rates. On average, women married before men and a high percentage of adult women were married or lived in consensual unions.[11] In this context, figures indicating changes in size and composition of the household suggest that the decline occurred during the last decades, and the increase of nuclear units has probably resulted in lightening the reproductive burden of women.[12]

Despite normative assumptions and the constraints derived from high fertility rates, a closer examination of historical records and the use of oral sources show that women's work outside the household was not occasional or exceptional but rather part of the subsistence pattern of poor peasants. Moreover, the contracts between landlords and poor peasants often included the regular input of females in what was defined as 'women's work'. In consequence, women were responsible for dairy work and for cleaning, cooking and baking for the personnel of the estate. Rural women could also be employed as domestic servants in the landlord's household. Working relations in agriculture were rarely based on market principles alone. Payment in kind and direct exchanges were also common. For instance, the salary of the rural labourers usually included food and bread during working days. Milk and cheese could be used both as payment for labour or, conversely, as land rent.[13] In such circumstances the contribution of women in producing goods to be used in non-monetary exchanges was particularly important.

Rural women were also expected to work in harvesting, cleaning and storing. In periods of high seasonal demand, both females and males could be employed on the big estates.[14] In some cases female work outside the household has formed part of family strategies and has been paid as family wage to the head of the household. But individual salaries also existed. In spite of normative judgements and the definition of work tasks as feminine or masculine, the traditional gender division of labour in agriculture seems to have given women the opportunity to take on extra-household work and even access to salaried work.[15] However, in most cases this occurred in an unstable and discontinuous fashion and without altering the dominant norms and representations of the role of women.

The organisation of the agricultural work and variations in the demand for agricultural labour allowed a flexible interpretation of the gender division of labour, especially in situations of labour force scarcity. However, in a context of surplus labour in the agricultural sector, the normative aspects of the gender division of labour probably had a definite influence in generating female-dominated migratory flows from the rural areas to the cities. Despite differences between the Latin American countries, the factors behind rural–urban migration had a selective impact on the female population.

According to available records women in most Latin American countries dominated internal migration until the 1970s. In many cases this trend started in the inter-war period. For instance, in Mexico the ratio of men to women in the migrant population was 88:100 for the 1940s, 91:100 for the 1950s and 92:100 for the 1960s. In other countries migration, and fundamentally female migration, became intensified during the post-war period. In Chile, 23 per cent of all males and 24 per cent of females were counted as migrants in 1960.[16] According to the ECLAC (The United Nations Economic Commission for Latin America and the Caribbean), the migrant flows to the cities included an overwhelming majority of young people, and especially of young women. The migrants were a heterogeneous group regarding education, work experience and occupation level. There are indications, however, that the majority of the migrants had lower qualifications and formal education than the average for the population of their respective destinations, but higher than the non-migrant population in the areas of origin.[17] This relation was seen as a factor contributing to deepening existing differences between rural and urban areas and also as a sign of the gap between an urban modern life and the backwardness of the countryside.

Economic stagnation and increasing rural–urban differences are an important reason behind economic strategies based on the substitution of imports and the modernisation of agriculture, which were recommended, and in varying degree also implemented, in the region.[18] Import substitution increased the role of the state and of the public sector in shaping new work opportunities for women. Investment in infrastructure, education, health and administration generated a demand for female labour but, in contrast to the welfare states in Western Europe, the Latin American states took over a very reduced degree of responsibility for reproductive work. In the Latin American context, the responsibility for reproductive and care work remained an individual issue, thus increasing an urban labour market for domestic service.

Female work in Latin America has been characterised by the existence of a bipolar model of employment, in which the conditions of labour differ radically according to the level of income and class background. On one hand there is a group of well-educated women employed in formal work in the private and public sector. These women are well qualified and in many cases have benefited from a higher education, often to university level, as well as social guarantees and the access to social security. This group enters the labour market not only for economic reasons but also because of a need for personal realisation and as a result of class-related values and norms. These values are associated with patterns of social behaviour of an urban middle class involved in a modernisation project in the Latin American societies. However, within this project the responsibility for the household is still defined as a female area. Thus, conflicts between working life and family life have commonly been solved with the help of domestic servants. Therefore, women's involvement in the labour market has not only been characterised by gender segregation but also by a deeply rooted class differentiation. On an ideological level, this dual model of the labour market can be seen as an expression of the internal differentiation of gender and of a hierarchy based on a modernisation paradigm. The idea of modernity and its normative construction in terms of class and ethnic dichotomies is crucial to understanding how differences between women are established in Latin America.

During the 1960s the development of a labour market for women created simultaneously a specific demand for migrant female workers in the large cities. According to studies in several Latin American countries, migrant women tended to concentrate in large urban centres and, to a greater extent than other women, were congregated in a small number of activities principally in the service sector and in manual activities.[19] Employment opportunities in domestic service have been an important incentive to migrate for young rural women, as has the wish to gain access to a modern lifestyle in the cities.

Migrant women have, to a great extent, performed domestic service. These women usually lived in the home of their employers, a situation that seriously limits personal privacy, autonomy and the separation of work time and free time. Migrant women were often very young, and in fact many girls were compelled to leave their homes for domestic service in the cities. Their relative youth made migrant women and girls extremely vulnerable. Additionally, single mothers constituted an important share of migrant domestic workers often due to social and/or economic pressures in the society of origin. Single mothers and their children faced a very precarious situation. Rural–urban migration implies definitive change of residence and the permanent incorporation to urban living and working conditions. Nevertheless, during this period, the migrants usually maintained the links with their origin places, becoming a 'bridge' and a network for the newly arrived.

The employment conditions of domestic workers have often been characterised by paternalism and clientelism, that is, inserted in a set of non-formalised long-term defined commitments, obligations, expectations and demands. On an ideological level, the servile relations established between domestic workers and their employers was legitimised by prejudices against the migrants and stories of their ignorance. The employer was assumed to be a mentor and a guide in the process of transculturalisation, that is, of learning and adopting an urban way of life, that the migrant must go through before she or he gained the skills necessary for a modern life. The dichotomy between a traditional and modern life has been an important component of the conceptualisation of the differences between the rural and urban worlds. In a longer-term perspective, this can be seen as a factor contributing to the invisibility of domestic work and the exclusion of domestic workers from, among other things, the benefits of labour legislation. Labour legislation which, to a great extent, is aimed at protecting the reproductive rights of women, includes such important items as regulated working time, leisure, maternity leave and minimum wages. These rights, however, are guaranteed only to women who have formal contracts with their employers. Until very recently, domestic work has been excepted from important parts of the labour legislation and only partially recognised as work.[20]

To sum up, the traditional pattern of rural–urban migration is associated with structural changes in the Latin American economies. The impact of these changes is nevertheless clearly gendered which, first, is evidenced by the predominance of a female labour force surplus in the countryside. Second, the changes are manifested in the emergence of new and differentiated labour markets for women in urban areas. The integration into the labour market of migrant women is thus inscribed in a context where gender segregation, class differentiation and migrant status give female migrants a place in the lowest occupational categories, as is the case with domestic service, which is not only performed in unstable and informal conditions but is also not officially recognised as work and is to a great extent excepted by labour legislation.

Political crisis, economic adjustments and survival: women migrants at the end of the century

The 1990s can be characterised as a period of social and economic restructuring whereby democratisation and the incorporation of the Latin American economies into international trade in competitive terms appear as simultaneous but contradictory trends. Behind these changes we can see the reorganisation of the production processes, the incorporation of new technologies and the deregulation of the labour market. These changes have altered the composition of the labour market and particularly women's labour force participation. Moreover, among the most evident of the new phenomena in the region is the growing presence of women in the labour market. This trend is specially marked among young women, but even middle-aged and married women have increased participation rates.[21]

It is necessary to underline that the increased participation of women in the labour market is taking place in a situation of economic crisis and recession. Therefore the new forms of female work are, in many cases, inserted in strategies for survival and characterised by precariousness and poverty. In this context, new migratory flows appear as a component in these survival strategies. This is the case, for example, for young women both from urban and rural areas who migrate searching for jobs either as temporary workers in export agriculture (*temporeras*), as factory workers in assembly industry (*maquiladoras*) in Northern Mexico or who form part of migratory flows between the Central American countries.

In the case of Chile, the expansion of agricultural exports is to a great extent based on female temporary workers. Both in fruit production and in horticulture there are some production tasks which are almost exclusively performed by women. For instance, harvesting and packaging of fruit for export have become typical female jobs which attract seasonal labourers both from other rural areas and from urban settlements during the peak periods. Seasonal work is usually paid on a piecework basis and therefore the experience and skill of the workers influence earnings. Women are considered particularly suitable to perform these tasks because of their 'natural' inclination to handle with care. Thus, the competence of women is not recognised as such but is defined as a 'natural' component of femininity. However, despite their experience and qualifications, women are seldom promoted to managerial positions and therefore are commonly supervised by men.[22]

The unstable demand for labour has given rise to employment patterns where periodical unemployment is combined with peak periods that absorb a significant amount of migrant labourers. For the migrant workers, this means long periods in search of work that follows the agricultural cycles of the different regions of the country. In contrast to earlier migration, the new patterns are not associated with a permanent change of residence. The lack of infrastructure and very precarious accommodation during the work season do not allow permanent arrangements. This is particularly difficult for migrant women who, while lacking access to nurseries or to an established network, are forced to leave their children for long periods or to rely on very uncertain childcare arrangements during their working periods.[23] Studies carried on in other Latin American countries underline the increase of these new patterns of female migration associated with agricultural export and based on assumptions about the natural competence of female workers.[24]

Another example of the new migration pattern is associated with the expansion of the assembly (*maquila*) industry on the northern border of Mexico and in the recently emerging free zones in Central America. In the mid-1990s Costa Rica, El Salvador, Guatemala, Honduras and Nicaragua increased their share of assembly production.[25] The assembly industry has been associated with the development of new employment opportunities for women and the emergence of a new destination for female migrants. Recent research results show an increased number of women among Central American migrants. Regional flows have traditionally been directed to the USA, but Costa Rica has become an important pull area due to relatively high salary levels and work opportunities, especially in non-agricultural activities for women. Both the education level and participation rates among this group of female migrants are higher than the average for women in the host societies.[26]

According to recent studies, the majority of assembly workers have newly migrated from urban areas and had a higher-than-average level of formal education compared to the adult population in their respective countries of origin. Guatemala is an exception to this, since most of the assembly workers are of rural origin and have low levels of formal education.[27] Two main groups are distinguished among the migrant workers: young, unmarried women without children and aged between 15 and 24 years form the first and largest category. Women older than 25 who are married and/or have children compose a second and increasing group.[28]

It has been pointed out that in *maquila* production, gender is a factor leading to worsening working conditions for women. Gender inequalities are reproduced during the working process and expressed in the subordinated position of women in workplaces. As in agriculture, work is paid on a piecework basis, but since women and men perform different tasks there are important wage differences between women and men. Wage differentials, working hierarchies, the lack of access to management positions and the fact that women tend to be concentrated in unskilled tasks are all signs of the vulnerable position of women involved in assembly production.[29] An interesting trend manifested in Mexico during the last few years is the increasing share of male workers in *maquila* production.[30] Women still constitute the majority of the *maquila* workers, but the masculinisation of the *maquila* raises a number of questions about their quality of life and the future effects on their labour conditions and household strategies.

The new patterns of migration emerging after the debt crisis of the 1980s crystallised during the 1990s. This period is often associated with an expansion of salaried work among women. However, regarding women's labour force participation it is necessary to distinguish between a structural trend initiated in the 1960s in such countries as Argentina, Colombia, Uruguay, Chile and Panama and a new, conjunctural process which also takes place in Bolivia, Guatemala, Honduras and Nicaragua. Both models of insertion are nevertheless found in more or less degree in most countries in the region.[31] In the first case the new female work is mostly concentrated in urban areas and in the formal sector of the economy; in the second case, the incorporation of women occurred in a context of informalisation and precariousness. The debt crisis and the adjustment process that followed increased the structural heterogeneity of the labour market, worsening the underutilisation of the labour force. The capacity of the public sector to absorb labour declined and instability increased. In this context, the feminisation of the labour force and the increased participation of women in various forms of remunerated work are signs not only of the gendered impact of the crisis but also of women's flexibility and capacity to adapt to these new conditions.

Demographic transformations in the regions are key to understanding current patterns of female employment and migration and also to explaining women's capacity to adapt to new working conditions. Compared to 1950, Latin American women in the 1990s gave birth to fewer children

(3.1) and they did so at a later stage of the life cycle. Women have increased their life expectancy by eighteen years and they are likely to see their children reach adulthood due to the rapid decline in infant mortality.[32] Additionally, most women live in urban areas, principally large cities, and belong to nuclear family units.[33] An increasing trend particularly in urban areas are the female-headed households, which in 1990 reached 23 per cent of the total.[34] Many authors related this process to the economic crisis and the search for alternative solutions to everyday subsistence. In this process women have moved outside the domestic sphere into the public, organising themselves in soup kitchens and other collective actions.[35] On the whole, differences between the conditions of women in the various Latin American countries and between rural and urban areas persist and have even deepened. Thus, while the demographic transition has been completed in the majority of the countries in the region which show low mortality and birth rates, there are other countries with a predominance of rural population where high birth rates are combined with low mortality, resulting in a high population growth.[36]

The persistence of differences between rural and urban areas is particularly striking in the case of women. In general, rural women have higher fertility, less access to health care services, less education and lower rates of participation in the labour market. Despite the statistical bias derived from underregistration, lower levels of activity are undoubtedly also linked to a greater informalisation of women's work in rural areas and in many cases also to normative values that still make women define themselves as housewives rather than rural workers.[37]

To conclude, the labour market for women, as well as women's mobility, has undergone important changes. The economic crisis and the implementation of export-based strategies have shaped new forms of labour market insertion for women. These new strategies have benefited from class differentiation, gender segregation and especially from the vulnerability of women with migrant status. Demographic factors and particularly declining fertility rates have helped to broaden women's options, increasing the possibility of their adapting to new working conditions. Fewer children, a longer life expectancy and the shortening of the reproductive period have enabled women to have a more flexible working life.

Change and continuity in patterns of female migration at the end of the century

The changing patterns of female migration during the period present a complex picture where great variations and contrasts are linked with considerable similarities. Differences in the economic structure of each country, class bias and urban–rural bias shape a heterogeneous framework to women's labour and also to migration. On the whole, we can see that internal migration in Latin America has increased in variety and complexity. While rural–urban migration in the past was oriented to service work in the cities and particularly to domestic work, modern migration flows are linked to the export production and to the most expansive economic sectors. Widespread servile relations of labourer to employer have been replaced by capitalist relations and wages based on piecework. This fact, however, does not mean substantial improvements for the migrants. Wage inequalities between women and men, precarious jobs and vulnerability are still characterising the working conditions of migrant women. The same is true regarding access to social guarantees and work rights. Although migrants are now employed in different economic sectors where both orientation of production and the organisation of work is different, the labour conditions of women have not undergone any significant changes in terms of equity. On the contrary, many studies indicate that the subordinate condition of women is a factor giving them comparative advantages in relation to men.

Regarding the socio-demographic changes that have occurred, the figures indicate that adolescents no longer dominate migratory flows. Older women, married women and unmarried mothers comprise an increased share of the migrant workers. The migratory flows to the large cities have declined while temporary movements such as interurban migration, rural–rural flows and the combination of urban residence with rural employment have increased. Overall, migration is rarely linked to permanent resident changes but implies constant mobility in searching for work opportunities. These conditions imply increased instability for migrant women and impact on the ways in which wage work and household work are combined. It is a remarkable paradox that the incorporation of older and married women occurs in a context of greater instability. Undoubtedly, this is linked to the increased importance of the women's wages for the family income. In many cases, this is a key factor in introducing changes in gender relations within the household and negotiations of rights and responsibilities amongst the household members. On an ideological level, this is manifested by a weakened representation of the man as the natural 'breadwinner' and greater acceptance of a two-income model.[38]

An important factor behind the transformations in patterns of labour and migration relates to women's increased formal education and declining fertility rates. Available data shows that educational differences between migrants and other workers are no longer important. In fact, in many cases the migrants have a higher education level than other workers. These aspects have altered traditional patterns, giving women new options and also contributing to the development of social identities separated from or less tied to motherhood and family life. Urbanisation has been an important factor in this process, expanding the access to education for women as well as improving their opportunities in the labour market. However, a striking fact among Latin American women in general is the lack of correspondence between educational levels, occupational achievements and income. This is even more striking in the case of migrant women.[39] Despite inequalities derived from a migrant status, the growing heterogeneity of the migrant women as a group, as well as the character of the new migration flow, no longer gives ground for definite categorisations. Differentiation models codified in terms of modernity or tradition are less suitable when female migrants become a more heterogeneous group in demographic, educational and spatial terms.

Continuity in patterns of migration is found in the fact that gender segregation appears to be determinant in both traditional and new migratory flows. However, vulnerability is associated not only with gender segregation but also with class differentiation. The existence of a gendered division of labour and the development of a gender-segregated and class-stratified labour market at both the society of origin and of destination seems to be a key factor determining the scope and composition of female migration in both periods. In spite of the changes in women's labour force participation, patterns of residence and reproductive behaviour segregation and subordination of women are still unchanged. Therefore, the analysis of the paradoxes of continuity and changes giving origin to new patterns of female migration indicates that an unfinished task for the Latin American societies is the construction of a gender order which better recognises and values the contribution of women to society.

Notes

1 See for instance P. de los Reyes, 'I skärningspunkten mellan genus och etnicitet: Ett ekonomisk historiskt perspektiv på invandrarkvinnor i svenskt arbetsliv', *Arbetsmarknad & arbetsliv*, 1998, 1, pp. 335–356.

2 P. de los Reyes, 'Det problematiska systerskapet', *Historisk tidskrift*, 1998, 3.

3 L. Lean Lin, 'The Status of Women and International Migration', in United Nations, *International Migration Policies and the Status of Female Migrants*, New York, UN, 1995.

4 ibid. See also X. Aranda, 'Las mujeres madres solteras y las jefas de hogar rurales', in X. Valdes and A. M. Arteaga *et al.*, *Mujeres, relaciones de género en la agricultura*, Santiago, CEDEM, 1995.

5 United Nations, *International Migration Policies and the Status of Female Migrants*, New York, UN, 1995.

6 In 1950 only 25 per cent of the population lived in cities: Uruguay (53 per cent), Argentina (50 per cent) and Chile (43 per cent) were the most urbanised countries in the region. FLACSO, *Mujeres Latinoamericanas en cifras: Tomo Comparativo*, Santiago, 1995.

7 R. Prebich, 'The Economic Development of Latin America and its Principal Problems', *Economic Bulletin for Latin America*, 1962, vol. VII, pp. 1–22.

8 ECLA/FAO, 'An Agricultural Policy to expedite the Economic Development of Latin America', *Economic Bulletin for Latin America*, 1961.

9 FLACSO, *Mujeres Latinoamericanas en cifras*, p. 44.

10 ibid.

11 ibid., pp. 54–56. See also United Nations, *The World's Women*, New York, UN, 1995.

12 ECLAC, *Family and Future: a Regional Programme in Latin America and the Caribbean*, Santiago, 1995.
13 See for instance C. Tuijtelaar de Quiton and M. Rodriguez Amurrio, *La Campesina de Carrasco*, La Paz, Ciplade, 1994; X .Valdes *et al.*, *Historias testimoniales de mujeres en el campo*, Santiago, CEDEM, 1983; S. Bradshaw, 'Women in Chilean Rural Society', in D. Hojman (ed.), *Neo-liberal Agriculture in Rural Chile,* London, Macmillan, 1990, pp. 110–126.
14 See for instance Valdes *et al.*, *Historias testimoniales.*
15 P. de los Reyes, *The Rural Poor: Agricultural Changes and Survival Strategies in Chile 1973–1989*, Uppsala, Uppsala Studies in Economic History, 1992.
16 ECLAC, 'Internal Migration', *Economic Bulletin for Latin America*, 1973, no. XVIII.
17 ibid.
18 Taking into consideration the diversity of models used to pursue the industrialisation goal I prefer to use the term 'strategy' in plural.
19 X. Aranda, *Empleo, migración rural y estructura productiva agrícola*, Santiago, FLACSO, 1982. O. de Oliveira, 'Migración femenina, organización familiar y mercados laborales en Mexico', *Revista de Comercio Exterior*, 1984, vol. 34. J. Elizaga, *Migraciones a las areas metropolitanas de America Latina*, Santiago, CELADE, 1970.
20 FLACSO, *Mujeres latinoamericanas en cifras*, p. 150.
21 I. Arriagada, 'Changes in the Female Labour Market', *Cepal Review*, 1994, 53, p. 95.
22 de los Reyes, *The Rural Poor.* See also J. Medel *et al.*, *Las temporeras y su vision del trabajo*, Santiago, CEDEM, 1989.
23 Accidents are often reported from the fruit district during the peak season. A demand of high priority among seasonal workers is the creation of nurseries close to their workplaces. See G. Fallabella, 'Organisarse y sobrevivir en Santa Maria', 1991, paper presented at the 47th International Congress of Americanists, New Orleans, July 1991.
24 A. Barrón, *Migraciones y empleo agricola en los cultivos no tradicionales*, Centro de Estudios Históricos de la Cuestion Agraria Mexicana, Mexico, 1995. S. Lara, 'Incorporacion de la Mujer indigena al sector hostícola de exportación en Mexico 1920–1990', 1991, paper presented at the 47th International Congress of Americanists, New Orleans, July 1991. Proyecto Estado de la Region, *Estado de la Region en Desarrollo Humano Sostenible*, Informe 1, Editorama, 1999.
25 ECLAC, *Centroamerica: El empleo femenino en la industria maquiladora de exportacion*, Santiago, United Nations, 1994.
26 Proyecto Estado de la Region, *Estado de la Region*, pp. 369–371.
27 ibid. See also S. González *et al.*, *Mujer, migracion y maquila en la frontera norte*, El Colegio de Mexico, 1995.
28 ECLAC, *Centroamerica*, pp. 33–35.
29 A critical review of the literature and research on the *maquila* in Mexico is found in K. Kopinak, 'Gender as a Vehicle for the Subordination of Women Maquiladora Workers in Mexico', *Latin American Perspectives*, Winter 1995, 84, 22, 1, pp. 30–48.
30 T. Alegría *et al.*, 'Restructuring of Production and Territorial Change: a Second Industrialisation Hub in Northern Mexico', *Cepal Review*, 1997, 61, pp. 187–204.
31 P. de los Reyes, 'Mujeres Latinoamericanas a fines del siglo XX: En busca de un nuevo contrato de género?' in M. C. Medina (ed.), *America Latina: Y las mujeres qué?* Gothenburg, HAINA, 1998, pp. 261–289.
32 FLACSO, *Mujeres latinoamericanas en cifras*, pp. 35–62, 113–134. The figure corresponds to an average for eighteen Latin American countries. For an historical analysis see de los Reyes, 'Mujeres Latinoamericanas'.
33 V. Ramirez, *Cambios en la familia y en los roles de la mujer*, CELADE, 1995.

34 FLACSO, *Mujeres Latinoamericanas en cifras*, p. 37. An interesting analysis of this trend is found in ECLAC, *Family and Future*.

35 S. Rowbotham and S. Mitter, *Dignity and Daily Bread: New Forms of Economic Organising among Poor Women in the Third World and the First*, London, Routledge, 1994.

36 This is the case of Bolivia, el Salvador, Guatemala, Honduras, Nicaragua and Paraguay. FLACSO, *Mujeres Latinoamericanas en cifras*, pp. 34–37.

37 On this point see the discussion on gender roles and rural work in de los Reyes, *The Rural Poor*, pp. 156–160.

38 ibid., pp. 161–170. See also ECLAC, *Family and Future*, pp. 44–59.

39 FLACSO, *Mujeres Latinoamericanas en cifras*. See also I. Szasz, 'Women and Migrants: Inequalities in the Labour Market of Santiago, Chile', *Cepal Review*, August 1996, 56, pp. 185–195.

Bibliography

Abdulrahim, D. (1993) 'Defining Gender in a Second Exile: Palestinian Women in West Berlin' in Buijs, G. (ed.) *Migrant Women: Crossing Boundaries and Changing Identities*, Oxford, Berg: 55–82.

Abe, T. (1989) *Nihon ni okeru Sanchi Men'orimonogyō no Tenkai*, Tokyo, Tokyo University Press.

Abel, M. and Folbre, N. (1990) 'A Method for Revising Estimates: Female Participation in the US Before 1940', *Historical Methods* 23: 167–176.

Akenson, D. H. (1994) *The Irish Diaspora: a Primer*, Belfast, Institute of Irish Studies.

Alegría, T. *et al.* (1997) 'Restructuring of Production and Territorial Change: a Second Industrialisation Hub in Northern Mexico', *Cepal Review* 61: 187–204.

Alford, K. (1984) *Production or Reproduction? An Economic History of Women in Australia, 1788–1850*, Melbourne, Oxford University Press.

Alonso Ruiz, B. (1991) *El arte de la cantería. Los maestros trasmeranos de la Junta de Voto*, Santander, Universidad de Cantabria.

Anderson, B. (2000) *Doing the Dirty Work: the Global Politics of Domestic Labour*, London, Zed Books.

Anderson, M. (1971) *Family Structure in Nineteenth-century Lancashire*, Cambridge, Cambridge University Press.

Anderson, M. and Morse, D. J. (1993) 'High Fertility, High Emigration, Low Nuptiality: Adjustment Processes in Scotland's Demographic Experience, 1861–1914, Part II'. *Population Studies* 47: 319–343.

Aranda, X. (1982) *Empleo, migración rural y estructura productiva agrícola*, Santiago, FLACSO.

Aranda, X. (1995) 'Las mujeres madres solteras y las jefas de hogar rurales' in Valdes, X. and Arteaga, A. M. *et al. Mujeres, relaciones de género en la agricultura*, Santiago, CEDEM.

Arriagada, I. (1994) 'Changes in the Female Labour Market', *Cepal Review* 53: 91–110.

Assion, P. (ed.) (1991) *Über Hamburg nach Amerika: Hessisiche Auswandernde in den Hamburger Schiffslisten 1855 bis 1866*, Marburg, Germany, Institut für Europäische Ethnologie und Kulturforschung der Universität Marburg.

Audenino, P. (1990) 'Le custodi della montagna: donne e migrazioni stagionali in una communità alpina' in Corti, P. (ed.) 'Società rurale e ruoli femminili in Italia tra Ottocento e Novecento', *Annali dell' Istituto 'Alcide Cervi'*, 12: 265–288.

Auerbach, I. (1993) *Auswanderung aus Kurhessen: Nach Osten oder Westen?*, Marburg, Hessisches Staatsarchiv Marburg.

Aymer, P. L. (1997) *Uprooted Women: Migrant Domestics in the Caribbean*, Westport, CT and London, Praeger.

Bacci, M. L. (1972) 'The Countries of Emigration' in Bacci, M. L. (ed.) *The Demographic and Social Pattern of Emigration from Southern European Countries,* Florence, Dipartimento Statistico-Matematic dell'Università di Firenze: 33–4.

Baily, S. L. (1985) 'Patrones de residencia de los italianos en Buenos Aires y Nueva York: 1880–1914', *Estudios Migratorios Latinoamericanos* 1 (December): 8–47.

Baily, S. L. (1999) *Immigrants in the Lands of Promise: Italians in Buenos Aires and New York City, 1870–1914*, Ithaca, NY, Cornell University Press.

Baines, D. (1985) *Migration in a Mature Economy: Emigration and Internal Migration in England and Wales, 1861–1900*, Cambridge, Cambridge University Press.

Baines, D. (1991) *Emigration from Europe, 1815–1930*, London, Macmillan.

Baldasser, L. (2001) *Visits Home: Ethnicity, Identity and Place in the Migration Process*, Melbourne, University of Melbourne Press (forthcoming).

Banfield, E. (1958) *The Moral Basis of a Backward Society*, Glencoe, IL, The Free Press.

Barbalet, M. (1983) *Far From a Low Gutter Girl: the Forgotten World of State Wards South Australia 1887–1940*, Melbourne, Oxford University Press.

Barbič, A. and Miklavčič-Brezigar, I. (1999) 'Domestic Work Abroad: a Necessity and an Opportunity for Rural Women from the Goriška Borderline Region of Slovenia' in Momsen, J. H. (ed.) *Gender, Migration and Domestic Service,* London, Routledge, 164–178.

Barnes, T. (forthcoming) 'Virgin Territory? Travel and Migration by African Women in 20th-century Southern Africa' in Geiger, S., Allman, J. and Musisi, N. (eds) *Women and African Colonial History*, Bloomington, Indiana University Press.

Barrón, A. (1995) *Migraciones y empleo agricola en los cultivos no tradicionales*, Centro de Estudios Históricos de la Cuestion Agraria Mexicana, Mexico.

Barth-Scalmani, G. (1995) 'Salzburger Handelsfrauen, Frätschlerinnen, Fragnerinnen: Frauen in der Welt des Handels am Ende des 18. Jahrhunderts', *L'Homme Zeitschrift für Feministische Geschichtswissenschaft* 6 jg, heft 1: 23–45.

Basch, L. G., Glick-Schiller, N. and Szanton Blanc, C. (1994) *Nations Unbound: Transnational Projects, Postcolonial Predicaments, and Deterritorialized Nation-states*, Reading, Gordon and Breach.

Bauböck, R. (1999) 'Immigration Control without Integration Policy: an Austrian Dilemma' in Brochmann, G. and Hammar, T. (eds) *Mechanism of Immigration Control: A Comparative Analysis of European Regulation Policies*, Oxford/New York, Berg: 97–134.

Berg, M. (1988) 'Women's Work, Mechanization and the Early Phases of Industrialisation in England' in Pahl, R. (ed.) *On Work: Historical, Comparative and Theoretical Approaches*, Oxford, Blackwell: 61–94.

Betts, L. (1904) 'Italian Peasants in a New Law Tenement', *Harper's Bazaar* 38: 104.

Bideau, A. and Brunet, G. (1996) 'Stay or Leave? Individual Choice and Family Logic: the Destinations of Children Born in the Valserine Valley (French Jura) in the Eighteenth and Nineteenth Centuries', *The History of the Family: an International Quarterly* 1, 2: 159–168.

Bjerén, G. (1997) 'Gender and Reproduction' in Hammar, T. *et al.* (eds) *International Migration, Immobility and Development: Multidisciplinary Perspectives*, Oxford, Berg: 219–246.

Blaikie, J. A. D. (1991) 'The Country and the City: Sexuality and Social Class in Victorian Scotland' in Kearns, G. and Withers, C. M. J. (eds) *Urbanising Britain: Essays on Class and Community in the Nineteenth Century*, Cambridge, Cambridge University Press: 80–102.

Blaschke, M. and Harzig, C. (1990) (eds) *Frauen wandern aus: deutsche Migrantinnen im 19. und 20. Jahrhundert*, Bremen, Universität Bremen.

Blessing, P. (1985) 'Irish Emigration to the United States, 1800–1920: an Overview' in Drudy, P. J. (ed.) *The Irish in America: Emigration, Assimilation and Impact*, Cambridge, Cambridge University Press: 11–37.

Bochsler, R. and Gisiger, S. (1989) *Dienen in der Fremde. Dienstmädchen und ihre Herrschaften in der Schweiz des 20. Jahrhunderts*, Zürich, Chronos.

Bonaich, E. and Modell, J. (1980) *The Economic Basis of Ethnic Solidarity: Small Businesses in the Japanese American Community*, Berkeley and Los Angeles, University of California Press.

Bovensiepen, R. (1909) *Die kurhessische Gewerbepolitik und die wirtschaftliche Lage des zünftigen Handwerks in Kurhessen von 1816–1867*, Marburg, Germany, Elwert.

Boyd Caroli, B. (1973) *Italian Repatriation from the United States, 1900–1914*, New York, Center for Migration Studies.

Boyd Caroli, B., Harney, R. F. and Tomasi, L. F. (eds) (1978) *The Italian Immigrant Woman in North America*, Toronto, The Multicultural History Society of Ontario: 79–101.

Bozzoli, B. with Nkotsoe, M. (1991) *Women of Phokeng*, Johannesburg, Ravan Press.

Bradley, H. (1989) *Men's Work, Women's Work: a Sociological History of the Sexual Division of Labour in Employment*, Cambridge, Polity.

Bradshaw, S. (1990) 'Women in Chilean Rural Society' in Hojman, D. (ed.) *Neo-liberal Agriculture in Rural Chile*, London, Macmillan: 110–126.

Braun, M. (1992) *De prijs van de liefde. De eerste feministische golf, het huwelijksrecht en de vaderlandse geschiedenis*, Amsterdam, Spinhuis.

Bredbenner, C. L. (1998) *A Nationality of Her Own: Women, Marriage and the Law of Citizenship*, Berkeley, University of California Press.

Breitenbach, E. and Gordon, E. (eds) (1992) *Out of Bounds: Women in Scottish Society, 1800–1945*, Edinburgh, Edinburgh University Press.

Brettell, C. B. (1986) *Men who Migrate, Women who Wait: Population and History in a Portuguese Parish*, Princeton, NJ, Princeton University Press.

Brüggemeier, F. J. (1984) *Leben vor Ort. Ruhrbegleute und Ruhrbergbau 1889–1919*, Munich, C. H. Beck.

Buijs, G. (1993) (ed.) *Migrant Women: Crossing Boundaries and Changing Identities*, Oxford, Berg.

Bundy, C. and Beinart, W. (1987) *Hidden Struggles in Rural South Africa*, Johannesburg, Ravan Press.

Burawoy, M. (1976) 'The Functions and Reproduction of Migrant Labor: Comparative Material from Southern Africa and the United States', *American Journal of Sociology* 81 (March): 1076–1087.

Bustos, M. (1991) *Burguesía de negocios y capitalismo en Cádiz: los Colarte (1650–1750)*, Cádiz, Diputatión Provincial de Cadiz.

Cerase, F. P. (1967) 'Su una tipologia di emigrati ritornati: il ritorno di investimento', *Studi emigrazione* 4, 10: 327–344.

Cerase, F. P. (1971) *L'emigrazione di ritorno: Innovazione o reazione? L'esperienza dell'emigrazione di ritorno dagli Stati Uniti d'America*, Roma, Istituto Gini.

Cerase, F. P. (1974) 'Expectations and Reality: a Case Study of Return Migration from the United States to Southern Italy', *International Migration Review* 8: 245–262.

Chamberlain, M. (1997) 'Gender and the Narratives of Migration', *History Workshop Journal* 43: 87–108.

Chant, S. (ed.) (1992) *Gender and Migration in Developing Countries*, London, Belhaven.

Chant, S. and Radcliffe, S. A. (1992), 'Migration and Development: the Importance of Gender' in Chant, S. (ed.) *Gender and Migration in Developing Countries*, London, Belhaven: 1–29.

Chapin, R. C. (1909) *The Standard of Living Among Workingmen's Families in New York City*, New York, Charities Publication Committee.

Chatelain, A. (1969) 'Migrations et domesticité féminine urbaine en France, XVIIIe siècle – XX siècle', *Revue d'Histoire Économique et Sociale* 47, 4: 506–528.

Cheng, S-J. A. (1999) 'Labor Migration and International Sexual Division of Labor: a Feminist Perspective' in Kelson, G. A. and Delaet, D. (eds) *Gender and Immigration*, London, Macmillan: 38–59.

Chin, K. S., Yoon, I. and Smith, D. (1996) 'Immigrant Small Business and International Economic Linkage: a Case of the Korean Wig Business in Los Angeles, 1968–1977', *International Migration Review*, XXX, 2: 485–510.

Ciccotosto, E. and Bosworth, M. (1990) *Emma: a Translated Life*, Fremantle, Australia, Fremantle Arts Centre Press.

Cinel, D. (1991) *The National Integration of Italian Return Migration, 1870–1929*, Cambridge, Cambridge University Press.

Clarke, P. (1985) *The Governesses: Letters from the Colonies 1862–1882*, Hawthorn, Victoria, Hutchinson.

Coghlan, T. A. (1918) *Labour and Industry in Australia: From the First Settlement of 1788 to the Establishment of the Commonwealth in 1901*, vol. 3, London and Melbourne, Oxford University Press.

Cohen, M. (1993) *Workshop to Office: Two Generations of Italian Women in New York City, 1900–1950*, Ithaca, NY, Cornell University Press.

Cohen, R. (ed.) (1995) *The Cambridge Survey of World Migration*, Cambridge, Cambridge University Press.

Cohen, R. (1995) 'Rethinking "Babylon": Iconoclastic Conceptions of the Diasporic Experience', *New Community* 21, 1: 5–18.

Cohen, R. (1997) *Global Diasporas: an Introduction*, Seattle, University of Washington Press.

Cohn R. (1995) 'A Comparative Analysis of European Immigrant Streams to the United States during the Early Mass Migration', *Social Science History* 19, 1: 63–89.

Cornell, L. and Hayami, A. (1986) 'The Shūmon Aratame Chō: Japan's Population Registers', *Journal of Family History* 11, 4 (November): 311–328.

Cortés Echánove, L. (1954) *Nacimiento y crianza de personas reales en la Cortede España*, Madrid, Consejo Superior de Investigaciones Cientificas.

Corti, P. (1990) 'Donne che vanno, donne che restano. Emigrazione e comportamenti femminili', *Annali dell'Istituto 'Alcide Cervi'* 12: 213–235.

Corti, P. (1993) 'Societés sans hommes et intégrations des femmes à l'étranger: Le cas de l'Italie', *Revue européenne des migrations internationales* 9, 2: 113–128.

Corti, P. (1997) 'Circuiti migratori e consuetudini alimentari nella rappresentazione autobiografica degli emigranti piemontesi', in Capatti, A., De Bernardi, A. and Varni, A. (eds) *L'alimentazione nella storia dell'Italia contemporanea, Storia d'Italia, Annali*, Turin, Einaudi.

Crehan, K. (1992) 'Rural Households: Survival and Change' in Berstein, H., Crow, B. and Johnson, H. (eds) *Rural Livelihoods: Crises and Responses*, Oxford, Oxford University Press and The Open University: 87–110.

Curthoys, A. (1984) 'History in a Vacuum: a Review of Katrina Alford, *Production or Reproduction? An Economic History of Women in Australia, 1788–1850*, Oxford University Press, 1984', *Hecate* 10, 1.

Daly, M. E. (1987) 'Women in the Irish Workforce from Pre-industrial to Modern Times', *Saothar* 7.

Daly, M. E. (1997) *Women and Work in Ireland*, Dublin, Economic and Social History Society of Ireland.

Damousi, J. (1997) *Depraved and Disorderly: Female Convicts, Sexuality and Gender in Colonial Australia*, Melbourne, Cambridge University Press.

Daniels, C. R. (1989) 'Between Home and Factory: Homeworkers and the State' in Boris, E. and Daniels, C. R. (eds) *Homework: Historical and Contemporary Perspectives on Paid Labor at Home*, Urbana, University of Illinois Press.

Daniels, K. (1998) *Convict Women*, Sydney, Allen & Unwin.

Darbyshire, D. E. (1991) *In Time for Lunch: the Personal Diary and the Official Journal of Douglas E. Darbyshire, Surgeon-in-charge of the Young Women Emigrants Sailing in the S.S. Cornwall from England to Australia, 1898*, Fremantle, Fremantle Arts Centre Press.

Darroch, A. G. (1981) 'Migrants in the Nineteenth Century: Fugitives or Families in Motion?', *Journal of Family History* 6: 257–277.

Davis, J. (1973) *Land and Family in Pisticci*, London School of Economics Monographs on Social Anthropology, 48, New York, Humanities Press.

de los Reyes, P. (1992) *The Rural Poor: Agricultural Changes and Survival Strategies in Chile 1973–1989*, Uppsala, Uppsala Studies in Economic History.

de los Reyes, P. (1998) 'Det problematiska systerskapet', *Historisk tidskrift* 3, 98.

de los Reyes, P. (1998) 'I skärningspunkten mellan genus och etnicitet: Ett ekonomisk historiskt perspektiv på invandrarkvinnor i svenskt arbetsliv', *Arbetsmarknad and arbetsliv* 1, 98: 335–356.

de los Reyes, P. (1998) 'Mujeres Latinoamericanas a fines del siglo XX: En busca de un nuevo contrato de género?' in Medina, M. C. (ed.) *America Latina: Y las mujeres qué?* Gothenburg, HAINA: 261–289.

de Oliveira, O. (1984) 'Migración femenina, organización familiar y mercados laborales en Mexico', *Revista de Comercio Exterior* 34.

Dekker, R. and van de Pol, L. (1989), *The Tradition of Female Transvestism in Early Modern Europe*, London, Macmillan.

Del Carria, R. (1975) *Proletaria senza rivoluzione* (4 vols), Rome, Sanelli.

del Fabbro, R. (1996) *Transalpini: Italienische Arbeitswanderung nach Süddeutschland im Kaiserreich 1870–1918*, Osnabrück, Universitätsverlag Rasch.

Delaney, E. (1998) 'State, Politics and Demography: the Case of Irish Emigration, 1921–71', *Irish Political Studies* 13: 25–49.

Delaney, E. (2000) *Demography, State and Society: Irish Migration to Britain, 1921–71*, Liverpool and Kingston/Montreal, Liverpool University Press/McGill-Queen's University Press.

Delaney, E. (2001) *Irish Emigration since 1921*, Dublin, Economic and Social History Society of Ireland.

Della Peruta, F. (1985) *Società e classi popolari nell'Italia dell'Ottocento*, Syracuse, Ediprint.

Denig, C. (1995) *Utrecht van het ancien régime tot nieuwe tijd. De bewoning van de Utrechtse binnenstad in haar ruimtelijke structuur, 1793–1891*, Utrecht, Matrijs.

Devine, T. M. (1978) 'Social Stability and Agrarian Change in the Eastern Lowlands of Scotland, 1810–1840', *Social History* 3: 331–346.

Devine, T. M. (1988) *The Great Highland Famine: Hunger, Emigration and the Scottish Highlands in the Nineteenth Century*, Edinburgh, John Donald.

Devine, T. M. (1989) 'Social Responses to Agrarian "Improvement": the Highland and Lowland Clearances in Scotland' in Houston, R. A. and Whyte, I. D. (eds) *Scottish Society*, Cambridge, Cambridge University Press: 148–168.

Diner, H. R. (1983) *Erin's Daughters in America: Irish Immigrant Women in the 19th Century*, Baltimore, MD, Johns Hopkins University Press.

Dionigi, A., Dossetti, M. and Ottonelli, S. (1988) 'Società ed emigrazioni nell'alta valle Varaita in età moderna', *Bolletino Storico Bibliografico Subalpino*, 86: 117–169.

Drudy, P. J. (1985) 'Irish Population Change and Emigration since Independence' in Drudy, P.J. (ed.) *The Irish in America: Emigration, Assimilation and Impact*, Cambridge, Cambridge University Press: 63–85.

Durán, M. A. (1982) 'Una lectura económica de Fray Luis de León' in *Nuevas perspectivas sobre la mujer*, Seminario de Estudios de la Mujer de la Universidad Autónoma de Madrid, Madrid.

Duroux, R. (forthcoming) 'The Temporary Migration of Males and the Power of Females in a Stem-family Society: the Case of 19th-century Auvergne', *The Journal of Family History*.

ECLAC (1973) 'Internal Migration', *Economic Bulletin for Latin America* XVIII.

ECLAC (1994) *Centroamerica: El empleo femenino en la industria maquiladora de exportacion*, Santiago, United Nations.

ECLAC (1995) *Family and Future: a Regional Programme in Latin America and the Caribbean*, Santiago.

ECLA/FAO (1961) 'An Agricultural Policy to Expedite the Economic Development of Latin America', *Economic Bulletin for Latin America.*

Ehmer, J. (1976) 'Frauenarbeit und Arbeiterfamilie in Wien', *Geschichte und Gesellschaft* 3/4: 438–473.

Ehmer, J. (1994) *Soziale Traditionen in Zeiten des Wandels. Arbeiter und Handwerker im 19. Jahrhundert*, Frankfurt a.M. and New York, Campus.

Ehmer, J. (1996) 'Zur socialen Schichtung der Wiener Bevölkerung 1857 bis 1910? in Melinz, G. and Zimmermann, S. (eds) *Wien – Prag – Budapest. Urbanisierung, Kommundpolitik, gesellschaftliche Konflikte (1867–1918)*, Vienna, Promedia: 73–83.

Ehmer, J. (1997) 'Worlds of Mobility: Migration patterns of Viennese Artisans in the Eighteenth Century' in Crossick, G. (ed.) *The Artisan and the European Town, 1500–1900*, Aldershot and Vermont, Scolar Press: 172–199.

Elder, G. H., Jr (1978) 'Family History and the Life Course' in Hareven, T. K. (ed.) *Transitions: the Family and the Life Course in Historical Perspective*, New York, Academic Press.

Elder, G. H., Jr (1985) 'Perspectives on the Life Course' in Elder, G. H. (ed.) *Life Course Dynamics: Trajectories and Transitions*, Ithaca, NY, Cornell University Press.

Elder, G. H., Jr (1987) 'Families and Lives: some Developments in Life-course Studies', *Journal of Family History* 12: 179–199.

Elizaga, J. (1970) *Migraciones a las areas metropolitanas de America Latina*, Santiago, CELADE.

Engelsing, R. (1973) 'Das häusliche Personal in der Epoche der Industrialisierung' in Engelsing, R. (ed.) *Zur Sozialgeschichte deutscher Mittel- und Unterschichten*, Göttingen, Vandenhoeck & Ruprecht: 225–261.

Ewen, E. (1985) *Immigrant Women in the Land of Dollars: Life and Culture on the Lower East Side, 1890–1925*, New York, Monthly Review Press.

Faist, T. (1997) 'The Crucial Meso-level' in Hammar, T. *et al.* (eds) *International Migration, Immobility and Development: Multidisciplinary Perspectives*, Oxford, Berg: 187–218.

Fassmann, H. (1985) 'A Survey of Patterns of Migration in Austria, 1850–1900' in Hoerder, D. (ed.) *Labour Migrations in the Atlantic Economies: the European and North American Working Class during the Period of Industrialisation*, Westport, CT and London, Greenwood Press: 69–94.

Fawcett, J. T., Khoo, S-E. and Smith, P. C. (1984) *Women in the Cities of Asia: Migration and Urban Adaption*, Boulder, CO, Westview Press.

Fay-Sallois, F. (1980) *Les nourrices à Paris au XIXe siècle*, Paris, Payot.

Federico, G. (1997) *An Economic History of the Silk Industry, 1830–1930*, Cambridge, Cambridge University Press.

Ferenczi, I. and Willcox, W. (1929) *International Migrations, Vol. I, Statistics*, New York, National Bureau for Economic Research.

Ferrie, J. P. (1999) *Yankeys Now: Immigrants in the Antebellum United States, 1840–1860*, New York, Oxford University Press.

Fildes, V. (1988) *Wet-nursing: a History from Antiquity to the Present*, Oxford, Basil Blackwell.

Finer, M., and McGregor, O. R. (1974) 'The History of the Obligation to Maintain', Appendix 5 to Department of Health and Social Security, *Report of the Committee on One-parent Families*, London, vol. 2.

Fisher, S. (1982) 'The Pastoral Interest and Sydney's Public Health', *Historical Studies* 20: 78.

Fitzpatrick, D. (1984) *Irish Emigration, 1801–1921*, Dublin, Economic and Social History Society of Ireland.

Fitzpatrick, D. (1986) '"A Share of the Honeycomb": Education, Emigration and Irishwomen', *Continuity and Change* 1: 217–234.

Fitzpatrick, D. (1987) 'The Modernisation of the Irish Female' in O'Flanagan, P., Ferguson, P. and Whelan, K. (eds) *Rural Ireland, 1600–1900: Modernisation and Change*, Cork, Cork University Press: 162–180.

Fitzpatrick, D. (1989) 'Emigration, 1801–70' in Vaughan, W. E. (ed.) *A New History of Ireland, V: Ireland under the Union, I (1801–70)*, Oxford, Clarendon Press: 562–622.

Fitzpatrick, D. (1996) 'Emigration, 1871–1921' in Vaughan, W. E (ed.) *A New History of Ireland, VI: Ireland under the Union, II (1871–1921)*, Oxford, Clarendon Press: 606–652.

FLACSO (1995) *Mujeres Latinoamericanas en cifras. Tomo Comparativo*, Santiago.

Foerster, R. (1968, first published 1919) *The Italian Emigration of our Times*, New York, Russell & Russell.

Fox, C. (1991) *Working Australia*, North Sydney, Allen & Unwin.

Francks, P. G. (1990) 'Peasantry, Proletariat or Private Enterprise? The Japanese Farmer in the Industrialisation Process', *Japan Forum* 2, 1: 91–104.

Freeman, S. T. (1979) *The Pasiegos: Spaniards in No Man's Land*, Chicago, Chicago University Press.

Friedman-Kasaba, K. (1996) *Memories of Migration: Gender, Ethnicity, and Work in the Lives of Jewish and Italian Women in New York, 1870–1924*, Albany, State University of New York Press.

Fries, H. (1993) *Kurrimurri. Erinnerungen an die Kannenbäcker in Höhr-Grenzhausen*, Stadt Höhr-Grenzhausen.

Gabaccia, D. (1984) *From Sicily to Elizabeth Street: Housing and Social Change Among Italian Immigrants: 1880–1930*, Albany, State University of New York Press.

Gabaccia, D. (1987) 'In the Shadows of the Periphery: Italian Women in the Nineteenth Century' in Boxer, M. J. and Quataert, J. H. (eds) *Connecting Spheres: Women in the Western World, 1500 to the Present*, New York, Oxford University Press: 166–175.

Gabaccia, D. (ed.) (1989) *Immigrant Women in the United States: a Selectively Annotated Multidisciplinary Bibliography*, New York, Greenwood Press.

Gabaccia, D. (ed.) (1992) *Seeking Common Ground: Multidisciplinary Studies of Immigrant Women in the United States*, Westport, CT, Greenwood Press.

Gabaccia, D. (1994) *From the Other Side: Women, Gender and Immigrant Life in the U.S., 1820–1990*, Bloomington, Indiana University Press.

Gabaccia, D. (1996) 'Women of the Mass Migrations: from Minority to Majority, 1820–1930' in Hoerder, D. and Moch, L. P. (eds) *European Migrants: Global and Local Perspectives*, Boston, Northeastern University Press: 90–111.

Gabaccia, D. (1997) 'The "Yellow Peril" and the "Chinese of Europe": Global Perspectives on Race and Labor, 1815–1930' in Lucassen, J. and Lucassen, L. (eds) *Migration, Migration History, History: Old Paradigms and New Perspectives*, Bern, Peter Lang AG.

Gabaccia, D. (1998) 'Italian-American Cookbooks: from Oral to Print Culture', *Italian Americana* XVI, I (Winter): 15–23.

Gabaccia, D. (1998) *We Are What We Eat: Ethnic Food and the Making of Americans*, Cambridge, MA, Harvard University Press.

Gabaccia, D. (2000) *Italy's Many Diasporas*, London, UCL Press.

Galush, W. J. (1990) 'Purity and Power: Chicago Polonian Feminists, 1880–1914', *Polish American Studies* 67: 5–24.

García Lomas, A. (1977) *Los pasiegos. Estudio crítico, etnográfico y pintoresco (años 1011 a 1960*), Santander, Estudio.

Giles, W., Mussa, H. and van Esterik, P. (eds) (1996) *Development and Diaspora: Gender and the Refugee Experience*, Dundas, Ontario, Artemis Enterprises.

Gilkey, G. (1967) 'The United States and Italy: Migration and Repatriation, *Journal of Developing Areas* 2: 23–35.

Gillmor, D. A. (1985) *Economic Activities in the Republic of Ireland: a Geographical Perspective*, Dublin, Gill & Macmillan.

Glenn, E. N. (1986) *Issei, Nisei, War Bride: Three Generations of Japanese American Women in Domestic Service*, Philadelphia, PA, Temple University Press.

Gletter, M. (1972) *Die Wiener Tschechen um 1900*, Munich and Vienna, R. Oldenbourg Verlag.

Glick-Schiller, N., Basch, L. and Blanc-Szanton, C. (eds) (1992) *Towards a Transnational Perspective on Migration: Race, Class, Ethnicity, and Nationalism Reconsidered*, New York, Academic Press.

González, S. *et al.* (1995) *Mujer, migracion y maquila en la frontera norte*, El Colegio de Mexico.

Gordon, E. and Breitenbach, E. (eds) (1990) *The World is Ill Divided: Women's Work in Scotland in the Nineteenth and Twentieth Centuries*, Edinburgh, Edinburgh University Press.

Gothard, J. S. (1989) '"Radically unsound and mischievous": female migration to Tasmania, 1856–1863', *Australian Historical Studies* 23: 386–404.

Gothard, J. S. (1991) '"Pity the poor immigrant": assisted single female migration to colonial Australia' in Richards, E. (ed.), *Poor Australian Immigrants in the Nineteenth Century*, Canberra, Research School of Social Sciences.

Gothard, J. S. (2001) *Blue China: Single Female Migration to Colonial Australia*, Melbourne, Melbourne University Press.

Gould, J. D. (1980) 'Emigration, the Road Home: Return Migration from the U.S.A.', *Journal of European Economic History*, 9 (Spring): 41–112.

Gray, M. (1973) 'Scottish Emigration: the Social Impact of Agrarian Change in the Rural Lowlands, 1775–1875', *Perspectives in American History* 7: 95–174.

Green, N. L. (1997) *Ready-to-Wear; Ready-to-Work: a Century of Industry and Immigrants in Paris and New York*, Durham, NC, Duke University Press.

Guinnane, T. W. (1992) 'Age at Leaving Home in Rural Ireland', *The Journal of Economic History* 52, 3: 651–674.

Guinnane, T. W. (1997) *The Vanishing Irish: Households, Migration, and the Rural Economy in Ireland, 1850–1914*, Princeton, NJ, Princeton University Press.

Guy, J. (1990) 'Gender Oppression in Southern Africa's Precapitalist Societies' in Walker, C. (ed.) *Women and Gender in Southern Africa to 1945*, Cape Town and London, David Philip and James Currey: 33–47.

Haan, A. de (1997) 'Migration as a Family Strategy: Rural–Urban Labor Migration in India during the Twentieth Century', *The History of the Family: an International Quarterly* 2, 4: 481–505.

Hahn, S. (1989) 'Frauenwerbstätigkeit in Wiener Neustadt 1869–1880' in Verband Österreichischer Geschichtsvereine (ed.) *Bericht über den siebzehnten Österreichischen Historikertag*, Vienna.

Hahn, S. (1993) 'Fremde Frauen. Migration und Erwerbstätigkeit von Frauen am Beispiel von Wiener Neustadt', *Zeitgeschichte* 5, 6: 139–157.

Hahn, S. (forthcoming) 'Different Ways – Common Experiences: Labour Migration in Nineteenth-century Austria' in Ebeling, D. and King, S. (eds) *Community, Locality and Life-cycle: Migration Strategies in Modern and Early Modern Europe*, Oxford, Berghahn.

Hahn, S. and Flanner, K. (eds) (1994) *Die 'Wienerische Neustadt'. Handwerk, Handel und Militär in der Steinfeldstadt*, Vienna-Cologne-Weimar, Böhlau.

Hahn, S. and Sprengnagel, G. (1987) 'Nomitave Record Linkage aus Massenquellen des 19. Jahrhunderts. Aufbau und Dokumentation der Datenbank "Wiener Neustadt im Maschinenzeitalter" in Hausmann, F., Härtel, R. and Kropac, I. H. (eds) *Datennetze für die historischen Wissenschaften? Probleme und Möglichkeiten bei Standardisierung und Tranfer maschinenlesbarer Daten*, Graz, Leykam: 113–128.

Hahn, S., Maderthaner, W. and Sprengnagel, G. (1989) *Aufbruch in der Provinz. Niederösterreichische Arbeiter im 19. Jahrhundert*, Vienna, Verlag für Gesellschaftskritik.

Hamano, K., Kurosu, S. and Morimoto, S. (1998) 'Tokugawa Nōson wa "Kaikon Shakai" Ka? Nōshū Nishijō mura, Shōgai Mikonritsu no Suikei' [Were Tokugawa agricultural villages "universal marriage" societies? An estimation of the celibacy rate for Nishijō village Nobi region]', EurAsian Project on Population and Family History, *Working Paper Series* No. 6.

Hamilton, P. (1985) *'No Irish need apply': Aspects of the Employer–Employee Relationship in Australian Domestic Service 1860–1900*, London, Working Papers in Australian Studies.

Hammerton, A. J. (1979) *Emigrant Gentlewomen: Genteel Poverty and Female Migration 1830–1914*, Canberra, Australian National University Press/London, Croom Helm.

Hannan, D. (1969) 'Migration Motives and Migration Differentials among Irish Rural Youth', *Sociologia Ruralis* 9: 195–210.

Harada, S. (1928, repr. 1968) *Labour Conditions in Japan*, New York, Columbia University Press.

Hardach-Pinke, I. (1993) *Die Gouvernante: Geschichte eines Frauenberufs*, Frankfurt am Main, Campus.

Hareven, T. K. (ed.) (1978) *Transitions: the Family and the Life Course in Historical Perspective*, New York, Academic Press.

Hareven, T. K. (1987) 'Family History at the Crossroads', *Journal of Family History* 12: ix–xxiii.

Harney, R.F. (1978) 'Boarding and Belonging: Thoughts on Sojourner Institutions', *Urban History Review* 2: 8–37.

Harney, R. F. (1978) 'Men Without Women: Italian Migrants in Canada, 1885–1930' in Caroli, B. B., Harney, R. F. and Tomasi, L. F. (eds) *The Italian Immigrant Woman in North America*, Toronto, Multicultural History Society of Ontario: 79–101.

Hart, P.D.'t (1990) *Utrecht en de cholera 1832–1910*, Utrecht, Stichtse Historische Reeks 15.

Harzig, C. (1995) 'Die Analytische Kategorie "Geschlect" [Gender] in der Historischen Migrationsforschung', *Gesellschaft für Historische Migrationsforschung, Bulletin*, Nr. 1, Osnabrück, Institut für Migrationsforschung und Interkulturelle Studien (IMIS), Universität Osnabrück.

Harzig, C. (1999) 'A Migrant is a Migrant is a Migrant: Immigration Policies in Post-World-War-II Europe', *Magazine of History* 14, 1: 22–25.

Harzig, C. (1999) '"The Movement of 100 Girls". 1950s Canadian Immigration Policy and the Market for Domestic Labour', *Zeitschrift für Kanada Studien*, 19, 2: 131–146.

Harzig, C., Knothe, M. A., Matovic, M., Mageean, D. and Blaschke, M. (eds) (1997) *Peasant Maids, City Women: from the European Countryside to Urban America*, Ithaca, NY and London, Cornell University Press.

Hayami, A. (1979) 'Thank you Francisco Xavier: an Essay in the Use of Microdata for Historical Demography of Tokugawa Japan', *Keiō Economic Studies* XVI, 1–2: 65–81.

Hayami, A. (1980) 'Kyōto Machi Kata no Shūmon Aratame Chō [The temple registration records of Kyoto townsmen *Nihon*: Shijo Tachiuri Naka no Machi] in *Kenkyū Kiyō* [Research Bulletin], (Tokugawa Rinsei Shi Kenkyū Sho), pp. 502–541.

Hayami, A. (1985) 'Rural Migration and Fertility in Tokugawa Japan: the Village of Nishijō 1773–1868' in Hanley, S. and Wolf, A. (eds) *Family and Population in East Asian History*, Stanford, CA, Stanford University Press.

Hayami, A. (1992) *Kinsei Nōbi Chihō no Jinkō, Keizai, Shakai* [Population, economy and society of the early modern Nobi region], Tokyo, Sōbunsha.

Heijs, E. (1995) *Van vreemdeling tot Nederlander. De verlening van het Nederlanderschap aan vreemdelingen 1813–1992*, Amsterdam, Spinhuis.

Helstosky, C. (1998) 'The Tradition of Invention: Reading History through "La Cucina Casareccia Napoletana"', *Italian Americana* 16, 1: 7–23.

Henkes, B. (1990) 'Changing Images of German Maids during the Inter-war Period in the Netherlands: from Trusted Help to Traitor in the Nest' in Thompson, P. and Samuel, R. (eds) *The Myths We Live By*, London, Routledge: 225–239.

Henkes, B. (1993) 'German Maids in the Prosperous Guilderland and the Land of Moral Threats: Nation-images and National Identity during the Interwar-Period' in Galema, A., Henkes, B. and Te Velde, H. (eds) *Images of the Nation: Different Meanings of Dutchness, 1870–1940*, Amsterdam, Rodopi.

Henkes, B. (1998) *Heimat in Holland. Deutsche Dienstmädchen 1920–1950*, Straelen/ Niederrhein, Straelener Manuskripte Verlag.

Herr, E. (1995) 'The Census, Estimation Biases, and Female Labor-force Participation Rates in 1880 Colorado', *Historical Methods* 28: 167–182.

Herrera Heredia, A. (1967) 'Apuntes para la historia del Consulado de la Universidad de cargadores a Indias en Sevilla y en Cádiz', *Anuario de Estudios Americanos*, Sevilla, XXVII: 219–279.

Herrera Heredia, A. (1979) *Inventario de los fondos de Consulados del Archivo General de Indias*, Madrid, Ministerio de Cultura.

Hicks, N. (1978) *'This Sin and Scandal': Australia's Population Debate 1891–1911*, Canberra, Australian National University Press.

Higgs, E. (1983) 'Domestic Servants and Households in Victorian England', *Social History* 8: 201–210.

Higgs, E. (1987) 'Women, Occupations and Work in the Nineteenth-century Censuses', *History Workshop Journal* 23: 59–80.

Hilden, P. (1979) 'Family History vs. Women in History: a Critique of Tilly and Scott', *International Labor and Working Class History* 16 (Fall): 1–11.

Hill, B. (1994) 'Rural–urban Migration of Women and their Employment in Towns', *Rural History* 5, 2: 185–194.

Hill, B. (1996) *Servants: English Domestics in the Eighteenth Century*, Oxford, Clarendon.

Hillmann, F. (1996) *Jenseits der Kontinente. Migrationsstrategien von Frauen nach Europa*, Paffenweiler, Centaurus Verlag.

Hindson, D. (1987) *Pass Controls and the Urban African Proletariat in South Africa*, Johannesburg, Ravan Press.

Hoban, M. (1984) *Fifty-one Pieces of Wedding Cake: a Biography of Caroline Chisholm*, Melbourne, Polding Press.

Hobart Houghton, D. and Walton, E. M. (1952) *The Economy of a Native Reserve: Keiskammahoek Rural Survey*, vol. 11, Pietermaritzburg, Shuter & Shooter.

Hobsbawm, E. (1994) *Age of Extremes: the Short Twentieth Century 1914–1991*, London, Abacus.

Hochstadt, S. (1999) *Mobility and Modernity: Migration in Germany 1820–1989*, Ann Arbor, University of Michigan Press.

Hoerder, D. (1997) 'Segmented Macrosystems and Networking Individuals: the Balancing Functions of Migration Processes' in Lucassen, J. and Lucassen, L. (eds) *Migration, Migration History, History: Old Paradigms and New Perspectives*, Bern, Peter Lang AG: 73–84.

Hoerder, D. (1999) 'From Immigration to Migration Systems: New Concepts in Migration History', *Magazine of History* 14, 1: 5–12.

Hoerder, D. (forthcoming) *Global Migrations*, Durham, NC, Duke University Press.

Holcombe, L. (1983) *Wives and Property: Reform of the Married Women's Property Law in Nineteenth-century England*, Toronto and Buffalo, University of Toronto Press.

Holmes, C. (1988) *John Bull's Island: Immigration and British Society, 1871–1971*, London, Macmillan.

Hondagneu-Sotelo, P. (1999) 'Gender and Contemporary U.S. Immigration', special issue, *American Behavioral Scientist* 42: 4.

Horn, P. (1990) *The Rise and Fall of the Victorian Servant*, Gloucestershire, Alan Sutton (first edition 1975).

Horrell, S. and Humphries, J. (1995) 'Women's Labour Force Participation and the Transition to the Male-Breadwinner Family, 1790–1865', *Economic History Review* 48: 89–117.

Houston, R. A. (1985) 'Geographical Mobility in Scotland, 1652–1811: the Evidence of Testimonials', *Journal of Historical Geography* 11: 379–394.

Houston, R. A. (1989) 'Women in the Economy and Society of Scotland, 1500–1800' in Houston, R. A. and Whyte, I. D., *Scottish Society*, Cambridge, Cambridge University Press: 118–47.

Houston, R. A. and Whyte, I. D. (eds) (1989) *Scottish Society, 1500–1800*, Cambridge, Cambridge University Press.

Houston, R. A. and Withers, C. W. J. (1990) 'Population Mobility in Scotland and Europe, 1600–1900: a Comparative Perspective', *Annales de Demographie Historique* 31: 285–308.

Houstoun, M. F. *et al.* (1984) 'Female Predominance of Immigration to the United States since 1930: a First Look', *International Migration Review* 28: 908–963.

Hubbard, W. H. (1984) *Auf dem Weg zur Großstadt. Eine Socialgeschichte der Stadt Graz 1850–1914*, Vienna, Verlag für Geschichte und Politik.

Hufton, O. (1995) *The Prospect Before Her: a History of Women in Western Europe, Vol. 1: 1500–1800*, London, HarperCollins.

Hunter, J. (1996) 'Continuity and Change in the Japanese Labour Market: Rural Impoverishment and the Geographical Origins of Female Textile Workers' in Metzger-Court, S. and Pascha, W. (eds) *Japan's Socio-economic Evolution: Continuity and Change*, Folkestone, Kent, Japan Library.

Indra, D. (1999) *Engendering Forced Migration: Theory and Practice*, New York and Oxford, Berghahn.

Ingrao, C. (1987) *The Hessian Mercenary State*, Cambridge, Cambridge University Press.

International Migration Review (1984) 'Special Issue: Women in Migration', 18:4.

Izzard, W. (1985) 'Migrants and Mothers: Case-studies from Botswana', *Journal of Southern African Studies* 11, 2: 258–280.

Jabavu, N. (1982) *The Ochre People*, Johannesburg, Ravan Press.

Jackel, S. (ed.) (1982) *A Flannel Shirt and Liberty: British Emigrant Gentlewomen in the Canadian West, 1880–1914*, Vancouver and London, University of British Columbia Press.

Jackson, J. and Moch, L. P. (1996) 'Migration and the Social History of Modern Europe' in Hoerder, D. and Moch, L. P. (eds) *European Migrants: Global and Local Perspectives*, Boston: Northeastern University Press: 52–69.

Jackson, J. A. (1986) 'The Irish in Britain' in Drudy, P. J. (ed.) *Ireland and Britain since 1922*, Cambridge, Cambridge University Press.

Jackson, J. H. (1982) 'Migration in Duisburg, 1867–1890: Occupational and Familial Contexts', *Journal of Urban History* 8, 3: 235–270.

Jackson, P. (1984) 'Women in Nineteenth-century Irish Emigration', *International Migration Review* 18: 1004–1020.

Jansen, W. (1987) *Women Without Men*, Leiden, E. J. Brill.

John, M. and Lichtblau, A. (1990) *Schmelztiegel Wien – einst und jetzt. Geschichte und Gegenwart der Zuwanderung nach Wien*, Vienna, Böhlau.

Johnson, D. (1985) *The Interwar Economy in Ireland*, Dublin, Economic and Social History Society of Ireland.

Johnson, J. H. (1990) 'The Context of Migration: the Example of Ireland in the Nineteenth Century', *Transactions of the Institute of British Geographers* 15: 259–276.

Joksch, J. (n.d.) 'Nur ein Kindermädchen (um 1885)' in Klucsarits, R. and Kürbisch, F. G. (eds) *Arbeiterinnen kämpfen um ihr Recht*, Wuppertal, Paul Hammer Verlag.

Jongilanga, J. D. (1982) *Ukuqawuka kwembeleko*, Lovedale: Lovedale Press.

Jordon, E. (1989) 'The Exclusion of Women from Industry in Nineteenth-Century Britain', *Comparative Studies in Society and History* 31: 273–296.

Kamphoefner, W. D. (1991) 'German–American Return Migration' in Vecoli, R. J. and Sinke, S. (eds) *A Century of European Migrations, 1830–1930*, Urbana, University of Illinois Press.

Kamphoefner, W. D., Helbich, W. and Sommer, U. (eds) (1991) *News from the Land of Freedom: German Immigrants Write Home*, Ithaca, NY, Cornell University Press.

Kelson, G. A. and Delaet, D. (eds) (1999) *Gender and Immigration*, London, Macmillan.

Kennedy, K. A., Giblin, T. and McHugh, D. (1988) *The Economic Development of Ireland in the Twentieth Century*, London, Routledge.

Kennedy, L. (1989) *The Modern Industrialisation of Ireland, 1940–1988*, Dublin, Economic and Social History Society of Ireland.

Kennedy, L. and Clarkson, L. A. (1993) 'Birth, Death and Exile: Irish Population History, 1700–1921' in Graham, B. J. and Proudfoot, L. J. (eds) *An Historical Geography of Ireland*, London, Academic Press.

Kertzer, D. I. and Saller, R. P. (eds) (1991) *The Family in Italy: from Antiquity to the Present*, New Haven, CT, Yale University Press.

Kessner, T. and Boyd Caroli, B. (1978) 'New Immigrant Women at Work: Italians and Jews in New York City, 1880–1905', *Journal of Ethnic Studies* 5: 19–32.

Khoo, S-E., Smith, P. C. and Fawcett, J. T. (1984) 'Migration of Women to Cities: the Asian Situation in Comparative Perspective', *International Migration Review* 18: 1247–1263.

Kiddle, M. (1950) *Caroline Chisholm*, Melbourne, Melbourne University Press.

King, E. (1993) *The Hidden History of Glasgow's Women: the New Factor*, Edinburgh, Mainstream Publishing.

King, R. and O'Connor, H. (1996) 'Migration and Gender: Irish Women in Leicester', *Geography* 81: 316–317.

King, S. (1997) 'Migrants on the Margin? Mobility, Integration and Occupations in the West Riding, 1650–1820', *Journal of Historical Geography* 23: 284–303.

Kingston, B. (1974) 'Poor Mary Ann: Domestic Service as a Career for Girls in Australia in the Late Nineteenth Century', *Refractory Girl* 7: 4–9.

Kingston, B. (1975) *My Wife, My Daughter and Poor Mary Ann*, Melbourne, Nelson.

Kleyn, J. de (1965) *Volksaardewerk in Nederland 1600–1900*, Zeist, De Tijdstroom: 36–37.

Knapp, U. (1984) *Frauenarbeit in Deutschland*, Munich, Minerva.

Kofman, E. (1999) 'Female Birds of Passage – a Decade Later: Gender and Immigration in the European Union', *International Migration Review* 33: 269–299.

Kopinak, K. (1995) 'Gender as a Vehicle for the Subordination of Women Maquiladora Workers in Mexico', *Latin American Perspectives* 84, 22, 1: 30–48.

Kraus, K. (1987) 'Der Meldezettel' in Kraus, K. *Sittlichkeit und Kriminalität*, Frankfurt am Main, Suhrkamp.

Kuhn, A. and Wolpe, A. (1978) *Feminism and Materialism: Women and Modes of Production*, London, Routledge & Kegan Paul.

Kukowski, M. (1995) *Pauperismus in Kurhessen: Ein Beitrag zur Enstehung und Entwicklung der Massenarmut in Deutschland 1815–1855*, Darmstadt and Marburg: Hessischen Historischen Kommission Darmstadt und der historischen Kommission für Hessen.

Landes, D. (1993) 'The Round of Horological Migrations' in *Le migrazioni in Europa, secc. XIII-XVIII*, Istituto internazionale di Storia economica F. Datini, 25: 561–566.

LaSorte, M. (1985) *La Merica: Images of Italian Greenhorn Experience*, Philadelphia, PA, Temple University Press.

Lauby, T. and Stark, O. (1988) 'Individual Migration as a Family Strategy: Young Women in the Philippines', *Population Studies* 42: 473–486.

Lawson, V.A. (1998) 'Hierarchical Households and Gendered Migration in Latin America: Feminist Extensions to Migration Research', *Progress in Human Geography* 22: 39–53.

Lean Lin, L. (1995) 'The Status of Women and International Migration' in United Nations, *International Migration Policies and the Status of Female Migrants*, New York, United Nations.

Leddy, M. J. (1997) *At the Border Called Hope: Where Refugees are Neighbours*, Toronto, HarperCollins.

Lee, E. (1999) 'Immigrants and Immigration Law: a State of the Field Assessment', *Journal of American Ethnic History* 18, 4: 85–114.

Leneman, L. (1997) '"A Tyrant and Tormentor": Violence against Wives in Eighteenth- and Early Nineteenth-Century Scotland', *Continuity and Change* 12: 31–54.

León, F. L. de (1980) [1570] *La perfecta casada*, Madrid, Espasa-Calpe.

Light, I. and Karageorgis, S. (1994) 'The Ethnic Economy' in Smelser, N. J. and Swedberg, R. (eds) *The Handbook of Economic Sociology*, Princeton, NJ, Princeton University Press.

Lintelman, J. K. (1995) 'Making Service Serve Themselves: Immigrant Women and Domestic Service in North America, 1850–1920' in Hoerder, D. and Nagler, J. (eds) *People in Transit: German Migrations in Comparative Perspective 1820–1930*, Cambridge, Cambridge University Press.

List, E. (1993) *Die Präsenz des Anderen. Theorie und Geschlechterpolitik*, Frankfurt am Main, Suhrkamp.

Luby, J. and Stark, O. (1988) 'Individual Migration as a Family Strategy: Young Women in the Philippines', *Population Studies* 42: 473–486.

Lucassen, J. (1994) 'The Netherlands, the Dutch, and Long Distance Migration in the Late Sixteenth to Early Nineteenth Centuries' in Kloek, E., Teeuwen, N. and Huisman, M. (eds) *Women of the Golden Age: an International Debate on Women in Seventeenth-Century Holland, England and Italy*, Hilversum, Verloren.

Lucassen, J. and Lucassen, L. (eds) (1997) *Migration, Migration History, History: Old Paradigms and New Perspectives*, Bern, Peter Lang AG.

Lucassen, J. and Penninx, R. (1994) *Nieuwkomers, nakomelingen, Nederlanders. Immigranten in Nederland 1550–1993*, Amsterdam, Spinhuis: 99–111.

Lucassen, L. (1990) *En men noemde hen zigeuners . . . De geschiedenis van Kaldarasch, Ursari, Lowara en Sinti in Nederland (1750–1944)*, Amsterdam, IISG.

Lynn, R. (1968) *The Irish Brain Drain*, Dublin, Economic and Social Research Institute.

McAllister, P. (1980) 'Work, Homestead and the Shades: the Ritual Interpretation of Labour Migration among the Gcaleka' in Mayer, P. (ed.) *Black Villagers in Industrial Society*, Cape Town, Oxford University Press.

McBride, T. M. (1976) *The Domestic Revolution: the Modernisation of Household Service in England and France 1820–1920*, London, Holmes & Meier.

McBride, T. (1977) 'The Modernization of Women's Work', *Journal of Modern History* 49: 231–245.

McCants, A. (1992) 'Internal Migration in Friesland, 1750–1805', *Journal of Interdisciplinary History* 22, 3: 387–409.

McConville, C. (1988) 'Peopling the Place Again' in Burgmann, V. and Lee, J. (eds) *A Most Valuable Acquisition: a People's History of Australia Since 1788,* Melbourne, McPhee Gribble/Penguin.

Macdonald, C. (1983) 'Ellen Silk and her Sisters: Female Emigration to the New World' in London Feminist History Group, *The Sexual Dynamics of History: Men's Power, Women's Resistance*, London and Leichhardt, New South Wales, Pluto Press.

Macdonald, C. (1990) *A Woman of Good Character: Single Women as Immigrant Settlers in Nineteenth-century New Zealand*, Wellington, Allen & Unwin.

McDonogh, W. (1986) *Good Families of Barcelona: a Social History of Power in the Industrial Era*, Princeton, NJ, Princeton University Press.

Macry, P. (1997) 'Rethinking a Stereotype: Territorial Differences and Family Models in the Modernization of Italy', *Journal of Modern Italian Studies* 2, 2: 188–214.

Madgwick, R. B. (1937) *Immigration into Eastern Australia 1788–1851*, Sydney, Sydney University Press.

Mager, A. (1999) *Gender and the Making of a South African Bantustan: a Social History of the Ciskei, 1945–1959*, Portsmouth, London, Cape Town: Heinemann, James Currey, David Philip.

Mager, A. and Minkley, G. (1993) 'Reaping the Whirlwind: the East London Riots of 1952' in Bonner, P., Delius, P. and Posel, D. (eds) *Apartheid's Genesis: 1935–1962*, Johannesburg, Ravan Press: 229–251.

Manona, C.W. (1980) 'Marriage, Family Life and Migrancy in a Ciskei Village' in Mayer, P. (ed.) *Black Villagers in Industrial Society*, Cape Town, Oxford University Press.

Manso, J. (1979) [1798] *Estado de las Fábricas, Comercio, Industria y Agricultura en las Montañas de Santander,* Martínez Vara, T. (ed.), Santander, Librería Estudio.

Mantecón, T. (1997) *La muerte de Antonia Isabel Sánchez. Tiranía y escándalo en una sociedad rural del Norte español en el Antiguo Régimen,* Alcalá de Henares, Centro de Estudios Cervantinos.

Marks, S. and Richardson, P. (1984) *International Labour Migration: Historical Perspectives*, London, Maurice, Temple & Smith.

Martin, S. F. (1995) *Refugee Women*, London, Zed Books.

Matovic, M. (1997) 'Maids in Motion: Swedish Women in Dalsland' in Harzig, C. (ed.) *Peasant Maids–City Women: from the European Countryside to Urban America,* Ithaca, NY, Cornell University Press.

Mayer, P. (1978) 'Migrant Labour: Some Perspectives from Anthropology', vol. 3, 'Wives of Migrant Workers', Rhodes University, Grahamstown, Institute of Social and Economic Research.

Mayer, P. (1980) (ed.) *Black Villagers in Industrial Society*, Cape Town, Oxford University Press.

Mayer, P. and Mayer, I. (1972) 'Report on the Self Organisation by Youth among the Xhosa-speaking Peoples of the Ciskei and Transkei', Part 2, Rhodes University, Grahamstown, Institute of Social and Economic Research.

Mayer, P. and Mayer, I. (1974) *Townsmen or Tribesmen*, Cape Town, Oxford University Press.

Medel, J. *et al.* (1989) *Las temporeras y su vision del trabajo*, Santiago, CEDEM.

Meijide Pardo, A. (1960) 'La emigración gallega intrapeninsular en el siglo XVIII', *Estudios de Historia Social de España*, Madrid, Consejo Superior de Investigaciones Científicas, vol. IV, 2: 463–606.

Meillassoux, C. (1981) *Maidens, Meal, and Money: Capitalism and the Domestic Economy*, Cambridge, Cambridge University Press.

Meldrum, T. (2000) *Domestic Service and Gender 1660–1750: Life and Work in the London Household*, London, Pearson.

Miellet, R. (1993) *Honderd jaar grootwinkelbedrijf in Nederland*, Zwolle, Catena.

Miller, K. A. (1985) *Emigrants and Exiles: Ireland and the Irish Exodus to North America*, Oxford, Oxford University Press.

Miller, K. A. with Doyle, D. N. and Kelleher, P. (1995) '"For love and liberty": Irish Women, Migration and Domesticity in Ireland and America, 1815–1920' in O'Sullivan, P. (ed.) *Irish Women and Irish Migration*, London, Leicester University Press: 41–61.

Milton, N. (1987) 'Essential Servants: Immigrant Domestics on the Canadian Prairies, 1885–1930' in Armitage, S. and Jameson, E. (eds) *The Women's West*, Norman and London, University of Oklahoma Press.

Mitchison, R. and Leneman, L. (1989) *Sexuality and Social Control: Scotland 1660–1780*, Oxford, Blackwell.

Mitterauer, M. (1992) 'Gesindedienst und Jugendphase im europäischen Vergleich' in M. Mitterauer, *Familie und Arbeitsteilung. Historischvergleichende Studien*, Vienna, Cologne, Weimar, Böhlau.

Mizumoto, K. (1997) *Kinsei no Goson Jiji to Yukusei* [Self government and administration in early modern villages], Tokyo, Tokyo Daigaku Shuppankai.

Moch, L. P. (1992) *Moving Europeans: Migration in Western Europe since 1650*, Bloomington: Indiana University Press.

Model, S. (1989) 'The Effects of Ethnicity in the Workplace on Blacks, Italians, and Jews in New York, 1910', *Journal of Urban History* 16: 29–51.

Modell, J. and Hareven, T. K. (1973) 'Urbanization and the Malleable Household: an Examination of Boarding and Lodging in American Families', *Journal of Marriage and the Family* 35: 467–479.

Möker, U. (1977) *Nordhessen im Zeitalter der Industriellen Revolution*, Cologne, Böhlau Verlag.

Molony, B. (1991) 'Activism Among Women in the Taishō Cotton Textile Industry' in Bernstein, G.L. (ed.) *Recreating Japanese Women, 1600–1945*, Berkeley, University of California Press.

Momsen, J. H. (1992) 'Gender Selectivity in Caribbean Migration' in Chant, S. (ed.) *Gender and Migration in Developing Countries*, London, Belhaven Press.

Momsen, J. H. (ed.) (1999) *Gender, Migration and Domestic Service*, London, Routledge.

Moore, H. and Vaughan, M. (1994) *Cutting Down Trees*, Portsmouth and London, Heinemann and James Currey.

Moore, H. L. (1988) *Feminism and Anthropology*, Oxford, Polity Press.

More, L. B. (1907) *Wage Earners' Budgets*, Greenwich House Series of Social Studies 1, New York, Henry Holt.

Mori, Y. (1984) 'Seishigyō' [The paper industry]' in Kodama, K. (ed.) *Sangyoshi II* [Industrial history], Tokyo, Yamakawa Shuppansha: 346–364.

Morishita, T. (1995) *Nihon Kinsei Koyō Rōdōshi no Kenkyū* [research on the history of hired labour in early modern Japan], Tokyo, Tōkyō Daigaku Shuppankai.

Morokvasic, M. (1983) 'Women in Migration: Beyond the Reductionist Outlook' in Phizacklea, A. (ed.) *One Way Ticket: Migration and Female Labour*, London and Melbourne, Routledge & Kegan Paul.

Morokvasic, M. (1984) 'Birds of Passage are also Women . . .', *International Migration Review* XVIII: 886–907.

Moser, P. (1993) 'Rural Economy and Female Emigration in [sic] the West of Ireland, 1936–56', *UCG Women's Studies Review* 2.

Moya, J. C. (1998) *Cousins and Strangers: Spanish Immigrants in Buenos Aires, 1850–1930*, Berkeley, University of California Press.

Mullan, B. P. (1989) 'The Impact of Social Networks on the Occupational Status of Migrants', *International Migrations* 27, 1: 69–86.

Müller, H. (1981) *Dienstbare Geister. Leben und Alltagswelt städtischer Dienstboten*, Berlin, Dietrich Reimer Verlag.

Müller, W., Willms, A. and Handl, J. (1983) *Strukturwandel der Frauenarbeit 1880–1980*, Frankfurt am Main and New York, Campus.

Muraskin, W. (1974) 'The Moral Basis of a Backward Sociologist: Edward Banfield, the Italians and the Italian-Americans', *American Journal of Sociology* 79: 1484–1496.

Murray, N. (1978) *The Scottish Hand Loom Weavers, 1790–1850: a Social History*, Edinburgh, John Donald.

Nagata, M. L. (1997) 'Who Are You? Servant Origins and Social Mobility in Early Modern Japan', EurAsian Project on Population and Family History, *Conference Paper Series* No. 18.

Nagata, M. L. (1998) 'Name Changing Patterns and the Stem Family in Early Modern Japan: Shimomoriya' in Fauve-Chamoux, A. and Ochiai, E. (eds) *House and the Stem Family in EurAsian Perspective*, Proceedings of the C18 Session Twelfth International Economic History Congress: 291–319.

Nagata, M. L. (1999) 'Balancing Family Strategies with Individual Choice: Name Changing in Early Modern Japan', *Japan Review* 11: 145–166.

Nagata, M. L., Kurosu, S. and Hayami, A. (1998) 'Niita and Shimomoriya of the Nihonmatsu Domain in the Northeastern Region of Tokugawa Japan' EurAsian Project on Population and Family History, *Working Paper Series* No. 20.

Nakamura, M. (1976) *Rōdōsha to Nōmin*, vol. 29 of *Nihon no Rekishi*, Tokyo, Shōgakkan.

Nakamura, M. (ed.) (1994) *Technology Change and Female Labour in Japan*, Tokyo, United Nations University Press.

Nakamura, M. and Molteni, C. (1994) 'Silk-reeling Technology and Female Labour' in Nakamura, M. (ed.) *Technology Change and Female Labour in Japan*, Tokyo, United Nations University Press: 25–58.

Nakamura, T. (1981) *Economic Growth in Prewar Japan*, New Haven, CT, Yale University Press.

Narimatsu, S. (1985) *Kinsei Tōhoku Nōson no Hitobito: Ōshu Asaka-gun Shimomoriyamura* [the people of an early modern northeastern agricultural village: Shimomoriya village, Asaka district, Mutsu province], Kyoto, Mineruva Shobō.

Narimatsu, S. (1992) *Edo Jidai no Tōhoku Nōson: Nihonmatsu Han Niita mura* [a north-eastern agricultural village in the Edo period: Niita village in Nihonmatsu domain], Tokyo: Dōbunkan.

Nishikawa, S. *et al.* (eds) (1996) *Nihon Keizai no 200 Nen*, Tokyo, Nihon Hyōronsha.

Nolan, J. (1989) *Ourselves Alone: Women's Emigration from Ireland 1885–1920*, Lexington, University of Kentucky Press.

Nugent, W. (1989) 'Frontiers and Empires in the Late Nineteenth Century', *Western Historical Quarterly* 20: 393–408.

Nugent, W. (1996) 'Demographic Aspects of European Migration Worldwide' in Hoerder, D. and Moch, P. L. (eds) *European Migrants: Global and Local Perspectives*, Boston, Northeastern University Press.

Ó Gráda, C. and Walsh, B. M. (1994) 'The Economic Effects of Emigration: Ireland' in Asch, B. J. (ed.) *Emigration and its Effects on the Sending Country*, Santa Monica, Rand: 97–152.

Ochiai, E. (1998) 'Two Types of Stem Household System in Japan: the *ie* in global perspective' in Fauve-Chamoux, A. and Ochai, E. (eds) *House and the Stem Family in EurAsian Perspective, Proceedings of the C18 Session Twelfth International Economic History Congress*: 215–224.

Odencrantz, L. C. (1919) *Italian Women in Industry: a Study of Conditions in New York City*, New York, Russell Sage Foundation.

O'Farrell, P. (1986) *The Irish in Australia*, Kensington NSW, New South Wales University Press.

Okabe, B. *et al.* (1981) *Kōriyama-shi Shi*, vol. 2 [Koriyama city history] Koriyama City.

Ōkōchi, K. and Matsuo, H. (1976) *Nihon Rōdō Kumiai Monogatari – Shōwa*, Tokyo, Chikuma Shobō.

Ooms, H. (1996) *Tokugawa Village Practice*, Los Angeles, University of California Press.

Oris, M. (1996) 'Fertility and Migration in the Heart of the Industrial Revolution', *The History of the Family: an International Quarterly* 1, 2: 169–182.

Orth, K. (1993) *'Nur weiblicher Besuch'. Dienstbotinnen in Berlin 1890–1914*, Frankfurt am Main and New York, Campus.

Ortoleva, P. (1992) 'La tradizione e l'abbondanza: Riflessioni sulla cucina degli italiani d'America', *Altreitalie* 7: 31–52.

Oto, O. (1996) *Kinsei Nomin to Ie-Mura-Kokka* [Early modern peasants and family, village, nation], Tokyo, Yoshikawa Kobunkan.

Ottmüller, U. (1978) *Die Dienstbotenfrage. Zur Sozialgeschichte der doppelten Ausnutzung von Dienstmädchen im deutschen Kaiserreich*, Münster, Verlag Frauenpolitik.

Oxley, D. (1996) *Convict Maids: the Forced Migration of Women to Australia*, Cambridge, Cambridge University Press.

Papa, A. (1969) 'Guerra e terra', *Studi storici* 10: 3–45.

Paul, K. (1996) 'A Case of Mistaken Identity: the Irish in Postwar Britain', *International Labour and Working-class History* 49: 116–142.

Pedraza, S. (1991) 'Women and Migration: the Social Consequences of Gender', *Annual Review of Sociology* 17: 302–325.

Pedraza-Bailey, S. (1990) 'Immigration Research: a Conceptual Map', *Social Science History* 14, 1: 43–67.

Peires, J. (1989) *The Dead Will Arise*, Johannesburg, Ravan Press.

Penninx, R. (1994) *Raster en Mozaiek. Uitgangspunten voor onderzoek naar internationale migratie, etnische processen en sociale ongelijkheid*, Amsterdam, UvA.

Perco, D. (ed.) (1984) *Balie di latte. Una forma peculiare di emigrazione temporanea*, Milan, Feltre.

Peteni, R. L. (1979) *Hill of Fools: a Novel of the Ciskei*, Cape Town, David Philip.

Petit, J. J. M. (1930) *De burgerlijke rechtstoestand der gehuwde vrouw*, Zwolle, Tjeenk Willink.

Phizacklea, A. (ed.) (1983) *One Way Ticket: Migration and Female Labour*, London and Melbourne, Routledge & Kegan Paul.

Pierenkemper, T. (1988) '"Dienstbotenfrage" und Dienstmädchenmarkt am Ende des 19. Jahrhunderts', *Archiv für Sozialgeschichte* 28: 173–201.

Piore, M. J. (1979) *Birds of Passage: Migrants and Industrial Societies*, Cambridge, Cambridge University Press.

Pitrè, G. (1978, orig. published 1870–1913) *Proverbi siciliani*, Palermo, 'Il Vespro'.

Plenge, J. (1898) *Westerwälder Hausierer und Landgänger*, Leipzig, Dunder & Humblot.

Pooley, C. and D'Cruze, S. (1994) 'Migration and Urbanization in North-West England circa 1760–1830', *Social History* 19, 3: 339–358.

Pooley, C. and Turnbull, J. (1998) *Migration and Mobility in Britain Since the 18th Century*, London, UCL Press.

Pooley, C. G. and Whyte, I. D. (eds) (1991) *Migrants, Emigrants and Immigrants: a Social History of Migration*, London, Routledge.

Portes, A. (1994) 'The Informal Economy and its Paradoxes' in Smelser, N. J. and Swedberg, R. (eds) *The Handbook of Economic Sociology*, Princeton, NJ, Princeton University Press.

Potts, L. (1990) *The World Labour Market: a History of Migration*, London, Zed Books.

Poynton, C. (1990) 'The Privileging of Representation' in Threadgold, T. and Cranny Francis, A. (eds) *Feminine, Masculine and Representation*, Sydney, Allen & Unwin: 231–255.

Prebich, R. (1962) 'The Economic Development of Latin America and its Principal Problems', *Economic Bulletin for Latin America* 7: 1–22.

Prodolliet, S. (1999) 'Ohne Migrantinnen geht wirtschaftlich nichts', *Wiederspruch* 19, 37: 95–106.

Ramella, F. (1984) *Terra e telai: sistemi di parentela e manifattura nel Biellese dell'Ottocento*, Turin, Einaudi.

Ramirez, V. (1995) *Cambios en la familia y en los roles de la mujer*, CELADE.

Rath, J. (1991) *Minorisering: de sociale constructie van 'etnische minderheden*, Utrecht, SUA.

Raum, O. F. and de Jager, E. J. (1972) *Transition and Change in a Rural Community*, Fort Hare, South Africa, Fort Hare University Press.

Ravenstein, E. G. (1885) 'The Laws of Migration', *Journal of the Statistical Society* 48: 167–235 (Part I) and (1889) 52: 241–305 (Part II).

Reader, D. H. (1961) *The Black Man's Portion: History, Demography and Living Conditions of East London*, Pietermaritzburg, Oxford University Press.

Reeder, L. (forthcoming) 'When the Men Left Sutera: Sicilian Women and Mass Migration 1880–1920', in Gabaccia, D. and Iacovetta, F. (eds) *Foreign, Female and Fighting Back.*

Reith, R. (1994) 'Arbeitsmigratin und Gruppenkultur deutscher Handwerksgesellen im 18. und frühen 19. Jahrhundert' in Haupt, H-G. and Marschalck, P. (eds) *Städtische Bevölkerungsentwicklung in Deutschland im 19. Jahrhundert*, St. Katharinen, Scripta Mercaturae Verlag: 1–26.

Richards, E. (1989) 'Annals of the Australian Immigrant' in Richards, E., Reid, R. and Fitzpatrick, D. (eds) *Visible Immigrants: Neglected Sources for the History of Australian Immigration*, Canberra, Research School of Social Sciences.

Rigler, E. (1976) *Frauenleitbild und Frauenarbeit in Österreich vom ausgehenden 19. Jahrhundert bis zum Zweiten Weltkrieg*, Vienna, Verlag für Geschichte und Politik.

Rodenburg, J. (1997) *In the Shadow of Migration: Rural Women and their Households in North Tapanuli, Indonesia*, Leiden, KITLV Press.

Rommes, R. (1998) *Oost, west, Utrecht best? Driehonderd jaar migratie en migranten in de stad Utrecht (begin 16e – begin 19e eeuw)*, Utrecht, Amsterdamse Historische Reeks.

Rosoli, G. (ed.) (1978) *Un secolo di emigrazione italiana, 1876–1976*, Rome, Centro Studi Emigrazione.

Ross, L. (1912) *Weibliche Dienstboten und Dienstbotenhaltung in England*, Tübingen, Verlag J. C. B. Mohr.

Rowbotham, S. and Mitter, S. (1994) *Dignity and Daily Bread: New Forms of Economic Organising among Poor Women in the Third World and in the First*, London, Routledge.

Rowe, C. J. (1890) 'Housekeeping Troubles in the Australian Colonies', *Westminster Review*, 134: 509–514.

Rudd, J. 'The Emigration of Irish Women', *Social Studies* 9: 3–11.

Rudd, J. (1988) 'Invisible Exports: the Emigration of Irish Women this Century', *Women's Studies International Forum* 11: 307–311.

Saitō, O. (1985) *Purōto Kogyōka no Jidai* [The age of protoindustrialisation], Tokyo, Nihon Hyōronsha.

Saitō, O. (1986) 'The Rural Economy: Commercial Agriculture, By-employment and Wage Work' in Jansen, M. B. and Rozman, G. (eds) *Japan in Transition: from Tokugawa to Meiji*, Princeton, NJ, Princeton University Press.

Sanger Evans, M. (1891) 'Domestic Servants in Australia: a Rejoinder', *Westminster Review*, 136: 46–53.

Sarasúa, C. (1988) 'Understanding Intra-family Inequalities: the Montes de Pas, Spain, 1700–1900', *The History of the Family* 3, 2: 173–197.

Sarasúa, C. (1994) *Criados, nodrizas y amos. El servicio doméstico en la formación del mercado de trabajo, Madrid, 1758–1868*, Madrid, Siglo XXI.

Sarti, R. (1997) 'Notes on the Feminization of Domestic Service: Bologna as a Case Study (18th-19th Centuries)', *Acta demographica* XIII: 125–163.

Schenk-Sandbergen, L. (ed.) (1995) *Women and Seasonal Labour Migration*, New Delhi, Sage.

Schiller, N. G., Basch, L. and Blanc-Szanton, C. (1992) 'Towards a Definition of Transnationalism', *Annals of the New York Academy of Science*, vol. 645, July 6, *Towards a Transnational Perspective on Migration*, 645: ix–xiv, 1–24.

Schneider, A. (1992) 'L'etnicità, il cambiamento dei paradigmi e le variazioni nel consumo di cibi tra gli italiani a Buenos Aires', *Altreitalie* 7 (January–June): 71–83.

Schöttes, M. and Schuckar, M. (eds) (1994) *Frauen auf der Flucht*, 2 vols, Berlin, Edition Parabolis.

Schrover, M. (1996) 'Omlopers in Keulse potten en pottentrienen uit het Westerwald' in 't Hart, M., Lucassen, J. and Schmal, H. (eds) *Nieuwe Nederlanders. Vestiging van migranten door de eeuwen heen*, Amsterdam, IISG/SISWO.

Schrover, M. (1998) 'Gescheiden werelden in een stad. Duits ondernemerschap in Utrecht in de negentiende eeuw' in Rath, J. and Kloosterman. R. (eds) *Rijp en Groen, Het zelfstandig ondernemerschap van immigranten in Nederland,* Amsterdam, Spinhuis: 39–60.

Schrover, M. (1998) 'Groepsvorming onder Duitse aardewerkhandelaren in 19e-eeuws Holland en Utrecht', *Historisch tijdschrift Holland* 2: 94–112.

Schulz, M. (ed.) (1992) *Fremde Frauen. Von der Gastarbeiterin zur Bürgerin*, Frankfurt am Main, Verlag für Interkulturelle Kommunikation.

Schurer, K .(1991) 'The Role of the Family in the Process of Migration' in Pooley, C. G. and Whyte, D. (eds) *Migrants, Emigrants and Immigrants: a Social History of Migration*, London, Routledge.

Schwarz, L. (1999) 'English Servants and their Employers during the Eighteenth and Nineteenth Centuries', *Economic History Review* 52, 2: 236–256.

Seller, M. S. (1986) 'The Uprising of the Twenty Thousand: Sex, Class, and Ethnicity in the Shortwaist Makers' Strike of 1909' in Hoerder, D. (ed.) *'Struggle a Hard Battle': Essays on Working-class Immigrants*, DeKalb, IL, Northern Illinois University Press.

Sen, S. (1998) 'Gendered Exclusion: Domesticity and Dependence in Bengal' in Janssens, A. (ed.) *The Rise and Decline of the Male Breadwinner Family?*, *International Review of Social History* Supplement, Cambridge, Cambridge University Press: 65–86.

Serle, G. (1963) *The Golden Age: a History of the Colony of Victoria, 1851–1861*, Melbourne, Melbourne University Press.

Seymour, S. M. (1960) *Native Law in South Africa*, Cape Town and Johannesburg, Juta.

Sharpe, P. (1994) 'Female Emigration Schemes to Australia in the 1830s', *Essex Journal* (Spring).

Sharpe, P. (1996) *Adapting to Capitalism: Working Women in the English Economy, 1700–1850*, London, Macmillan.

Shōji, K. *et al.* (1982) *Nihonmatsu-shi Shi* [Nihonmatsu city history], Nihonmatsu City.

Silverman, S. F. (1968) 'Agricultural Organization, Social Structure and Values in Italy: Amoral Familism Reconsidered', *American Anthropologist* 70: 1–20.

Simon, R. J. and Brettell, C. B. (eds) (1986) *International Migration: the Female Experience*, Totowa, NJ, Rowman & Allanheld.

Simons, H. J. (1968) *African Women: their Legal Status in South Africa*, London, C. Hurst.

Simonton, D. (1998) *A History of European Women's Work 1700 to the Present*, London and New York, Routledge.

Sinclair, W. A. (1981) 'Women at Work in Melbourne and Adelaide since 1871', *Economic Record* 57, 159: 344–353.

Sinclair, W. A. (1982) 'Women and Economic Change in Melbourne 1871–1921', *Historical Studies* 20, 79: 278–291.

Sinke, S. (1999) 'Migration for Labor, Migration for Love: Marriage and Family Formation', *Magazine of History* 14, 1:17–21.

Sinke, S. with Gross, S. (1992) 'The International Marriage Market and the Sphere of Social Reproduction: a German Case Study' in Gabaccia, D. (ed.) *Seeking Common Ground: Multidisciplinary Studies of Immigrant Women in the United States*, Westport, CT: Greenwood Press.

Smethurst, R. J. (1986) *Agricultural Development and Tenancy Disputes in Japan, 1870–1940*, Princeton, NJ, Princeton University Press.

Smith, B. (1988), *A Cargo of Women: Susannah Watson and the Convicts of the Princess Royal*, Kensington NSW, New South Wales University Press.

Smith, J., Wallerstein, I. and Evers, H. (eds) (1984) *Households and the World Economy*, Beverly Hills: Sage Publications.

Smith, J. E. (1985) *Family Connections: a History of Italian and Jewish Immigrant Lives in Providence, Rhode Island, 1900–1940*, Albany, State University of New York Press.

Smout, T. C. (1976) 'Aspects of Sexual Behaviour in Nineteenth-Century Scotland' in Maclaren, A. A. (ed.) *Social Class in Scotland: Past and Present*, Edinburgh, John Donald: 55–85.

Smyth, W. J. (1992) 'Irish Emigration, 1700–1920' in Emmer, P. C. and Mörner, M. (eds) *European Expansion and Migration*, Oxford, Berg: 49–78.

Sogner, S. (1993) 'Young in Europe around 1700: Norwegian Sailors and Servant Girls Seeking Employment in Amsterdam' in Bardet, J.-P., Lebrun, F. and Le Mée,

R. (eds) *Mesurer et comprendre. Mélanges offert à Jacques Dupaquier*, Paris, Presses Universitaires de France.

Soldevilla Oria, C. (1996) *La emigración de Cantabria a América. Hombres, mercaderías y capitales*, Santander, Estudio.

Somogyi, S. (1973) 'L'alimentazione nell'Italia unita', vol. V: *I Documenti* in Romano, R. and Vivanti, C. (eds) *Storia d'Italia*, Turin, Einaudi: 841–887.

Spiegel, A. (1980) 'Rural Differentiation and the Diffusion of Migrant Labour Remittance in Lesotho' in Mayer, P. (ed.) *Black Villagers in Industrial Society*, Cape Town, Oxford University Press: 109–169.

Stanley, L. (ed.) (1984) *The Diaries of Hannah Cullwick, Victorian Maidservant*, London, Virago Press.

Struck, W. H. (1966) *Die Auswanderung aus dem Herzogtum Nassau (1806–1866)*, Wiesbaden, Steiner.

Sugihara, K. (1989) 'Japan's Industrial Recovery, 1931–6' in Brown, I. (ed.) *The Economies of Africa and Asia in the Inter-war Depression*, London, Routledge.

Sumiya, M. (1976) *Nihon Chinrōdō no Shiteki Kenkyū*, Tokyo, Ochanomizu Shobō.

Swaisland, C. (1993) 'Female Migration and Social Mobility: British Female Domestic Servants to South Africa, 1860–1914' in Buijs, G. (ed.) *Migrant Women: Crossing Boundaries and Changing Identities*, Oxford, Berg.

Swaisland, C. (1993) *Servants and Gentlewomen to the Golden Land: the Emigration of Single Women from Britain to Southern Africa, 1820–1939*, Oxford and Pietermaritzburg, Berg/University of Natal Press.

Symonds, D. A. (1997) *Weep Not for Me: Women, Ballads and Infanticide in Early Modern Scotland*, University Park, Pennsylvania State University Press.

Szasz, I. (1996) 'Women and Migrants: Inequalities in the Labour Market of Santiago, Chile', *Cepal Review* 56: 185–195.

Taeuber, I. B. (1955) 'Population and Labour Force in the Industrialisation of Japan, 1850–1950' in Kuznets, S. *et al. Economic Growth: Brazil, India, Japan*, Durham, NC, Duke University Press: 326–341.

Takizawa, H. (1974) 'Meiji Makki Suwa Seishigyō ni okeru Kuriito Kōjo no Chingin Taikei', *Kōnan Keizaigaku Ronshū* 15, 3: 67–92.

Tam, V. C. W. (1999) 'Foreign Domestic Helpers in Hong Kong and their Role in Childcare Provision' in Momsen, J. H. (ed.) *Gender, Migration and Domestic Service*, London, Routledge.

Tedebrand, L.-G. (1976) 'Sources for the History of Swedish Emigration' in Runblom, H. and Norman, H. (eds) *From Sweden to America: a History of the Migration*, Minneapolis, University of Minnesota Press.

Teti, V. (1987) 'Noti sui comportamenti delle donne sole degli "americani" durante la prima emigrazione in Calabria', *Studi emigrazione* 24: 13–46.

Thadani, V. N. and Todaro, M. P. (1984) 'Female Migration: a Conceptual Framework' in Fawcett, J. T., Khoo, S-E. and Smith, P. C. (eds) *Women in the Cities of Asia: Migration and Urban Adaption*, Boulder, CO, Westview Press.

Tichy, M. (1984) *Alltag und Traum. Leben und Lektüre der Dienstmädchen im Wien der Jahrhundertwende*, Vienna, Cologne, Graz, Böhlau.

Tilly, L. (1979) 'Individual Lives and Family Strategies in the French Proletariat', *Journal of Family History* l, 4: 137–152.

Tilly, L. (1987) 'After Family Strategies, What?' *Historical Methods* 20: 123–125.

Tilly, L. (1992) *Politics and Class in Milan, 1881–1901*, New York: Oxford University Press.

Tilly, L. and Scott, J. (1978) *Women, Work and Family*, New York, Holt, Rinehart & Winston.

Travers, P. (1995) 'Emigration and Gender: the Case of Ireland, 1922–60' in O'Dowd, M. and Wichert, S. (eds) *Chattel, Servant or Citizen: Women's Status in Church, State and Society*, Belfast, Institute of Irish Studies: 187–199.

Travers, P. (1995) '"There Was Nothing for Me There": Irish Female Migration, 1922–71' in O'Sullivan, P. (ed.) *Irish Women and Irish Migration*, London, Leicester University Press: 146–167.

Tsurumi, E. P. (1990) *Factory Girls: Women in the Thread Mills of Meiji Japan*, Princeton, NJ, Princeton University Press.

Tsuya, N. O. and Kurosu, S. (1998) 'Patterns and Covariates of Fertility in 18th and 19th Century Rural Japan: Evidence from Two Northeastern Villages', EurAsian Project on Population and Family History, *Working Paper Series* No. 16.

Twopeny, R. E. N. (1973) [1883] *Town Life in Australia*, Harmondsworth, Penguin.

Tyree, A. and Donato, K. (1986) 'A Demographic Overview of the International Migration of Women' in Brettell, C. and Simon, R. J. (eds) *International Migration: the Female Experience*, Totowa, NJ, Rowman & Allanheld: 21–44.

Umemura, M. (1961) *Chingin – Koyō – Nōgyō*, Tokyo, Ōmeidō: 82–5.

United Nations (1995) *International Migration Policies and the Status of Female Migrants*, New York.

United Nations (1995) *The World's Women*, New York.

Ushijima, T. and Abe, T. (1996) 'Mengyō', in Nishikawa, S. *et al.* (eds) *Nihon Keizai no 200 Nen*, Tokyo, Nihon Hyōronsha.

Valdes, X. *et al.* (1983) *Historias testimoniales de mujeres en el campo*, Santiago, CEDEM.

van de Pol, L. C. (1994) 'The Lure of the Big City: Female Migration to Amsterdam' in Kloek, E., Teeuwen, N. and Huisman, M. (eds) *Women of the Golden Age: an International Debate on Women in Seventeenth-century Holland, England and Italy*, Hilversun, Verloren: 73–86.

van der Horst, G. and Lucassen, L. (1998) *Nieuw in Leiden. Plaats en betekennis van Vreemdelingen in een Hollandsee stad (1918–1955)*, Leiden, Primavera Pers.

van Eijl, C. (1994) *Het werkzame verschil. Vrouwen in de slag om arbeid 1898–1940*, Hilversum, Verloren.

Van Hear, N. (1998) *New Diasporas: the Mass Exodus, Dispersal and Regrouping of Migrant Communities*, Seattle, University of Washington Press.

van Hulzen, A. (1987) *Utrecht en het verkeer 1850–1910*, Baarn, Bosch en Keuning.

van Maenen, A. J. Fr. (1959) *Petrus Regout 1801–1878. Een bijdrage tot de sociaal-economische geschiedenis van Maastricht*, Nijmegen, Centrale Drukkerij.

van Maurik, J. (1901) *Toen ik nog jong was*, Amsterdam, Van Holkema and Warendorf.

van Poppel, F. (1992) *Trouwen in Nederland. Een historisch-demografische studie van de 19e en vroeg-20e eeuw*, AAG Brijdragen 33, Wageningen, Landbouwuniversiteit.

van Rijnsoever, G.J. (1947) *Sint Maarten in de Tolsteeg. Geschiedenis van de Sint Martinusparochie te Utrecht*, Utrecht, Spectrum.

Van-Helten, J. J. and Williams, K. (1983) '"The Crying Need of South Africa": the Emigration of Single British Women to the Transvaal, 1901–10', *Journal of Southern African Studies* 10, 1.

Vaughan, W. E. and Fitzpatrick, A. J. (eds) (1978) *Irish Historical Statistics: Population, 1821–1971*, Dublin, Royal Irish Academy.

Waldinger, R. (1996) *Still the Promised City? African-Americans and New Immigrants in Postindustrial New York*, Cambridge, MA and London, Harvard University Press.

Walker, C. (1990) 'Gender and the Development of the Migrant Labour System *c.*1850–1930' in Walker, C. (ed.) *Women and Gender in Southern Africa,* Cape Town and London, David Philip and James Currey.

Walkowitz, J.R. (1992) *City of Dreadful Delight: Narratives of Sexual Danger in Late Victorian London,* London, Virago.

Walser, K. (1986) *Dienstmädchen. Frauenarbeit und Weiblichkeitsbilder um 1900,* Frankfurt am Main, Verlag Neue Kritik.

Walsh, B. M. (1974) 'Expectations, Information and Human Migration: Specifying an Econometric Model of Irish Migration to Britain', *Journal of Regional Science* 14: 107–120.

Walter, B. (1989) *Gender and Irish Migration to Britain,* Cambridge, Geography Working Paper No. 4, Anglia Higher Education College.

Walter, B. (1991) 'Gender and Recent Irish Migration to Britain' in King, R. (ed.) *Contemporary Irish Migration,* Dublin, Geographical Society of Ireland: 11–20.

Wegge, S. A. (1998) 'Chain Migration and Information Networks: Evidence From Nineteenth-century Hesse-Cassel', *Journal of Economic History* 58: 957–986.

Wegge, S. A. (1999) 'Network Strategies of Nineteenth-century Hesse-Cassel Emigrants', mimeo.

Wegge, S. A. (2000) 'Self-selection of Nineteenth-century German Emigrants: Evidence from the Principality of Hesse-Cassel', mimeo, revised May 2000.

Wehner, S. (1995) 'German Domestic Servants in America 1850–1914: a New Look at German Immigrant Women's Experiences' in Hoerder, D. and Nagler, J. (eds) *People in Transit: German Migrations in Comparative Perspective 1820–1930,* Cambridge, Cambridge University Press.

Wehner-Franco, S. (1994) *Deutsche Dienstmädchen in Amerika, 1850–1914,* Münster, Waxmann.

Weinberg, S. S. (1992) 'The Treatment of Women in Immigration History: a Call for Change?', *Journal of American Ethnic History* II: 25–46 and in Gabaccia, D. (ed.) *Seeking Common Ground: Multidisciplinary Studies of Immigrant Women in the United States,* Westport, CT, Praeger.

Whatley, C. A. (1994) 'Women and the Economic Transformation of Scotland, *c.*1740–1830', *Scottish Economic and Social History* 14: 19–40.

Whyte, I. D. (1989) 'Proto-industrialisation in Scotland' in Hudson, P. (ed.) *Regions and Industries,* Cambridge, Cambridge University Press: 228–251.

Whyte, I. D. (1991) 'Migration in Early-Modern Scotland and England: a Comparative Perspective' in Pooley, C. G. and Whyte, I. D. (eds) *Migrants, Emigrants and Immigrants: a Social History of Migration,* London, Routledge: 87–105.

Whyte, I. D. and Whyte, K. A. (1988) 'The Geographical Mobility of Women in Early Modern Scotland' in Leneman, L. (ed.) *Perspectives in Scottish Social History: Essays in Honour of Rosalind Mitchison,* Aberdeen, Aberdeen University Press: 83–106.

Wierling, D. (1987) *Mädchen für alles: Arbeitsalltag und Lebensgeschichte städtischer Dienstmädchen um die Jahrhundertwende,* Bonn, Verlag J.H.W. Dietz Nachf.

Wigen, K. (1995) *The Making of a Japanese Periphery, 1750–1920,* Berkeley, University of California Press.

Willcox, W. F. (1931) *International Migrations, Vol. II, Interpretations,* New York, National Bureau for Economic Research.

Willett, M. H. (1902) *The Employment of Women in the Clothing Trade,* Columbia University Studies in History, Economics and Public Law 16, New York, Columbia University Press.

Wilson, M., Kaplan, S., Maki, T. and Walton, E. M. (eds) (1952) *Social Structure: Keiskammahoek Rural Survey*, vol. 111, Pietermaritzburg, Oxford University Press.

Withers, C. W. J. (1985) 'Highland Migration to Dundee, Perth and Stirling, 1753–1891', *Journal of Historical Geography* 11: 395–418.

Withers, C. W. J. and Watson, A. J. (1991) 'Stepwise Migration and Highland Migration to Glasgow, 1852–1898', *Journal of Historical Geography* 17: 35–55.

Worthington, A. W. (1867) 'On the Unequal Proportion Between the Male and Female Population of Some Manufacturing and Other Towns', *Journal of the Statistical Society of London* 30: 68–79.

Wyman, M. (1993) *Round-Trip to America: the Immigrants Return to Europe, 1880–1930*, Ithaca, NY, Cornell University Press.

Yagi, T. (1981) 'Kinsei Mura to Seikatsu: Nōson Yojō Rōdō wa Dekasegi ni [early modern village life: surplus farm labour moves to outside work], in Tatsuno-shi Shi Hensan Senmon Iinkai (ed.) *Tatsuno-shi Shi* [Tatsuno city history] Vol. 2, Tatsuno City.

Yamada, M. (1934) *Nihon Shihonsugi Bunseki*, Tokyo, Iwanami Shoten.

Yáñez, C. (1996) *Saltar con red: La temprana emigración catalana a América, 1830–1870*, Madrid, Alianza.

Yeoh, B. S. A. and Huang, S. (1999) 'Singapore Women and Foreign Domestic Workers: Negotiating Domestic Work and Motherhood' in Momsen, J.H. (ed.) *Gender, Migration and Domestic Service*, London, Routledge.

Young, K. *et al.* (1981) *Of Marriage and the Market: Women's Subordination in International Perspective*, London, CSE Books.

Zappi, E. (1991) *If Eight Hours Seem Too Few: Mobilization of Women Workers in the Italian Rice Fields*, Albany, State University of New York Press.

Zinn, D. L. (1994) 'The Sengalese Immigrants in Bari: What Happens when the Africans Peer Back' in Benmayor, R. and Skotnes, A. (eds) *Migration and Identity*, Oxford, Oxford University Press: 53–69.

Zolberg, A. R. (1989) 'The Next Waves: Migration Theory for a Changing World', *International Migration Review* 22: 405–406.

Zolberg, A. R. (1997) 'The Great Wall against China: Responses to the First Immigration Crisis, 1885–1925' in Lucassen, J. and Lucassen, L. (eds) *Migration, Migration History, History: Old Paradigms and New Perspectives*, Bern, Peter Lang.

Zwaal, P. (1993) *Frisdranken in Nederland. Een twintigste eeuwse produktgeschiedenis*, Rotterdam, Stichting BBM.

Index

Page references for figures, maps, plates and tables are given in *italics*

acculturation process 85–6
adultery 267
African National Congress Youth League 263–4
Afro-Atlantic system 17
age 30; Hessians 174, *175*, 180; Japanese service migration 69, *70*; Latin America 280, 282, 284, 286; Wiener Neustadt domestic service 113–114, *114*, *115*, 118–20, *119*
agriculture: Ireland 212, 216, 218; Japan 244, 255n; Latin America 275, 277–8, 279, 283; Scotland 128, *133*, 137; temporary migration 32, 85, *see also* farm families
Alberdi, Juan Bautista 191
Alford, Katrina 156
allocation 86
amankazana 268–70
Argentina: fertility rate 278; Italians 190, 191, 200–1, 203
Aruba 10
Asia 1, 9
assembly industry 283–4
Assion, P. 166, 167, 171
asylum-seekers 2
Auerbach, I. 166–7, 178
Australia 2, 6, *149*, 158; domestic service 147–8; Irish 209; Italians 203; single women 145, 146, 147, 148–51, 153–6
Aymer, Paula 10

Baily, Samuel 195, 200
Baines, D. 165
Barbados 8
Barbalet, Margaret 147
Barnes, Teresa 9
Belgians 102
bigamy 140–2
Bohemia-Moravia 116
Bolivia 278
Bovensiepen, R. 166
brain drain 19
Brazil, Italians 190, 191, 203
Bredbenner, C. L. 24
Brettell, Caroline 10
bride ships 145
Britain 20; immigration policies 214, 219; Irish 209, 210–11, 213–15, 220; left behind 59n; standard of living 217–18, *see also* England; Scotland
British: Australia 145, 146, 150–6; South Africa 158; Utrecht 99

Cádiz 30, 40–1, 45
California 17
Canada 2; Caribbean domestics 19; Italians 190, 191, 194; settler migrations 17; single women 145, 156–8; software programmers 19
Caribbean 1, 3, 10, 19
Caroli, Betty Boyd 195
caste 9
Catholics *see* Roman Catholic Church
chain migration 100, 182–3
Chamberlain, Mary 8
Chapin, Robert 201, 202
children: Scotland 135–6; trade migration 93–4; wages 202, *see also* daughters; sons
Chile 280, 283
Chisholm, Caroline 148
Ciccotosto, Emma 197–8
Ciskei reserve 259–62, *260*; East London 262–4; family and marriage 265–70
citizenship 24, 105n
Coghlan, T. A. 153
community formation 20–2
construction industry, Italians 192, 194
control: Ciskei 261, 263, 265, 267–8, 270; Ireland 213–15, 220; Mediterranean societies 191; Spain 32–3; Wiener Neustadt 6, 122
Corti, Paola 51
Curthoys, Ann 148

Daly, M. E. 217, 218
daughters 73–4, *73*, 180, 244–58
de Valera, Eamon 214–15
decision-making strategies 22–5, 188n
dekasegi 244
Delaet, D. 4, 7
diasporas 22
distance 6, 30, 115–16; and household position 120–1, *121*; and occupational position 116–18, *117*
divorce 7
dockworkers 30, 40–2; families 46–50; hiring process 42–4, *43*; living conditions 45–6; wages, benefits, pensions 44–5
domestic service 6, 38, 109–11, 155–6, 158; Australia 147–8, 152, 153, 154, 156; Canada 19; East London 263; Germans

100, 224–5, 230–1; Hong Kong 1; Irish 218, 219; Latin America 279, 280–2; Scotland 128, *133*; Wiener Neustadt 112–21, *see also* wet nurses
Donato, K. 18, 21
dual Euro-Atlantic system 17
Duroux, Rose 51

East London 261–4
Eastern Europe 7
economic strategies 60, 237, 238, 244–5, 248–53, 276
economy: Ireland 215–17; Latin America 277–8, 280, 282
education 276, 286
Elder, G. H., Jr 134
emigration policies: Germany 167, 183, 238–9, 240; Ireland 213–15, 220
emotional impact 9–10
employment *see* occupations
empowerment 7, 11
England, internal migration 165
Ennepetalers 100–2
European Community 2
extra-marital relations 267

factory work 153, 191, 192, *see also* textile industry
families: Ciskei 265; dockworkers 46–50; German 164; migration 17, 19; Scotland 134–6; and temporary migration 50–4; transnationalism 195–203, 203–4; unification policies 19; wet nurses 39–40
family breakdown 6, 7, 8, 140–1, 259, 267–71
family migration 188n, 191
family networks 182–3
family strategies 5, 128, 259; farm families 244–5, 248–53; Hessians 171–3, *173*; Japanese service migration 60, 80, 81–2; Spain 50–4
farm families 244–5, 248–53, 254–5
female migration: historical analysis 3–8; historiography 148–51
femininity 9, 233–6, 239–41, 283
Ferenczi, I. 163
fertility rates 278–9, 284–5, 286
filemakers 100–2
Filipinas 1, 4, 22, 23
Fitzpatrick, D. 212
followers 16–17, 19, 20
Fox, Charlie 147–9
France 20
Friedman-Kasaba, Kathie 7, 11

Gabaccia, D. 4
Galicia 32
Germans 18, 19, 224–5, 240–1; aspirations 225–7; combating immorality 234–6; migration control 236–40; motivation 232–4; protection of girls 227–30; push and pull factors 230–1; United States 164, 165–6; in Utrecht 85, 97, 98–102, *see also* Hessians; Westerwalders
Germany: emigration policies 231; family unification policies 19; immigrant communities 20; internal migration 165; labour migration 18; war brides 19, *see also* Hesse-Cassel
globalisation 275

governesses 153
government *see* emigration policies; immigration policies
Great Britain *see* Britain

Habsburg Empire 109
Haitians 22
Hamilton, Paula 148
Hannan, D. 216
Hareven, T. K. 134
Harzig, C. 11
hatmakers 102
hawkers 139–40
Hayami Akira 62
Heimatrecht 122–3
Hesse-Cassel 164, 166, *167*, 186–7n
Hessians 165, 183–4; age *175*; cash statistics *176*; data 166–7; daughters 180; emigrant permit lists 167–8, *169*, 170–1, *170*; family networks 182–3; family strategies 171–3, *173*; occupations *177*; widows 178; wives and mothers 174, 177; women travelling alone 180–1; year of departure *179*
Hill, B. 110
Hillmann, F. 23
Hochstadt, S. 165
Hoerder, D. 16, 17, 23–4
homeworkers 200
house-maids *see* domestic service
household 265
household position: Japanese service migration 60–1, 72–4, *73*, 74–5, *75*; Wiener Neustadt 120–1, *121*
Hubbard, William 116
Hufton, Olwen 9
human rights 2
Hungarians 115

identity 8–12, 21
illegal migration 2, 7
immigrant assimilation 163–4
immigrant communities 20–2, 85–6, 276
immigration policies 24–5; Australia 145, 146, *149*, 150, 151–2, 153, 154–5, 158; Britain 211, 214, 219; Netherlands 91–2
immorality 234–6
import substitution 280
India 9
Indians 19
Indonesia 10
Indra, Doreen 4
industrialisation 62, 80, 224
infertility 8
internal migration 10, 165; Habsburg Empire 108–23; Hessians 181, 183; Ireland 186n, 210; Japan 60–82, 244–55; Latin America 275–87; South Africa 259–71; Spain 29–54
International Ladies Garment Workers Union 19
International Migration Review 15
intra-American system 17
Ireland: emigration policies 213–15, 220; internal migration 186n, 210; migration 6–7; socioeconomic change 215–19
Irish 165, 209–13, *210*, *211*, *212*, 219–20; agricultural work 128; Australia 156; remittances 22; Scotland 130
Italians 164, 192, *193*, 194–5, *194*; International Ladies Garment Workers Union 19; transnationalism 2–3, 190–1, 195–204

Italy 3
Izzard, W. 5

Jabavu, Noni 264
Jackel, Susan 145, 156
Japan *61*; agriculture 255–6n; data and methodology 63–5; service migration 60–3, 65–82; textile industry 245, *246*, 247, *247*, *248*; textile migration 244–5, 248–55
Jews 7, 19
Joksch, Josefine 108, 123n
Jongilanga, J. D. 264

Kelson, G. A. 4, 7
Kingston, Bev 147
Korea 19
Kraus, Karl 122
Kukowski, M. 166

labour migration 1–3, 17–18, 60, *see also* service migration; trade migration
labour organisations 9, 19
Lanheses 10
Latin America 1, 275; change and continuity 285–7; import substitution and urbanisation 277–82, 287n; political crises and economic adjustments 282–5
Leddy, Mary Jo 20
left behind 10; Italy 190, 191, 197–8; Spain 51–2, 59n
Leneman, L. 135
life cycle 276
Lin, L. Lean 276
lobola 265–6, 267, 268
Lucassen, J. 85–6
Lutherans 98

Madgwick, R. B. 150, 154
Madrid 30, 34–5, 36
maids *see* domestic service
maquila production 283–4
marital breakdown 6, 7, 8, 140–1, 259, 267–71
marital status 276; Japanese service migration 69, 71–2, *71*, 75–6; Wiener Neutstadt domestic service *118*, 120–1, *120*, *121*, *see also* single women
marriage: Australia 145, 154, 155; Ciskei 265–70; Irish 6, 218–19; Latin America 279; Russian-Jewish women 7; Scotland 138–42; war brides 19
married women 174, 177
masculinity 8–9
Meijide Pardo, A. 32
mental maps 17
metal workers 100–2
Mexico 278, 280, 284
migration 1–3, 15–16; gender differences 29–30, 275–7; historical analysis 3–8; and identity 8–12; indicators 130–4, *131*, *132*; systems theory 16–19; women's roles and functions 19–20, *see also* labour migration
migration policies *see* emigration policies; immigration policies
Milton, Norma 156
Mitchison, R. 135
Mitterauer, Michael 116
modernity 8, 9
Möker, U. 166
Momsen, J. H. 3, 10
La Montaña 33, 40
Montañeses: dockworkers 40–50; wet nurses 33–40
Moore, H. 259
Moore, Henrietta 5
morality 213, 214–15, 220, 227–30
Morokvasic, Mirjana 15, 148, 150
mothers 8, *see also* single mothers

Nagoya 78
Nairobi 7
Nakamura, Takafusa 254
Netherlands 20, *99*; German maids 9, 18, 224–40; German trade migration 85, 87, 89–95, *see also* Utrecht
networks 61, 121–2, 134, 182–3
New Zealand 150, 158
niche formation 86, 104
Nigeria 9
Nihonmatsu 62–4, 65
Niita 62, 63, 79–80; age of service migration 69, *70*; changes in service migration 67, *68*; destinations 77–8; marital status 71–2, *71*; probability of service migration 65, *66*; relations to head of household 72–4, *73*; return migration 74–6, *75*
Nishijō 62, 63, 78, 79, 80–1; age of service migration 69, *70*; destinations 77–8, *77*, *79*; marital status 71, *71*; probability of service migration 65, *66*; relations to head of household 73–4, *73*; return migration 74–6, *75*
North America 16, 209, *see also* Canada; United States
nursing 219

occupations 163, 164; East London 262; Hessians *177*, 178, 180–1; Ireland 216–17, 218; Latin America 278, 279, 280–1, 283–4, *see also* agriculture; domestic service; factory work
Ochiai, Emiko 69
O'Farrell, Patrick 156
Ōgaki 78
Ōsaka 78, *248*

Pardo Bazán, Emilia 34
Pasiego women 33–40, *35*
patriarchy: Ciskei 259, 261, 265–6, 270; Italy 191, 192
pawn service 67, *68*, 69, 74, 80
peasants 29, 30–1
Pedraza-Bailey, S. 16
Penninx, R. 85–6
Phizacklea, Anne 5
pioneers 16–17, 19, 145
Poles 22
political persecution 19, 26n
Portugal 10, 57n
Portuguese 220
Precognitions 129
pregnancy 8, 9, 135–6
problem solving 259
prostitutes 7, 9
psychological impacts 10
push–pull paradigm 16; German maids 227, 230–1; Latin America 275

race 9
railway workers 99
Ravenstein, E. G. 30, 116, 165
refugees 4, 18–20
regional migration 9, 111, 115–16
religion 21, 98, *see also* Roman Catholic Church
religious organisations 225, 227–30, 234–5, 236, 239
remittances: Italians 197, 198; Japanese textile migration 248–53, 255
research methodology: Japan 63–5; Scotland 129, 134; Westerwalders 87
restricted migration 2
return migration 18, 164; German maids 238–9; Hessians 183; Irish 211; Italians 195, 198–9; Japanese service migration 74–6, *75*, 80
Richards, Eric 150
Rodenburg, J. 10
Roman Catholic Church: Ireland 213, 214–15, 220; Spain 32, 33; Utrecht 98, 100, 103

Saitō, Osamu 62, 80
Santander 30, *31*, 33
Sarti, R. 110
Schwarz, L. 110
Scotland 6, 127–8, 142; case studies 134; indicators of mobility 130–4, *131*, *132*; marriages 138–40; Precognitions 129; separations, bigamy and remarriage 140–2; weavers and wanderers 137–8; women, children and families 134–6
seasonal migration: Italians 192, 203; Westerwalders 102
self-organisation 86
Senegal 8–9
separation *see* family breakdown; transnationalism
service migration 64, 79–82; age 69, *70*; destinations *61*, 76–8, *77*, *79*; marital status 69, 71–2, *71*; motivation 65, *66*, 67, *68*, 69; relation to head 72–4, *73*; return 74–6, *75*
settler migrations 17
sexuality 191, 192, 228, 259; control 267–8, 270
Sharpe, P. 110
Shimomoriya 62, 63, 64, 79–80; age of service migration 69, *70*; changes in service migration 67, *68*; destinations 77–8; marital status 71–2, *71*; probability of service migration 65, *66*; relations to head of household 72–4, *73*; return migration 74–6, *75*
Sinclair, W. A. 147
single mothers 8, 177, 276, 281
single women 19, 145, 156–8; Australia 146, 147, 148–51, 151–2, 153–6; Ciskei 268–9; German maids 224–43; Hessians 180–1; Irish 209
Smith, Babette 145
social capital 23
social control *see* control
social criticism 51
social mobility 61
soldiers 55n, 99–100
sons 72–3, *73*, 180
South Africa 9, 158, 259, *260*, 270, *see also* Ciskei reserve
Spain 3, 30–1, *31*, 50–4; dockworkers 40–50; wet nurses 33–40

Sugihara, Kaoru 252
Swaisland, Cecillie 158
Sweden 11, 20

Takegahana 78
temporary migration 2, 30–1, 54–5n; dockworkers 40–50; family impact 50–4; gender pattern 31–3; Portugal 57n; wet nurses 33–40, *see also* seasonal migration; textile migration
Texas 17
textile industry: Italians 194, 200; Japan 245, *246*, 247, *247*, *248*, 251; Scotland 128, 132, *133*, 137; Utrecht 100
textile migration 244–5, 247, *248*; forces for change 253–5; savings and remittances 248–53
thwala 266–7
trade migration 85; Westerwalders 89–91, 104–5; women 91–5
transnationalism 2–3, 21–2, 25, 190; Italians 190–1, 191–2, 195–203, 203–4
Turks 19
Tyree, A. 18, 21

United Kingdom *see* Britain
United States: citizenship 24; Germans 165–6, 183–4; immigration 1, 2, 6; Irish 210, 211; Italians 190, 191, *193*, 194, 195–203; return migration 195; settler migration 17; women immigrants 4, 18, 20, 164, 187–8n
unmarried mothers 8, 177, 276, 281
unmarried women *see* single women
unskilled work 218, 219
urbanisation 3, 210, 224, 239, 286, 287n
Uruguay 278
Utrecht 85, *96*, 97; immigrant communities 98–102; religion 98; Westerwalders 102–3, 104

Van-Helten, Jean Jacques 158
Vaughan, M. 259
Vienna 108–9, 110, 111, 116, 123n

wage service 67, *68*, 69
Waldinger, R. 86
war brides 19
warrior service 67, *68*, 80, 81
weavers 137
Weinberg, S. S. 10–11
Westerwald *88*
Westerwalders 85, 87, 89–91, 104–5; research methodology 87; in Utrecht 102–3; women 91–5, *92*
wet nurses 5–6, 30, 33–6, *35*, 55n; families 39–40; hiring process 36–7; living conditions 39; working conditions 37–9
white widows 190, 191, 197–8
widows 4, 95, 178
Wiener Neustadt 109, 112–13; domestic service 111; household position 113–15, *114*, *115*, 120–1, *121*; marital status *118*, 120, *120*; municipal surveillance 121–3; occupational position 116–18, *117*; region of origin 115–16
Willcox, W. 163
Williams, Keith 158

Zinn, Dorothy Louise 8–9